WE WERE THERE

WE WERE THERE

An eyewitness history of
the twentieth century

EDITED BY ROBERT FOX

THE OVERLOOK PRESS
NEW YORK

This edition first published in the United States in 2010 by

The Overlook Press, Peter Mayer Publishers, Inc.
141 Wooster Street
New York, NY 10012
www.overlookpress.com
For bulk and special sales, please contact sales@overlookny.com

Designed by Sue Lamble
Printed in the United States of America
ISBN 978-1-59020-422-1
10 9 8 7 6 5 4 3 2 1

Contents

Illustrations

The Wright Brothers' first powered flight at Kitty Hawk, North Carolina, on 17 December 1903. (© *CORBIS*)

The suffragette Emily Wilding Davison is fatally injured at the Epsom Derby in 1913. (*Hulton Archive/Getty Images*)

Archduke Franz Ferdinand and his wife on a visit to Sarajevo on 28 June 1914, moments before being assassinated, an event which precipitated the First World War. (*Hulton Archive/Getty Images*)

Ernest Shackleton's ship, the *Endurance*, trapped in pack-ice in 1915. (© *Frank Hurley/Royal Geographic Society 2005*)

British soldiers going 'over the top', September 1918. (*Hulton Archive/ Getty Images; stereograph by H. D. Girdwood*)

The funeral procession of Italian-born film actor Rudolph Valentino coming up Broadway, New York, on 1 September 1926 (*Hulton Archive/Getty Images*)

Crowds gather in Wall Street, New York, on 24 October 1929, as news of the collapse of the financial market spreads through the city. (*Hulton Archive/Getty Images*)

The burning of the Reichstag in Berlin on 27 February 1933, a pivotal event in the establishment of Nazi Germany. (*akg-images*)

A man bows into the wind in the tempest that devastated Oklahoma and New Mexico on 14 April 1935. (© *CORBIS*)

Hiroshima in ruins after the dropping of the atom bomb on 6 August 1945. (*Time & Life Pictures/Getty Images; photograph by Bernard Hoffman*)

Inhabitants of Budapest demonstrating against the Soviet-backed
    Hungarian regime, 1956. (*Time & Life Pictures/Getty Images;*
    photograph by Michael Rougier)
The Mint 400 Bikers Race, 1971, across the Mojave Desert, Nevada.
    (*Time & Life Pictures/Getty Images; photograph by Bill Eppridge*)
Communist Khmer Rouge soldiers driving through Phnom Penh,
    Cambodia, during their takeover in April 1975. (*AFP/Getty Images*)
Chinese army tanks in Tiananmen Square, Beijing, in June 1989.
    (*AP/PA Photos; photograph by Jeff Widener*)
Members of the Afghan Mujahedin guerrilla group in 1989. (*Getty*
    Images; photograph by David Stewart-Smith)
The iconic 110-storey Twin Towers of the World Trade Center,
    11 September 2001. (*AP/PA Photos; photograph by Marty*
    Lederhandler)

Introduction

The eyewitness reports and memoirs in this collection all aim at the same magical effect of giving the reader the sensation of being there at great and curious events, and with extraordinary people. This is the essence of storytelling ever since humans had the ability to communicate in speech and script.

I have chosen a selection of reports and testimonies from across the last century (with a handful before and after). It was a great time for news and for reporting, but this book is not exclusively about professional reporting and journalism. Some of the most poignant entries come from the private moments of confidence to diaries, letters and journals. Some tackle great and cataclysmic events; others speak of domestic joys and grief.

Much of the choice is coloured by my life over the past 43 years or so as a journalist, traveller and amateur historian. In some ways this is the scrapbook of imagination and memory. The pieces are chosen because of what they have conjured in the mind's eye of people, places and happenings that fascinate in themselves, or fascinate in the manner of their telling. Each piece is either remarkable in the way it is related, or speaks of remarkable occurrences and personalities. I hope, too, that each tells a complete story in itself.

I believe that all good reporters, and storytellers, are born not made. Certainly professional reporters and correspondents must have some training in how to shape a report, observe the rules of grammar and the strictures of the law – especially on libel and defamation – and the peculiar customs and mannerisms dictated by the whims of an editor or a publication's house style. But all good reporters need the same quality of driving curiosity, a dash of recklessness even, to find things out and then spill the beans as forcefully as possible.

This book teems with natural storytellers. Some are professional journalists and writers. Some of the very best are amateurs who found themselves in the right place, or the wrong one maybe, at the right time – and became highly accomplished reporters almost by accident. A favourite of mine is the Welsh poet W. H. Davies, the first minstrel hobo of the railway age. In the late nineteenth century he crisscrossed North America, illegally hitchhiking on freight trains. He came to grief when his leg was crushed by a train in Ontario; thereafter he was slowed down by a heavy wooden leg. He collected his memoirs in *Autobiography of a Super Tramp*, which with the generous backing of George Bernard Shaw was published in 1907. I have selected his description of the technique of 'hopping box cars'. Davies shows himself a natural wandering troubadour of the railroad, an inspiration to generations including Bob Dylan and Jack Kerouac. The rock band Supertramp took their name as homage to his book.

Ernest Hemingway, a legendary reporter in every sense, shows the touch of the true storyteller in just a few lines. Take the opening of his most famous despatch from World War II, the D Day landings in Normandy, which was published a month later in *Collier's Magazine*. 'No one remembers the date of the battle of Shiloh. But the day we took Fox Green beach was the sixth of June ...' In just a few lines you are with him bouncing up and down in the landing craft in rough sea as it drives towards the beach, the faces of the GIs under their steel helmets turning grey with seasickness and apprehension .

Hemingway had a real reporter's eye for detail. His account of the rout of hundreds of thousands of Italian soldiers in driving rain and mud at Caporetto in 1917 makes one of the most vivid passages in his novel *A Farewell to Arms*. These were scenes he witnessed as an ambulance driver on the Carso front; they are among the best of all surviving descriptions of that terrible war.

I have chosen a number of pieces that were written or composed well after the event, but they are great distillations of the experience of being there on the spot as it happened. John Dos Passos compiled in his documentary novel *USA* a brilliant account of the funeral of the silent movie *divo* Rodolfo Valentino – possibly the first tickertape funeral in history. It has all the punch and immediacy of a report in that morning's newspaper.

Distillation of the moment is the key. Some of the pieces, the poetry especially, are chosen because they are items of testimony, and they bear witness in themselves, encapsulating the whole mood of the time. Isaac Rosenberg's 'Break of Day in the Trenches' celebrates a fleeting thought that captures a whole experience. In a different way the Dust Bowl Ballads of Woody Guthrie chronicle the disaster and diaspora of a whole generation of poor dirt farmers of the American Midwest in the Depression.

Some, like the Dust Storm Disaster (14 April 1935), are remarkably accurate in their detail. This is all the more impressive as reporters are notorious for exaggeration. We all like to embellish stories, and there is a bit of Baron Munchhausen in most of us. Journalism of most cultures and languages has a maxim along the lines of the Fleet Street adage, 'never let the facts get in the way of a good story.' The Italian is somewhat more elegant and piquant: 'Se non è vero, è ben trovato' (if it isn't true, it is none the less well found). With many great reporters it is hard to detect when the fine line, a wafer-thin caesura, is transgressed between strict fact and a touch of romancing and embellishment. One of the best storytellers, and reporters, I ever knew was René Cutforth. He'd been a schoolmaster, a professional soldier, and gun runner before he settled down, if that is the right word, and became a reporter for BBC radio Newsreel, which took him off to the Korean War. He saw himself more as a spinner of yarns and less a professional journalist, a 'hack'. He was a freebooter who wouldn't survive a second today in mainstream media with its codes of conduct and health and safety regulations. As he spun out his shaggy dog stories of reminiscence, fact and fiction merged, and the audience didn't seem to care. He was a surprisingly sharp prose stylist, too. When the BBC asked him to narrate his autobiography for radio, somebody fortunately had the wit to put them into a small book, for the tapes of that unforgettable gravelly voice are long gone. I have included his electric description of the wild celebrations in the small German town of Lublar as the Second World War came to an end in 1945.

Reporters have suffered the same fate and reputation as the chroniclers of the Middle Ages, often portrayed as gossips at worst and purveyors of rough-hewn truths at best. What they write, according to some academics, can only be a first draft of what will become finely honed and considered history. The patronising term 'scribbler' or 'hack' says it all. What we reporters, yes 'hacks', deliver are graffiti on the walls of the collective memory. Our scribbles are to history, according to this point of view, as doggerel is to the sonnet or the epic poem. In the introduction to an anthology of reportage published in the 1980s, the editor, a professor of English Literature, suggested that reporting was too fleeting and ephemeral to be considered great art. I disagree.

Some pieces of eyewitness reporting in this book do reach the heights of great literary art and great history. They reveal a central truth about the human condition. None is more powerful than the telling of the experience of prisoners in Auschwitz by Primo Levi. Primo Levi wrote down his reflections on surviving the death camp and his long odyssey to reach home in Italy several years later and published them in two books, *If This Is a Man* and *The Truce*. They are among the greatest pieces of factual description and witness in the canon of western literature. Reporting by Levi's pen becomes testimony, and great literature and history.

Coincidentally Primo Levi's distant kinsman Carlo Levi also managed the same feat of alchemy, turning reportage into great literature in his memoir of exile by the Fascists in the 1930s to the depths of Italy's impoverished south, *Christ Stopped at Eboli*. He describes the peasants of Aliano in Basilicata with their superstitions, witchcraft and spells, in poetic detail. Some 45 years later I visited Aliano. Some of Levi's peasants were still living there, now a great age, and the buildings and the surrounding hills were exactly as he depicted them.

History, wrote the great historian and resistance hero Marc Bloch, consists of 'momentary convulsions' and 'long developments'. Bloch proved himself a wonderful reporter when he described the collapse of the French forces in May 1940 in his searing polemic 'Strange Defeat', written weeks after his escape from Dunkirk and subsequent return to France.

How does the reporter capture the scale, the impact, the texture of a momentary, and momentous, convulsion? John Updike addressed the dilemma squarely in his brilliant account of the attack on the World Trade

Center on September 11th 2001. 'Suddenly summoned to witness something great and horrendous, we keep fighting not to reduce it to our own smallness,' he begins. 'From the view-point of a tenth floor apartment in Brooklyn Heights, where I happened to be visiting some kin, the Destruction of the World Trade Center twin towers had the false intimacy of television, on a day of clear reception.'

Giving the story some shape, getting to the heart of the matter, capturing the colour and momentum – these are the things uppermost in my mind whenever I report from the field. What is this really about, what is the truth at its heart, why does it matter – why is it news ? Like the late great journalist James Cameron I also worry that I am going to miss the crucial point entirely each time I open the laptop and hit the keyboard to create and file a new story. He put it more elegantly: 'every time I put a new sheet in my typewriter, I think this time they'll find me out.'

Generally I am as worried about what I have missed as I am about what I have uncovered, reported and revealed. Nearly thirty years ago I was witness to the first battle in the Falklands Campaign in 1982, at a sheep ranching settlement called Goose Green. The events were dramatic enough as battle ebbed and flowed for nearly 24 hours across an area roughly the size of three municipal golf courses. Given the small numbers involved, somewhat under 2,000 people all told, Argentine and British forces and some 120 Falkland Island settlers, one would imagine it is pretty easy to work out the details of exactly what happened that blustery autumn day, 28 May 1982. Yet to this day I have not met a single person who can tell me exactly what happened at every major juncture in that drama. Each person has a crucial detail, to be sure, but they are tiles in a mosaic whose outline is clear, but whose overall form and content remain a mystery.

The sense shared by many writers and reporters of not quite having the final word is neatly expressed by Hemingway at the end of his famous D Day despatch. 'But if you want to know how it was in an LCV(P) on D Day when we took Fox Green Beach and Easy Red beach on the sixth of June, 1944, then this is as near as I can come to it.' In one sentence he sums up the feeling shared by all good reporters that we can never be omniscient – only the most monumental egotists among us or the clinically insane would disagree.

Many of the pieces in this collection deal with war: the drama, the effects and victims, the aftermath. It is inevitable that this should be so in any panoramic reflection of the 20th century, named by the historian Eric Hobsbawm 'the age of extremes' with its two great global conflicts, strings of rebellions, terrible civil wars, and the ragged brushfire struggles of national liberation and insurgency. But the quieter moments, the odd pieces of eyewitness account of domestic life and social manners touch the heart and catch the inner eye as much as the *sturm und drang* of the battlefield. We eavesdrop, for example, on the private worries of Nella Last, from eking out rations to coping with her dreary marriage and her own depression, as she recorded them faithfully in her diary entries for Mass Observation, the extraordinary social scrapbook that recorded how people coped in the Second World War.

A similar favourite is the opening speech of the prosecuting counsel Mervyn Griffith-Jones in the trial of Penguin Books for obscenity for publishing the unexpurgated edition of D. H. Lawrence's *Lady Chatter-ley's Lover*. Quite unintentionally it is a wonderful piece of testimony to a bygone age. Britain was on the cusp of the Swinging Sixties, miniskirts, the Beatles, the pill and psychedelia. 'Would you approve of your young sons, young daughters – because girls can read as well as boys – reading this book? Is it a book you would have lying around in your own house? Is it a book that you would even wish your wife or your servants to read?'

A very different scene of domestic life is depicted in one of the last entries of the collection, the despatches via the Internet of the Baghdad housewife who called herself Riverbend. New media delivered some very remarkable eyewitness accounts of the last days of Saddam Hussein and the appalling aftermath in Iraq. Riverbend loses members of her family in the anarchy of kidnapping and sectarian revenge attacks as order fell apart in the Iraqi capital under American occupation. Yet she managed to keep the family together, and is still writing her e-mail diary to the outside world.

Equally remarkable is the journal, again transmitted via e-mail, of a man, an architect by profession I believe, who called himself Salam Pax, the Baghdad Blogger. He records the precise moment of the American forces entering the capital, and from the inside chronicles the cycle of elation and despair of his family friends as they realise that their deliverance is being overtaken by disaster.

Traditional mainstream media and journalism has been slow to grasp how the new means of communication – chat rooms and the net, text messaging and video phoning – has enfranchised a huge global pool of eyewitness reporters and 'citizen journalists' whose news and views otherwise would never have been heard. New means have brought new modes of conveying reports and reflections, the cryptographic styles of text speech by the telephone, and now the staccato paragraphs of Twitter. Twitter messages to and from Tehran and the other great cities of Iran made, or at least sustained, an incipient revolution during the elections of 2009. I have included several bursts of Twitter from Tehran gathered by a translator calling himself Nite Owl and relayed to the world on the Internet and by mobile phone. They are both eyewitness reports and testaments to a great drama, and a momentous convulsion for millions of young Iranians.

In collecting many of these pieces I have been travelling in the company of friends – and a few heroes. Among the heroes is Ernie Pyle, who told the story from ground level in the company of GI Joe, his emblematic American infantry soldier, slogging with him through the mud and rain of Northern Europe and dying with him within sight of the end of the Second World War at Okinawa in April 1945. Then there are the travellers like Eric Newby, a delightfully gentle character whom I met several times, and the great wizard of the tales of the exotic, from soccer wars to the wild life in Africa and Asia, Ryszard Kapuscinski. He is a companion of the imagination, in the manner of his tall stories and embellishments, and as great a romancer as René Cutforth, whom I knew well and found one of the most beguiling conversationalists I have ever encountered.

Friends and colleagues like Anthony Loyd of *The Times*, one of the bravest journalists around, Robert Fisk, Patrick Cockburn and John Simpson, companions of the road, are here. Their company and added insights as we have gone about discovering and then telling the story have made doing so all the more rewarding and exhilarating.

And that is why we do it. Reporters, the hawkers of the eyewitness business, do it because we are hooked on the sheer thrill of finding out, getting it straight, then getting the story back to the newsdesk and the readers. One of the greatest eyewitness reporters of my generation is Kurt Schork of Reuters, who was killed in Sierra Leone in the summer of 2000. Because he was a wire man reporting for an agency, his byline was hardly known to a world audience, though his words and despatches graced papers and journals and news stations by the thousand. He was fearless in body and spirit, and his prose from the field of action had a strange elegance. I have chosen one of his most famous pieces, the story of a Muslim and Serb couple shot by snipers in the no man's land of the Siege of Sarajevo in May 1993.

Kurt led the life he did, because he liked it and it liked him. At times it seems more an addiction than a choice; the compulsion to tell it how it is.

Robert Fox
London, N1
2009

Editorial Note

The extracts selected for this book come from a wide variety of printed and manuscript sources. We have adopted a degree of standardisation so that the reader will not be unduly distracted by often markedly different forms and styles, and such things as typographical conventions, spellings, capitalisation and (to a lesser extent) punctuation have been gently harmonised. To avoid confusion, the names of individuals and place names have also been regularised as far as possible to the most commonly accepted forms. In those instances, however, where the style adopted seems particularly characteristic and a part of the flavour of the piece, the original forms have been left unchanged.

Minor cuts, for ease of reading, have been made silently. We have also excised chapter numbers and headings where they disrupt the narrative flow. Significant cuts, however, have been marked with ellipses and substantive emendations or editorial interpolations in quoted matter have been placed in square brackets. The footnotes are confined to elucidating otherwise obscure remarks in the eyewitness accounts, and are not intended to be in any way comprehensive.

Most of the material in this volume has been extracted from original sources, but inevitably there is some overlap with other anthologies. There are a number of famous eyewitness accounts that have earned their place in any such collection, and readers will expect to see them in this one. Three anthologies in particular were helpful in suggesting some of the set pieces included in this book: *The Faber Book of Reportage* (1987), edited by John Carey, *The Mammoth Book of How it Happened* (1998–2006), edited by Jon E. Lewis, and *Eyewitness to America* (1997), edited by David Colbert.

VISIONS OF THE FUTURE

The twentieth century was born on a tide of hope and apprehension. Europe was already locked in an arms race which many feared, and a manic few hoped, might lead to war, and both Europe and the United States continued to carve out new colonies and spheres of interest across the globe – in Africa, South America, the Mediterranean, the Pacific, the South Seas and Asia. World history happened in the midst of an explosion of new ideas and visions of the future.

Transatlantic Triumphs and Disasters

Two major scientific breakthroughs took place at the beginning of the century – radium and relativity. Radium, a radioactive metallic element which was to become vital in medicine, was discovered in 1898 by the French physicist **Pierre Curie** *and his Polish wife,* **Marie.** *Working jointly, they finally managed to prove its existence in 1902 by preparing a decigram of pure radium and determining its atomic weight. Before that they had spent four years in a shed, sifting through tons of pitchblende, which contained both polonium and radium, and which had to be brought from the St Joachimsthal mines in Bohemia, where uranium salts were extracted for the making of glass. Pierre and Marie had to pool their savings to buy this material and transport it to Paris. The shed in which they worked at the Faculty of Medicine had an earth floor and was furnished with some old kitchen tables and a rusty stove. This is Marie's description of their working life during that time.*

We had no money, no laboratory and no help in the conduct of this important and difficult task. It was like creating something out of nothing, and if Casimir Dluski once called my student years 'the heroic years of my sister-in-law's life', I may say without exaggeration that this period was, for my husband and me, the heroic period of our common existence ...

And yet it was in this miserable old shed that the best and happiest years of our life were spent, entirely consecrated to work. I sometimes passed the whole day stirring a boiling mass, with an iron rod nearly as big as myself. In the evening I was broken with fatigue ...

I came to treat as many as 20 kilograms of matter at a time, which had the effect of filling the shed with great jars of precipitates and liquids. It was killing work to carry the receivers, to pour off the liquids and to stir, for hours at a stretch, the boiling matter in a smelting basin ...

At this period we were entirely absorbed by the new realm that was, thanks to an unhoped-for discovery, opening before us. In spite of the difficulties of our working conditions, we felt very happy. Our days were spent at the laboratory. In our humble shed there reigned a great tranquillity: sometimes, as we watched over some operation, we would walk up and down, talking about work in the present and in the future; when we were cold a cup of hot tea taken near the stove comforted us. We lived in our single preoccupation as if in a dream ...

We saw only very few persons at the laboratory; among the physicists and chemists there were a few who came from time to time, either to see our experiments or to ask for advice from Pierre Curie, whose competence in several branches of physics was well known. Then took place some conversations before the blackboard – the sort of conversation one remembers well because it acts as a stimulant for scientific interest and the ardour for work without interrupting the course of reflection and without troubling that atmosphere of peace and meditation which is the true atmosphere of a laboratory.

> *The Curies began to talk about radium as if it were a child about to be born. Marie is reported to have wondered 'what It will be like, what It will look like', while Pierre hoped that it would have a very beautiful colour. Forty-five months after they had first posited the existence of the element, they found out. Returning on impulse after a long day's work, they saw the particles glowing in the darkness with a phosphorescent bluish outline. As a couple they shared a Nobel prize in 1903, and after her husband's death in an accident Marie was awarded a further Nobel prize in 1911 for isolating radium and polonium.*
>
> *Meanwhile, in 1905 – 'the miraculous year', the physicist Albert Einstein proposed his special theory of relativity – the notion that the wavelength of light emitted by atoms was influenced by gravity. Though it would be another ten years before his general theory was formulated, 1905 marked the beginning of a huge advance in human understanding of the universe – equivalent in genius to the discoveries of Galileo and Newton.*

On 17 December 1903, at Kitty Hawk, North Carolina, the Wright broth-ers made the first powered flight. There were only a handful of witnesses, including the lifeguards at the Kill Devil Hills Life Saving Station, and at first the press did not believe the story. The plane weighed 745 pounds, less than half the weight of a modern car, and was powered by a 12- horsepower engine. This account comes from **Orville Wright**'s *diary.*

When we got up a wind of between 20 and 25 miles was blowing from the north. We got the machine out early and put out the signal for the men at the station ... After running the engine and propellers a few minutes to get them in working order, I got on the machine at 10.35 for the first trial ... On slipping the rope the machine started off increasing in speed to prob-ably 7 or 8 miles. The machine lifted from the truck just as it was enter-ing on the fourth rail. Mr Daniels took a picture just as it left the tracks. I found the control of the front rudder quite difficult on account of its being balanced too near the centre and thus had a tendency to turn itself when started so that the rudder was turned too far on one side and then too far on the other. As a result the machine would rise suddenly to about 10 feet and then as suddenly, on turning the rudder, dart for the ground. A sudden dart when out about 100 feet from the end of the tracks ended the flight. Time about twelve seconds (not known exactly as watch was not promptly stopped). The lever for throwing off the engine was broken, and the skid under the rudder cracked. After repairs, at twenty minutes after eleven o'clock Will made the second trial. The course was about like mine, up and down but a little longer over the ground though about the same in time. Distance not measured but about 175 feet. Wind speed not quite so strong. With the aid of the station men present, we picked the machine up and carried it back to the starting ways. At about twenty minutes till twelve o'clock I made the third trial. When out about the same distance as Will's, I met with a strong gust from the left which raised the left wing and sidled the machine off to the right in a lively manner. I immediately turned the rudder to bring the machine down and then worked the end control ... At just twelve o'clock Will started on the fourth and last trip.

The machine started off with its ups and downs as it had before, but by the time he had gone over 300 or 400 feet he had it under much better control, and was travelling on a fairly even course. It proceeded in this manner till it reached a small hummock out about 800 feet from the starting ways, when it began its pitching again and suddenly darted into the ground. The front rudder frame was badly broken up, but the main frame suffered none at all. The distance over the ground was 852 feet in 59 seconds. The engine turns was 1071, but this included several seconds while on the starting ways and probably about a half-second after landing. The jar of landing had set the watch on machine back so that we have no exact record for the 1071 turns. Will took a picture of my third flight just before the gust struck the machine. The machine left the ways successfully at every trial, and the tail was never caught by the truck as we had feared.

After removing the front rudder, we carried the machine back to camp. We set the machine down a few feet west of the building, and while standing about discussing the last flight, a sudden gust of wind struck the machine and started to turn it over. All rushed to stop it. Will who was near one end ran to the front, but too late to do any good. Mr Daniels and myself seized spars [uprights] at the rear, but to no purpose. The machine gradually turned over on us. Mr Daniels, having had no experience in handling a machine of this kind, hung on to it from the inside, and as a result was knocked down and turned over and over with it as it went. His escape was miraculous, as he was in with the engine and chains. The engine legs were all broken off, the chain guides badly bent, a number of uprights, and nearly all the rear ends of the ribs were broken.

On 15 April 1912 the liner Titanic, *on her maiden voyage, hit an iceberg and sank. Though the ship was British, many prominent Americans were on board, and of 2,224 passengers, 1,513 lives were lost – mostly from among those travelling steerage. The ship, which her owners had boasted was 'unsinkable', went down in a matter of hours, and there were spaces in lifeboats and collapsible rafts for only 1,178 people. It was one of the biggest disasters, and scandals, of peacetime maritime history.* **Harry Senior**, *a fireman, described the first impact of the iceberg.*

I was in my bunk when I felt a bump. One man said, 'Hello. She has been struck.' I went on deck and saw a great pile of ice on the well deck before the forecastle, but we all thought the ship would last some time, and we went back to our bunks. Then one of the firemen came running down and yelled, 'All muster for the lifeboats.' I ran on deck, and the captain said, 'All firemen keep down on the well deck. If a man comes up I'll shoot him.'

Then I saw the first lifeboat lowered. Thirteen people were on board, eleven men and two women. Three were millionaires, and one was Ismay [J. Bruce Ismay, managing director of the White Star Line; a survivor].

Then I ran up on the hurricane deck and helped to throw one of the collapsible boats on to the lower deck. I saw an Italian woman holding two babies. I took one of them, and made the woman jump overboard with the baby, while I did the same with the other. When I came to the surface the baby in my arms was dead. I saw the woman strike out in good style, but a boiler burst on the *Titanic* and started a big wave. When the woman saw that wave, she gave up. Then, as the child was dead, I let it sink too.

I swam around for about half an hour, and was swimming on my back when the *Titanic* went down. I tried to get aboard a boat, but some chap hit me over the head with an oar. There were too many in her. I got around to the other side of the boat and climbed in.

Harold Bride was one of the Titanic's *wireless operators. He gave this account to the* New York Times.

'We've struck an iceberg,' the captain said, 'and I'm having an inspection made to tell what it has done for us. You'd better get ready to send out a call for assistance. But don't send it until I tell you.'

The captain went away, and in ten minutes, I should estimate the time, he came back. We could hear a terrible confusion outside; there was not the least thing to indicate that there was any trouble. The wireless was working perfectly.

'Send the call for assistance,' ordered the captain, barely putting his head in the door.

'What call shall I send?' Phillips asked.

'The regulation international call for help. Just that.'

Then the captain was gone. Phillips began to send 'CQD'. He flashed away at it and we joked while he did so. All of us made light of the disaster.

We joked that way while he flashed signals for about five minutes. Then the captain came back.

'What are you sending?' he asked.

'CQD,' Phillips replied.

The humour of the situation appealed to me. I cut in with a little remark that made us all laugh, including the captain.

'Send SOS,' I said. 'It's the new call, and it may be your last chance to send it.'

Phillips, with a laugh, changed the signal to SOS. The captain told us we had been struck amidships, or just back of amidships. It was ten minutes, Phillips told me, after he had noticed the iceberg, that the slight jolt that was the collision's only signal to us occurred. We thought we were a good distance away.

We said lots of funny things to each other in the next few minutes. We picked up, first, the steamship *Frankford*. We gave her our position and said we had struck an iceberg and needed assistance. The *Frankford* operator went away to tell his captain.

He came back and we told him we were sinking by the head. By that time we could observe a distinct list forward.

The *Carpathia* answered our signals. We told her our position and said we were sinking by the head. The operator went to tell the captain and in five minutes returned and told us that the captain of the *Carpathia* was putting about and heading for us ...

[Phillips] was a brave man. I learned to love him that night, and I suddenly felt for him a great reverence to see him standing there sticking to his work while everybody else was raging about. I will never live to forget the work of Phillips for the last awful fifteen minutes.

I thought it was about time to look about and see if there was anything to catch that would float. I remembered that every member of the crew had a special lifebelt and ought to know where it was. I remembered mine was under my bunk. I went and got it. Then I thought how cold the water was.

I remembered that I had some boots and I put those on, and an extra jacket, and I put that on. I saw Phillips standing out there still sending away, giving the *Carpathia* details of just how we were doing.

We picked up the *Olympic* and told her we were sinking by the head, and were about all down. As Phillips was sending the message, I strapped his lifebelt to his back. I had already put on his overcoat.

I wondered if I could get him into his boots. He suggested with a sort of laugh that I look out and see if all the people were off in boats, or if any boats were left, or how things were.

I saw a collapsible boat near a funnel and went over to it. Twelve men were trying to boost it down to the boat deck. They were having an awful time. It was the last boat left. I looked at it longingly a few minutes. Then I gave them a hand, and over she went. They all started to scramble in on the boat deck, and I walked back to Phillips. I said the last raft had gone.

Then, came the captain's voice, 'Men, you have done your full duty. You can do no more. Abandon your cabin. Now it's every man for himself. You look out for yourselves. I release you. That's the way of it at this kind of a time. Every man for himself.'

I looked out. The boat deck was awash. Phillips clung on, sending and sending. He clung on for about ten minutes, or maybe fifteen minutes after the captain had released him. The water was then coming into our cabin.

While he worked something happened I hate to tell about. I was back in my room, getting Phillips's money for him, and as I looked out the door I saw a stoker, or somebody from below decks, leaning over Phillips from behind. He was too busy to notice what the man was doing. The man was slipping the lifebelt off Phillips's back.

He was a big man, too. As you can see, I am very small. I don't know what it was I got hold of. I remembered in a flash the way Phillips had clung on – how I had to fix that lifebelt in place, because he was too busy to do it.

I knew that man from below decks had his own lifebelt and should have known where to get it.

I suddenly felt a passion not to let that man die a decent sailor's death. I wish he might have stretched rope or walked a plank. I did my duty. I hope I finished him. I don't know. We left him on the cabin floor of the wireless room and he was not moving.

From aft came a tune from the band. It was a ragtime. I don't know what. Then there was 'Autumn'. Phillips ran aft, and that was the last I ever saw of him.

I went to the place I had seen the collapsible boat on the boat deck, and to my surprise I saw the boat, and the men still trying to push it off. I guess there wasn't a sailor in the crowd. They couldn't do it. I went up to them and was just lending a hand when a large wave came awash of the deck. The big wave carried the boat off. I had hold of an oarlock and I went with it. The next I knew I was in the boat. But that was not all. I was in the boat, and the boat was upside-down, and I was under it. And I remember realising I was wet through and that whatever happened I must not breathe, for I was under water. I knew I had to fight for it, and I did. How I got out from under the boat I do not know but I felt a breath of air at last. There were men all around me – hundreds of them. The sea was dotted with them, all depending on their lifebelts. I felt I simply had to get away from the ship. She was a beautiful sight then. Smoke and sparks were rushing out of her funnel. There must have been an explosion, but we heard none. We only saw the big stream of sparks. The ship was turning gradually on her nose – just like a duck that goes for a dive. I had only one thing on my mind: to get away from the suction. The band was still playing. I guess all of them went down. They were playing 'Autumn' then. I swam with all my might. I suppose I was 150 feet away when the *Titanic*, on her nose, with her afterquarter sticking straight up in the air, began to settle – slowly.

One of the passengers, **Mrs D. H. Bishop**, *witnessed the last moments of the great liner from one of the lifeboats.*

We did not begin to understand the situation till we were perhaps a mile or more away from the *Titanic*. Then we could see the rows of lights along the decks begin to slant gradually upward from the bow. Very slowly the lines of light began to point downward at a greater and greater angle. The sinking was so slow that you could not perceive the lights of the deck changing their position. The slant seemed to be greater about every quarter of an hour. That was the only difference.

In a couple of hours, though, she began to go down more rapidly. Then the fearful sight began. The people in the ship were just beginning to realise how great their danger was. When the forward part of the ship dropped suddenly at a faster rate, so that the upward slope became marked, there was a sudden rush of passengers on all the decks towards the stern. It was like a wave. We could see the great black mass of people in the steerage sweeping to the rear part of the boat and breaking through into the upper decks. At the distance of about a mile we could distinguish everything through the night, which was perfectly clear. We could make out the increasing excitement on board the boat as the people, rushing to and fro, caused the deck lights to disappear and reappear as they passed in front of them.

This panic went on, it seemed, for an hour. Then suddenly the ship seemed to shoot up out of the water and stand there perpendicularly. It seemed to us that it stood upright in the water for four full minutes.

Then it began to slide gently downwards. Its speed increased as it went down head first, so that the stern shot down with a rush.

The lights continued to burn till it sank. We could see the people packed densely in the stern till it was gone ...

As the ship sank we could hear the screaming a mile away. Gradually it became fainter and fainter and died away. Some of the lifeboats that had room for more might have gone to their rescue, but it would have meant that those who were in the water would have swarmed aboard and sunk her.

Social Revolution in Edwardian Britain

When Edward VII came to the British throne following the death of Queen Victoria in 1901, not a great deal was expected of him. He was already close on sixty, was no intellectual and was easily bored. His liaisons were many, his tastes were raffish and his boon companions disreputable. Nevertheless he proved a success as king. He enjoyed company, got on well with foreign statesmen and looked good in uniform. In retrospect the Edwardian age has acquired a golden glow, a sort of Indian summer before the horrors of the Great War, but in fact it was a time of turbulence and increasing tension. The 'Second Industrial Revolution', from 1870 onwards, introduced ever more new technologies and mechanisation. The Education Act of 1902 raised hopes and aspirations. Trade unions and workers' 'combinations' became increasingly active and powerful, using strikes to force concessions on pay and conditions of work. The women's suffrage movement was becoming militant, and the Labour Party, returned in numbers for the first time at the general election of 1906, heralded a move towards class politics.

At Tonypandy in Wales, on 9 November 1910, the government sent in the troops to break up a strike by miners. They went in on the orders of the young home secretary, Winston Churchill. The special correspondent of the Manchester Guardian, ***J. V. Radcliffe****, reported.*

The centre stretch of the Rhondda valley, where it lies deep between mountain slopes all autumn brown and ashen grey, was in wild turmoil late last night and early this morning. Strikers and policemen were in furious conflict, stones were thrown in showers, truncheons were drawn and vigorously used, colliery property was smashed, and more than a hundred strikers and six or seven policemen were injured, some of them badly. What set the bad spirit abroad cannot be known. It seemed to fall with the gathering darkness. High above the Llwynypia pit is a frowning head of rock, which the clouds wrapped round last night in sullen gloom, and if they had distilled riot and fury down its threatening front the effect in the valley could scarcely have been more sombre and wild. The first mutterings of trouble were heard about nine o'clock. Four thousand men marched to the pit and halted at its gate. This was a repetition so far of the morning and midday marches, but the temper of the men underwent a sudden change. Some youths showed the first symptoms of what was stirring. They made a rush towards the gates, where the police kept guard. It was not a formidable movement, and the police withstood the shock without a tremor, but the repulse set more evil designs on foot. A sober-minded collier very bravely ventured to set himself against the current of feeling. Climbing a bank, he began a speech of counsel to his fellow workmen to act humanely and justly. The counsel was too quiet for distempered minds, and if it had any effect at all it was only to divert attention from the colliery gates and their police guard to the long line of palisading that shuts off the pit yard from the road.

One common motive actuated the thousands of men massed together. It was to get to the electric powerhouse, to drive out the men in charge and stop the machinery. The powerhouse since Sunday has been manned by under-managers and other officials of the Glamorgan Colliery Company, with Mr Llewellyn, the general manager, at their head. The regular enginemen and stokers have been frightened away. The power station is the citadel of the situation so far as the Glamorgan Company is concerned. It supplies the power for pumping and ventilating five pits. The pits, at any rate, will be in danger of flooding, the ventilation has already ceased, and as a consequence the fate of hundreds of horses is only a matter of hours. To stop every bit of work at the collieries, to stop the pumping as well as the ventilating, was what one man called the trump card that the strikers were now to play. They rushed at the palisading to tear it down. They dared not push it before them lest they should fall with it on the railway below. It had to come down on the road. Thick stumps were snapped and props and stays torn up by the pulling of thousands of hands, and the men began to swarm into the pit yard. The brightly lighted power station was in front of them, and to hinder their advance only the railway, a line of trucks, and a score or two of policemen advancing in scouting order. Not one of the strikers got behind the line of trucks. Big, active men more than their match physically drove them violently back, and they did not try that way any more. Worse things were in store. Stone-throwing began. The road that skirts the colliery is cut low down on the hillside. Another road descends the hill to join it fast by the colliery, and for 150 yards it overlooks the colliery entrance. A band of strikers had taken up places here as well as on the slope between the two highways. Stones were plentiful, and big and small, just as they came to hand, they were hurled at the policemen at the gates.

The policemen were unfortunately conspicuous. The light from the power station, without which the men there could not work, shone on the silver facings of their helmets and made them an easy mark. Man after man was hit, and when the line was weakened and another attempt was made to carry the pit by storm the policemen gave way, and the strikers were already within the gates when re-inforcements came from another part of the yard. These men had their truncheons drawn, and laying freely about them they drove the crowd beyond the gates and some distance along the lower road. The men on the higher road were at the moment beyond reach, but when the stone-throwing commenced Captain Lionel Lindsay, chief constable of the county, called his men together and led them in a charge up the hill. The attacking force consisted of 118 men, every one of them 6 foot tall or thereabouts. With their truncheons in their hands they advanced with long swinging strides. The colliers did not wait. They preferred throwing stones from a distance to a personal encounter, in which, indeed, they would have been completely overmatched. They scuttled off as fast as their legs would carry them, but not fast enough for all to escape the horrid thud of truncheons on their heads and shoulders. It was a wild, headlong flight for safety, only limited by the necessity for the policemen to remain in touch with their base. Even after this there was no quietness. The strikers re-formed once and again, and other though minor charges were made. The night passed into morning, and still the road was in turmoil. About four o'clock there was a second but this time half-hearted attempt to storm the powerhouse. It was easily defeated.

Daylight revealed in a striking manner the part of the conflict that darkness had hidden. Most fearful-looking of the wreckage was the litter of stones, half-bricks, and bits of rock that lay all about the colliery gate. It was appalling to think of enduring that merciless, invisible hail. In less profusion, the missiles lay a considerable distance along the road, and a walk up to the hill showed where the supply had come from and the commanding position the throwers held. The best-placed would be 30 or 40 feet above the heads of the police and scarcely more than a street's width from them. Standing in a body, as they were obliged to do, and picked out by the colliery lights, the police were completely exposed, a mark for any coward who chose to aim from a distance.

The powerhouse itself, though it stands well back from the road, had not escaped scot-free. A number of its windows were perforated by stones, but no one inside was hurt. Those of its garrison who were struck were hit while passing to and from the boilers. Twenty men who are really prisoners in this building are waging a hard, unresting struggle against a flood of water in the mine. Amateurs at stoking as they are, they find it almost beyond their power to keep a sufficient head of steam to run the pumping machinery. None of them has slept since Sunday night, and weariness compels them to lie down sometimes on the hard concrete floor, but the rest is brief. They are doing all that men can do to save the pits, and are just keeping the water down. If it overflows the dam it will invade the steam coal pit, and incalculable damage may be done and some three hundred horses drowned. As it is three fates threaten the horses – by starvation, asphyxiation or drowning – and one can scarcely tell which is coming fastest ...

There was hope for a time during the afternoon that troops would not be necessary to enforce order in the valley. The morning had passed quietly, and the afternoon was occupied chiefly, so far as the strikers were concerned, with a mass meeting at which ten thousand were present, and a huge parade round the district. The long delay in the arrival of troops known to have started for the coalfield caused wonder and surprise, and the explanation came later in the afternoon. The strike leaders received a telegram from Mr Winston Churchill inviting them to meet him in London tomorrow. The home secretary's telegram added (according to a statement made by the strike leaders) that he was reluctant to have troops quartered in the valley, and that if quietness were maintained the troops on the way would not be sent to their destination. It was extremely unfortunate that this telegram had not arrived in time to be read at the mass meeting. The strike leaders met immediately afterwards to consider what reply they should send, and decided to accept Mr Churchill's offer and to advise the men to keep the peace.

There were, however, no effective means of promulgating their decision, and tonight Tonypandy has been the scene for hours of a terrible uproar. Rioting broke out again as soon as twilight fell. It began down at the Llwynypia (Glamorgan Colliery) pit. The police in strong force were again on duty at the gates and in the yard concentrating their force so as to defend the powerhouse. A great crowd drew up in the road. All at once stones began to hurtle through the air. Another attack was made on the palisading, and the wreckage of last night was piled up in the road to prevent the mounted police from charging. The fusilade on the police was unendurable. The chief constable took advantage of a temporary cessation of the onslaught to make a last appeal for order. The reply was another volley of stones.

The chief constable himself was hit and knocked to the ground. There was a menacing rush to the gates, and the police replied by drawing their staves and charging. They drove the men before them until they had cleared a good space, and just the same as last night it was necessary to clear the higher road with truncheons. This space the police resolved to defend. Their line was weakened by being extended, but they were in a less vulnerable position. On each side of them was a desperate crowd, but for a time they won a breathing space. The tale of the injured has yet to be told, however. Nobody knows how many are injured, but news comes from the pit that nine constables are lying there in a serious condition. The riot is spreading throughout the town, and it is unsafe to venture into the street. A fellow journalist has just come in bleeding from a wound in the head, inflicted by a stone. He was a stranger, and that alone seems to account for the attack. A reckless crowd is marching through the streets. There seem to be no police about. The rioters swarm down the main street ...

The town was awake all night. Excitement and fear kept many out of bed, and only the dawn scattered the prevailing alarm. All night long men were boarding up the shattered shop fronts and carts were going round for the sweepings of plate glass that littered the main street for three-quarters of a mile. Now and again there was the heavy tramp of large bodies of police going or returning from the Glamorgan pit at Llwynypia, but nothing occurred to remove or increase the anxious suspense. Today is also full of fear. The few shops that escaped damage yesterday are being barricaded today, and the night is awaited with dread. Soldiers have arrived. A squadron of the 18th Hussars reached Pontypridd early this morning, and after a rest a troop came here by road, a distance of 7 miles, while the other troop went to Aberdare. Their places at Pontypridd were taken by another squadron brought from Cardiff, where they had been overnight. The troop here rode through the town about one o'clock to their quarters at the New Colliery offices. The Metropolitan Mounted Constabulary have also arrived. Superficially there is nothing but curiosity in the minds of the slow-moving crowds that are in the streets, but the same could have been said yesterday, and those who know the temper of the Rhondda miners predict more trouble. Let us hope the prophets of evil are wrong.

The right to vote had always been contentious. As early as 1429, an Act passed in Henry VI's reign declared that 'great, outrageous and excessive numbers of people ... of small substance and no value' were voting at elections. By 'people' the Act naturally meant 'men'. It was not until the Great Reform Act of 1832 – the first major step forward since the time of Cromwell – that the urban franchise was made uniform at the £10 householder level, and even then, while radicals were pressing for more, men like Lord Macaulay insisted that universal suffrage was 'utterly incompatible with the very existence of civilisation'.

The campaign to give the vote to women was well under way by the later nineteenth century, but it was not until 1918 that this was granted, and then only to women over thirty. The term 'suffragette' was coined by the Daily Mail *to describe the militant group of feminists led by Emmeline Pankhurst and her daughters Christabel and Sylvia, who founded the Women's Social and Political Union in 1903. They led an increasingly spectacular series of protests to gain votes for women. The authorities responded with arrests and prison sentences, the women with hunger strikes, leading to the notorious 'Cat and Mouse' Act of 1913, which allowed hunger-striking prisoners to be freed and then rearrested once their health had improved. It was as a demonstration against this Act that Emily Wilding Davison made a lone attempt to disrupt the chief event of the racing calendar, the Epsom Derby, on 5 June of that year. The* **Manchester Guardian** *recorded what happened from several eyewitnesses.*

'They had just got round the Corner, and all had passed but the king's horse, when a woman squeezed through the railings and ran out into the course. She made straight for Anmer, and made a sort of leap for the reins. I think she got hold of them, but it was impossible to say. Anyway the horse knocked her over, and then they all came down in a bunch. They were all rolling together on the ground. The jockey fell with the horse, and struck the ground with one foot in the stirrup, but he rolled free. Those fellows know how to tumble. The horse fell on the woman and kicked out furiously, and it was sickening to see his hoofs strike her repeatedly. It all happened in a flash. Before we had time to realise, it was over. The horse struggled to its feet – I don't think it was hurt – but the jockey and the woman lay on the ground. The ambulance men came running up, put them on stretchers and carried them away. Most of the other jockeys saw nothing of it. They were far ahead. It was a terrible thing.'

This was an account given to me [writes a representative of the *Manchester Guardian*] by a man who was standing behind the rails quite near to the place where the woman rushed out. It conflicts in some detail with descriptions given by other people in the tightly-packed crowd at the Corner. Another version has it that the woman did not come from behind the rails, but had managed to stay outside when the mounted policemen cleared the course, and had concealed herself by crouching down, and that she ran towards the horse bending low without trying to seize the reins.

All the accounts agree that she was struck with terrible force by the galloping horse, and that she rolled several yards before the horse lost its footing and fell upon her. The jockey, said one man, 'flew from the horse's back like a stone from a sling', and it was doubtless only owing to his jockey's skill in knowing just how to fall that he was not far more seriously injured.

Anmer was the last of the string, and the last but one was Mr Bronson's Agadir, ridden by Earl. The woman just missed Agadir, and Earl was the only jockey who got a glimpse of what happened. The race had been over for some moments before the news reached the stands and the king learned what had befallen his jockey. He was standing in the Jockey Club at the time, and soon afterwards he looked on with great concern at the spectacle of the jockey, bleeding and with closed eyes, carried past on a stretcher towards the hospital. The king then went to tell the queen what had happened. The doctor afterwards reported to the king that Jones had had a wonderful escape. One of his arms was injured and he was bruised all over, and one of his ribs was broken.

The woman was far more seriously hurt, and the first report that spread about the course was that she was killed. She turned out to be one of the best-known of the militant suffragists, Miss Emily Wilding Davison. It is said that underneath her jacket was found a suffragette flag tied round her body. A house surgeon at the Epsom Cottage Hospital a couple of hours after the accident reported that she was suffering from severe concussion of the brain. 'She has lain unconscious since the time of her admission,' he said, 'and it is impossible to say for a few hours whether her life will be saved.'*

The first clue to her identity was the finding of a paper in her possession bearing the words 'WSPU Helpers'.

The people who were near enough to see what happened could not believe at first that the woman ran out deliberately. They thought she must have had the idea that all the horses had gone by, and had rushed on the course, as everyone does, as soon as the racers have passed. The only alternative to this theory in the mind of the crowd was that it was the deed of a mad person or a suicide, for it was about as dangerous a thing to do as it would be to throw oneself in the track of an express train.

The Manchester Guardian *supported the cause of votes for women. In 1913 it promoted the inquiry into the conditions for women at work by the Women's Industrial Council, and on 28 May 1913 published, from firsthand accounts, a report of women in domestic service, under the headline 'The Most Despised Form of Employment'.*

---

* In fact, she died of her injuries.

The servants were addressed by a set of twenty-four questions, of which two of the most striking were: (1) 'Would you advise any young friend to go into service? If not, why not?' and (2) 'What do you think could be done to make domestic service a more desirable occupation?' and the answers so far received, especially in reply to these cited questions, provide an unequivocal condemnation of our whole system of household organisation. The enquiries were sent forth broadcast throughout the United Kingdom, and have reached every grade of domestic service, from the 'between-maid' earning £12 a year to the butler who has visited fourteen countries, and who, according to his wife, a cook-housekeeper, 'is an honoured correspondent of many of the intellectual giants of the world'. From these varying social levels the answer returned is clear, decisive and, for the most part, reasoned; the profession is felt to be undesirable, if not repulsive, under its present conditions.

A cook of twenty-four years who has been ten years at work laments: 'When you are in domestic service you are not treated as human beings, and you are never able to go anywhere for a pleasure-trip the same as your girl friends, but have to stay in and work while your mistress takes her pleasure.' And then, with unexpected organising instinct, she adds that Sunday work might be better arranged: 'If they [i.e. the family] had cold supper we could have everything ready, and we could take it in turns and one come in early one Sunday and the other the next to clear and wash up, and then we should have Sunday a little different to a weekday.'

A children's nurse, aged thirty-two, replies to the question: 'How long holidays have you in the year?' 'One day in two years,' and sets down as her 'free time' in the day, 'An hour if the baby is asleep, not unless.' A lady's maid who has been fifteen years in household service, prompted thereto by 'a great desire to travel in foreign countries', remarks: 'For many nights in succession I do not go to bed till the early hours of the morning, but the day's work is expected just the same, and you are not expected to be tired.' And in answer to the question: 'How much free time have you each day in the house?' she states laconically, 'None.' A maid in a country vicarage has no time to herself on Sunday, but is constrained to attend church three times in the day, which necessitates changing her dress eight times. She notes that she 'cannot get out at all, not allowed even in an adjoining garden from the house', yet she would advise any young friend to go into service when she 'can get a little more liberty'.

Modern 'unrest' in the household can no longer be explained as an unreasonable revolt proceeding from elementary school education with a top dressing of Women's Suffrage Movement since a high degree of thoughtfulness characterises these replies, while in some cases a remarkable impartiality in judgement and a sense of fair play are displayed. There is, moreover, frequent allusion to the 'better living' in domestic service and occasional recognition of the advantages of an employment which fits a woman for married life, 'what lies before the majority of us', as a young cook sagely remarks. Still, the unanimous opinion is that present restrictions render domestic service 'the most despised form of employment'. 'We are treated much as though we were in prison'; 'we are kept in the house from week's end to week's end'; 'servants have it continually impressed upon them that they are inferior, and eventually do come inferior to what they were'; 'a girl in service is ignored by people in her own social scale'; 'the servant girl has less chance of marriage than any other' – such is the monotonous dirge that resounds through these papers.

A somewhat unexpected fact that comes to light is the resentment against the modern Sunday with its influx into the household of weekend visitors, varied entertainments and resultant extra work for the servants, and the desire for 'a quiet old-fashioned Sunday where there is not so much company going on' seems pretty general. Indeed, there appears to be a stirring of sentiment in several directions with regard to Sabbath observances. 'A girl should be allowed to follow her own religion,' remarks a kitchen-maid of twenty years, and a housemaid, aged twenty-one, says, 'We should not be asked if we have been to church.' Another young maid comments plaintively, 'We should not be made to go to church in bonnets,' and an upper housemaid of demurer years thinks that a servant ought not to be 'compelled to wear black to go to church'.

A more serious indictment against the employers is voiced in the oft-repeated assertion that mistresses lack in consideration for and courtesy to their maids, complaints which culminate in such observations as: (1) A parlourmaid, who remarks, 'I think in our days dogs are treated far better than human beings, as we are not allowed to use the bath, but in my last situation four dogs were bathed weekly and my share of the bath was to keep it clean after them'; and (2) a cook, who states, 'My sister and I were in separate situations in the Midlands. Though we knew no one else, yet we were not allowed to have each other in the kitchen.'

Imperial Dreams in the Antarctic

The Antarctic was the setting for one of the last great dramas of the imperial age. While the theory of a great frozen zone around the South Pole was proposed by Greek geographers in the fifth century BC, the discovery of the landmass itself did not take place until 1820, when three different expeditions recorded sightings. Sealers, whalers and other commercial vessels visited the region throughout the nineteenth century but by the end of it even the outline of the coast was only vaguely comprehended, and no attempt had been made to penetrate the interior.

In 1895 the Sixth Geographical Congress identified Antarctica as the last great challenge for explorers, and the two decades that followed witnessed some of the most extraordinary feats of endurance in the history of exploration. There were no fewer than sixteen expeditions between 1897 and 1917, including de Guerlache's Belgian expedition which explored the Antarctic peninsula and Borchgrevink's British expedition which was the first to winter ashore on the continent. But what really fired the imagination of imperial nations was the race for the Pole.

Captain Robert Falcon Scott, of the British Royal Navy, was every inch the Victorian explorer-hero. Between 1901 and 1904 his National Antarctic Expedition made the first extensive land explorations on the continent, and he soon became locked in intense rivalry with his fellow explorers in the effort to be first to the South Pole. With him on that journey was Ernest Shackleton, who suffered badly from scurvy. They were forced to turn back well short of their goal, and subsequently, in the Nimrod expedition of 1907–9, Shackleton nearly scooped the prize himself, crossing the Ross Ice Shelf and making the first ascent on to the vast polar plateau before turning *back only 97 miles from the Pole. When Scott set off for the Pole again in 1910, it was not only the pressure of Shackleton's near-miss that drove him, but the fact that it had become a genuine race with the tough and thoroughly professional Norwegian explorer Roald Amundsen, and while Scott's* Terra Nova *expedition went equipped for a wide-ranging scientific and exploratory programme, Amundsen had only one goal – the South Pole itself.*

The tragedy of the gifted amateur Scott, beaten to the post by a ruthless Norwegian professional, became part of the British national psyche for decades. After wintering at opposite ends of the Ross Ice Shelf, the two parties set out. Both suffered setbacks from the weather and frostbite, but Amundsen's team of Arctic veterans, skilfully using dogs to haul their sledges, were always to have the advantage over the less experienced Britons who were man-hauling theirs. **Amundsen** *completed his round land trip in ninety-nine days – he had scheduled one hundred. Here he describes reaching the Pole.*

We had a great piece of work before us that day: nothing less than carrying our flag further south than the foot of man had trod. We had our silk flag ready; it was made fast to two ski-sticks and laid on Hanssen's sledge. I had given him orders that as soon as we had covered the distance to 88°S, which was Shackleton's furthest south, the flag was to be hoisted on his sledge. It was my turn as forerunner, and I pushed on. There was no longer any difficulty in holding one's course; I had the grandest cloud-formations to steer by, and everything now went like a machine. First came the forerunner for the time being, then Hanssen, then Wisting, and finally Bjaaland. The forerunner who was not on duty went where he liked; as a rule he accompanied one or other of the sledges. I had long ago fallen into a reverie – far removed from the scene in which I was moving; what I thought about I do not remember now, but I was so preoccupied that I had entirely forgotten my surroundings. Then suddenly I was roused from my dreaming by a jubilant shout, followed by ringing cheers. I turned round quickly to discover the reason of this unwonted occurrence, and stood speechless and overcome.

I find it impossible to express the feelings that possessed me at this moment. All the sledges had stopped, and from the foremost of them the Norwegian flag was flying. It shook itself out, waved and flapped so that the silk rustled; it looked wonderfully well in the pure, clear air and the shining white surroundings; 88°23' was passed; we were further south than any human being had been. No other moment of the whole trip affected me like this. The tears forced their way to my eyes; by no effort of will could I keep them back. It was the flag yonder that conquered me and my will. Luckily I was some way in advance of the others, so that I had time to pull myself together and master my feelings before reaching my comrades. We all shook hands, with mutual congratulations; we had won our way far by holding together, and we would go farther yet – to the end.

We did not pass that spot without according our highest tribute of admiration to the man, who – together with his gallant companions – had planted his country's flag so infinitely nearer to the goal than any of his precursors. Sir Ernest Shackleton's name will always be written in the annals of Antarctic exploration in letters of fire. Pluck and grit can work wonders, and I know of no better example of this than what that man has accomplished.

Scott reached the Pole a month after Amundsen. His exhausted and demoralised five-man party began the return journey which became a running battle against bad weather and bad luck. Scott's journals, brilliantly and movingly written, were found in the tent on the Ross Ice Shelf where he and the remainder of his party perished shortly after 29 March 1912. By 16 March he already knew what the outcome would be.

Friday, 16 March or Saturday 17: Lost track of dates, but think the last correct. Tragedy all along the line. At lunch, the day before yesterday, poor Titus Oates said he couldn't go on; he proposed we should leave him in his sleeping-bag. That we could not do, and we induced him to come on, on the afternoon march. In spite of its awful nature for him he struggled on and we made a few miles. At night he was worse and we knew the end had come.

Should this be found I want these facts recorded. Oates's last thoughts were of his mother, but immediately before he took pride in thinking that his regiment would be pleased with the bold way in which he met his death. We can testify to his bravery. He has borne intense suffering for weeks without complaint, and to the very last was able and willing to discuss outside subjects. He did not – would not – give up hope till the very end. He was a brave soul. This was the end. He slept through the night before last, hoping not to wake; but he woke in the morning – yesterday. It was blowing a blizzard. He said, 'I am just going outside and may be some time.' He went out into the blizzard and we have not seen him since.

I take this opportunity of saying that we have stuck to our sick companions to the last. In case of Edgar Evans, when absolutely out of food and he lay insensible, the safety of the remainder seemed to demand his abandonment, but Providence mercifully removed him at this critical moment. He died a natural death, and we did not leave him till two hours after his death. We knew that poor Oates was walking to his death, but though we tried to dissuade him, we knew it was the act of a brave man and an English gentleman. We all hope to meet the end with a similar spirit, and assuredly the end is not far.

I can only write at lunch and then only occasionally. The cold is intense, −40° at midday. My companions are unendingly cheerful, but we are all on the verge of serious frostbites, and though we constantly talk of fetching through I don't think any one of us believes it in his heart.

We are cold on the march now, and at all times except meals. Yesterday we had to lay up for a blizzard and today we move dreadfully slowly. We are at no. 14 pony camp, only two pony marches from One Ton Depot. We leave here our theodolite, a camera and Oates's sleeping-bags. Diaries etc., and geological specimens carried at Wilson's special request, will be found with us or on our sledge ...

Monday, 19 March: Lunch. We camped with difficulty last night, and were dreadfully cold till after our supper of cold pemmican and biscuit and half a pannikin of cocoa cooked over the spirit. Then, contrary to expectation, we got warm and all slept well. Today we started in the usual dragging manner. Sledge dreadfully heavy. We are 15½ miles from the depot and ought to get there in three days. What progress! We have two days' food, but barely a day's fuel. All our feet are getting bad – Wilson's best, my right foot worst, left all right. There is no chance to nurse one's feet till we can get hot food into us. Amputation is the least I can hope for now, but will the trouble spread? That is the serious question. The weather doesn't give us a chance – the wind from N to NW and −40° temperature today.

Wednesday, 21 March: Got within 11 miles of depot Monday night; had to lay up all yesterday in severe blizzard. Today forlorn hope, Wilson and Bowers going to depot for fuel.

Thursday, 22 and 23 March: Blizzard bad as ever – Wilson and Bowers unable to start – tomorrow last chance – no fuel and only one or two of food left – must be near the end. Have decided it shall be natural – we shall march for the depot with or without our effects and die in our tracks.

Thursday, 29 March: Since the 21st we have had a continuous gale from WSW and SW. We had fuel to make two cups of tea apiece and bare food for two days on the 20th. Every day we have been ready to start for our depot 11 miles away, but outside the door of the tent it remains a scene of whirling drift. I do not think we can hope for any better things now. We shall stick it out to the end, but we are getting weaker, of course, and the end cannot be far.

It seems a pity, but I do not think I can write more.

R. SCOTT

For God's sake look after our people.

The rear party left by Scott at the coast had set out to find him but had narrowly missed doing so because of the blizzards. Their ship had to return to New Zealand before the pack ice closed in, but a number of the party, including **Apsley Cherry-Garrard**, *stayed on through a third Antarctic winter. It was Cherry-Garrard who eventually found the bodies of Scott and his companions on 12 November 1912. He describes the moment in* The Worst Journey in the World.

That scene can never leave my memory. We with the dogs had seen Wright turn away from the course by himself and the mule party swerve right-handed ahead of us. He had seen what he thought was a cairn, and then something looking black by its side. A vague kind of wonder gradually gave way to a real alarm. We came up to them all halted. Wright came across to us. 'It is the tent.' I do not know how he knew. Just a waste of snow: to our right the remains of one of last year's cairns, a mere mound: and then 3 feet of bamboo sticking quite alone out of the snow: and then another mound, of snow, perhaps a trifle more pointed. We walked up to it. I do not think we quite realised – not for very long – but someone reached up to a projection of snow, and brushed it away. The green flap of the ventilator of the tent appeared, and we knew that the door was below.

Two of us entered, through the funnel of the outer tent, and through the bamboos on which was stretched the lining of the inner tent. There was some snow – not much – between the two linings. But inside we could see nothing – the snow had drifted out the light. There was nothing to do but to dig the tent out. Soon we could see the outlines. There were three men here.

Bowers and Wilson were sleeping in their bags. Scott had thrown back the flaps of his bag at the end. His left hand was stretched over Wilson, his lifelong friend. Beneath the head of his bag, between the bag and the floor-cloth, was the green wallet in which he carried his diary. The brown books of diary were inside: and on the floor-cloth were some letters.

Everything was tidy. The tent had been pitched as well as ever, with the door facing down the sastrugi, the bamboos with a good spread, the tent itself taut and shipshape. There was no snow inside the inner lining. There were some loose pannikins from the cooker, the ordinary tent gear, the personal belongings and a few more letters and records – personal and scientific. Near Scott was a lamp formed from a tin and some lamp wick off a finnesko. It had been used to burn the little methylated spirit which remained. I think that Scott had used it to help him to write up to the end. I feel sure that he had died last – and once I had thought that he would not go so far as some of the others. We never realised how strong that man was, mentally and physically, until now.

We sorted out the gear, records, papers, diaries, spare clothing, letters, chronometers, finnesko, socks, a flag. There was even a book which I had lent Bill for the journey – and he had brought it back. Somehow we learned that Amundsen had been to the Pole, and that they too had been to the Pole, and both items of news seemed to be of no importance whatever. There was a letter there from Amundsen to King Haakon. There were the personal chatty little notes we had left for them on the Beardmore – how much more important to us than all the royal letters in the world.

We dug down the bamboo which had brought us to this place. It led to the sledge, many feet down, and had been rigged there as a mast. And on the sledge were some more odds and ends – a piece of paper from the biscuit box: Bowers's meteorological log: and the geological specimens, 30 pounds of them, all of the first importance. Drifted over also were the harnesses, ski and ski-sticks.

Hour after hour, so it seemed to me, Atkinson sat in our tent and read. The finder was to read the diary and then it was to be brought home – these were Scott's instructions written on the cover. But Atkinson said he was only going to read sufficient to know what had happened – and after that they were brought home unopened and unread. When he had the outline we all gathered together and he read to us the message to the public, and the account of Oates's death, which Scott had expressly wished to be known.

We never moved them. We took the bamboos of the tent away, and the tent itself covered them. And over them we built the cairn.

I do not know how long we were there, but when all was finished, and the chapter of Corinthians had been read, it was midnight of some day. The sun was dipping low above the Pole, the Barrier was almost in shadow. And the sky was blazing – sheets and sheets of iridescent clouds. The cairn and cross stood dark against a glory of burnished gold.

Cherry-Garrard was haunted for the rest of his life by the experience of finding Scott, and his account of the expedition in The Worst Journey in the World *is a fitting memorial – a masterpiece of travel writing as enduring as Scott's own journal.*

A fittingly heroic climax to the period came with **Ernest Shackleton's** *Imperial Trans-Antarctic Expedition of 1914–17. The aim was to cross the whole Antarctic continent, and a separate party, in the* Aurora, *sailed to the Ross Ice Shelf to establish depots for Shackleton and his team, who were to begin their crossing from the Weddell Sea. They never even started. By January 1915, Shackleton's ship, the* Endurance, *had become wedged in the pack-ice which was thickening for winter, and was eventually lost altogether. The crew had to make their way across the ice, dragging the ship's boats until they reached Elephant Island, off the Antarctic peninsula, where they camped on a spur of land backed by soaring cliffs and glaciers in ever-worsening conditions. On this voyage Shackleton was to prove himself a born survivor and – more importantly – a born leader. Though he could not* *match Scott as a writer, his description of the ice closing in on the* Endurance *is a memorable one, and Frank Hurley's photographs are, quite simply, unforgettable.*

This morning, our last on the ship, the weather was clear, with a gentle south-south-easterly to south-south-westerly breeze. From the crow's nest there was no sign of land of any sort. The pressure was increasing steadily, and the passing hours brought no relief or respite for the ship. The attack of the ice reached its climax at 4 p.m. The ship was hove stern up by the pressure, and the driving floe, moving laterally across the stern, split the rudder and tore out the rudder post and stern post. Then, while we watched, the ice loosened and the *Endurance* sank a little. The decks were breaking upwards and the water was pouring in below. Again the pressure began, and at 5 p.m. I ordered all hands on to the ice. The twisting, grinding floes were working their will at last on the ship. It was a sickening sensation to feel the decks breaking up under one's feet, the great beams bending and then snapping with a noise like heavy gunfire. The water was overmastering the pumps, and to avoid an explosion when it reached the boilers I had to give orders for the fires to be drawn and the steam let down. The plans for abandoning the ship in case of emergency had been made well in advance, and men and dogs descended to the floe and made their way to the comparative safety of an unbroken portion of the floe without a hitch. Just before leaving, I looked down the engine room skylight as I stood on the quivering deck, and saw the engines dropping sideways as the stays and bed plates gave way. I cannot describe the impression of relentless destruction that was forced upon me as I looked down and around. The floes, with the force of millions of tons of moving ice behind them, were simply annihilating the ship.

Essential supplies had been placed on the floe about 100 yards from the ship, and there we set about making a camp for the night. But about 7 p.m., after the tents were up, the ice we were occupying became involved in the pressure and started to split and smash beneath our feet. I had the camp moved to a bigger floe about 200 yards away, just beyond the bow of the ship. Boats, stores and camp equipment had to be conveyed across a working pressure ridge. The movement of the ice was so slow that it did not interfere much with our short trek, but the weight of the ridge had caused the floes to sink on either side and there were pools of water there.

A pioneer party with picks and shovels had to build a snow causeway before we could get all our possessions across ...

At midnight I was pacing the ice, listening to the grinding floe and to the groans and crashes that told of the death agony of the *Endurance*, when I noticed suddenly a crack running across our floe right through the camp. The alarm whistle brought all hands tumbling out, and we moved the tents and stores lying on what was now the smaller portion of the floe to the larger portion. Nothing more could be done at that moment, and the men turned in again; but there was little sleep. Each time I came to the end of my beat on the floe I could just see in the darkness the uprearing piles of pressure ice, which toppled over and narrowed still further the little floating island we occupied. I did not notice at the time that my tent, which had been on the wrong side of the crack, had not been erected again. Hudson and James had managed to squeeze themselves into other tents, and Hurley had wrapped himself in the canvas of No. 1 tent. I discovered this about 5 a.m. All night long the electric light gleamed from the stern of the dying *Endurance*. Hussey had left this light switched on when he took a last observation, and, like a lamp in a cottage window, it braved the night until in the early morning the *Endurance* received a particularly violent squeeze. There was a sound of rending beams and the light disappeared. The connection had been cut.

Morning came in chill and cheerless. All hands were stiff and weary after their first disturbed night on the floe. Just at daybreak I went over to the *Endurance* with Wild and Hurley, in order to retrieve some tins of petrol that could be used to boil up milk for the rest of the men. The ship presented a painful spectacle of chaos and wreck. The jib boom and bowsprit had snapped off during the night and now lay at right angles to the ship, with the chains, martingale and bobstay dragging them as the vessel quivered and moved in the grinding pack. The ice had driven over the forecastle and she was well down by the head. We secured two tins of petrol with some difficulty, and postponed the further examination of the ship until after breakfast. Jumping across cracks with the tins, we soon reached camp, and built a fireplace out of the triangular watertight tanks we had ripped from the lifeboat. This we had done in order to make more room. Then we pierced a petrol tin in half a dozen places with an ice axe and set fire to it. The petrol blazed fiercely under the 5-gallon drum we used as a cooker, and the hot milk was ready in quick time. Then we three ministering angels went round the tents with the life-giving drink, and were surprised and a trifle chagrined at the matter-of-fact manner in which some of the men accepted this contribution to their comfort. They did not quite understand what work we had done for them in the early dawn, and I heard Wild say, 'If any of you gentlemen would like your boots cleaned just put them outside!' This was his gentle way of reminding them that a little thanks will go a long way on such occasions.

The cook prepared breakfast, which consisted of biscuit and hoosh, at 8 a.m., and I then went over to the *Endurance* again and made a fuller examination of the wreck. Only six of the cabins had not been pierced by floes and blocks of ice. Every one of the starboard cabins had been crushed. The whole of the after part of the ship had been crushed concertina fashion. The forecastle and the Ritz were submerged, and the wardroom was three-quarters full of ice. The starboard side of the wardroom had come away. The motor engine forward had been driven through the galley. Petrol cases that had been stacked on the foredeck had been driven by the floe through the wall into the wardroom and had carried before them a large picture. Curiously enough, the glass of this picture had not been cracked, whereas in the immediate neighbourhood I saw heavy iron davits that had been twisted and bent like the ironwork of a wrecked train. The ship was being crushed remorselessly.

On Elephant Island the men lived in makeshift shelters provided by upturned lifeboats. Shackleton knew that they could survive only a few months at most, so he decided to sail one of the ship's boats, the James Caird, *to South Georgia, 800 miles to the north-east, to get help from the whaling stations there. Leaving Frank Wild, his faithful second-in-command, in charge of the Elephant Island party, and taking with him the one potentially mutinous member of the crew, Shackleton and his party set sail. Here the somewhat diffident executive officer of the* Endurance, **Frank Worsley**, *came into his own. He was a brilliant small-boat navigator, but even so the task was an almost impossible one: using only a sextant and intermittent sightings of the sun, he had to work out how to reach one small island in the vast space of the South Atlantic.*

Worsley was a natural raconteur, and his account of perhaps the most challenging small-boat voyage in history is one of the best adventure stories ever. He knew only too well what he and the scratch crew of the James Caird *were up against, as they fought their way through the most powerful ocean swells in the world, the rollers of the South Atlantic.*

In the afternoon the swell settled and lengthened out – the typical deep-sea swell of these latitudes. Offspring of the westerly gales, the great unceasing westerly swell of the Southern Ocean rolls almost unchecked around this end of the world in the Roaring Forties and the Stormy Fifties. The highest, broadest and longest swells in the world, they race on their encircling course until they reach their birthplace again, and so reinforcing themselves sweep forward in fierce and haughty majesty. 400, a thousand yards, a mile apart in fine weather, silent and stately they pass along. Rising 40 or 50 feet and more from crest to hollow they rage in apparent disorder during heavy gales. Fast clippers, lofty ships and small craft are tossed on their foaming, snowy brows, and stamped and battered by their ponderous feet, while the biggest liners are playthings for these real leviathans of the deep, with a front of a thousand miles. Smitten, pounded and smothered by them, many a good ship has foundered with all hands; a tossing lifebuoy or a grating alone remaining to mark their grave.

At times, rolling over their allotted ocean bed, in places four miles deep, they meet a shallow of 30 to a hundred fathoms – the Birdwood Bank, near Cape Horn, the Agulhas off the Stormy Cape and others. Their bases retarded by the bank – their crests sweep up in furious anger at this check, until their front forms an almost perpendicular wall of green rushing water that smashes on a ship's deck, flattening steel bulwarks, snapping 2-inch steel stanchions, and crushing deck-houses and boats like egg-shells. These blue water hills in a very heavy gale move as fast as 25 statute miles an hour, but striking the banks, the madly leaping crests falling over and onward, probably attain a momentary speed of 50 miles or more. The impact of hundreds of tons of solid water at this speed can only fairly be imagined. Even on deeper banks they may be seen 'topping up', for the disturbance of these huge rollers extends down a thousand feet at times. Born of the fierce, gloomy nor'wester, harrowed, combed and scourged by the devilish wrathful squalls of their sire, the sou'wester, they keep, in the main, to their easterly course. Even when meeting the sudden blast of the sou'easter's fury they still hold mightily on their way, their great crests blown back in long white streamers – the manes of the galloping white horses. Their sou'east foe may lead the attack for two or three days, and apparently stay their career, but they are never quite subdued, for as the gale eases they can still be seen moving east, though slowly, and when their head wind has died away, there they are, still pressing onward, unbeaten. They had only been hidden and disguised by the surface tumult of the sou'easter.

So we held our way; in those valleys and on those ridges alternately. First, half becalmed – a hill of water ahead, another astern – the following hill lifts us, and the boat slides with increasing speed down the ever-steepening slope, till with a sudden upward swoop, the sea boiling white around and over us, we are on the summit with a commanding view of a panorama of dark grey and indigo-blue rollers, topped and broken with white horses. The crest passing leaves the boat apparently stationary, gravity now holding her back till the next hollow reaches us, and so on *ad nauseam*.

There was little variety, during bad weather, in our conversation. We spoke in set phrases: 'What's it like?' – an enquiry regarding the weather from the watch coming on or someone below to the helmsman. 'There's a hell of a sea.' 'She steers like a Dutch galliot.' 'Eight bells.' 'The sun's coming out, Skipper.' 'Look out for a big 'un!' 'Pump ship!!' 'Balers!!!' 'Reef the mainsail!' 'Keep her north-east.' 'Curse these stones.' 'And this is how the poor live.' 'A life on the ocean wave. Bah!' 'Hoosh!!'

Thanks to Worsley, the Shackleton party made South Georgia in just under a fortnight. Their troubles were far from over. They were forced to land on the west side of the island, in the uninhabited King Haakon Bay, which meant that to reach the whaling stations on the east side, they would have to climb the formidable Allardyce range of mountains that runs down the spine of South Georgia. This would have been a formidable task in daylight and good weather – with winter upon them and short of food and clothes it was well-nigh impossible. On 19 May, at 3 a.m., Shackleton, Worsley and Tom Crean set out for the saddle they had seen from the boat – the only possible crossing-point – and after many wrong turnings and retracing of steps in deep snow, they found themselves, at 6 a.m. the following day, looking down on Fortuna Bay, and beyond it some glimpses of Stromness Bay and their goal. It was three in the afternoon by the time the three men reached the whaling station, 'ragged, filthy and evil-smelling: hair and beards long and matted with soot and blubber; unwashed for three months, and no bath or change of clothing for seven months. Fortunately', commented Worsley, 'we had no vermin.'

As a result of their epic journey, all Shackleton's crew were eventually rescued. The Endurance *adventure marked the climax of the heroic age – an exercise in sustained fortitude that never received the attention it deserved because, by the time it took place, the world was at war.*

The Balkans and the Coming of War

The period leading up to the First World War was characterised by the growing strength of some of the European powers and the weakness of others. Following its defeat by Russia in 1876–7, Turkey had been forced to grant independence to Romania, Serbia and Bulgaria, and from that moment on the 'Eastern Question' – the future of the Ottoman empire – dominated and divided Europe. As Turkish power waned, Russia increasingly competed with the Austrian empire for influence in the Balkans, and ultimately for control of Constantinople. Tension rose in 1908, when the Austro-Hungarian empire annexed Bosnia, an Ottoman territory that had been under Austrian administration since 1878, and Europe came to the brink of war. Russia pulled back when Germany offered to support its Austrian ally, but there was to be no further compromise. Russia would resist any Austrian advance into the Balkans.

*This bellicose jockeying for power in a historically unstable part of Europe went hand in hand with a rise in nationalism, fuelled by the emergence of an independent Greece in 1830, the rash of popular revolutions for political change in 1848 and the waning power of the Ottoman Turks. Among the reinvigorated nationalist causes was that of Albania, and one of its more exotic champions was an English spinster, **Edith Durham**. She travelled extensively throughout Albania and across the southern Balkans, giving, in her masterpiece* High Albania *(1909), a remarkable account of the lives of the mountain tribes living north of Scutari, who were governed, for the most part, by the notion of blood-vengeance and a distinctive oral code of law – the Canon of Lek.*

For all their habits, laws and customs, the people, as a rule, have but one explanation: 'It is in the Canon of Lek', the law that is said to have been laid down by the chieftain Lek Dukaghin. Lek is fabled to have legislated minutely on all subjects. For example, a man told me that Lek had ordered that men should walk the length of one gun-barrel apart, lest in turning the barrel should accidentally strike the next man, for a blow even by chance must be avenged. And this law was to keep peace. Similarly women must walk the length of one distaff apart – they always spin on the march.

Of Lek himself little is known. His fame among the tribes that still bear his name far exceeds that of Skenderbeg, and the fog of mythology is thick round him. He has left no mark on European history – is a purely local celebrity – but must have been of insistent individuality to have so influenced the people that 'Lek said so' obtains far more obedience than the Ten Commandments. The teachings of Islam and of Christianity, the sharia and Church law, all have to yield to the Canon of Lek ...

The most important fact in north Albania is blood-vengeance, which is indeed the old, old idea of purification by blood. It is spread throughout the land. All else is subservient to it.

'What profit is life to a man if his honour be not clean?' To cleanse his honour no price is too great. And in the mountains the individual is submerged in tribe. He is answerable, too, for the honour of his *mehala*, sometimes indeed of his whole *fis*.

Blood can be wiped out only with blood. A blow also demands blood, so do insulting words. One of the worst insults is the marrying of a girl betrothed to one man, to another. Nothing but blood can cleanse it.

Abduction of a girl demands blood, as does of course adultery. This does not appear to be common. It entails so much blood that 'the game is not worth the candle'. The blood taken need not be that of the actual offender. It must be male blood of his house or tribe. The usage differs in various districts, and will be noted in the accounts of them.

A man is answerable, too, for his guest, and must avenge a stranger that has passed but one night beneath his roof, if on his journey next day he be attacked. The sacredness of the guest is far-reaching. A man who brought me water from his house, that I might drink by the way, said that I now ranked as his guest, and that he should be bound by his honour to avenge me should anything happen to me before I had received hospitality from another.

Blood-vengeance, slaying a man according to the laws of honour, must not be confounded with murder. Murder starts a blood feud. In blood-vengeance the rules of the game are strictly observed. A man may not be shot for vengeance when he is with a woman nor with a child, nor when he is met in company, nor when *besa* (oath of peace) has been given. The two parties may swear such an oath for a few weeks if they choose, for business purposes. There are men who, on account of blood, have never been out alone for years.

When the avenger has slain his victim, he first reaches a place of safety, and then proclaims that he has done the deed. He wishes all to know his honour is clean. That he is now liable to be shot, and, if the blood be taken within the tribe, to heavy punishment also, is of minor moment to him.

In the Dukaghini tribes the council has power not merely to burn his house, but to destroy his crops, fell his trees, slaughter his beasts and condemn him to leave his land unworked. An incredible amount of food-stuff is yearly wasted, and land made desolate.

The house is perhaps not merely the home of himself, his wife and children, but that of a whole family community, forty or fifty people. The law is carried out to the last letter. It crushes the innocent along with the guilty; it is remorseless, relentless. But 'It is the Canon and must be obeyed.'

A man can save his house only if he can return to it and defend it successfully for three days, so that no one can approach near enough to set fire to it. A 'very brave man' was pointed out to me in Berisha, who has three times been condemned to have his house burnt, and each time saved it thus. A man can also save his property by inviting to the house the head of another *mehala*, who must then declare himself house lord and take command. The house is then, for the time being, his; he summons his own men to defend it, a regular battle may take place and the house be saved. But it is usual at once to call a council of elders to stop the warfare. In such a case it is usual to burn only the house, and spare the crop and other property (Berisha).

The Canon of Lek has but two punishments, fine and burning of property. Neither death nor imprisonment can be inflicted. Prison there is none. Death would but start a new feud. And Lek's object appears to have been to check feud ...

A woman is never liable for blood-vengeance, except in the rare case of her taking it herself. But even then there seems to be a feeling that it would be very bad form to shoot her. I could not hear of a recent case. I roused the greatest horror by saying that a woman who commits a murder in England is by law liable to the same punishment as a man. Shala is a wild tribe; it shoots freely. But a Shala man said, 'It is impossible. Where could a man be found who would hang a woman? No mountain man would do it. It is a bad law. You must be bad people.' He was as genuinely shocked as is a suburban mission meeting over the sacrifices of Dahomey. The tribe cannot punish bloodshed within the family group, e.g. if one cousin in a communal house kill another. The head of the house is arbiter. A man said naïvely on this subject, 'How can such a case be punished? A family cannot owe itself blood?' To him the 'family' was the entity; the individual had no separate existence. Marriage is arranged entirely by the head of the house. The children are betrothed in infancy or *in utero*. Even earlier. A man will say to another with whom he wishes to be allied, 'When your wife has a daughter I want her for my son.' A wife is always bought. The infant comes into the world irrevocably affianced, and part of the purchase-money is at once paid. She can marry no other man, is sent to her unknown husband when old enough, and the balance of the price handed over. The husband is bound to take her, no matter what she is like, or fall into blood with her family. The girl may – but it requires much courage on her part – refuse to marry the man. In that case she must swear before witnesses to remain virgin all her life. Should she break this vow, endless bloodshed is caused. If her father sell her to another it entails two bloods – blood between her family and her first betrothed's, and blood between her husband's and her betrothed's. Should she make a runaway match there is triple blood, as her family is at blood also with her husband's. In such cases the woman is furiously blamed. 'She knew the laws, and the amount of blood that must be shed.'

The most singular part of the business is the readiness with which most youths accept the girl bought for them. I never heard of one refusing, though I met several 'Albanian virgins', girls who had sworn virginity to escape their betrothed.

*The crisis unleashed by the Balkan Wars, during which Turkey lost almost all its European territories and the Balkan states divided up the spoils between them, began the slide into war, but it was not the trigger. The last day of 'peace' was 28 June 1914, the feast day of St Vitus, and a day of national celebration for Serbian nationalists. On that day the heir to the Austro-Hungarian throne, Archduke Franz Ferdinand, visited Sarajevo, capital of the recently annexed Bosnia-Hercegovina, and was assassinated, together with his wife, by Gavrilo Princip, of the Young Bosnia underground movement. **Borijove Jevtic**, one of the conspirators, describes how the plot was hatched and executed.*

A tiny clipping from a newspaper mailed without comment from a secret band of terrorists in Zagreb, capital of Croatia, to their comrades in Belgrade, was the torch which set the world afire with war in 1914. That bit of paper wrecked old proud empires. It gave birth to new, free nations.

I was one of the members of the terrorist band in Belgrade which received it and, in those days, I and my companions were regarded as desperate criminals. A price was on our heads. Today my little band is seen in a different light, as pioneer patriots. It is recognised that our secret plans hatched in an obscure café in the capital of old Serbia, have led to the independence of the new Yugoslavia, the united nation set free from Austrian domination.

The little clipping was from the *Srobobran*, a Croatian journal of limited circulation, and consisted of a short telegram from Vienna. This telegram declared that the Austrian archduke Franz Ferdinand would visit Sarajevo, the capital of Bosnia, on 28 June, to direct army manoeuvres in the neighbouring mountains.

It reached our meeting place, the café called Zeatna Moruana, one night the latter part of April 1914 ... At a small table in a very humble café, beneath a flickering gas jet we sat and read it. There was no advice or admonition sent with it. Only four letters and two numerals were sufficient to make us unanimous, without discussion, as to what we should do about it. They were contained in the fateful date, 28 June.

How dared Franz Ferdinand, not only the representative of the oppressor but in his own person an arrogant tyrant, enter Sarajevo on that day? Such an entry was a studied insult.

The date of 28 June is engraved deeply in the heart of every Serb, so that the day has a name of its own. It is called the *Vidovdan*. It is the day on which the old Serbian kingdom was conquered by the Turks at the battle of Amselfelde in 1389. It is also the day on which in the Second Balkan War the Serbian arms took glorious revenge on the Turk for his old victory and for the years of enslavement.

That was no day for Franz Ferdinand, the new oppressor, to venture to the very doors of Serbia for a display of the force of arms which kept us beneath his heel.

Our decision was taken almost immediately. Death to the tyrant!

Then came the matter of arranging it. To make his death certain twenty-two members of the organisation were selected to carry out the sentence. At first we thought we would choose the men by lot. But here Gavrilo Princip intervened. Princip is destined to go down in Serbian history as one of her greatest heroes. From the moment Ferdinand's death was decided upon he took an active leadership in its planning. Upon his advice we left the deed to members of our band who were in and around Sarajevo under his direction and that of Gabrinovic, a linotype operator on a Serbian newspaper. Both were regarded as capable of anything in the cause.

The fateful morning dawned. Two hours before Franz Ferdinand arrived in Sarajevo all the twenty-two conspirators were in their allotted positions, armed and ready. They were distributed 500 yards apart over the whole route along which the archduke must travel from the railway station to the town hall.

When Franz Ferdinand and his retinue drove from the station they were allowed to pass the first two conspirators. The motor cars were driving too fast to make an attempt feasible and in the crowd were Serbians: throwing a grenade would have killed many innocent people.

When the car passed Gabrinovic, the compositor, he threw his grenade. It hit the side of the car, but Franz Ferdinand with presence of mind threw himself back and was uninjured. Several officers riding in his attendance were injured.

The cars sped to the town hall and the rest of the conspirators did not interfere with them. After the reception in the town hall General Potiorek, the Austrian commander, pleaded with Franz Ferdinand to leave the city, as it was seething with rebellion. The archduke was persuaded to drive the shortest way out of the city and to go quickly.

The road to the manoeuvres was shaped like the letter V, making a sharp turn at the bridge over the river Nilgacka. Franz Ferdinand's car could go fast enough until it reached this spot but here it was forced to slow down for the turn. Here Princip had taken his stand.

As the car came abreast he stepped forward from the kerb, drew his automatic pistol from his coat and fired two shots. The first struck the wife of the archduke, the archduchess Sofia, in the abdomen. She was an expectant mother. She died instantly.

The second bullet struck the archduke close to the heart.

He uttered only one word, 'Sofia' – a call to his stricken wife. Then his head fell back and he collapsed. He died almost instantly.

The officers seized Princip. They beat him over the head with the flat of their swords. They knocked him down, they kicked him, scraped the skin from his neck with the edges of their swords, tortured him, all but killed him.

Then he was taken to the Sarajevo gaol. The next day he was transferred to the military prison and the round-up of his fellow conspirators proceeded, although he denied that he had worked with anyone.

He was confronted with Gabrinovic, who had thrown the bomb. Princip denied he knew him. Others were brought in, but Princip denied the most obvious things.

The next day they put chains on Princip's feet, which he wore till his death.

His only sign of regret was the statement that he was sorry he had killed the wife of the archduke. He had aimed only at her husband and would have preferred that any other bullet should have struck General Potiorek.

The Austrians arrested every known revolutionary in Sarajevo and among them, naturally, I was one. But they had no proof of my connection with the crime. I was placed in the cell next to Princip's, and when Princip was taken out to walk in the prison yard I was taken along as his companion.

THE GREAT WAR

How it Began

*In Britain it was 'Tommy Atkins' who first went to war – that veteran of Kiplingesque legend who had seen service with the regular army on the plains of India, the sands of Egypt and the veld of South Africa. The British Expeditionary Force numbered about eighty thousand soldiers, most of whom, whatever their quarrels with the status quo at home, went in the belief that they were fighting (as the British slogan had it) for 'Honour, Justice, Truth and Right'. A few, like the poet **Alfred Lichtenstein**, seemed to realise the enormity of what lay ahead, though for him the war was brutally short. He wrote these lines as he left for the front on 7 August 1914. Seven weeks later he was killed.*

Leaving for the Front*
Before I die I must just find this rhyme.
Be quiet, my friends, and do not waste my time.

We're marching off in company with death.
I only wish my girl would hold her breath.

There's nothing wrong with me. I'm glad to leave.
Now mother's crying too. There's no reprieve.

And now look how the sun's begun to set.
A nice mass-grave is all that I shall get.

Once more the good old sunset's glowing red.
In thirteen days I'll probably be dead.

---

* Translated from the German by Patrick Bridgwater.

Behind the tangled barbed wire and assorted artillery, both armies dug in. Christmas 1914 brought a spontaneous truce for the day, at least on some parts of the Western Front. It is recalled here in two accounts, the first by **Lieutenant Johannes Niemann** *of the 133rd Royal Saxon Regiment, who describes the jumpiness that accompanied the 'truce' – and the famous football match that followed.*

We came up to take over the trenches on the front between Frelinghien and Houplines, where our regiment and the Scottish Seaforth Highlanders were face to face. It was a cold starry night and the Scots were a hundred or so metres in front of us in their trenches where, as we discovered, like us they were up to their knees in mud. My company commander and I, savouring the unaccustomed calm, sat with our orderlies round a Christmas tree we had put up in our dugout.

Suddenly, for no apparent reason, our enemies began to fire on our lines. Our soldiers had hung little Christmas trees covered with candles above the trenches and our enemies, seeing the lights, thought we were about to launch a surprise attack. But by midnight it was calm once more. Next morning the mist was slow to clear and suddenly my orderly threw himself into my dugout to say that both the German and Scottish soldiers had come out of their trenches and were fraternising along the front. I grabbed my binoculars and looking cautiously over the parapet saw the incredible sight of our soldiers exchanging cigarettes, schnapps and chocolate with the enemy. Later a Scottish soldier appeared with a football which seemed to come from nowhere and a few minutes later a real football match got under way. The Scots marked their goal mouth with their strange caps and we did the same with ours. It was far from easy to play on the frozen ground, but we continued, keeping rigorously to the rules, despite the fact that it only lasted an hour and that we had no referee. A great many of the passes went wide, but all the amateur footballers, although they must have been very tired, played with huge enthusiasm. Us Germans really roared when a gust of wind revealed that the Scots wore no drawers under their kilts – and hooted and whistled every time they caught an impudent glimpse of one posterior belonging to one of 'yesterday's enemies'. But after an hour's play, when our commanding officer heard about it, he sent an order that we must put a stop to it. A little later we drifted back to our trenches and the fraternisation ended.

The game finished with a score of three goals to two in favour of Fritz against Tommy.

The experience of Captain Stockwell's company was collected as part of a superb eyewitness compendium by **Captain J. C. Dunn**, *Medical Officer of the Royal Welch Fusiliers, called* The War the Infantry Knew. *The Royal Welch Fusiliers was the regiment of Siegfried Sassoon and Robert Graves, and the latter became a close friend of Dunn's. Though not as famous as the works of the two poets, Dunn's book is an astonishing record of the war, recalling what happened in the front line for the duration, from 1914 to 1918.*

I think I and my company have just spent one of the most curious Christmas Days we are ever likely to see. It froze hard on Christmas Eve, and in the morning there was a thick ground-fog. I believe I told you the Saxons opposite had been shouting across in English. Strict orders had been issued that there was to be no fraternising on Christmas Day. About 1 p.m., having seen our men get their Christmas dinners, we went into our shelter to get a meal. The sergeant on duty suddenly ran in and said the fog had lifted and that half a dozen Saxons were standing on their parapet without arms. I ran out into the trench and found that all the men were holding their rifles at the ready on the parapet, and that the Saxons were shouting, 'Don't shoot. We don't want to fight today. We will send you some beer.' A cask was hoisted on to the parapet and three men started to roll it into the middle of no man's land. A lot more Saxons then appeared without arms. Things were getting a bit thick. My men were getting a bit excited, and the Saxons kept shouting to them to come out. We did not like to fire as they were all unarmed, but we had strict orders and someone might have fired, so I climbed over the parapet and shouted, in my best German, for the opposing captain to appear. Our men were all chattering and saying, 'The captain's going to speak to them.' A German officer appeared and walked out into the middle of no man's land, so I moved out to meet him amidst the cheers of both sides. We met and formally saluted. He introduced himself as Count Something-or-other, and seemed a very decent fellow. He could not talk a word of English. He then called out to his subalterns and formally introduced them with much clicking of heels and saluting. They were all very well turned out, while I was in a goatskin coat. One of the subalterns could talk a few words of English, but not enough to carry on a conversation. I said to the German captain, 'My orders are to keep my men in the trench and allow no armistice. Don't you think it is dangerous, all your men running about in the open like this? Someone may open fire.' He called out an order and all his men went back to their parapet, leaving me and the five German officers and a barrel of beer in the middle of no man's land. He then said, 'My orders are the same as yours, but could we not have a truce from shooting today? We don't want to shoot, do you?' I said, 'No, we certainly don't want to shoot, but I have my orders to obey.' So then we agreed not to shoot until the following morning when I was to signal that we were going to begin. He said, 'You had better take the beer. We have lots.' So I called up two men to take the barrel to our side. As we had lots of plum puddings I sent for one and formally presented it to him in exchange for the beer. He then called out, 'Waiter,' and a German private whipped out six glasses and two bottles of beer, and with much bowing and saluting we solemnly drank it amid cheers from both sides. We then all formally saluted and returned to our lines. Our men had sing-songs, ditto the enemy.

*National myths were forged and destroyed in a war that brought the Russian, Austrian, Turkish and German empires to an end and created new countries from the Balkans to the south Pacific. One of the most potent was the story of Australian nationhood, baptised in the blood of a futile bid to capture the Dardanelles and thus to command the sea route to Constantinople (Istanbul) on the Gallipoli peninsula. The Ottoman empire had joined the Austro-German alliance in November 1914, in return for a promise that Macedonia would be restored to Turkish rule. During the nine-month battle for Gallipoli, which the Turks eventually won, the Australians and New Zealanders of the Anzacs took more than twenty-six thousand casualties, killed and wounded, out of a force of thirty-six thousand. The British and the Turks fared even worse. **Captain T. A. White** of the Australian Imperial Force recalls the day of the landings on Gallipoli.*

Dawn, 25 April: Ominous and thrilling sounds in the distance. We all knew that our 1st Division mates were in it, and became impatient to join them. Passing Cape Helles we could see the battle and the shelling of the village of Sedd-el-Bahr. At 4.30 p.m. we dropped anchor off Anzac Cove. On all sides battleships were bombarding the distant hills; nearer in towards the shore were transports discharging their troops into destroyers, which then darted towards the shore to discharge the men into rowing boats. Shells were bursting around and over the vessels and boats and we could hear the crackling of machine-guns and rifles.

At 9.30 p.m. destroyers came alongside. In the dark the laden men climbed down the gangways and unsteady ladders, feeling uncomfortable in spite of our practice, until we felt our legs gripped by the friendly hands of the sailors. As each destroyer received its complement it rushed towards the shore and soon came within range of the enemy bullets. Nearer the beach the men climbed into the boats and were towed by launches or rowed to the shore. Several were wounded and a few killed on the destroyers and in the boats.

The rendezvous of the battalion was on the slope of Ari Burnu and from there at daybreak next morning, wet with dismal rain that had been falling since midnight, we moved in file on Monash Valley. Spreading out and lying down in the scrub we found bullets coming in all directions.

During the morning the swarms of Turks coming down were shelled by our warships and this caused them to break up into small parties of threes and fours and to advance these driblets down in short rushes to minimise losses. In this way, in spite of heavy casualties, they soon became overwhelming. All day long we were losing cobbers and stretcher-bearers were kept busy. At times the noise was deafening. Orders of a most contradictory nature came along from both flanks and worried us considerably. One officer of the 1st Brigade, utterly worn out and unnerved by thirty hours' fighting, continually stood upon a conspicuous point and waving two revolvers shouted, 'Five rounds rapid, and charge!' For hours he led a charmed life.

Both sides were trying to entrench within 40 yards of one another on the same narrow ridge and every now and again the digging was interrupted to 'Stand-to' and our positions were so precarious that the enemy only needed to drive our thin line back a few yards in order to hurl us over into the valley. But our men were so solid that every Turkish attempt failed. All through the afternoon charge after charge was made. Sergeant Shapley (just promised his commission for splendid work) would jump on his parapet, followed by his platoon, charge into the scrub with fixed bayonets, yelling 'Imshi! Imshi!' and, after each successful charge, he would stand and cheer regardless of the enemy.

The Turks now quailed considerably, but further reinforcements and darkness increased their valour, and again they came on, determined to clear us off the peninsula. After sounding our 'Cease Fire' they advanced to the weirdest accompaniment ever heard in battle. Bugles called eerily along the whole front, advancing and retiring, blaring suddenly close up and then in the dark distance, the echoes repeating in the gullies, while crashes of rifles and machine-guns occasionally drowned the efforts of the musicians. There was no tune about it – simply weird blasts, whistle-blowing and shouting – the blasts apparently being signals in Morse. If those signals were orders to drive us into the sea, they were of little avail. Our bullets mowed down line after line.

The stalemate ended in December 1915 when, following huge casualties and no ground gained, it was decided to withdraw. The veteran war correspondent **H. W. Nevinson** *describes the evacuation.*

The stores began to go first, slowly. Various ruses and accidents served to deceive the enemy, who even thought that the increased number of ships off the bay signified a strongly renewed attack about Christmas. To maintain this apprehension, parties of our men were taken off at night and returned by day, like a stage army. On the final day, an ironic order commanded that the immemorial custom of our men showing themselves on the skyline should be carefully maintained, and we all did our best to serve our country by walking everywhere round Suvla in the enemy's sight. Orders were further received that mule-carts were to be driven slowly up and down. The mules were singular fine animals; happily all were saved at Suvla, and nearly all at Anzac. Native Indians managed them as though mules were well-trained dogs, and served with great patience and fortitude, even under the severe trial of tempest and frost.

After the strain of carefully organised preparations, the excitement of the final hours was extreme, but no signs of anxiety were shown. Would the sea remain calm? Would the moon remain veiled in a thin cloud? Would the brigades keep time and place? Our own guns continued firing duly till the moment for withdrawal came. Our rifles kept up an intermittent fire, and sometimes came sudden outbursts from the Turks. An aeroplane whirred overhead, but was invisible. We could not be sure it was our own until we saw a green star blaze for a few seconds just below Saturn. On the earth a few fires still blazed where camps or dugouts were once inhabited, but gradually they went out. Only far off the hospital tents along the curving shore showed lights, and there were only two of these. The sea glimmered white through a moonlit haze, and over its surface thin black lines kept moving. Could an enemy see, or could he possibly miss the significance of those thin black lines?

Mules neighed, chains rattled, steamers hooted low and sailor men shouted into megaphones language strong enough to carry a hundred miles. Still the enemy showed no sign of life or hearing, though he lay almost visible in the moonlight across the familiar scene of bay and plain and hills to which British soldiers have given such unaccustomed names. So the critical hours went by slowly, and yet giving so little time for all to be done. At last the final bands of silent defenders began to come in from the nearest lines. Sappers began to come in, cutting all telephone wires and signals on their way. Some sappers came after arranging slow fuses to kindle our few abandoned stores of biscuits, bully beef and bacon left in the bends of the shore. Silently the staffs began to go. The officers of the beach party, who had accomplished such excellent and sleepless work, collected. With a smile they heard the distant blast of Turks still labouring at the trenches – a peculiar instance of labour lost. Just before three a pinnace took me off to one of the battleships. At half-past three the last-ditchers put off. From our familiar northern point of Suvla Bay itself, I am told, the general commanding the 9th Army Corps was himself the last to leave, motioning his chief of staff to go first. So the Suvla expedition came to an end after more than five months of existence. I do not discuss policy, but the leaving of the existence well became it.

In Istanbul, Turkish families waited for news from the front. In his Portrait of a Turkish Family, *__Irfan Orga__ left a remarkable account of his family's*

*life during this, the last great war of the Ottoman empire. He recalls the visit
to a Captain Ali with his mother to hear about the death of his father on the
march to the Dardanelles front.*

Then the man called Ali, who was a captain, plunged into conversation to
tell her this story.

On the march to the Dardanelles my father had suffered badly from
foot trouble. He had to march day and night, night and day, and his feet
began to swell and in the end they had had to cut his torn boots off him.
The two feet were found to be badly infected right up to the ankles and
soaked in fresh, bright blood. He had been left by the roadside, as was the
custom, and they had called back down the lines that a wounded man
lay under a tree. And eventually this message would reach the end of
the marching lines where a horse-drawn cart lumbered for the express
purpose of picking up the sick and wounded. But if the cart was already
full to overflowing with all the other sick soldiers who had dropped out on
the way? Ah well – in that case a man just lay by the side of the road under
the blazing sun and waited for the next lot of marching soldiers to take up
the same old cry, that a man lay wounded under the trees by the side of an
alien road. Down, down the weary lines the cry would go, but perhaps by
the time the sick-cart reached the spot a man would be dead and there was
not much point in carrying a dead man – when there were so many living
who still might be saved. But of course, Captain Ali hastened to assure my
mother that my father was picked up and taken to a base hospital – where
he died.

As he told her all these unsavoury things, his pale face flickered and his
eyes were loath to meet hers – for how could he tell this white, courageous
woman that neither he nor anyone else knew where her husband had
died? But she persisted in subjecting herself to this useless agony, demand-
ing the name of the hospital – as if the young captain could have told her,
even supposing he knew. He was infinitely patient, holding himself stiffly
to attention, assuring her that everything that could have been done had
been done. And in the end she had to be contented, for there was nothing
else he could tell her. So she thanked him and he saluted her, as one brave
soldier to another, and she took my hand and we began the long trudge
back to the station.

She did not speak to me at all but walked as if mechanically propelled, never slackening or altering her pace, although my small legs were breaking under me. I begged her to sit down, to let me rest, crying in my tiredness and with cold, for the day had become overcast and all signs of spring had left the air. I tottered beside her and plucked at her skirt and she looked at me, as if she did not recognise me, as if I had brought her back from some far place, and I cried all the more bitterly in this new loneliness. Then I saw expression creep into her dead eyes and she caught me to her and sat down with me in a ditch.

'Poor tired boy!' she said over and over again, as though she knew no other words or as though this repetition would still remembrance of something else, something that lurked in the foreground of the mind and would not be pushed back, back with all those other memories that could not be looked upon because they were still too new.

She put her arms around me and repeated her meaningless refrain and frightened me unendurably, for her arms held no security and her voice no comfort and I did not know if she was speaking to me or to some image of my father, whom she held in her empty, rocking arms.

The Western Front

Robert Graves, *writer and poet, had just left his school, Charterhouse, when England declared war on Germany. He decided immediately to enlist and a few months later found himself in France as an officer with the Royal Welch Fusiliers. Those were the early days of trench warfare, 'the days', he says in Goodbye to All That, 'of the jam-tin bomb and the gas-pipe trench-mortar: still innocent of Lewis or Stokes guns, steel helmets, telescopic rifle-sights, gas-shells, pill-boxes, tanks, well-organised trench-raids or any of the later refinements ...' Graves's tour guide to the forward positions was none other than Captain J. C. Dunn (see p. 47).*

I had expected a grizzled veteran with a breastful of medals; but Dunn was actually two months younger than myself – one of the fellowship of 'only survivors'. Captain Miller of the Black Watch in the same division was another. Miller had escaped from the rue du Bois massacre by swimming down a flooded trench. Only survivors had great reputations. Miller used to be pointed at in the streets when the battalion was back in reserve billets. 'See that fellow? That's Jock Miller. Out from the start and hasn't got it yet.' Dunn did not let the war affect his morale at all. He greeted me very easily with: 'Well, what's the news from England? Oh, sorry, first I must introduce you. This is Walker – clever chap from Cambridge, fancies himself as an athlete. This is Jenkins, one of those elder patriots who chucked up their jobs to come here. This is Price – joined us yesterday, but we liked him at once: he brought some damn good whisky with him. Well, how long is the war going to last, and who's winning? We don't know a thing out here. And what's all this talk about war-babies? Price pretends ignorance on the subject.' I told them about the war, and asked them about the trenches.

'About trenches,' said Dunn. 'Well, we don't know as much about trenches as the French do, and not near as much as Fritz does. We can't expect Fritz to help, but the French might do something. They are too greedy to let us have the benefit of their inventions. What wouldn't we give for their parachute-lights and aerial torpedoes! But there's never any connection between the two armies, unless a battle is on, and then we generally let each other down.

'When I came out here first, all we did in trenches was to paddle about like ducks and use our rifles. We didn't think of them as places to live in, they were just temporary inconveniences. Now we work here all the time, not only for safety but for health. Night and day. First, at firesteps, then at building traverses, improving the communication trenches, and so on; last comes our personal comfort – shelters and dugouts. The territorial battalion that used to relieve us were hopeless. They used to sit down in the trench and say: "Oh, my God, this is the limit." Then they'd pull out pencil and paper and write home about it. Did no work on the traverses or on fire positions. Consequence – they lost half their men from frost-bite and rheumatism, and one day the Germans broke in and scuppered a lot more of them. They'd allowed the work we'd done in the trench to go to ruin, and left the whole place like a sewage farm for us to take over again. We got sick as muck, and reported them several times to brigade headquarters; but they never improved. Slack officers, of course. Well, they got smashed, as I say, and were sent away to be lines-of-communication troops. Now we work with the First South Wales Borderers. They're all right. Awful swine, those territorials. Usen't to trouble about latrines at all; left food about to encourage rats; never filled a sandbag. I only once saw a job of work that they did: a steel loop-hole for sniping. But they put it facing square to the front, and quite unmasked, so two men got killed at it – absolute death-trap. Our chaps are all right, but not as right as they ought to be. The survivors of the show ten days ago are feeling pretty low, and the big new draft doesn't know a thing yet.'

'Listen,' said Walker, 'there's too much firing going on. The men have got the wind up over something. If Fritz thinks we're jumpy, he'll give us an extra bad time. I'll go up and stop them.'

Dunn went on: 'These Welshmen are peculiar. They won't stand being shouted at. They'll do anything if you explain the reason for it – do and die, but they have to know their reason why. The best way to make them behave is not to give them too much time to think. Work them off their feet. They are good workmen, too. But officers must work with them, not only direct the work. Our timetable is: breakfast at eight o'clock in the morning, clean trenches and inspect rifles, work all morning; lunch at twelve, work again from one till about six, when the men feed again. "Stand-to" at dusk for about an hour, work all night, "stand-to" for an hour before dawn. That's the general programme. Then there's sentry-duty. The men do two-hour sentry spells, then work two hours, then sleep two hours. At night, sentries are doubled, so working parties are smaller. We officers are on duty all day, and divide up the night into three-hourly watches.' He looked at his wristwatch. 'By the way,' he said, 'that carry-ing-party must have brought up the RE stuff by now. Time we all got to work. Look here, Graves, you lie down and have a doss on that bunk. I want you to take the watch before "stand-to". I'll wake you up and show you around. Where the hell's my revolver? I don't like to go out without it. Hello, Walker, what was wrong?'

Walker laughed. 'A chap from the new draft. He had never fired on his musketry course at Cardiff, and tonight he fired ball for the first time. It went to his head. He'd had a brother killed up at Ypres, and sworn to avenge him. So he blazed off all his own ammunition at nothing, and two bandoliers out of the ammuntion-box besides. They call him the "Human Maxim" now. His foresight's misty with heat. Corporal Parry should have stopped him; but he just leant up against the traverse and shrieked with laughter. I gave them both a good cursing. Some other new chaps started blazing away too. Fritz retaliated with machine-guns and whizz-bangs. No casualties. I don't know why. It's all quiet now. Everybody ready?'

Graves and Dunn recorded the experience of young officers in the line, increasingly reluctant warriors. In Her Privates We, *a brilliant autobiog-raphy very thinly disguised as a novel,* **Frederic Manning**, *an Australian adventurer, tells how it felt to be a private soldier.*

A couple of days later, in the small hours of the morning, Bourne was on the firestep; and Corporal Jakes was asleep in the same bay. The weather had become much clearer. After a time Bourne seemed to forget his own existence; not that he was dreaming, or was unaware of the world about him, for every nerve was stretched to the limit of apprehension. Staring into the darkness, behind which menace lurked, equally vigilant and furtive, his consciousness had pushed out through it, to take possession, gradually, and foot by foot, of some 40 or 50 yards of territory within which nothing moved or breathed without his knowledge of it. Beyond this was a more dubious obscurity, into which he could only grope without certainty. The effort of mere sense to exceed its normal function had ended, for the moment at least, not only in obliterating his own identity, and merging it with those objects of sense which he did actually perceive, but in dissolving even their objective reality into something incredible and fantastic. He had become so accustomed to them that they had ceased to have any reality or significance for him. The night was quiet. Puddles and flat wet surfaces reflected what was no more than a reminiscence of light. Against the skyline he could see strands of wire, and the uprights leaning awry; and beyond them little waifs of diaphanous mist drifting into the darkness. The darkness itself changed continually, clearing at times to a curious transparency, and then clouding again. The moon was behind a bank of cloud in the west; but the stars sparkled with the brilliance they gain from frost. At intervals the silence became so intense that he almost expected it to crack like ice. Then the whine of a shell would traverse it, or several in succession pass overhead, a pack in full cry; and there were dull explosions, or the sudden stutter of a machine-gun in the distance. The mind, so delicately sensitive to the least vibration from the outer world, no longer recorded it in the memory, unless it had some special relevance. The sound for which he was waiting was that of a stumble in the dark, or of a shaken, creaking wire; and that for which his eyes sought, where dark-ness swallowed up the travelling wraiths of mist, was a crawling shadow advancing stealthily towards him. It was such an unearthly stillness, that he almost prayed for something to happen, so that he might kill, or be killed. Sooner or later it would come, out of the hostile night. He waited in motionless expectancy, his tin-hat tilted forward slightly over his eyes and gleaming very faintly, as his waterproof groundsheet, worn cape-wise and tied at the neck with a bootlace through two of its eyelets, gleamed also, from the damp air which had condensed on it.

Corporal Jakes slept. Bourne could hear his breathing; but for that matter he could hear his own breathing, as though it came from a third man. Then, within that territory, which had become as it were his whole mind, something shifted; and he drew in his breath quickly, all his previously passive awareness concentrating itself purposively on one point. It was almost imperceptible, as though a clod of mud had shifted a little; but it continued, something separated itself from the mass, and the intaken breath escaped from him in a sigh of disgust, as a rat came hurrying, with a quick dainty movement of its twinkling feet, towards him. Seeing him, it stopped, a few yards from the parapet, its muzzle twitching sensitively, sat up, sleek and well fed, to stroke its whiskers with its forepaws; and then, avoiding the puddles and shell-holes, turned aside in a direction parallel to the trench, not taking a straight path, but picking its way delicately along the ridges, as though to keep its feet dry.

> *For the French forces on the Western Front, the battle became focused on the complex of fortresses round Verdun, itself a fortress-city. Life in the trenches for the French* poilu *was every bit as grim as for the Tommies of the British armies and the French soldiers had, in* **Henri Barbusse**, *a chronicler as accomplished and brutally honest as Robert Graves and Frederic Manning.* Under Fire *was published in 1916, as the battle for Verdun reached its height. Barbusse himself, who became a pacifist, describes the scene unforgettably.*

Half-drowsing, half-asleep, sometimes opening our eyes only to shut them again, paralysed, exhausted and cold, we experience the incredible renewal of light.

Where are the trenches?

We can see lakes and between them lines of stagnant, milky water.

There is even more water than we thought. The water has got everywhere, spreading all around, and the prediction of the men last night has been realised: there are no trenches – the trenches are under those canals. The world is flooded. The battlefield is not asleep, it is dead. Somewhere over there life may go on, but we cannot see that far.

I half get up, painfully, swaying like an invalid, to look around. My coat weighs me down with its dreadful burden. Beside me are three monstrously shapeless forms. One of them – Paradis, under an extraordinary crust of mud, with a swelling around his waist in place of his cartridge belt – also rises. The others are asleep and motionless.

And then what is this silence? It is prodigious. There is no noise, except from time to time the falling of a sod of earth into the water, in the midst of this fantastic paralysis of the world. No one is shooting: no shells, because they would not explode; no bullets, because the men ...

The men! Where are the men?

Bit by bit we start to see them. There are some not far from us, spread out, asleep, caked in mud from head to foot, changed almost into things.

Some distance away I can make out others, curled up and stuck like snails along a rounded embankment half covered in water – a motionless line of crude shapes, parcels next to one another, dripping with mud and water, the colour of the earth that surrounds them.

Making an effort to break the silence I ask Paradis, who is also looking in that direction: 'Are they dead?'

'We'll go and look in a while,' he whispers. 'Let's stay here for a bit longer. In a while we'll feel more like going.'

We exchange a glance and then turn to those who have also come to rest here. Our faces are so weary that they are no longer faces: something dirty, smudged and bruised, with bloodshot eyes, on top of us. We have seen each other in every guise since the beginning, yet we can no longer recognise one another.

Paradis turns away and looks at something else. Suddenly I notice that he has started to tremble. He extends a huge arm, encrusted with mud.

'Look there ... there ...' he says.

There are shapes, round reefs floating on the water overflowing from one trench in the midst of a particularly uneven, humpy patch of ground. We drag ourselves over to it. They are men who have drowned.

Their heads and arms are under water, but you can see their backs with the leather of their equipment emerging on the surface of the pasty liquid, while their blue cloth trousers are blown up with the feet attached crosswise to these balloon legs, like the rounded black feet stuck on the shapeless legs of clowns or puppets. From one sunken head the hair is standing upright like waterweed. Here there is a face almost emerging, its head stranded on the edge while the body vanishes into the murky depths. It is looking upwards, its eyes two white holes, its mouth one black one. The puffy yellow skin of this mask looks soft and wrinkled, like cold pastry.

The men there were on watch. They could not haul themselves out of the mud. All their efforts to escape from the ditch with its sticky embankment, slowly, fatally filling up with water, only served to drag them further back towards the bottom. They died holding on for support to the earth as it slid away from them.

Here are our front lines, and there the German ones, equally silent and submerged.

We go over to these soft ruins, passing through what was only yesterday a zone of terror, the dreadful space at the edge of which the forward thrust of our last attack had to come to a halt. Here, for a year and a half, bullets and shells were continually exchanged, their crossed fire furiously raking the ground from one horizon to another.

Now it is a supernatural field of rest. Everywhere the landscape is dotted with sleeping figures, or others who are gently moving, raising an arm, lifting their heads, starting to live again – or in the process of dying.

The enemy trench is finally collapsing into itself at the bottom of great undulations and marshy craters, filled with mud, through which it forms a line of puddles and wells. In places you can see the still-overhanging edges move, break up and slide down. At one point you can lean over it.

There are no bodies in this whirlpool of mire, but over there, worse than a body, is a lone arm, naked and pale as stone, emerging from a hole that can be vaguely distinguished in the wall, under the water. The man was buried in his shelter and only had time to reach out his arm.

An anonymous correspondent for the **New York Times** *witnessed, in the searchlight, the French shelling of the Meuse dykes on 12 April. Hundreds of Germans drowned.*

Then a dense thundercloud covers everything. The searchlight's rays beat vainly against its yellowish walls. The glass trembles in my hand.

Like a nightmare vision, conjured by magic amid the smoke, a horrible scene is revealed, first dimly, then clearer, and finally very distinct in the sharp white light.

The field, the dark line and the rushing ants have disappeared. In their place a ragged hollow, wherein blocks of earth, like huge tree-trunks, roll and quiver.

Among them the tiny dark things are writhing like fallen leaves fluttered by the breeze. Those shapeless objects are German soldiers.

As the smoke clears I distinguish arms raised in agony or supplication. Some try to crawl upward. They form heaps, sliding back together as one mounts another and drags him down.

Meanwhile from the right of the scene, what seems to be an immense black snake creeps forward. In the ray of the light it glimmers, and the observer beside me mutters, 'My God.'

It reaches the lip of the hollow, and the mass of crawling men quiver with a new agitation. It is the water of the Meuse overwhelming the German survivors, already dazed and disabled by the same concentration of melinite that ruptured the river's dykes. With frantic gestures the Germans fight upward, there comes a flash, and another cloud patch, half-veiling the chaos of earth and water, and drowning men.

Then the shells begin to fall rapidly, and the searchlight abandons the struggle against the smoke, swinging higher along the bare hillside. A few moments later it returns. I see a placid pool glimmering beneath the ray, save where an occasional spot of blackness is floating motionless.

I look at my watch. Three hours have passed since we entered the post. That is what I saw of the greatest battle for Verdun.

*For the Royal Navy the major clash of the war at sea was off Jutland at the end of May 1916, when the German Grand Fleet sailed into the North Sea to challenge the British blockade. This was the biggest battle of ironclad warships to date, and it ended with both sides pulling back after inflicting heavy damage. The German navy was not defeated, but the blockade went on. **Bill Fell** was an eighteen-year-old midshipman in HMS Warspite.*

I'd had forenoon watch on the bridge and, at about 12.30, I went down below and cut and made some sandwiches. I then ran off to my action station, the transmitting station, right in the bowels of the ship, five decks down. Three heavy armoured hatches rang shut above us. We then got orders that the enemy were in sight. Then 'ranges' and 'elevations and bearings' began to come in. My job was on a bearing plot, a very simple device on which I had to plot the rate of change of bearing so that the guns could follow it. The senior midshipman down below was plotting the mean of the ranges that were coming down to him from the rangefinders. Shortly after 4 p.m. we opened fire at 18,000 yards (just over 10 miles) on the battle-cruiser *Von der Tann*. There were corrections straight away because we were short: we went up 800 yards. Then all of a sudden there was a monumental crump which sounded as if all the tea trays in the world, full of crockery, had been dropped on our heads; the whole ship rattled and shook. We realised we'd been hit by something pretty big. We were only just recovering from that when there was an even worse crash which knocked us off our stools. I was dazed and when I sat up I was in water. Apart from one stuttering light in the corner it was pitch dark. Worst of all was the complete silence. No sound of the engines, no sound of the action, no sound except for swishing water.

After a moment, I noticed that down all the voice pipes was spurting a good old sluice of water – so we were slowly flooding. I think we all began to come to about the same time and two young midshipmen, who had only been on the ship a couple of weeks, began to whimper a bit. The senior midshipman went across and banged their two heads together and dropped them back into the water. Well, that solved that problem.

We then went back to trying to do our job, but of course no information was coming down. Then, reassuringly, the engines started and we found a few lamps and got them going. But we were still anxious about our situation. The senior midshipman found his way to the voice pipe and called up 'Foretop? Foretop?' He then paused. 'What another one gone up? Splendid!' He was in fact speaking to a mythical Foretop through a wrecked voice pipe. Of course we didn't realise that, and so our morale shot up. After that we waited and waited for about an hour and a half. Then we heard banging on the hatches and someone let us out.

I didn't recognise the ship when I got up on deck. She was a shambles, every single boat had gone, splinters everywhere, funnels were riddled or falling down. She was a hell of a mess. Thirty dead and wounded. A cordite fire had broken out in the starboard 6-inch battery and many had been burnt. She was right down in the water with the quarterdeck nearly awash. I went up on the bridge and Captain Philpotts turned to me and said, 'How did you like that, boy?' I said, 'Not much, sir.'

We were now out of the action and on our own. We had suffered a jammed helm probably from being put hard over at 24 knots and we'd done an unrehearsed complete circle within 10,000 yards of Scheer's line around the sinking *Warrior*. We'd become an irresistible target and we'd been hit eighty-seven times, thirteen of which had been big-calibre hits. Everyone else had disappeared and we were ordered back to Rosyth. The constructor came up on the bridge and told the captain that we could not exceed 8 knots otherwise we'd sink. The captain rang down to the engine room: '12 knots.'

We were attacked the following morning by a U-boat. A torpedo was fired at us and we all watched as it ran from the stern parallel with us about 40 feet away to disappear ahead. The U-boat broke surface very close and we nearly rammed her. In fact people were throwing wreckage at her, from the upper deck. She had lost buoyancy and so was too close to fire. We were very lucky! Then two little torpedo boats came out to join us and we were very relieved to see them.

I don't think we gave any thought to how we would be received at home. But as we passed up the Firth of Forth and under the bridge, all the railway people were lined along it. To our dismay they shouted 'Cowards! Cowards, you ran away!' and chucked lumps of coal at us. We were received at Rosyth with very, very great disapproval by the local people. They were all in mourning, black hats and black arm-bands. They all felt the Grand Fleet had suffered complete defeat and that some ships, like the *Warspite*, had run away. That was the news that had reached Scotland and it was twenty-four hours before things got better, when the other ships returned and more facts were known.

The Battle of the Somme

More than six hundred thousand were killed at Verdun, which was only saved by the attack launched by the British on the Somme on 1 July 1916. The Somme offensive was arguably the great turning-point for the British on the Western Front – at least as far as future generations and their perceptions were concerned. There were over four hundred thousand casualties, and by the end of it people were beginning to question the bloodletting. By now the British force, under General Rawlinson, was a new form of citizen army, recruited by Lord Kitchener, then minister for war, with one of the iconic posters of the campaign proclaiming, 'Your country needs you!' Around twenty thousand British soldiers were killed on the first day of the Somme offensive alone, and some forty thousand wounded. The fighting went on for months. The Ulster Division was decimated, and, at Beaumont-Hamel, of the 801 men of the Newfoundland Regiment that went over the top that morning, only sixty-eight responded to the roll-call the next day.

Sergeant Major Ernest Shepard, later the matchless illustrator of such children's classics as Winnie-the-Pooh *and* The Wind in the Willows, *describes his experience of that day in his diary.*

A lovely day, intensely hot. Lot of casualties in my trench. The enemy are enfilading us with heavy shell, dropping straight on us. A complete trench mortar battery of men killed by one shell, scores of dead and badly wounded in trench, now 1 p.m. Every move we make brings intense fire, as trenches so badly battered the enemy can see all our movements. Lot of wounded in front we got in, several were hit again and killed in trench. We put as many wounded as possible in best spots in trench and I sent a lot down, but I had so many of my own men killed and wounded that after a time I could not do this. Sent urgent messages to Brigade asking for RAMC bearers to be sent to evacuate wounded, but none came, although Brigade said they had been despatched. Meanwhile the enemy deliberately shelled the wounded between the trenches with shrapnel, thus killing, or wounding, again most of them. Our own regimental stretcher-bearers worked like niggers to take cases away. Counted all Dorsets at 1 p.m. Total fifty-three all ranks. At 3 p.m. the Manchesters went through the Russian Sap and made an attack, captured a portion of the Leipzig Redoubt. Brigade sent message to say we would be relieved by 15th Highland Light Infantry as soon as possible. Meanwhile we were to hold tight.

We needed to; literally we were blown from place to place. Men very badly shaken. As far as possible we cleared trenches of debris and dead. These we piled in heaps, enemy shells pitching on them made matters worse.

Wounded suffering agonies. I got them water from bottles of dead, a few managed to crawl away to the Aid Post in wood. At dusk we got more wounded in from the front. At 8 p.m. we got shelled intensely, and continued at intervals. I had miraculous escapes. The HLI arrived at midnight. I handed care of wounded to them, and took remnants of B and C Companies, only ten NCOs and men, back via Mounteagle and Rock St., through Wood Post and over same track (Dumbarton) through Blighty Wood, down the valley to Crucifix Corner. Arrived there at 1 a.m. on Sunday 2 July.

Robert Graves was wounded at Bazentin, during the complicated and disastrous attack on the Fricourt sector.

The German batteries were handing out heavy stuff, 6- and 8-inch, and so much of it that we decided to move back 50 yards at a rush. As we did so, an 8-inch shell burst three paces behind me. I heard the explosion, and felt as though I had been punched rather hard between the shoulder-blades, but without any pain. I took the punch merely for the shock of the explosion; but blood trickled into my eye and, turning faint, I called to Moodie: 'I've been hit.' Then I fell. A minute or two before I had got two very small wounds on my left hand; and in exactly the same position as the two that drew blood from my right hand during the preliminary bombardment at Loos. This I took as a lucky sign, and for further security repeated to myself a line of Nietzsche's, in French translation: 'Non, tu ne me peux pas tuer!' It was the poem about a man on the scaffold with the red-bearded executioner standing over him. (My copy of Nietzsche's poems, by the way, had contributed to the suspicions of my spying activities. Nietzsche, execrated in the newspapers as the philosopher of German militarism, was more properly interpreted as a William le Queux mystery-man – the sinister figure behind the Kaiser.)

One piece of shell went through my left thigh, high up, near the groin; I must have been at the full stretch of my stride to escape emasculation. The wound over the eye was made by a little chip of marble, possibly from one of the Bazentin cemetery headstones. (Later, I had it cut out, but a smaller piece has since risen to the surface under my right eyebrow, where I keep it for a souvenir.) This, and a finger-wound which split the bone, probably came from another shell bursting in front of me. But a piece of shell had also gone in 2 inches below the point of my right shoulder-blade and came out through my chest 2 inches above the right nipple.

My memory of what happened then is vague. Apparently Dr Dunn came up through the barrage with a stretcher-party, dressed my wound, and got me down to the old German dressing-station at the north end of Mametz Wood. I remember being put on the stretcher, and winking at the stretcher-bearer sergeant who had just said: 'Old Gravy's got it, all right!' They laid my stretcher in a corner of the dressing-station, where I remained unconscious for more than twenty-four hours.

Late that night, Colonel Crawshay came back from High Wood and visited the dressing-station; he saw me lying in the corner, and they told him I was done for. The next morning, 21 July, clearing away the dead, they found me still breathing and put me on an ambulance for Heilly, the nearest field hospital. The pain of being jolted down the Happy Valley, with a shell-hole at every 3 or 4 yards of the road, woke me up. I remember screaming. But back on the better roads I became unconscious again. That morning, Crawshay wrote the usual formal letters of condolence to the next of kin of the six or seven officers who had been killed. This was his letter to my mother:

22 July 1916

Dear Mrs Graves,

I very much regret to have to write and tell you your son has died of wounds. He was very gallant, and was doing so well and is a great loss.

He was hit by a shell and very badly wounded, and died on the way down to the base, I believe. He was not in bad pain, and our doctor managed to get across and attend to him at once.

We have had a very hard time, and our casualties have been large. Believe me, you have all our sympathy in your loss, and we have lost a very gallant soldier.

Please write to me if I can tell you or do anything.

Yours sincerely,

C. CRAWSHAY, LT-COL.

Then he made out the official casualty list – a long one, because only eighty men were left in the battalion – and reported me 'died of wounds'.

*During the Somme campaign, the British used aerial reconnaissance on a wider scale than ever before. The planes flew above the artillery, and attempted to photograph the German positions and the muzzle flashes of their guns. One of the pioneers of this kind of flying was **Cecil Lewis**, who had managed to join the Royal Flying Corps in 1915 by lying about his age – he was not yet seventeen – and whose memoir,* Sagittarius Rising, *is one of the masterpieces in the literature of flying. He was ordered to take off at dawn on 1 July 1916, and for him it was far from a fine day.*

The zero hour of the Somme offensive drew nearer. The troops, sent down for a long rest before it, had learned with us the new co-operative methods of contact patrol, and had now returned to the lines, ready for the attack. The guns were all in position, and most of the squadron spent all their time ranging them. I happened to be the exception, for I was put on to photography.

The whole section of our front, from Thiepval, down past Boisselle, round the Fricourt salient, and on to Montauban, was to be photographed every day, in order that headquarters might have accurate information of the effects of the bombardment. This aimed at destroying all the enemy first- and second-line trenches, and so making the attack easy for the infantry.

In this it was only partially successful, for the Germans had constructed concrete redoubts and defences that remained to a large extent intact, even after the terrific bombardment. Fricourt, which stood on a sharp rise, was in reality an impregnable concrete fort, bristling with machine guns. It was only evacuated when the advance, more successful on either side of it, pinched it off, and forced those in Fricourt itself to retire.

At leisure we had photographed the line before the bombardment started. But during this last week the weather was poor. On two days, low clouds and rain prevented us getting any photos at all. The 3rd and 15th Corps, for whom we were working, got in a panic. It was essential to know the effect of the shelling. Photos were to be got at all costs.

We went out in the afternoon. The clouds forced us down to 2,000 feet. A terrific bombardment was in progress. The enemy lines, as far as we could see, were under a white drifting cloud of bursting high explosive. The shell-bursts were continuous, not only on the lines themselves, but on the support trenches and communications behind.

At 2,000 feet we were in the path of the gun trajectories, and as the shells passed, above or below us, the wind eddies made by their motion flung the machine up and down, as if in a gale. Each bump meant that a passing shell had missed the machine by 4 or 5 feet. The gunners had orders not to fire when a machine was passing their sights, but in the fury of the bombardment much was forgotten – or perhaps the fact that we were not hit proves the orders were carried out. If so, they ran it pretty fine.

Grimly I kept the machine on its course above the trenches, waiting, tense and numb, for a shell to get us, while Sergeant Hall (who got a DCM and a commission for his work that week) worked the old camera handle, changed the plates, sighted, made his exposures. I envied him having something to do. I could only hold the machine as steady as possible and pray for it to be over. At last, after an hour, I felt a tap on my shoulder. Gratefully I turned for home.

Just above us the heavy cloud-banks looked like the bellies of a school of whales huddled together in the dusk. Beyond, a faintly luminous strip of yellow marked the sunset. Below, the gloomy earth glittered under the continual scintillation of gunfire. Right round the salient down to the Somme, where the mists backed up the ghostly effect, was this sequined veil of greenish flashes, quivering. Thousands of guns were spitting high explosive, and the invisible projectiles were screaming past us on every side. Though they were our own guns, their muzzles were towards us, and suddenly I knew it was at us they were firing. The malevolent fury of the whole bombardment was concentrated on us! Of course it was ridiculous; but for about a minute I was in the grip of nightmare terror. The machine lurched and rolled. It was us they were after! It was us!

In another minute we were through the danger zone; but the vivid memory haunted me back to the aerodrome. Even there we could hear the thud and rumble of the guns, even back in England they were hearing it. For seven nights and days it went on. After dark, we used to come out and watch. Continual summer lightning, flickering and dancing in the eastern sky. Voluminous and austere bursts of thunder rolling by on the night wind. The others used to laugh: 'The old Hun's fairly going through it.' But I could not forget its blind fury, and pitied the men who for a week lived under that rain. I suppose I was many times nearer death than on that particular evening; but for me it remains, none the less, the most fearful moment of the war.

Most miserable, and bewildering, was the fate of the deserters. All armies in the conflict shot deserters, some more than others – the British shot hundreds, the Germans, thousands. Four brothers of the Bickersteth family went to war in France and Belgium: one was killed, and all were decorated and commended for gallantry. The three surviving brothers became bishops, and served in the Second World War in the chaplaincy. They left an extraordinary set of letters from both wars which were woven into diary form by their mother. On 5 July 1917, the **Revd Julian Bickersteth MC**, *chaplain of the 56th London Division, wrote this intensely moving account of the treatment of one particular deserter. It begins with no hint of the drama to come.*

Let me try to describe to you the man, before I tell you more. Heavily built, rather vacant-eyed, low forehead, very dirty in appearance in spite of all efforts of the military police to make him clean himself; his utterance was indistinct and his mastery of the English language somewhat limited. His previous history was typical, I suppose, of many others, but not without its sadness. Our modern civilisation had done little for him. His father, a 'cabby' in East London, had died when he was a boy of thirteen. His mother, reduced in her circumstances, lived afterwards in one room. The boy was sent out to 'do what he could for himself'. He lived from hand to mouth. He learned enough to avoid the police, to get enough to eat, but his home ties soon began to mean less and less to him. Occasionally he brought his mother home a few pence to add to the limited family exchequer. On this effort he dwelt in his reminiscences to me with pride. Who knows it may stand before the Judgement Seat for much; it meant at least a spark of filial duty. But with no one to help him much, he drifted into bad company and before he was twenty found himself in prison.

On coming out the first time, he still kept in touch with his mother, but a second conviction soon after meant a longer time in prison and when at last he was free again his mother had moved from the single room she occupied before he went to prison, and from that day to this he had never seen her again. He never found out, or troubled to find out, where she had gone. His two sisters had several years before gone into service and disappeared from the family circle. The Military Service Act caught him in its meshes and he became a soldier. During his training in the East End, he found one good woman who lived next door to the military depot or guard room, who used to give him meals on credit. The address of this woman he remembered, but not her name. Accustomed always to do as he pleased, he had deserted twice before he left England and was brought across under arrest. Escaping soon after, he was caught and sent up to the line, only to escape on the way, and when apprehended, we had to send our battalion military police to fetch him – not a very propitious entry into the regiment.

This was six months ago, and from that day to this he has almost the whole time been in our guard room.

This was the man I had to tackle with only twelve hours more left to live. There were not a few who said he was mad, or at least that there was something wrong with his brain, but our doctor had been unable to certify that he was in any way not responsible for his actions, and certainly he was quite intelligent in a good many ways. He could read and write well.

He sat down heavily on a chair. The room was furnished with a small round table, three chairs and a wire bed raised 6 inches from the ground. I took a chair and sat next to him. 'I am going to stay with you and do anything I can for you. If you'd like to talk, we will, but if you would rather not, we'll sit quiet.' Two fully armed sentries with fixed bayonets stand one by the door and the other by the window. The room is only 9 feet by 10 feet. Anything in the nature of a private talk seems likely to be difficult. An appeal that the sentries might be removed is not accepted. There are no bars to the window and the prisoner might seek to make an end of himself. So I sit on silently. Suddenly I hear great heaving sobs, and the prisoner breaks down and cries. In a second I lean over close to him, as he hides his face in his hands, and in a low voice I talk to him. He seems still a little doubtful about his fate, and I have to explain to him what is going to happen tomorrow morning. I tell him about Morris and of how many splendid men have 'passed on'; what fine company he will find on the other side.

After a time he quietens down and his tea comes up – two large pieces of bread and butter, a mess tin half-full of tea and some jam in a tin. One of the sentries lends me his clasp knife so that I may put jam on his bread, for the prisoner of course is not allowed to handle a knife. After his tea is over, I hand him a pipe and tobacco. These comforts, strictly forbidden to all prisoners, are not withheld now. He loved a pipe – and soon he is contentedly puffing away.

Times goes on. I know that he must sleep, if possible, during the hours of darkness, so my time is short. How can I reach his soul? I get out my Bible and read to him something from the gospel. It leaves him unmoved. He is obviously uninterested and my attempt to talk a little about what I have read leaves him cold. Where is my point of contact? I make him move his chair as far away from the sentry as possible, and speaking in a very low voice close to him, I am not overheard; but of what to speak? There is no point of contact through his home, which means nothing to him. I get out an army prayer book, which contains at the end about 130 hymns, and handing him the book, ask him to read through the part at the end so that if he can find a hymn he knows, I can read it to him. He hits 'Rock of Ages' and asks, not if I will read it to him, but if we can sing it. The idea of our solemnly singing hymns together while the two sentries eye us coldly from the other side of the room seems to me so incongruous that I put him off with the promise of a hymn to be sung before he goes to sleep, but he is not satisfied and he returns to the suggestion again. This time I had enough sense, thank goodness, to seize on 'the straw'; and we sat there and sang hymns together – for three hours or more.

The curious thing about this extraordinary man is that he takes command of the proceedings. He chooses the hymns. He will not sing any one over twice. He starts the hymn on the right note, he knows the tunes and pitches them all perfectly. Music has evidently not been denied him. The words mean nothing to him, or else he is so little gifted with imagination that the pathos of such lines as 'Hold thou thy Cross before my closing eyes' and many similar lines, which in my view of the morrow should cut deep, leave the prisoner unmoved.

Oh how we sang! – hymn after hymn. He knew more tunes than I did. After half an hour away for some dinner, I returned to the little room and in the rapidly fading light went on with the hymn-singing. I brought him a YMCA hymn book which contained several hymns not in the other. He was delighted, and we sang 'Throw out the life-line', 'What a friend we have in Jesus' and others. When 10.30 p.m. came I was anxious to see the prisoner sleeping for his own sake, though I was willing to go on singing hymns if he wanted to. His stock, however, was nearly exhausted, as he would never sing the same hymn twice over. So we agreed to close the singing, but he would sing one of the hymns he had already sung, a second time as a last effort. So he chose 'God be with us till we meet again'. He sang it utterly unmoved. While I was ruminating over how to make use of the hymns for getting a little further on he said, 'We haven't finished yet; we must have "God save the king",' and then and there we rose to our feet, and the two military police, who had replaced the ordinary guards and had been accommodated with two chairs, had to get up and stand rigidly to attention while the prisoner and I sang lustily three verses of the national anthem. A few seconds later the prisoner was asleep ...

All night I sat by his side. One sentry played patience, the other read a book. Once or twice the prisoner woke up, but he soon slept again. At 3 a.m. I watched the first beginnings of dawn through the window. At 3.30 a.m. I heard the tramp, tramp of the firing party marching down the road.

A few minutes later, the sergeant major brought me a cup of tea and I had a whispered consultation with him as to how long I could let the prisoner sleep. A minute or two later I was called down to the APM, and he gave me some rum to give the prisoner if he wanted it. It was a dark morning, so he did not want the prisoner awakened for another ten minutes. I went up again, and at the right time awakened him. While his breakfast was being brought up, we knelt together in prayer. I commended him to God and we said together the Lord's Prayer, which he knew quite well and was proud of knowing. Then he sat down and ate a really good breakfast – bread and butter, ham and tea.

When he had finished, it was just four o'clock and I poured into his empty mug a tablespoon of rum, but when he had tasted it, he wouldn't drink any of it. 'Is it time to go?' he said. 'Yes, it is time. I will stay close to you.' Down the narrow stairs we went, and through the silent streets of the village our weird little procession tramped. First, a burly military policeman, then the prisoner, unbound, and myself, followed close on our heels by two more policemen, the APM, the doctor and one other officer. We had about 300 yards to go to a deserted and ruined house just outside the village. I held the prisoner's arm tight for sympathy's sake. Reaching the house, the police immediately handcuffed the man and the doctor blindfolded him. He was breathing heavily and his heart going very quickly, but outwardly he was unmoved. I said a short prayer and led him the ten or twelve paces out into the yard, where he was at once bound to a stake. I whispered in his ear, 'Safe in the arms of Jesus,' and he repeated quite clearly, 'Safe in the arms of Jesus.' The APM motioned me away. In three or four seconds the firing party had done their work. Poor lads – I was sorry for them. They felt it a good deal, and I followed them out of the yard at once and spoke to them and handed them cigarettes.

The War in Italy

Italy had entered the war on the side of the Allies in 1915. On 24 October 1917, the Austro-Hungarian and German forces launched an onslaught on the Italians with the aim of reaching the Tagliamento river. In November the Italian line on the Isonzo broke and some three hundred thousand Italians were taken prisoner, while as many more deserted. At least twenty thousand had been killed in the previous week's fighting, and there had already been eleven battles in that impossible terrain, but the name of this, the twelfth, would enter the Italian political lexicon: it was the battle of Caporetto. Though the Italians rallied to stop the enemy forces near Venice, Caporetto was a national trauma for a country that had been in existence for less than sixty years.

The hero of Caporetto was the young Erwin Rommel who single-handedly took nine thousand Italian prisoners and was given an immediate battlefield promotion to captain. There were also no fewer than four Nobel laureates for literature on the battlefields of northern Italy. One of them was the American writer **Ernest Hemingway***, who had volunteered for ambulance duty and was badly wounded twice. Born in 1899, he did not reach Italy until 1918, so was not present at Caporetto; nevertheless it became one of the set pieces in his great documentary novel* A Farewell to Arms *(1929), and in the following passages he vividly evokes the sensations of rout and defeat.*

It stormed all that day. The wind drove down the rain and everywhere there was standing water and mud. The plaster of the broken houses was grey and wet. Late in the afternoon the rain stopped and from out No. 2

post I saw the bare wet autumn country with clouds over the tops of the hills and the straw screening over the roads wet and dripping. The sun came out once before it went down and shone on the bare woods beyond the ridge. There were many Austrian guns in the woods on that ridge but only a few fired. I watched the sudden round puffs of shrapnel smoke in the sky above a broken farmhouse near where the line was; soft puffs with a yellow-white flash in the centre. You saw the flash, then heard the crack, then saw the smoke ball distort and thin in the wind. There were many iron shrapnel balls in the rubble of the houses and on the road beside the broken house where the post was, but they did not shell near the post that afternoon. We loaded two cars and drove down the road that was screened with wet mats and the last of the sun came through in the breaks between the strips of matting. Before we were out on the clear road behind the hill the sun was down. We went on down the clear road and as it turned a corner into the open and went into the square arched tunnel of matting the rain started again.

The wind rose in the night and at three o'clock in the morning with the rain coming in sheets there was a bombardment and the Croatians came over across the mountain meadows and through patches of woods and into the front line. They fought in the dark in the rain and a counter-attack of scared men from the second line drove them back. There was much shelling and many rockets in the rain and machine-gun and rifle-fire all along the line. They did not come again and it was quieter and between the gusts of wind and rain we could hear the sound of a great bombardment far to the north.

The wounded were coming into the post, some were carried on stretchers, some walking and some were brought on the backs of men that came across the field. They were wet to the skin and all were scared. We filled two cars with stretcher cases as they came up from the cellar of the post and as I shut the door of the second car and fastened it I felt the rain on my face turn to snow. The flakes were coming heavy and fast in the rain.

When daylight came the storm was still blowing but the snow had stopped. It had melted as it fell on the wet ground and now it was raining again. There was another attack just after daylight but it was unsuccessful. We expected an attack all day but it did not come until the sun was going down. The bombardment started to the south below the long wooded ridge where the Austrian guns were concentrated. We expected a bombardment but it did not come. It was getting dark. Guns were firing from the field behind the village and the shells, going away, had a comfortable sound.

> No fewer than three Italian Nobel prize-winning poets were there on the Isonzo, and wrote about it. One of them, **Giuseppe Ungaretti**, powerfully evokes the desolation of the place, San Martino del Carso, and the increasing despair of the Italian soldiers, in a short poem written after the first huge losses in 1916.

Of these houses
nothing
but fragments of memory

Of all who
would talk with me not
one remains

But in my heart
no one's cross is missing

My heart is
The most tormented country of all

> Towards the end of hostilities, **Vera Brittain** received the news that her brother Edward, her closest friend as well as relation, had been killed on the Asiago during the Italian break-out at Vittorio Veneto in 1918. Throughout the war, millions had learned to dread the arrival of a telegram. Perhaps no one could have described the experience quite so poignantly.

By the following Saturday we had still heard nothing of Edward. The interval usually allowed for news of casualties after a battle was seldom so long as this, and I began, with an artificial sense of lightness unaccompanied by real conviction, to think that there was perhaps, after all, no news to come. I had just announced to my father, as we sat over tea in the dining room, that I really must do up Edward's papers and take them to the post office before it closed for the weekend, when there came the sudden loud clattering at the front-door knocker that always meant a telegram.

For a moment I thought that my legs would not carry me, but they behaved quite normally as I got up and went to the door. I knew what was in the telegram – I had known for a week – but because the persistent hopefulness of the human heart refuses to allow intuitive certainty to persuade the reason of that which it knows, I opened and read it in a tearing anguish of suspense.

'Regret to inform you Captain E. H. Brittain MC killed in action Italy 15 June.'

'No answer,' I told the boy mechanically, and handed the telegram to my father, who had followed me into the hall. As we went back into the dining room I saw, as though I had never seen them before, the bowl of blue delphiniums on the table; their intense colour, vivid, ethereal, seemed too radiant for earthly flowers.

Then I remembered that we should have to go down to Purley and tell the news to my mother.

Late that evening, my uncle brought us all back to an empty flat. Edward's death and our sudden departure had offered the maid – at that time the amateur prostitute – an agreeable opportunity for a few hours' freedom of which she had taken immediate advantage. She had not even finished the household handkerchiefs, which I had washed that morning and intended to iron after tea; when I went into the kitchen I found them still hanging, stiff as boards, over the clothes-horse near the fire where I had left them to dry.

Long after the family had gone to bed and the world had grown silent, I crept into the dining room to be alone with Edward's portrait. Carefully closing the door, I turned on the light and looked at the pale, pictured face, so dignified, so steadfast, so tragically mature. He had been through so much – far, far more than those beloved friends who had died at an earlier stage of the interminable war, leaving him alone to mourn their loss. Fate might have allowed him the little, sorry compensation of survival, the chance to make his lovely music in honour of their memory. It seemed indeed the last irony that he should have been killed by the countrymen of Fritz Kreisler, the violinist whom of all others he had most greatly admired.

And suddenly, as I remembered all the dear afternoons and evenings when I had followed him on the piano as he played his violin, the sad, searching eyes of the portrait were more than I could bear, and falling on my knees before it I began to cry 'Edward! Oh, Edward!' in dazed repetition, as though my persistent crying and calling would somehow bring him back.

Lawrence of Arabia and the Middle East

*In 1918 British and American newspaper readers were riveted by the adventures of one **Colonel T. E. Lawrence**, whose ability to penetrate the closed society of the bedouin Arabs had enabled him to reinvigorate the wilting Arab revolt against the Turks. The legend that arose of the romantic hero, dressed in flowing white robes and leading camel charges across the desert, was irresistible, and Lawrence himself, a scholar-adventurer who partly shunned and partly courted publicity, did little to resist it. Though the British empire forces, under General Allenby, had prevented Turkey from seizing the Suez Canal, it was not until 1917 that they were able, with the help of the Arabs, to push through Sinai and on to Jerusalem, and Lawrence was the key to this success. Operating in command of the emir Faisal's levies, he took a ragbag group of insurgents and used guerrilla tactics and fast, mobile operations to clear the way for Allenby's triumphal advance – a glaring contrast to the bloody and static confrontations on the Western and Eastern Fronts and at Gallipoli.*

The first big turning-point came when the Arab irregulars, led by Faisal and Lawrence, took the Ottoman naval base of Aqaba, by attacking it from the landward side after a wild march across the desert. Lawrence describes it himself in his racy account of the campaign, Revolt in the Desert *(1927).*

The Arabs passed before us into a little sunken place, which rose to a low crest; and we knew that the hill beyond went down in a facile slope to the main valley of Aba el-Lissan, somewhat below the spring. All our four hundred camel men were here tightly collected, just out of sight of the enemy. We rode to their head, and asked the Shimt what it was and where the horsemen had gone.

He pointed over the ridge to the next valley above us, and said, 'With Auda there': and as he spoke yells and shots poured up in a sudden torrent from beyond the crest. We kicked our camels furiously to the edge, to see our fifty horsemen coming down the last slope into the main valley like a runaway, at full gallop, shooting from the saddle. As we watched, two or three went down, but the rest thundered forward at marvellous speed, and the Turkish infantry, huddled together under the cliff ready to cut their desperate way out towards Maan in the first dusk, began to sway in and out, and finally broke before the rush, adding their flight to Auda's charge.

Nasir screamed at me, 'Come on,' with his bloody mouth; and we plunged our camels madly over the hill, and down towards the head of the fleeing enemy. The slope was not too steep for a camel-gallop, but steep enough to make their pace terrific, and their course uncontrollable: yet the Arabs were able to extend to right and left and to shoot into the Turkish brown. The Turks had been too bound up in the terror of Auda's furious charge against their rear to notice us as we came over the eastward slope: so we also took them by surprise and in the flank; and a charge of ridden camels going nearly 30 miles an hour was irresistible.

The Howeitat were very fierce, for the slaughter of their women on the day before had been a new and horrible side of warfare suddenly revealed to them. So there were only 160 prisoners, many of them wounded; and three hundred dead and dying were scattered over the open valleys.

A few of the enemy got away, the gunners on their teams, and some mounted men and officers with their Jazi guides. Muhammad ed-Dheilan chased them for 3 miles into Mreigha, hurling insults as he rode, that they might know him and keep out of his way. The feud of Auda and his cousins had never applied to Muhammad, the political-minded, who showed friendship to all men of his tribe when he was alone to do so. Among the fugitives was Dhaif-Allah, who had done us the good turn about the King's Well at Jefer.

Auda came swinging up on foot, his eyes glazed over with the rapture of battle, and the words bubbling with incoherent speed from his mouth. 'Work, work, where are words, work, bullets, Abu Tayi' ... and he held up his shattered field-glasses, his pierced pistol-holster, and his leather sword-scabbard cut to ribbons. He had been the target of a volley which had killed his mare under him, but the six bullets through his clothes had left him scatheless.

He told me later, in strict confidence, that thirteen years before he had bought an amulet Koran for £120 and had not since been wounded. Indeed, death had avoided his face, and gone scurvily about killing brothers, sons and followers. The book was a Glasgow reproduction, costing eighteenpence; but Auda's deadliness did not let people laugh at his superstition.

He was wildly pleased with the fight, most of all because he had confounded me and shown what his tribe could do. Muhammad was wroth with us for a pair of fools, calling me worse than Auda, since I had insulted him by words like flung stones to provoke the folly which had nearly killed us all: though it had killed only two of us, one Rueili and one Sherari.

On 9 December 1917 British and Allied troops entered Jerusalem, which the Ottomans had surrendered. **Ronald Storrs,** *who was to be made commissioner for the British mandate in Palestine by the League of Nations, gave a situation report in his journal on 21 December just after he arrived in the city. Here are a few of his impressions.*

21 December 1917: Hot bath from a little boiler heated by chips in the passage. Noticed for the first time the continuous firing of heavy guns (somewhere from the neighbourhood, as I learned afterwards, of the Mount of Olives), which seems to go on day and night. Llewellyn gave me some butter and half a ration for breakfast (the difficult meal), but there seems to be plenty of bread, at any rate in the hotel. Then round to Borton's office where were Gabriel Bey Haddad, his confidential secretary, and Albina, Mark's ex-dragoman or whatnot. Borton was discussing with Clayton the question of provisional law courts, which I should have given to an English expert to do, and a French to draft. I proposed seeing the chief of the municipality and the mufti and, neither being in nor to be found, spent a vagrant morning waiting for their arrival. Rain was falling 3 inches deep. I walked down with Said (who up to that moment imagined we were in Jaffa) to the Jaffa gate, turned to the left and into Morcos's Grand Hotel, quite unchanged since our visit. I found Morcos, asked for the old visitors' book, and there turned up our three names on 5 April

1910. Morcos's Hotel had been taken by the Americans for a hospital, and I visited and talked with a wounded Turkish officer whose shoulder had been shattered ...

Several Turkish officials have left their families in the city, confiding in the English name. I arranged to visit the mufti in his court next day at 9.30. Thence a longish walk to the Armenian Catholics where Monseigneur Joseph Kalebjian the patriarch vicar led me up to his bed-sitting room by the feeble gleam of a night light floating in a tumbler, all he has had in the house for the last three years. His cathedral is called the church of the Fourth Station, or of the Spasm, and is supposed to stand upon the spot where Mary suddenly came upon Christ carrying the cross, and swooned. On his appointment as *vicaire* in 1915, he found the convent 15,000 francs in debt and wholly without revenues; 'par conséquent il menait une vie pénible privée de tout confortable'; before the war, 'nos fidèles étaient presque cinquante personnes'; which the deportations from the north 'augmentèrent jusqu'à cent-trente'. There are also some four hundred chiefly women and children, in the parts beyond Jordan, wandering about in the last distress. I promised to do my best for this amiable and courageous man and walked back to the hotel through the moon- (but nothing else) lit bazaars, the most romantic and picturesque I know.

Gertrude Bell was a friend and colleague of T. E. Lawrence. Like him, she was a formidable scholar who had travelled extensively in the Middle East before the First World War. Like him, she became obsessed with placing the Hashemite dynasty on the throne of the new state of Iraq, and in 1916 became oriental secretary attached to military intelligence – a post she kept when she moved to Baghdad after it was captured in 1917, where as a fervent advocate of the Sharifian cause, she devoted herself to 'king-making' with dedicated enthusiasm. In 1921 King Faisal came to Baghdad, and Bell's dreams for the new king and country seemed to have been realised. She describes his arrival in late June 1921, in a letter to her father.

I must now give you an account of our doings. Overshadowing all else was the display at Ramadi. Fakhri Jamil Zadah and I left at 4 a.m. but Faisal was a little in front of us. We caught him up at Naqtah, half way to the Euphrates, and asked leave to go ahead so that I might photograph his arrival at Fallujah. Outside that village a couple of big tents were pitched in the desert and for several miles crowds of tribal horsemen gathered in and stood along the track as he passed ... Then we drove through Fallujah which was all decorated and packed with people. The tribesmen lined the road to the ferry some 6 miles – rode round, after and beside the cars (I was immediately behind Faisal) amid incredible clouds of dust ...

Under the steep edge of the Syrian desert were drawn up the fighting men of the Anazeh, horsemen and camel riders, bearing the huge standard of the tribe. We stopped to salute it as we passed. Ali Suleiman the chief of the Dulaim and one of the most remarkable men in Iraq came out of the Ramadi to meet us. He has been strongly and consistently pro-British ...

We drove to the Euphrates bank where Ali Suleiman had pitched a huge tent about 200 feet long with a dais at the upper end and roofed with tent cloth and walled with fresh green boughs. Outside were drawn up the camel riders of the Dulaim, their horsemen and their standard carried by a Negro mounted on a gigantic white camel; inside the tribesmen lined the tent five or six deep from the dais to the very end. Faisal sat on the high divan with Fahad on his right while Major Yetts and I brought up people to sit on his left – those we thought he ought to speak to. He was supremely happy, a great tribesman amongst famous tribes and, as I couldn't help feeling, a great Sunni among Sunnis ... Faisal was in his own country with the people he knew. I never saw him look so splendid. He wore his usual white robes with a fine black abba over them, flowing white headdress and silver-bound *aqal*. Then he began to speak, leaning forward over the small table in front of him, sitting with his hand raised and bringing it down on the table to emphasise his sentences. The people at the end of the tent were too far off to hear; he called them all up and they sat on the ground below the dais rows and rows of them, four or five hundred men. He spoke in the great tongue of the desert, sonorous, magnificent – no language like it. He spoke as a tribal chief to his feudatories. 'For four years', he said, 'I have not found myself in a place like this or in such company' – you could see how he was loving it. Then he told them how Iraq was to rise to their endeavours with himself at their head. 'O Arabs, are you at peace with one another?' They shouted, 'Yes, yes, we are at peace.' 'From this day – what is the date? and what is the hour?' Someone answered him. 'From this day, 25 July (only, he gave the Muhammadan date) and the hour of the morning four (it was eleven o'clock) any tribesman who lifts his hand against a tribesman is responsible to me – I will judge between you calling your sheikhs in council. I have my rights over you as your lord.' A grey-bearded man interrupted: 'And our rights?' 'And you have your rights as subjects which it is my business to guard.' So it went on, the tribesmen interrupting him with shouts, 'Yes, yes,' 'We agree,' 'Yes, by God.' It was the descriptions of great tribal gatherings in the days of ignorance, before the Prophet, when the poets recited verse which has come down to this day and the people shouted at the end of each phrase, 'The truth, by God the truth.'

When it was over Fahad and Ali Suleiman stood up on either side of him and said, 'We swear allegiance to you because you are acceptable to the British government.' Faisal was a little surprised. He looked quickly round to me smiling and then he said, 'No one can doubt what my relations are to the British, but we must settle our affairs ourselves.' He looked at me again, and I held out my two hands clasped together as a symbol of the union of the Arab and British governments. It was a tremendous moment, those two really big men who have played their part in the history of their time, and Faisal between them the finest living representative of his race – and the link ourselves. One after another Ali Suleiman brought up his sheikhs, some forty or fifty of them. They laid their hands in Faisal's and swore allegiance ...

The afternoon's ceremony was the swearing of allegiance on the part of the towns. From Fallujah to Qaim, the northern frontier, all the mayors, qadis and notables had come in. The place was a palace garden. There was a high dais built up against a blank house wall which was hung with carpets. On this Faisal and the rest of us sat while the elders and notables, sitting in rows under the trees, got up, stepped to the dais and laid their hands in his ... The beauty of the setting, the variety of dress and colour, the grave faces of the village elders, white-turbaned or draped in the red Arab kerchief, and the fine dignity with which Faisal accepted the homage offered to him made the scene almost as striking as that of the morning ...

We are now waiting for the Mosul and Hillah papers to come in to declare Faisal king. He may possibly be crowned next week. Isn't that very remarkable! Five weeks' work.

The Last Days

From the German trenches **Ernst Jünger** *gives a graphic account of the last days of fighting on the Western Front in his autobiography,* Storm of Steel. *Jünger was born in 1895 and ran away from school to join the Foreign Legion. He volunteered in 1914 and fought throughout the war. He is adept at evoking what it felt like to be in the heat of battle.*

I leapt into the nearest trench; plunging round the traverse, I ran into an English officer in an open jacket and loose tie; I grabbed him and hurled him against a pile of sandbags. An old white-haired major behind me shouted: 'Kill the swine!'

There was no point. I turned to the lower trench, which was seething with British soldiers. It was like a shipwreck. A few tossed duck's eggs, others fired Colt revolvers, most were trying to run. We had the upper hand now. I kept firing off my pistol as in a dream, although I was out of ammunition long ago. A man next to me lobbed hand grenades at the British as they ran. A steel helmet took off into the air like a spinning plate.

It was all over in a minute. The British leapt out of their trenches, and fled away across the field. From up on the embankment, a wild pursuing fire set in. They were brought down in full flight, and, within seconds, the ground was littered with corpses. That was the disadvantage of the embankment.

German troops were also down among them. An NCO stood next to me watching the fighting open-mouthed. I seized his rifle and shot an Englishman who was tangling with a couple of Germans. They stopped in bafflement at the invisible assistance, and then ran on.

Our success had a magical effect. There was no question of leadership, or even of separate units, but there was only one direction: forward! Every man ran forward for himself.

For my objective I selected a low rise, on which I could see the ruins of a house, a cross and the wreckage of an aeroplane. Others were with me; we formed a pack, and in our eagerness ran into the wall of flame laid down by our own artillery. We had to throw ourselves in a crater and wait while the shelling moved forward. Next to me there was a young officer from another regiment, who, like me, was delighted with the success of this first charge. In a few minutes, the intensity of our mutual enthusiasm gave us the feeling we'd known each other for years. Then we leapt up, and never saw each other again.

In 1917 the Americans entered the war on the Allied side. At that stage of the fighting, Russia was on the point of collapse, and her allies faced the prospect of a German offensive with an army strengthened by troops transferred from the Eastern Front. In March 1918 the Germans launched their attack, and the Allied line almost broke before the Americans had concentrated their men enough to join in the decisive Allied offensive of August–November 1918. **Corporal Elmer Sherwood** *from Indiana tells the story of the attack on the Saint-Mihiel salient, popularly known as 'the hernia of Saint-Mihiel', which had been held by the Germans for four years.*

12 September: The zero hour was 1.05 a.m., the heavy artillery starting it off. The earth seemed to give way when the rest of our guns joined in the stupendous and fierce barrage. The roar was so loud that we could scarcely distinguish the deep intonation of our own howitzers from the reports of the 75s.

For four hours the deafening roar continued as our messengers of death were hurled into enemy territory. Then at 5.00 our infantry preceded by tanks went over the top, making a picture of dash and activity.

Not content with ordinary progress the boys of our division leapt ahead of the clumsy tanks and pressed forward in irresistible waves to the German trenches.

The enemy artillery reply was feeble, though the infantry machine-gun and rifle-fire was more menacing.

Our artillery fire in the first place demoralised enemy resistance, and the Boche are surrendering in droves. Surely they must regret giving up these luxurious dugouts and trenches which they have lived in for four years. Many of them even have electric lights and good furniture 'requisitioned' from nearby French villages.

We must have slipped up on the enemy because they left a great deal of equipment, ammunition and food. Before we left the battery on detail work, two or three hundred prisoners passed our position. Up here in the advance we pass prisoners in droves of from ten to a hundred with a doughboy in the rear prodding the laggards with a bayonet whenever necessary.

A good many of the Germans are being utilised to carry back wounded. A sedate-looking officer wearing white gloves had to bow his back in the work just as his men did. It seemed to do these enemy enlisted men good to see their officers thus reduced to their own plane. Most of them became quite cheerful after they found that they weren't going to be scalped as they had been led to believe these aboriginal Americans were wont to do.

The condition of the roads is very bad and no man's land is a mess of shellholes and mud. A good many enemy dead are lying about and a few of our own men are lying where they were struck down by enemy fire this morning.

The doughboys are still advancing swiftly. In the air we are supreme. We are not in the position of the rat in the cage, as we were at Château-Thierry when enemy planes swooped down upon us and threw streams of machine-gun bullets into our ranks. This time the tables are turned. We see our aviators flying over the retreating enemy, dropping bombs and creating havoc.

No rest for the weary last night. By inches we progressed to Seicheprey, the town which saw such terrific fighting between the 26th Division and the Germans late last winter.

3 October: We are now hiking up to the line over newly captured territory. For four years this land had been in German hands.

A doughboy who was under fire for the first time Thursday was on the way back today on some detail. He told me that half of his company was wiped out by gas attack. These fellows, without actual battle experience, didn't detect gas in time, and the officers gave no command to put on masks. By the time they did get their masks on, if indeed they got them on at all, half of them were casualties; many of them died.

I feel sure that we are going to suffer heavy casualties in this drive, due to the nature of the German defence – enemy machine-guns scattered through the forests in front of us like snakes in the grass …

30 October: Last night Fritz put on a whale of a bombardment, and I don't see how any of us escaped to tell the story. In the thick of it our communications were knocked out and I was detailed to repair the telephone line. How kind they are to me! Well, I thought of all the mean things I'd done in my life, breathed a little prayer, climbed out of my foxhole and darted out into the inferno.

Flashes of exploding artillery at intervals lighted up the blackness of the night. Explosions of enemy shells on every hand and the scream of big ones going overhead to back areas added to the thunderous uproar so that I could not have heard my own voice had I dared to speak. Boy! I was glad when I came to that break in the line. I was splicing the wire when – Shriek! Bang! A ton of steel came over me. Just as I finished the job – hell's bells! – another hit knocked the line out in another place.

For once I lost my cocky self-assurance, and I wasn't so certain that I would ever see home and Mother again. But finally, after stumbling over the body of a dead German, I came upon the next break and spliced it in a hurry. Then I raced back to my hole after reporting communications in order.

Jack Skull has just been sent back to the hospital suffering from shell-shock. No wonder nerves give way and normal men go crazy.

On the Macedonian Front, the painter **Stanley Spencer**, *who had volunteered to join the fighting infantry from being an ambulance man, dreamed of the day of peace, an ideal that was to inspire many of his paintings. He wrote in his journal:*

The idea … occurred to me in thinking how marvellous it would be if one morning, when we came out of our dugouts, we found that somehow everything was peace and that war was no more. That was one thing – the thought of how we would behave.

*But it was left to **Isaac Rosenberg**, Stanley Spencer's contemporary at the Slade School of Art in London, to immortalise the abiding image of trench warfare on the Western Front. Perhaps the most neglected and most unusual of the British poets of the First World War, he was a practising Jew and a socialist. His poetry had a grander scope than that of most of his contemporaries. It was more international and reflected the experience of both sides. He died accidentally during the Arras offensive of 1918. His poem 'Break of Day in the Trenches', with its wry, universal appeal, is the quintessence of experience of all his fellow men – on all sides.*

The darkness crumbles away –
It is the same old druid Time as ever.
Only a live thing leaps my hand –
A queer sardonic rat –
As I pull the parapet's poppy
To stick behind my ear.
Droll rat, they would shoot you if they knew
Your cosmopolitan sympathies.
Now you have touched this English hand
You will do the same to a German –
Soon, no doubt, if it be your pleasure
To cross the sleeping green between.
It seems you inwardly grin as you pass
Strong eyes, fine limbs, haughty athletes
Less chanced than you for life,
Bonds to the whims of murder,
Sprawled in the bowels of the earth,
The torn fields of France.
What do you see in our eyes
At the shrieking iron and flame
Hurled through still heavens?
What quaver – what heart aghast?
Poppies whose roots are in man's veins
Drop, and are ever dropping;
But mine in my ear is safe,
Just a little white with the dust.

By October 1918 the German army on the Western Front was in retreat, while unrest at home turned to revolution. The Kaiser went into exile and the politicians hastily agreed to Allied terms for an end to the fighting. The Armistice came into force on 11 November, though many of those at the front did not realise at first that the war was over. **Captain J. C. Dunn** *of the Royal Welch Fusiliers, an astonishing survivor, faithfully recorded his own reactions and those of his fellows to the celebrations in London. Typically, when he published* The War the Infantry Knew *he refused to be credited as editor.*

During the closing weeks of the war I was in London, mending after being wounded at Messines at the end of September. The evening of 10 November was spent by most people in tense expectation that would have become wild ecstasy had news of the ceasefire come through. On the morning of the 11th all went to their accustomed place of work or resort, and made-believe to carry on as usual. In the middle of the morning the firing of maroons proclaimed that an armistice had been signed. Great numbers of the people were not aware of the changed meaning of the signal. Thinking it was a warning of the approach of German bombers, for such it had been for three years, they made for basements, cellars, underground railway stations and other like places of refuge. But soon everyone was in the streets cheering, yelling and dancing: hats were thrown in the air, and often lost, handkerchiefs were thrown from windows: from the innumerable temporary government offices paper forms, thousands and thousands of them, were floated out over the crowds below. Everything with which a noise could be made was in use. Some people went to the churches. No more work was done that day. Everyone was alternately anyone's host or guest. As the day advanced the vast number of men in uniform doubled, trebled, in the streets, for trains and vehicles of all sorts brought in men, with or without leave, from the camps for miles round. Every man in uniform was the centre of a demonstration. The jollity increased after dark. Bonfires were lighted in Trafalgar Square and other open spaces; any combustible was used, a motor lorry if nothing else was at hand.

The experience of one regimental officer, Moody, is typical. After three and a half years spent in France he had been sent home for six months' rest as an instructor at a corps school. 'With three colleagues, officers in the Royal Scots, Argyll and Sutherland Highlanders, and Rifle Brigade,

I went to see what London was doing on Armistice night. Parades had been ordered for next day, the 12th, but they were cancelled tacitly, then formally. We arrived in town early in the evening of the 11th in rain, and it continued to rain. Thinking it necessary to book a table for dinner we made a weary round of restaurants that were full up before coming to rest at a little place in Wardour Street, owned by a Frenchman. Very bedraggled we were, for the London populace was in a state of wild excitement, especially the feminine part, who seemed to think that anyone in uniform was fair game. The doors of the restaurant were closed immediately after we got in, and customers were told that Monsieur X, the proprietor, wished to make a speech. Standing on a table he spoke partly in French, partly in broken English, with much gesticulation. He said that the doors had been closed because of the crowds, and that it would be unsafe for those who had been fortunate enough to get in to leave until late at night. He had an eye to business! Dinner was ordered, but before the fish had been eaten it was obvious that no more food would be served owing to the waiters' preoccupation with the opening of champagne bottles. Songs were started by the French community and rendered with excessive noise, fervour overcoming the singers. The Scottish officers could not stand it; they insisted on providing real music; so every Scottish song ever written was given in turn. The popularity of the Scots overcame all thought of food. Everyone in uniform had to be the guest of the civilians. All present were soon on the best of terms. The scene of amity was indescribable. We danced. We toasted the *entente cordiale* many dozens of times. But as time wore on the novelty of the experience wore off; so we contrived to give our new-made friends the slip, and have a look at what the rest of London was doing.

'Outside, the scenes were extraordinary. Coventry Street and Leicester Square were packed with people of every description, whose chief object seemed to be to shake the hand of any serviceman. Girls formed rings, in the centre of which was pushed and pulled any officer or man they could seize. By this means the four of us got separated for a time, but by good luck we met again in Coventry Street. The feeling of the people was really genuine, there was no disorder. Everyone was extraordinarily kind and generous; it seemed that most of the better-off people were taking a personal interest in each soldier they met. About 1 a.m. on the 12th I found myself alone, having seen the going of my friends. Number One had taken strong objection to an undersized Jew, and expressed his intention to ask the little man "what he had done in the Great War". His victim, sensing that something out of the ordinary was about to happen, turned and bolted through the crowd closely pursued by Number One. Number Two disappeared on the roof of a private limousine, dancing a reel. Number Three was left giving a good exhibition of squad drill, using a squad of policemen who had just come out on duty from Vine Street. A space had been cleared, and the police were willingly carrying out his orders to the amusement of the crowd. Number Four, his hand black and swollen with much handshaking, arrived at the Piccadilly Hotel which was more than overcrowded. After a clean-up I descended to the grill room where most of the occupants seemed to be dancing on the tables, or steeplechasing over the furniture which had been pushed against the walls. I had not been in the room a second before a party of perfect strangers insisted that I had been a friend of the family for more years than they cared to remember, and compelled me to be their guest for the rest of the night. So there I was among about twenty people, being hilariously entertained. Having had nothing to eat since lunchtime I tried to impress on my new-made friends that food was all-important. The protest was ignored and more champagne was ordered.

'A day or so later the original party of four met again, and tried to reckon up the number of people who had ordered champagne on their behalf. It had been quite impossible to share in all that had been offered, many dozens of bottles must have been wasted.'

Russia: Defeat and the Coming of the Revolution

When war broke out in 1914, Russia was still an autocracy, her course determined by the tsar, Nicholas II. There was a parliament, the Duma, but it had few powers. There were political parties, including a Marxist Social Democratic Party whose left wing, the Bolsheviks, had opposed the war. Chaos reigned in the country and food ran short, except for the very rich. In March 1917 there were food riots in Petrograd, and the tsar was forced to abdicate.

As A. J. P. Taylor wrote, 'Such was the revolution of March 1917. The tsar had gone. Otherwise nothing had changed.' The leader of the provisional government which took over decided to continue the war and ordered a massive new offensive against the Germans which proved a catastrophic failure. The Russian troops on the Eastern Front had had enough. An early trickle of desertions became a torrent. There was nothing left to stem the German advance.

Florence Farmborough *went to live in Russia in 1908. She was twenty-one and worked in Kiev and Moscow as a tutor in English to several families. When war was declared in 1914, she was staying at the dacha belonging to a heart surgeon, Dr Pavel Sergeyvich Usov, and his family not far from Moscow. The whole family returned to the city, and Florence immediately volunteered for nursing duty. She joined a Red Cross unit which took her to the Austrian border on the South-West Front, and later to Romania. Her diary, which runs to more than four hundred thousand words and was never intended for publication, is an extraordinary document telling a little-known part of the story. In June 1917 she describes retreating with the wounded as the fighting reached her hospital on the Romanian Front.*

Wednesday, 21 June: Marching-orders had been received and we were to leave Loschina in the afternoon. Those wounded and too frail to stand the jolting of the *dvukolki* were carefully packed on stretchers attached to horses. Horse-drawn stretchers have proved to be an excellent way of traversing the well-trodden mountain paths, too narrow to admit any vehicle. Both Mak and Misha – the wounded transport men – were sent off early. Just before Mak was lifted into the *dvukolka* a shrapnel exploded near our camp and a largish piece of metal fell into his tent, while another bit wounded our horse Lebed [Swan]. Two more stomach cases had died; mercifully they had passed away quietly under heavy sedation. Our soldiers, under Smirnov's Christian guidance, buried the dead men, seven in all, and a wooden cross inscribed with their names was placed at the head of the brothers' grave. Our packing took time, as we had been stationed in Loschina since 6 June, but at 12.30 p.m. we set off. We drove to a lovely wood, some 4 *versts* from Bojikov and 7 from Podgaytsy. It was a beautiful day, but I was still so tired that I lay down and fell asleep while the tents were being erected. A light supper of eggs, black bread and cheese was served in picnic fashion. As twilight was falling, we sisters decided to seize the opportunity of a long night's sleep. In this tranquil spot, with the sweet, clean air of beech and pine trees around us, it was not difficult to find rest ...

Thursday, 6 July, Grabuvka: Before dinner, one of our doctors told us that the 90th Regiment has refused to remain in the front line and nearly 2 *versts* of trenches are completely unguarded. His voice was thick and unsteady. 'What can that mean?' someone asked. 'Mean?' he repeated heatedly. 'Why, any fool can see what that means! The enemy will occupy the empty trenches and our troops on either side will be obliged to retreat.' 'But surely re-inforcements will be sent to their aid?' The doctor thought for a while and then he said – very slowly: 'Reinforcements will be sent. But will they go?' ...

Saturday, 8 July: The firing has ceased. What the silence portends, no one can tell. We are all on the alert for marching-orders. Anna and I walked for a brief while in the small neighbouring wood. We found a few mushrooms, but they and the beautiful trees failed for once to revive our spirits. We looked at each other and each saw tears in the other's eyes, but we made no mention of them. For my part, I was deeply downhearted for the Russians, but I was homesick too, for no news had been received from my homefolk for a long time.

Sunday, 9 July: They brought a noisy volunteer with a comrade's bullet in his leg; the first thing he demanded was something to eat. I offered him our black bread and cheese, but no! it was not good enough. His friends went away and returned with white bread, butter and milk, which our kitchen could not supply. Another told us that things were going badly in the trenches and that he had heard that Tarnopol had been recaptured by the Germans. He was in very low spirits, so we did not believe his story, but when a second soldier came, with a hand-wound, self-inflicted, and told the same story, we were forced to believe there might be some truth in it.

Monday, 10 July: The 11th Donskaya Division came riding towards us, grisly, invulnerable Cossacks, their spears pointing skywards, sitting like silent, carved statues astride their panting horses. They – and they only – were bound westwards. We guessed their missions: to check the advance of the enemy at all costs; to put the German hordes to flight; to rally the desperately tired Russian infantry, and knout the cowardly deserters into submission.

As we drove through a village, flames suddenly shot up from a burning house; through the doorway several soldiers came running, a glowing firebrand lighting their way. Soon they had set fire to another house; bits of burning timber and debris flew up like rockets, illuminating the surroundings in brilliant relief. It was a tragic scene. The inhabitants passed us in their flight; frightened, defenceless peasant women, running, limping, breathing hard, uttering little smothered cries, intent on reaching the friendly woodlands, where they might find shelter.

The tsarist regime in Russia had been replaced by a provisional government committed to democratic institutions. The Bolsheviks, however, were aiming at communist dictatorship, and threw their weight behind the workers and soldiers committees ('soviets') that were challenging government authority. In an attempt to end a revolution that had barely started, the prime minister, Kerensky, ordered the arrest of leading Bolsheviks – including Trotsky, who had returned from America in May and had only just joined the party. His and Lenin's names were to dominate coming events. By mid-September

Trotsky, freed from prison, had become president of the Petrograd (St Petersburg) soviet, and Lenin, who had escaped to Finland, was planning his return, shorn of his customary red beard. At this point the Bolshevik party had a majority on the Petrograd and Moscow soviets and controlled the Red Guard, but they seemed at a loss as to what to do next, apart from indulging in a great many speeches and meetings throughout September and October.

The Bolshevik revolution itself was eventually precipitated by Kerensky. In a last-ditch attempt to overcome the opposition once and for all he sent, on 5 November, a detachment of cadets to occupy the offices of Pravda, *the Bolshevik newspaper, and seal the doors. It was Trotsky who defied him by ordering the seals to be broken. By that afternoon* Pravda *was once again on the streets.*

The climax came with the seizure of the Winter Palace. The American journalist and radical **John Reed**, *author of one of the most famous eyewitness accounts of the revolution,* Ten Days that Shook the World, *was in the crowd that poured into the palace, for the most part invited by the imperial servants. It is perhaps the most vivid part of his book, all the more effective because it is less coloured than many of his other set-piece descriptions by Bolshevik propaganda.*

Like a black river, filling all the street, without song or cheer we poured through the Red Arch, where the man just ahead of me said in a low voice: 'Look out, comrades! Don't trust them. They will fire, surely!' In the open we began to run, stooping low and bunching together, and jammed up suddenly behind the pedestal of the Alexander Column.

'How many of you did they kill?' I asked.

'I don't know. About ten ...'

After a few minutes huddling there, some hundreds of men, the army seemed reassured and without any orders suddenly began again to flow forward. By this time, in the light that streamed out of all the Winter Palace windows, I could see that the first two or three hundred men were Red Guards, with only a few scattered soldiers. Over the barricade of firewood we clambered, and leaping down inside gave a triumphant shout as we stumbled on a heap of rifles thrown down by the *yunkers* who had stood there. On both sides of the main gateway the doors stood wide open, light streamed out, and from the huge pile came not the slightest sound.

Carried along by the eager wave of men we were swept into the right-hand entrance, opening into a great bare vaulted room, the cellar of the east wing, from which issued a maze of corridors and staircases. A number of huge packing cases stood about, and upon these the Red Guards and soldiers fell furiously, battering them open with the butts of their rifles, and pulling out carpets, curtains, linen, porcelain plates, glassware ... One man went strutting around with a bronze clock perched on his shoulder; another found a plume of ostrich feathers, which he stuck in his hat. The looting was just beginning when somebody cried, 'Comrades! Don't touch anything! Don't take anything! This is the property of the people!' Immediately twenty voices were crying, 'Stop! Put everything back! Don't take anything! Property of the people!' Many hands dragged the spoilers down. Damask and tapestry were snatched from the arms of those who had them; two men took away the bronze clock. Roughly and hastily the things were crammed back in their cases, and self-appointed sentinels stood guard. It was all utterly spontaneous. Through corridors and up staircases the cry could be heard growing fainter and fainter in the distance, 'Revolutionary discipline! Property of the people ...'

We crossed back over to the left entrance, in the west wing. There order was also being established. 'Clear the palace!' bawled a Red Guard, sticking his head through an inner door. 'Come, comrades, let's show that we're not thieves and bandits. Everybody out of the palace except the commissars, until we get sentries posted.'

Two Red Guards, a soldier and an officer, stood with revolvers in their hands. Another soldier sat at a table behind them, with pen and paper. Shouts of 'All out! All out!' were heard far and near within, and the army began to pour through the door, jostling, expostulating, arguing. As each man appeared he was seized by the self-appointed committee, who went through his pockets and looked under his coat. Everything that was plainly not his property was taken away, the man at the table noted it on his paper, and it was carried into a little room. The most amazing assortment of objects were thus confiscated; statuettes, bottles of ink, bedspreads worked with the imperial monogram, candles, a small oil-painting, desk blotters, gold-handled swords, cakes of soap, clothes of every description, blankets. One Red Guard carried three rifles, two of which he had taken away from *yunkers*; another had four portfolios bulging with written documents. The culprits either sullenly surrendered or pleaded like children. All talking at once, the committee explained that stealing was not worthy of the people's champions; often those who had been caught turned around and began to help go through the rest of the comrades.

Yunkers came out, in bunches of three or four. The committee seized upon them with an excess of zeal, accompanying the search with remarks like, 'Ah, *provocateurs*! Kornilovists! Counter- revolutionists! Murderers of the people!' But there was no violence done, although the *yunkers* were terrified. They too had their pockets full of small plunder. It was carefully noted down by the scribe, and piled in the little room ... The *yunkers* were disarmed. 'Now, will you take up arms against the people any more?' demanded clamouring voices.

'No,' answered the *yunkers*, one by one. Whereupon they were allowed to go free.

We asked if we might go inside. The committee was doubtful, but the big Red Guard answered firmly that it was forbidden. 'Who are you anyway?' he asked. 'How do I know that you are not all Kerenskys?' (There were five of us, two women.)

'*Pazhal'st'*, *tovarishchi*! Way, comrades!' A soldier and a Red Guard appeared in the door, waving the crowd aside, and other guards with fixed bayonets. After them followed single-file half a dozen men in civilian dress – the members of the Provisional Government. First came Kishkin, his face drawn and pale, then Rutenberg, looking sullenly at the floor; Tereshchenko was next, glancing sharply around; he stared at us with cold fixity ... They passed in silence; the victorious insurrectionists crowded to see, but there were only a few angry mutterings. It was only later that we learned how the people in the street wanted to lynch them, and shots were fired – but the sailors brought them safely to Peter-Paul ...

In the meanwhile unrebuked we walked into the palace. There was still a great deal of coming and going, of exploring new-found apartments in the vast edifice, of searching for hidden garrisons of *yunkers* which did not exist. We went upstairs and wandered through room after room. This part of the palace had been entered also by other detachments from the side of the Neva. The paintings, statues, tapestries and rugs of the great state apartments were unharmed; in the offices, however, every desk and cabinet had been ransacked, the papers scattered over the floor, and in the living rooms beds had been stripped of their coverings and wardrobes wrenched open. The most highly prized loot was clothing, which the working people needed. In a room where furniture was stored we came upon two soldiers ripping the elaborate Spanish leather upholstery from chairs. They explained it was to make boots with ...

The old palace servants in their blue and red and gold uniforms stood nervously about, from force of habit repeating, 'You can't go in there, *barin*! It is forbidden ──' We penetrated at length to the gold and malachite chamber with crimson brocade hangings where the ministers had been in session all that day and night, and where the *shveitzari* had betrayed them to the Red Guards. The long table covered with green baize was just as they had left it, under arrest. Before each empty seat was pen and ink and paper; the papers were scribbled over with beginnings of plans of action, rough drafts of proclamations and manifestos. Most of these were scratched out, as their futility became evident, and the rest of the sheet covered with absent-minded geometrical designs, as the writers sat despondently listening while minister after minister proposed chimerical schemes. I took one of these scribbled pages, in the handwriting of Konovalov, which read, 'The Provisional Government appeals to all classes to support the Provisional Government ──'

All this time, it must be remembered, although the Winter Palace was surrounded, the government was in constant communication with the front and with provincial Russia. The Bolsheviks had captured the Ministry of War early in the morning, but they did not know of the military telegraph office in the attic, nor of the private telephone line connecting it with the Winter Palace. In that attic a young officer sat all day, pouring out over the country a flood of appeals and proclamations; and when he heard that the palace had fallen, put on his hat and walked calmly out of the building.

Civil war and famine followed the revolution. **Arthur Ransome***, who later became famous for his* Swallows and Amazons *children's books, was at that time the special correspondent of the* Manchester Guardian *and a sometime British secret agent. He reported from 'the Famine Region' on 11 October 1921, a terrible indictment of the revolution's brutal legacy.*

We went down to the shore of the Volga, down a rough broken street, past booths where you could buy white bread, and, not a hundred yards away, found an old woman cooking horse dung in a broken saucepan. Within sight of the market was a mass of refugees, men, women and children, with such belongings as they had retained in their flight from starvation, still starving, listlessly waiting for the wagons to move them away to more fortunate districts. Some of them are sheltered from the rain that is coming now, too late, by the roofs of open-sided sheds. Others are sitting hopelessly in the open, not attempting to move, not even begging. I shall never forget the wizened dead face, pale green, of a silently weeping little girl, whose feet were simply bones over which was stretched dry skin that looked like blue-black leather. And she was one of hundreds. A fortnight ago there were twenty thousand waiting beside the quays of Samara. Every day about fourteen hundred are taken off in wagons. There are, of course, no latrines ...

A little crowd was gathered beside a couple of wooden huts in the middle of the camp. I went up there and found that it was a medical station where a couple of doctors and two heroic women lived in the camp itself fighting cholera and typhus. The crowd I had noticed were waiting their turns for vaccination. At first the people had been afraid of it, but already there was no sort of difficulty in persuading them to take at least this precaution, though seemingly nothing will ever teach them to keep clean. The two women brought out a little table covered with a cloth and the usual instruments, and the crowd already forming into a line pressed forward. I called to Ercole and he set up his camera. One of the sisters called out: 'Lucky ones today; vaccination and having your pictures taken at the same time,' and while the camera worked, those behind urged those in front to be quick in taking their rags off, and to get on so that they too would be in time to come into the picture.

There were old men and women, girls and little ragged children. Shirt after shirt came off, showing ghastly bags of bones, spotted all over with bites and the loathsome scars of disease. And, dreadful as their condition was, almost all showed an interest in the camera, while I could not help reflecting that before the pictures are produced some at least of them will have left the camp and made their last journey into the cemetery over the way, the earth of which, as far as you could see, was raw with new-made graves.

In the siding beyond the camp was a refugee train, a sort of rolling village, inhabited by people who were for the most part in slightly better condition than the peasants flying at random from the famine. These were part of the returning wave of that flood of miserable folk who fled eastwards before the retreating army in 1915 and 1916, and are now uprooted again and flying westwards again with the whip of hunger behind them. To understand the full difficulty of Samara's problem it is necessary to remember the existence of these people who are now being sent back to the districts or the new states to which they belong. They have prior right to transport, and, in the present condition of Russian transport, the steady shifting of these people westwards still further lessens the means available for moving the immediate victims of the drought. I walked from one end of the train to the other. It was made up of cattle trucks, but these trucks were almost like huts on wheels, for in each one was a definite group of refugees and a sort of family life. These folks had with them their belongings, beds, bedding, chests of drawers, rusty sewing machines, rag dolls. I mention just a few of the things I happened to see. In more than one of the wagons I found three or four generations of a single family – an old man and his still more ancient mother struggling back to the village which they had last seen in flames as it was set on fire by the retreating army, anxious simply, as they said, 'to die at home', and with them a grandson, with his wife (married here) and their children. Families that had lost all else retained their samovar, the central symbol of the home, the hearth of these nomads; and I saw people lying on the platform with samovars boiling away beside them that must have come from west of Warsaw and travelled to Siberia and back. In the doorway of one truck I found a little boy, thinner than any child in England shall ever be, I hope, and in his hand was a wooden cage, and in the cage a white mouse, fat, sleek, contented, better off than any other living thing in all that train. There were a man and his wife on the platform outside. I asked them where they were going. 'To Minsk,' said the man, 'those of us who live; the children are dying every day.' I looked back at the little boy, warming his mouse in the sun. The mouse, at least, would be alive at the journey's end.

A Phoney Peace

The end of the Great War was supposed to usher in a period of peace and disarmament. The victorious allies met at Versailles in 1919 with the aim of replacing imperial regimes with a system of independent states, but as the allied powers all had different agendas the result was a messy compromise in which weak new democratic states were created and the defeated countries heavily penalised. In an effort to provide collective security, the League of Nations was formed, which Germany was allowed to join in 1926, and in 1928 the Kellogg–Briand pact was signed in Paris, committing all the signatories to the settling of disputes without resorting to war.

It was a nice if wistful idea. In many areas the war had never finished, and bitter social conflict and economic crisis ensured that it would be carried on by other means. In the British Isles, Ireland had been in a state of on-off insurrection against the Crown since the Easter Rising of 1916. This nationwide Irish Rebellion was planned by the Irish Republican Brotherhood to take advantage of British participation in the World War, and Sir Roger Casement, former British consul in the Congo, was instrumental in raising a prisoner-of-war force in Germany to carry it out. He was hanged for treason in the same year, but soldiers returning from France fashioned what would become the IRA into a highly skilled guerrilla force. Violence rose in a crescendo in 1921. **D. F. Boyd**, *special correspondent of the* Manchester Guardian, *describes the torching of the Custom House, one of the Dublin landmarks, on 26 May.*

Sinn Fein today in broad daylight burned down the Custom House, ambushed several lorries of Crown forces, and held up the Central Fire

Station. This *coup*, which must have been planned with much care, happened shortly after 1 p.m.

Before that hour a force of Sinn Feiners walked into the Custom House – a large, impressive building – ordered the staff out, and set fire to it. Under the arches which support the Great Northern Railway an ambushing party remained. Three lorries, unaware of the affair, passed and were engaged. Furious fights followed, both here and on the quays, where a tender full of Black-and-Tans had been passing.

A business man who was indoors at the moment says he heard three explosions and then a continual roar of small arms. He looked out and saw the police in the tender firing towards the Custom House and shouting madly. Another spectator, who was looking in the same direction but down Lower Abbey Street, saw the exchange of shots and saw one man, presumably trying to get out of harm's way, dash across the square in front of the Custom House. He was within a few feet of safety when he dropped on the pavement.

Meanwhile flames and great columns of smoke were bursting out of the Custom House windows. There were a few explosions and showers of cindered papers. The fight was still going on, and reinforcements of military and police began to arrive, but the fire call was not answered.

At the precise moment when the incendiaries began their work six or seven men entered the Central Fire Station, which is only a few yards from the Central Police Barracks, and held up the staff.

Not long after another journalist and myself in search of news knocked at the door of the fire station, and after a moment's scrutiny were allowed in. Firemen in their scarlet shirts and blue caps were standing about. One of them was attending to the telephone in the usual way, and among them moved a number of inconspicuous civilians, one of whom was a boy of perhaps fifteen or sixteen. After a few minutes one of them asked our names and occupations and wrote them down, but it was not until I noticed that one of the men had a bomb in his hand that I guessed what had happened. The party had locked one man in a room but touched nobody else, and behaved with politeness.

It appeared likely then that the military or police would come to the station to enquire after the brigade and that there would be a fight, for the phone man could be heard answering constant calls and offering no explanation. A loud knocking sounded at the door. It was opened and a policeman, dishevelled and very shaken, came in and walked to the watch room. The boy produced a large six-chambered revolver, and told the officer to put his hands up. At first the order seemed to amuse him, but he complied when the situation was explained by another raider. It was then learned that he had come for the brigade, but had been forced by the intense fire to take cover on the ground for nearly twenty minutes. Meanwhile the men ordered the motor ambulance out, filed into it, telling us not to move for ten minutes, and so went.

They had scarcely left when a party of auxiliary police in a car drove up and ordered the brigade out. It was just 1.45 when they got away, about three-quarters of an hour after the firing of the Custom House. The latter was now well alight. Great crowds had gathered on the O'Connell bridge and down the quays and side streets to watch it. Every now and then they retreated in panic before the auxiliaries, who constituted the cordon, and still at half-past two an occasional shot was fired, and there appeared to be no chance of saving the building, said to be worth £1 million.

It is surmounted by a dome sheathed in copper, and on the top of this stands a huge statue of Hope in stone. At the time of writing flames ring the dome, which springs directly from the entrance hall. At five o'clock the dome was still standing, but the front of the building was apparently absolutely gutted. The inside must be in the same state from front to back.

The Custom House, besides fulfilling its normal functions, also housed the Crown administrative departments of local government, income tax and old age pensions. It is, therefore, to a great extent the instrument of English government in Ireland, and shares such honours as there are with Dublin Castle.

BETWEEN THE WARS

Bright Young Things

Not surprisingly, the 1920s were a time of hedonistic escape from the carnage of the war years. The decade embraced jazz, dancing, the movies, the Bright Young Thing and the Flapper. The cinema was undoubtedly the most influential mass medium in the first half of the twentieth century, and in the 1920s it was the movies that encapsulated the aspirations of a generation. The great hero of the silent screen was Rodolfo Guglielmi, better known as Rudolph Valentino, the son of a vet in Castellaneta in south-east Italy. He had emigrated to America in 1913, and achieved worldwide fame through films such as The Four Horsemen of the Apocalypse *(1921),* The Sheikh *(1921) and* Blood and Sand *(1922). In 1926 he died of peritonitis in a New York hotel. He was thirty-one. In a brilliant essay,* **John Dos Passos** *recreated his life in the spotlight and the explosion of mass hysteria at his funeral procession.*

He hung around cabarets doing odd jobs, sweeping out for the waiters, washing cars; he was lazy handsome wellbuilt slender good tempered and vain; he was a born tangodancer.

Lovehungry women thought he was a darling. He began to get engagements dancing the tango in ballrooms and cabarets; he teamed up with a girl named Jean Acker on a vaudeville tour and took the name of Rudolph Valentino.

Stranded on the coast he headed for Hollywood, worked for a long time as an extra for 5 dollars a day; directors began to notice he photographed well.

He got his chance in *The Four Horsemen*

and became the gigolo of every woman's dreams.

Valentino spent his life in the colourless glare of klieg lights, in stucco villas obstructed with bric-a-brac, Oriental rugs, tigerskins, in the bridal-suites of hotels, in silk bathrobes in private cars.

He was always getting into limousines or getting out of limousines,

or patting the necks of fine horses.

Wherever he went the sirens of the motorcyclecops screeched ahead of him,

flashlights flared,

the streets were jumbled with hysterical faces, waving hands, crazy eyes; they stuck out their autographbooks, yanked his buttons off, cut a tail off his admirablytailored dress suit; they stole his hat and pulled at his necktie; his valets removed young women from under his bed; all night in nightclubs and cabarets actresses leching for stardom made sheepseyes at him under their mascaraed lashes.

He wanted to make good under the glare of the milliondollar searchlights

of El Dorado:

the Sheikh, the Son of the Sheikh;

personal appearances.

He married his old vaudeville partner, divorced her, married the adopted daughter of a millionaire, went into lawsuits with the producers who were debasing the art of the screen, spent a million dollars on one European trip;

he wanted to make good in the brightlights.

When the *Chicago Tribune* called him a pink powderpuff

and everybody started wagging their heads over a slavebracelet he wore that he said his wife had given him and his taste for mushy verse of which he published a small volume called *Daydreams* and the whispers grew about the testimony in his divorce case that he and his first wife had never slept together,

it broke his heart.

He tried to challenge the Chicago *Tribune* to a duel;

he wanted to make good

in heman twofisted broncobusting pokerplaying stockjuggling

America. (He was a fair boxer and had a good seat on a horse; he loved the desert like the sheikh and was tanned from the sun of Palm Springs.) He broke down in his suite in the Hotel Ambassador in New York: gastric ulcer.

When the doctors cut into his elegantlymoulded body, they found that peritonitis had begun; the abdominal cavity contained a large amount of fluid and food particles; the viscera were coated with a greenishgrey film; a round hole a centimetre in diameter was seen in the anterior wall of the stomach; the tissue of the stomach for one and onehalf centimetres immediately surrounding the perforation was necrotic. The appendix was inflamed and twisted against the small intestine.

When he came to from the ether, the first thing he said was, 'Well, did I behave like a pink powderpuff?'

His expensivelymassaged actor's body fought peritonitis for six days.

The switchboard at the hospital was swamped with calls, all the corridors were piled with flowers, crowds filled the street outside, filmstars who claimed they were his betrothed entrained for New York.

Late in the afternoon a limousine drew up at the hospital door (where the grimyfingered newspapermen and photographers stood around bored tired hoteyed smoking too many cigarettes making trips to the nearest speak exchanging wisecracks and deep dope waiting for him to die in time to make the evening papers), *and a woman, who said she was a maid employed by a dancer who was Valentino's first wife, alighted. She delivered to an attendant an envelope addressed to the filmstar and inscribed 'From Jean', and a package. The package contained a white counterpane with lace ruffles and the word 'Rudy' embroidered in the four corners. This was accompanied by a pillowcover to match over a blue silk scented cushion.*

Rudolph Valentino was only thirtyone when he died.

His managers planned to make a big thing of his highlypublicised funeral, but the people in the streets were too crazy.

While he lay in state in a casket covered with a cloth of gold, tens of thousands of men, women and children packed the streets outside. Hundreds were trampled, had their feet hurt by policehorses. In the muggy rain the cops lost control. Jammed masses stampeded under the clubs and the rearing hoofs of the horses. The funeral chapel was gutted, men and women fought over a flower, a piece of wallpaper, a piece of the broken plateglass window. Showwindows were burst in. Parked cars were overturned and smashed. When finally the mounted police after repeated charges beat the crowd off Broadway, where traffic was tied up for two hours, they picked up twentyeight separate shoes, a truckload of umbrellas, papers, hats, torn off sleeves. All the ambulances in that part of the city were busy carting off women who'd fainted, girls who'd been stepped on. Epileptics threw fits. Cops collected little groups of abandoned children.

The fascisti sent a guard of honour and the antifascists drove them off. More rioting, cracked skulls, trampled feet. When the public was barred from the undertaking parlours, hundreds of women groggy with headlines got in to view the poor body,

claiming to be exdancingpartners, old playmates, relatives from the old country, filmstars; every few minutes a girl fainted in front of the bier and was revived by the newspapermen who put down her name and address and claim to notice in the public prints. Frank E. Campbell's undertakers and pallbearers, dignified wearers of black broadcloth and tackersup of crape, were on the verge of a nervous breakdown. Even the boss had his fill of publicity that time.

It was two days before the cops could clear the streets enough to let the flowerpieces from Hollywood be brought in and described in the evening papers.

Many young Englishmen picked this moment to escape from a Europe overshadowed by war and the depression that followed it. Their aim was to earn a living from the journals of their adventures. One of the most engaging and eccentric among them was **Robert Byron**, *a historian and essayist by vocation, who journeyed from the Mediterranean to the Amu Darya, the river Oxus, which marks the northern frontier between Afghanistan and the then Soviet Union. It was a journey that never quite seemed to reach its destination. In its descriptions of the people and the architectural monuments encountered en route, however,* The Road to Oxiana *is a work of genius. Here Byron describes reaching the great palace of Ardeshir, near Ibrahimabad, in February 1933.*

The palace of Ardeshir assumed enormous dimensions as we crossed the river and could distinguish the smallness of two Kashgai tents encamped on a lawn below it. These tents were black and oblong, and were stretched over low stone walls. Dogs, children, lambs and chickens tottered about the grass, enlarging still further the uncouth skeleton above them. Two women wearing full pleated skirts were pounding corn on a cloth by means of pestles attached to long staves.

There was not time to measure the palace properly. But I soon saw that Dieulafoy's elevation was wrong. This is interesting, considering the importance of the building in the history of architecture and the fact that Dieulafoy's has so far been the only information available to writers on the subject.

The entrance was originally on the south, through a big barrel-vaulted *ivan*. Today what appears to be the main façade faces east, looking across the river towards the mouth of the gorge. Behind it, at either end, are two courts, the southern covering about half an acre, the northern rather less. These are divided from one another by a series of three domed chambers, which stretch right across the palace from side to side one behind the other. Only half the east chamber is still standing, with half its dome above it; so that the line of the façade appears at first sight to be interrupted by an open vestibule 30 feet across and 50 high. But one soon sees that really there is no façade at all – though I use the term for convenience – and that the whole of the east wall, having stood on the brink of the green slope now supporting the Kashgais, has gradually collapsed and taken the front of the first chamber with it.

The two inner chambers are also about 30 feet square, and their domes, resting directly on simple corner squinches, have the same diameter. The apex of each dome is pierced by a broad hole, round which the outside masonry projects upwards. At present these holes afford the only light there is; if they were originally enclosed, the chambers beneath must have been artificially lit, and each dome must have been surmounted by a sort of rough cupola, thus discovering a precedent for those extraordinary nipples on the Romanesque domes of Périgueux. The dome of the middle chamber is some 15 feet higher than the other two. Higher still is the elliptical cupola which separates it from the front dome, and which roofs the passage between the middle chamber and the outer ruined one. This passage is divided into two storeys; but a light well in the floor of the upper enables the hole in the cupola to illuminate the lower. A similar passage separates the middle and hinder chambers. This is roofed by a massive barrel vault and is entirely unlighted.

Dieulafoy makes all three domes the same height, and omits the cupolas of the passages altogether.

It would need a long time to make sense from the maze of internal walls and heaps of fallen masonry that occupy the two courts. One can see, however, that a barrel-vaulted room, or succession of rooms, ran beside the dome-chambers on the north. The vault is gone, but two of the transverse walls whose semicircular tops supported it still stand. These walls are pierced at the bottom by shallow archways like those of a bridge, whose curve, being less than that of the vault above, is rendered doubly hideous by a pier at the apex necessary to support the weight of the wall.

Most of the walls are about 5 feet thick. The stones are uncut and the mortar fills the gaps. Stucco adorned the three chambers, whose refinements are of two styles. One we call Romanesque: the squinches rest on a dog-tooth cornice; doorways with rounded tops are framed in concentric mouldings; and a similar niche in the south court has these mouldings also dog-toothed. The other is bastard Egyptian, copied from Persepolis: arched doorways are surmounted by horizontal canopies which are scalloped, as they spread forwards and outwards, with a radiating feather design. This convention is unattractive enough in its own country and original stone. As a third-hand reminiscence, in cheaper material, it foreshadows the taste of the London County Council in the early twentieth century.

Not everyone was quite so enamoured of literary travel. **Evelyn Waugh**, *who was sent as a special correspondent to Ethiopia, was a notoriously splenetic voyager. He sends up the whole genre of travel writing in a single paragraph in his impression of Etna at sunset in his first major travel book,* Labels.

I do not think I shall ever forget the sight of Etna at sunset; the mountain almost invisible in a blur of pastel grey, glowing on the tops and then repeating its shape, as though reflected, in a wisp of grey smoke, with the whole horizon behind radiant with pink light, fading gently into a grey pastel sky. Nothing I have ever seen in art or nature was quite so revolting.

The Great Depression

The Wall Street crash in the United States marked the beginning of the Great Depression. On 'Black Thursday', 24 October 1929, nearly thirteen million shares changed hands, and panic followed. **Elliott V. Bell**, *a reporter for the* New York Times, *tells the story.*

That day, 24 October 1929, was not the first of the big break in stocks, nor was it the last. Nevertheless, it was the most terrifying and unreal day I have ever seen on the Street, and it constitutes an important financial landmark, for that day marked the great decline in the prestige and power of Wall Street over national affairs.

The day was overcast and cool. A light north-west wind blew down the canyons of Wall Street, and the temperature, in the low fifties, made bankers and brokers on their way to work button their topcoats around them. The crowds of market traders in the brokers' boardrooms were nervous but hopeful as the ten o'clock hour for the start of trading approached. The general feeling was that the worst was over and a good many speculators who had prudently sold out earlier in the decline were congratulating themselves at having bought back their stocks a good deal cheaper. Seldom had the small trader had better or more uniform advice to go by.

The market opened steady with prices little changed from the previous day, though some rather large blocks, of twenty to twenty-five thousand shares, came out at the start. It sagged easily for the first half-hour, and then around eleven o'clock the deluge broke.

It came with a speed and ferocity that left men dazed. The bottom simply fell out of the market. From all over the country a torrent of selling orders poured on to the floor of the Stock Exchange and there were no buying orders to meet it. Quotations of representative active issues, like Steel (US Steel), Telephone (AT&T) and Anaconda, began to fall two, three, five and even ten points between sales. Less active stocks became unmarketable. Within a few moments the ticker service was hopelessly swamped and from then on no one knew what was really happening. By 1.30 the ticker tape was nearly two hours late; by 2.30 it was 147 minutes late. The last quotation was not printed on the tape until 7.08½ p.m., four hours, eight and a half minutes after the close. In the meantime, Wall Street had lived through an incredible nightmare.

In the strange way that news of a disaster spreads, the word of the market collapse flashed through the city. By noon great crowds had gathered at the corner of Broad and Wall Streets where the Stock Exchange on one corner faces Morgan's across the way. On the steps of the Sub-Treasury Building, opposite Morgan's, a crowd of press photographers and newsreel men took up their stand. Traffic was pushed from the streets of the financial district by the crush.

It was in this wild setting that the leading bankers scurried into conference at Morgan's in a belated effort to save the day. Shortly after noon Mr [Charles E.] Mitchell left the National City Bank and pushed his way west on Wall Street to Morgan's. No sooner had he entered than Albert H. Wiggin was seen to hurry down from the Chase National Bank, one block north. Hard on his heels came William C. Potter, head of the Guaranty Trust, followed by Seward Prosser of the Bankers Trust. Later George F. Baker Jr of the First National joined the group.

The news of the bankers' meeting flashed through the streets and over the news tickers – stocks began to rally – but for many it was already too late. Thousands of traders, little and big, had gone 'overboard' in that incredible hour between eleven and twelve. Confidence in the financial and political leaders of the country, faith in the 'soundness' of economic conditions had received a shattering blow. The panic was on.

At Morgan's the heads of six banks formed a consortium since known as the bankers' pool of October 1929 – pledging a total of $240 million or $40 million each, to provide a 'cushion' of buying power beneath the falling market. In addition, other financial institutions, including James Speyer and Company and Guggenheim Brothers, sent over to Morgan's unsolicited offers of funds aggregating $100 million. It was not only the first authenticated instance of a bankers' pool in stocks but by far the largest concentration of pool buying power ever brought to bear on the stock market – but in the face of the panic it was pitifully inadequate.

After the bankers had met, Thomas W. Lamont, Morgan's partner, came out to the crowd of newspaper reporters who had gathered in the lobby of his bank. In an understatement that has since become a Wall Street classic, he remarked: 'It seems there has been some disturbed selling in the market' ...

The days that followed are blurred in retrospect. Wall Street became a nightmarish spectacle.

The animal roar that rises from the floor of the Stock Exchange and which on active days is plainly audible in the Street outside, became louder, anguished, terrifying. The streets were crammed with a mixed crowd – agonised little speculators, walking aimlessly outdoors because they feared to face the ticker and the margin clerk; sold-out traders, morbidly impelled to visit the scene of their ruin; inquisitive individuals and tourists, seeking by gazing at the exteriors of the Exchange and the big banks to get a closer view of the national catastrophe; runners, frantically pushing their way through the throng of idle and curious in their effort to make deliveries of the unprecedented volume of securities which was being traded on the floor of the Exchange.

The ticker, hopelessly swamped, fell hours behind the actual trading and became completely meaningless. Far into the night, and often all night long, the lights blazed in the windows of the tall office buildings where margin clerks and bookkeepers struggled with the desperate task of trying to clear one day's business before the next began. They fainted at their desks; the weary runners fell exhausted on the marble floors of banks and slept. But within a few months they were to have ample time to rest up. By then thousands of them had been fired.

Agonising scenes were enacted in the customers' rooms of the various brokers. There traders who a few short days before had luxuriated in delusions of wealth saw all their hopes smashed in a collapse so devastating, so far beyond their wildest fears, as to seem unreal. Seeking to save a little from the wreckage, they would order their stocks sold 'at the market', in many cases to discover that they had not merely lost everything but were, in addition, in debt to the broker. And then, ironic twist, as like as not the next few hours' wild churning of the market would lift prices to levels where they might have sold out and had a substantial cash balance left over. Every move was wrong, in those days. The market seemed like an insensate thing that was wreaking a wild and pitiless revenge upon those who had thought to master it.

As the Depression bit deeper, more and more workers, in both the US and Britain, found themselves unemployed. By the early 1930s over twelve million people in the US were without work. Rural poverty was widespread. In the thirties the farmlands of Oklahoma were baked dry and torn up in a freak series of storms which turned large areas of country into a giant dust bowl. The farmers, the 'Okies', upped sticks with all they could load on to jalopies and trucks and headed for what they hoped would be better times and better pay in California. The singer **Woody Guthrie** *was born among the Okies, and he became their Homer with his famous Dust Bowl ballads. One of the most celebrated, still sung today, is 'Dust Storm Disaster'.*

On the 14th day of April of 1935,
There struck the worst of dust storms that ever filled the sky.
You could see that dust storm comin', the cloud looked deathlike black,
And through our mighty nation, it left a dreadful track.

From Oklahoma City to the Arizona line,
Dakota and Nebraska to the lazy Rio Grande,
It fell across our city like a curtain of black rolled down,
We thought it was our judgment, we thought it was our doom.

The radio reported, we listened with alarm,
The wild and windy actions of this great mysterious storm;
From Albuquerque and Clovis, and old New Mexico,
They said it was the blackest that ever they had saw.

In old Dodge City, Kansas, the dust had rung their knell,
And a few more comrades sleeping on top of old Boot Hill.

From Denver, Colorado, they said it blew so strong,
They thought that they could hold out, but they didn't know how long.

Our relatives were huddled into their oil boom shacks,
And the children they were crying as it whistled through the cracks.
And the family was crowded into their little room,
They thought the world had ended, and they thought it was their doom.

The storm took place at sundown, it lasted through the night,
When we looked out next morning, we saw a terrible sight.
We saw outside our window where wheat fields they had grown
Was now a rippling ocean of dust the wind had blown.

It covered up our fences, it covered up our barns,
It covered up our tractors in this wild and dusty storm.
We loaded our jalopies and piled our families in,
We rattled down that highway to never come back again.

> *Rural poverty was just as prevalent in Britain during the thirties. In 1967* ***Ronald Blythe***, *whose father had fought at Gallipoli in the Suffolk Regiment, published a history of a Suffolk village, based on the interviews he conducted with local people covering the previous half-century. Akenfield paints a grim picture of the poverty wages and grim conditions of the interwar years – a picture all too familiar to readers of William Cobbett, almost a century before. Here, the son of a village blacksmith from the Norfolk-Suffolk border recalls the rural depression of the early thirties.*

I was born during the bad times. My brothers and myself went to school for part of the day and to work for the rest of it. When we left school at half-past three we'd go gleaning, picking up beans and all such things as that. We'd most likely work till eight if it stayed light. We biked to school at Framlingham. It was 1934 time. Things weren't very sharp. Father was making out by killing pigs for Danny Linton at Pettistree, so we had to bike from school to home, eat some bread and cheese, or whatever there was – and there wasn't much – get an old sack and then bike on to Danny's farm to collect the pigs' insides. Then we biked home with them and tipped them out on the scullery floor and scraped them. We had to get them as white as a board, scratching out all the filth with the back of an old knife. Then we washed them in salty water and – hey presto! – sausage skins. But it wasn't the end. There were all these pails and pails of muck to be got rid of. We had to bike out of the village and bury it. On Saturdays we used to take a bundle of these skins to old Boot the butcher and he'd give us a three-cornered lump of brisket, all fat and bone, and weighing about a stone, in exchange. But even this is better than what happened in 1930, the big black year. In 1930 we had blackbird pie for Christmas dinner – and we had to catch the blackbirds before we had the pie! It had got to Christmas morning and we were going to make do when my father said, 'Come on, boys, let's try a blackbird!' We knocked a few over quite easy. I could take you to the spot where we did it. We cooked the pie in the brick oven.

This was the year my grandfather had to shut down the forge. He never went back to it. I used to walk by it, eyeing it and thinking. But nothing was rosy wherever you looked. Nearly everybody went out of business. Nothing was sold. People who had left school began to think about the Big House. You realised that it was there, with all the gardeners, grooms and maids and food. You have to face it, the Big House was then an asset to the village. It paid us to raise our hats, which is why we did it. I hear people run the gentry down now but they were better than the farmers in a crisis. Theirs was the only hand which fed us which we could see. So we bowed a bit; it cost nothing, even if it wasn't all courtesy. Nobody left, nobody went away. People were content. However hard up they were, they stayed content. The boys had the arse out of their trousers, no socks and the toes out of their boots. My brothers and myself were like this, yet so happy. I think other families were the same. The village kept close.

The Age of the Dictators

*The 1930s saw the rise of military dictatorship in Europe and the onset of wars in three continents. These were extremely bloody, indiscriminately violent since most victims were civilians, and harbingers of the enveloping global and regional conflicts to come. In 1933 **Patrick Leigh Fermor**, leaving school in England with not much to do, set out to walk across Europe. His destination was Constantinople – he insisted on calling the great Bosporus city by its old Greek name – and his book* A Time of Gifts *is a masterpiece of English descriptive writing. By this time, Hitler had come to power in Germany, though the young Leigh Fermor tried to ignore the increasing proliferation of Nazi street decoration and insignia. Here he describes arriving in Munich.*

I had expected a different kind of town, more like Nuremberg, perhaps, or Rothenburg. The neoclassical architecture in this boreal and boisterous weather, the giant boulevards, the unleavened pomp – everything struck chill to the heart. The proportion of storm troopers and SS in the streets was unusually high and still mounting and the Nazi salute flickered about the pavement like a tic douloureux. Outside the Feldherrnhalle, with its memorial to the sixteen Nazis killed in a 1923 street fight near by, two SS sentries with fixed bayonets and black helmets mounted guard like figures of cast iron and the right arms of all passers-by shot up as though in reflex to an electric beam. It was perilous to withhold this homage. One heard tales of uninitiated strangers being physically set upon by zealots. Then the thoroughfares began to shrink. I caught a glimpse down a lane of Gothic masonry and lancets and buttresses and further on copper domes hung in convolutions of baroque. A Virgin on a column presided over a slanting piazza, one side of which was formed by a tall, Victorian Gothic building whose great arched undercroft led to a confusion of lesser streets. In the heart of them stood a massive building; my objective, the Hofbräu- haus. A heavy arched door was pouring a raucous and lurching party of Brownshirts on to the trampled snow.

I was back in beer-territory. Half-way up the vaulted stairs a groaning Brownshirt, propped against the wall on a swastika'd arm, was unloosing, in a staunchless gush down the steps, the intake of hours. Love's labour lost. Each new storey radiated great halls given over to ingestion. In one chamber a table of SA men were grinding out '*Lore, Lore, Lore*', scanning the slow beat with the butts of their mugs, then running the syllables in double time, like the carriages of an express: 'UND – KOMMT – DER – FRÜHlingindastal! GRÜSS – MIR – DIE – LOREnocheinmal.' But it was certain civilian figures seated at meat that drew the glance and held it.

One must travel east for 180 miles from the Upper Rhine and 70 north from the Alpine watershed to form an idea of the transformation that beer, in collusion with almost non-stop eating – meals within meals dovetailing so closely during the hours of waking that there is hardly an interprandial moment – can wreak on the human frame. Intestine strife and the truce- less clash of intake and digestion wrecks many German tempers, twists brows into scowls and breaks out in harsh words and deeds.

The trunks of these feasting burghers were as wide as casks. The spread of their buttocks over the oak benches was not far short of a yard. They branched at the loins into thighs as thick as the torsos of ten-year-olds and arms on the same scale strained like bolsters at the confining serge. Chin and chest formed a single column, and each close-packed nape was creased with its three deceptive smiles. Every bristle had been cropped and shaven from their knobbly scalps. Except when five o'clock veiled them with shadow, surfaces as polished as ostriches' eggs reflected the lamplight. The frizzy hair of their wives was wrenched up from scarlet necks and pinned under slides and then hatted with green Bavarian trilbies, and round one pair of elephantine shoulders a little fox stole was clasped. The youngest of this group, resembling a matinée idol under some cruel spell, was the bulki- est. Under tumbling blond curls his china-blue eyes protruded from cheeks that might have been blown up with a bicycle pump, and cherry lips laid bare the sort of teeth that make children squeal. There was nothing bleary or stunned about their eyes. The setting may have reduced their size, but it keyed their glances to a sharper focus. Hands like bundles of sausages flew nimbly, packing in forkload on forkload of ham, salami, frankfurter, *Krenwurst* and *Blutwurst*, and stone tankards were lifted for long swallows of liquid which sprang out again instantaneously on cheek and brow. They might have been competing with stopwatches, and their voices, only partly gagged by the cheekfuls of good things they were grinding down, grew louder while their unmodulated laughter jarred the air in frequent claps. Pumpernickel and aniseed rolls and bretzels bridged all the slack moments but supplies always came through before a true lull threatened. Huge oval dishes, laden with *Schweinebraten*, potatoes, sauerkraut, red cabbage and dumplings, were laid in front of each diner. They were followed by colossal joints of meat – unclassifiable helpings which, when they were picked clean, shone on the scoured chargers like calves' pelvises or the bones of elephants. Waitresses with the build of weightlifters and all-in wrestlers whirled this provender along and features dripped and glittered like faces at an ogre's banquet. But all too soon the table was an empty bone-yard once more, sound faltered, a look of bereavement clouded those small eyes and there was a brief hint of sorrow in the air. But succour was always at hand; beldames barged to the rescue at full gallop with new clutches of mugs and fresh plate-loads of consumer goods; and the damp Laestrygonian brows unpuckered again in a happy renewal of clamour and intake.

I strayed by mistake into a room full of SS officers, *Gruppen-* and *Sturmbannführer*, black from their lightning-flash collars to the forest of tall boots underneath the table. The window embrasure was piled high with their skull-and-crossbones caps. I still hadn't found the part of this Bastille I was seeking, but at last a noise like the rush of a river guided me downstairs again to my journey's end.

On 27 February 1933, the German Reichstag, the parliament building, burned down, and Hitler tightened his grip on power in Berlin. The Nazis blamed a Dutch Communist, van der Lubbe, though it was more likely that the fire was started by the Nazis themselves as a pretext for outlawing political opposition. The correspondent **D. Sefton Delmer** *was soon on the scene,* *and gave an exemplary eyewitness report, carefully crafted with quotations taken on the spot.*

'This is a God-given signal! If this fire, as I believe, turns out to be the handiwork of Communists, then there is nothing that shall stop us now crushing out this murder pest with an iron fist.'

Adolf Hitler, fascist chancellor of Germany, made this dramatic declaration in my presence tonight in the hall of the burning Reichstag building.

The fire broke out at 9.45 tonight in the Assembly Hall of the Reichstag.

It had been laid in five different corners and there is no doubt whatever that it was the handiwork of incendiaries.

One of the incendiaries, a man aged thirty, was arrested by the police as he came rushing out of the building, clad only in shoes and trousers, without shirt or coat, despite the icy cold in Berlin tonight.

Five minutes after the fire had broken out I was outside the Reichstag watching the flames licking their way up the great dome into the tower.

A cordon had been flung round the building and no one was allowed to pass it.

After about twenty minutes of fascinated watching I suddenly saw the famous black motor car of Adolf Hitler slide past, followed by another car containing his personal bodyguard.

I rushed after them and was just in time to attach myself to the fringe of Hitler's party as they entered the Reichstag.

Never have I seen Hitler with such a grim and determined expression. His eyes, always a little protuberant, were almost bulging out of his head.

Captain Goering, his right-hand man, who is the Prussian minister of the interior, and responsible for all police affairs, joined us in the lobby. He had a very flushed and excited face.

'This is undoubtedly the work of Communists, Herr Chancellor,' he said.

'A number of Communist deputies were present here in the Reichstag twenty minutes before the fire broke out. We have succeeded in arresting one of the incendiaries.'

'Who is he?' Dr Goebbels, the propaganda chief of the Nazi Party, threw in.

'We do not know yet,' Captain Goering answered, with an ominously determined look around his thin, sensitive mouth. 'But we shall squeeze it out of him, have no doubt, doctor.'

We went into a room. 'Here you can see for yourself, Herr Chancellor, the way they started the fire,' said Captain Goering, pointing out the charred remains of some beautiful oak panelling.

'They hung cloths soaked in petrol over the furniture here and set it alight.'

We strode across another lobby filled with smoke. The police barred the way. 'The candelabra may crash any moment, Herr Chancellor,' said a captain of the police, with his arms outstretched.

By a detour we next reached a part of the building which was actually in flames. Firemen were pouring water into the red mass.

Hitler watched them for a few moments, a savage fury blazing from his pale blue eyes.

Then we came upon Herr von Papen, urbane and debonair as ever.

Hitler stretched out his hand and uttered the threat against the Communists which I have already quoted. He then turned to Captain Goering. 'Are all the other public buildings safe?' he questioned.

'I have taken every precaution,' answered Captain Goering. 'The police are in the highest state of alarm, and every public building has been specially garrisoned. We are waiting for anything.'

It was then that Hitler turned to me. 'God grant', he said, 'that this is the work of the Communists. You are witnessing the beginning of a great new epoch in German history. This fire is the beginning.'

And then something touched the rhetorical spring in his brain.

'You see this flaming building,' he said, sweeping his hand dramatically around him. 'If this Communist spirit got hold of Europe for but two months it would be all aflame like this building.'

By 12.30 the fire had been got under control. Two press rooms were still alight, but there was no danger of the fire spreading.

Although the glass of the dome has burst and crashed to the ground the dome still stands.

So far it has not been possible to disentangle the charred debris and see whether the bodies of any incendiaries, who may have been trapped in the building, are among it.

At the Prussian Ministry of the Interior a special meeting was called late tonight by Captain Goering to discuss measures to be taken as a consequence of the fire.

The entire district from the Brandenburg gate, on the west, to the river Spree, on the east, is isolated tonight by numerous cordons of police.

In Italy, Benito Mussolini established himself as dictator in 1922 when his Blackshirts marched on Rome. Il Duce flouted the League of Nations, allied himself with Germany and indulged imperial visions in Africa. In 1930 the **Duke of Pirajno**, *who had already spent several years working for the viceroy of Italian East Africa, was posted to the colony of Eritrea as regional commissioner. The duke, who had qualified as a doctor, must have been among the most humane and wise of all the servants of the Fascist empire. He describes the challenge that faced him in Eritrea.*

As soon as I arrived in Eritrea, in 1930, I was appointed regional commissioner for the western lowlands, a vast territory populated by seven different races, bounded on the west by the Anglo-Egyptian Sudan and on the south by Ethiopia from which it was separated by the river Setit.

In Agordat, where I had my residence, I occasionally deputised for the regional medical officer, who was a crack motor-driver and sometimes took part in races either in the colony or in the Sudan. On the whole, however, I was too busy to give as much time as I should have liked to dispensary work.

Nevertheless, it was at that time that I was obliged to run a long way after one patient – a patient I had never seen and who did his best to escape me. When, after a month's search, I finally caught up with him, guided by the traces of his torment and agony, he was dead. But even had I arrived in time I could have done nothing for him.

It was the period immediately preceding the war against Ethiopia which so scandalised the outraged virtue of the European colonial powers. The atmosphere in Africa was already tense and the Abyssinians, as though conscious of the gathering storm, were busy on the frontier, relieving their anxiety by making constant raids into our territory.

On one such raid two of the bandits – slaves who had escaped from their master to seek refuge in Eritrea – had killed a baby elephant in order to take his milk teeth, and had emasculated four children of a Cunama village because the people refused to help them.

With the aid of the armed bands of the Barentù and Tessenei the raiders were chased back over the river Setit and their chief, a half-caste named Zaccharias, was killed. As, however, some of the *shifta* still seemed to be in the frontier zone, I set out to comb the territory from the Setit to Mount Talasuba with the help of about fifteen armed men of the Cunama and Baria territories, four others from the uplands, led by a sergeant and Shumbashi Gabremariam.

It was not till the fourth day that we began to find the traces for which we were seeking. Then, in the direction of Motilè, we came upon the remnants of a recent fire and in the scattered ashes there was the imprint of an Abyssinian sandal. My men, who had begun to doubt the presence of the bandits and were becoming irritated and discontented at being asked to look for something that did not appear to exist, took heart at once like hounds. They spread instinctively in all directions, climbing up the slopes, sliding down rocks, following barely visible tracks under the acacia trees, pushing through grass as high as a man and forcing their way among thorn bushes which the rainy season had adorned with large white waxen flowers. At about midday, Lance-Corporal Taddé Bocú returned in a high state of excitement, stuttering, incoherent and quite unable to relate what he had just discovered. After an effective bout of cursing on the part of Gabremariam and some show of annoyance on mine, Taddé Bocú managed at last to put some sort of order into his tale.

In private life Taddé Bocú was an elephant tracker and this was a day of days, for he had found the tracks of an elephant.

Gabremariam was beside himself, and only my presence prevented him from jumping at the throat of the idiot who had not yet understood that we were looking for bandits and not elephants.

The unfortunate lance-corporal tried by gestures to stem the flow of his superior's curses and to beg leave to speak. Finally he was allowed to explain. He no longer stuttered; his musical Cunama speech flowed easily and was illustrated with such pantomime that the services of an interpreter were almost superfluous.

As the elephant tracker began his story Gabremariam became attentive and from time to time nodded his head, his brows drawn together. At intervals he signed to the man to stop and turned to me to interpret the extraordinary tale.

It seemed that after three hours' march to the east of the Shogotah marshland, Taddé Bocú had come upon the tracks of the Abyssinians. There were four of them, but there was also a fifth man who walked barefoot and whose left foot lacked the third toe. This was clearly Anto Alimatú, known in the Lakatakura as a man who prided himself on being an expert tracker, whereas his fellow countrymen, who knew him well, had nicknamed him *tila acoishah* which, in the language of the Cunama, means 'the hunter of fleas'. Three of the Abyssinians, according to Taddé Bocú, were of medium height, and one very tall and heavily built because his foot-marks sank into the earth, the left more than the right. The lance-corporal did not wish to commit himself entirely, but he thought that a wound in the leg or foot made him limp, for alongside the foot-marks there was also the mark of a stick on which the bandit probably leaned, particularly in the difficult places – and under a bush the Cunama had found a strip of bloodstained *futa* which he proceeded to wave under our noses.

> *Following his decision to invade Ethiopia in 1935, Mussolini rounded up known opponents to fascism and sent them into internal exile –* confino. *__Carlo Levi__, who had qualified as a doctor, was sent south from Turin to Lucania, now Basilicata, on the instep of the Italian peninsula. The peasants of the region were plagued by malaria, and most believed in witchcraft. 'We are not Christians,' one told him. 'Christ stopped at Eboli.' This became the title of a most memorable portrait of a world cut off from history, a remote and desperately poor corner of twentieth-century Europe. As late as 1980 several of the characters in the memoir were still living in Aliano (Gagliano in Levi's book), the principal village in which he was confined, their sheep and goats driven home each winter night to stables in the houses themselves. Levi, an accomplished artist, paints the landscape as he arrives in Lucania.*

I arrived at Gagliano one August afternoon in a rattling little car. I was wearing handcuffs and I was escorted by two stalwart servants of the state with vertical red bands on their trousers, and expressionless faces. I arrived reluctantly and ready for the worst, because sudden orders had caused me to leave Grassano, where I had been living and where I had learned to know the region of Lucania. It had been hard at first. Grassano, like all the villages hereabouts, is a streak of white at the summit of a bare hill, a sort of miniature imaginary Jerusalem in the solitude of the desert. I liked to climb to the highest point of the village, to the wind-beaten church, where the eye can sweep over an endless expanse in every direction, identical in character all the way around the circle. It is like being on a sea of chalk, monotonous and without trees.

The big event in Aliano was the Christmas festivities. The podestà, *the fascist mayor, Don Luigi, relaxed the curfew on the political detainees to allow them to go to midnight Mass.*

On the dot of midnight I was in front of the church, amid the crowd of villagers, all of us stamping our feet in the powdery snow. The sky was clear, with a few stars, and the Christ child was about to be born. But the bell failed to ring, the church door was padlocked, and of Don Trajella there was no sign. We waited half an hour in front of the locked door with mounting impatience. What was the matter? Was the priest ill or, as Don Luigi loudly insisted, drunk? Finally the mayor decided to send a boy to the priest's house to call him. A few minutes later Don Trajella appeared, coming down the path in high snow-boots with a big key in his hand. He went up to the church door, muttering some excuse or other for his lateness, turned the key in the padlock and hastened to light the candles on the altar. We all poured into the church and the Mass began, a poor, hurried Mass, without music or singing. At the end of the Mass, after the *Ite missa est*, Don Trajella came down from the altar, walked in front of the benches where we were sitting, and went up into the pulpit to preach the sermon.

'Beloved brethren!' he began. 'Beloved brethren! Brethren!' Here he stopped and began to search in his pockets, while incomprehensible mumblings issued from his lips. He put on his spectacles, took them off, put them on again, pulled out a handkerchief, wiped the perspiration from his face, raised his eyes to heaven, let them rest on his hearers, sighed, scratched his head in an agony of embarrassment, exclaimed 'Oh!' and 'Ah!', clasped and unclasped his hands, murmured a *pater*, and at last remained silent, with a look of despair. A murmuring rustled through the crowd. What was happening? Don Luigi turned red in the face and began to shout:

'He's drunk! And on Christmas Eve!'

'Beloved brethren!' said Don Trajella again. 'I came here, as your pastor, to talk to you, my beloved flock, on the occasion of this holy day, to bring you the message of a devoted shepherd, *solliciti et benigni et studiosi pastoris*. I had prepared, if I may say it in all humility, a fine sermon. I meant to read it to you because my memory is poor. I put it in my pocket, and now, alas, I can't find it; it's lost and I can't remember a single word of it. What can I do? What can I say to you, my faithful flock, you who are waiting to hear me? Alas, I have no words at all to say.' At this point Don Trajella relapsed into silence, with his eyes fixed dreamily on the ceiling. The peasants waited, uncertain and curious.

Don Luigi could no longer control himself; he got up angrily.

'It's a scandal! A desecration of the house of God! Fascists, come here!' The peasants did not know which way to look.

Don Trajella, as if awakened from a trance, knelt down in front of a wooden crucifix set on the edge of the pulpit and prayed with folded hands:

'Jesus, my Jesus, see into what a plight my sins have led me! Help me, Lord! Jesus, come to the rescue of Thy servant!' Then suddenly, as if he were touched by grace, the priest leapt to his feet, snatched up a piece of paper hidden at the foot of the crucifix and shouted: 'A miracle! A miracle! Jesus has heard me; Jesus has succoured me! I lost my sermon and he has helped me to find something better. What value could there have been in my poor words? Listen, rather, to words from afar!' And he began to read from the paper he had just found by the crucifix. But Don Luigi was not listening. He had let himself go in a tempest of icy anger and outraged religiosity.

'Fascists, come here! It's a sacrilege! Drunk in church, on Christmas Eve! Here, to me!' And beckoning to the seven or eight Fascist Scouts from the school among the congregation he began to sing 'Little Black Face'.

The Spanish Civil War

When General Franco launched his invasion of Spain from Spanish Morocco in July 1936, he expected a quick victory over the struggling Republican government. And indeed the rebellion quickly spread to the garrison towns of Seville, Cadiz, Burgos and Zaragoza. But resistance in Madrid and Barcelona, in particular, gave the government time to arm the militias, and the country was very quickly engulfed in civil war. Whether this was a war fought, as John Masters put it, 'between Communist beasts and Fascist swine, or between equally and therefore fatally divided Spaniards' will no doubt always be open to debate, but what is undeniable is that Franco's Falangists very quickly received the active support of Nazi Germany and Mussolini's Italy. Many onlookers saw the struggle in stark terms as a fight against the rising tide of fascism, and even as Britain and other countries preached non-intervention, Communist Russia began to send aid to the Republicans, and volunteers from over fifty countries flocked to join the International Brigade.

* **Arthur Koestler**, a Hungarian-born writer and journalist, who had been signed up to cover the war in Spain for the* News Chronicle, *was one of its early victims. He was captured when the Nationalists seized the port of Málaga in February 1937, and incarcerated for criticising the involvement of German and Italian forces in the fighting. He describes the scene in the courtyard of the jail after his arrival.*

Then I heard screams coming from the courtyard, and a young man, his naked torso streaming with blood, was led into the room. His face was battered, cut about and slashed; for a moment I thought the man must have been run over by a steam engine. Holding him by the armpits they dragged him across the room. He yelled and whimpered. The Falangists who were dragging him along spoke to him in honeyed tones: 'Hombre, we're not going to beat you any more.' The door closed after them, and a moment later there were sounds of ringing blows and dull thuds and kicks. The man groaned and cried by turns. He cried at regular intervals.

Then for a few seconds there was silence. All I could hear was quick, stertorous breathing. I don't know what they did to him in those few seconds. Then he screamed again in an unnaturally high-pitched shrill voice; and then at last he was silent. A few moments later the door flew open and they dragged him across the room in which I was sitting into the courtyard. I couldn't make out whether he was dead or merely unconscious. I did not care to look very closely.

Then a second victim was taken through the room to be subjected to the same treatment; and then a third.

Every time they went through the room the Falangists looked at me as though marking me down as their next victim, but they said nothing. After the third case, no more were brought in; I sat still and waited.

The Civil Guards sitting opposite me seemed to be disagreeably affected by these proceedings. While the tortures were going on in the next room they scrutinised my features keenly to watch my reaction; perhaps, too, with a faint stirring of pity. When the third victim was brought back, dead or unconscious, the elder of the Civil Guards shrugged his shoulders with a glance in my direction; it was an unconscious gesture of apology. In it was expressed the whole attitude towards life of a fifty-year-old gendarme who, on the one hand, had thirty years of service in a medieval country behind him and on the other probably had a wife, several underfed children and a pet canary. In it was expressed an entire human philosophy of shame, resignation and apathy. 'The world's like that,' he seemed to be saying, 'and neither I nor you will ever change it.' The shrug of the Civil Guard is more vivid in my memory than the screams of the tortured.

Isolated, and uncertain of his fate, Koestler gave way to a nervous craving for action which began with trying to decipher the inscriptions scratched on the cell walls. He comforted himself with the reflection that four days had passed since his arrest and that news of it would have reached England.

What I did not know was that the court martial in Málaga had already pronounced sentence of death on me without my being summoned before it.

The second thing that I did not know was that up to this time – Saturday, 13 February 1937 – five thousand men had been shot in Málaga since the fall of the town; six hundred from my prison alone.

The writer **George Orwell**, *then a convinced Communist, went to Spain with the object of writing newspaper articles, but was swept into the conflict after only two days in Barcelona. Within a week he was serving on the Aragon front, a corporal in the Youth Section of the militia of the Spanish* POUM *– an anti-Stalinist Labour party. His experience of action, described in* Homage to Catalonia, *was chaotic and dispiriting.*

We had been creeping forward for such an age that I began to think we had gone the wrong way. Then in the darkness thin parallel lines of something blacker were faintly visible. It was the outer wire (the Fascists had two lines of wire). Jorge knelt down, fumbled in his pocket. He had our only pair of wire-cutters. Snip, snip. The trailing stuff was lifted delicately aside. We waited for the men at the back to close up. They seemed to be making a frightful noise. It might be 50 yards to the Fascist parapet now. Still onwards, bent double. A stealthy step, lowering your foot as gently as a cat approaching a mousehole; then a pause to listen; then another step. Once I raised my head; in silence Benjamin put his hand behind my neck and pulled it violently down. I knew that the inner wire was barely 20 yards from the parapet. It seemed to me inconceivable that thirty men could get there unheard. Our breathing was enough to give us away. Yet somehow we did get there. The Fascist parapet was visible now, a dim black mound, looming high above us. Once again Jorge knelt and fumbled. Snip, snip. There was no way of cutting the stuff silently.

So that was the inner wire. We crawled through it on all fours and rather more rapidly. If we had time to deploy now all was well. Jorge and Benjamin crawled across to the right. But the men behind, who were spread out, had to form into single file to get through the narrow gap in the wire, and just at this moment there was a flash and a bang from the Fascist parapet. The sentry had heard us at last. Jorge poised himself on one knee and swung his arm like a bowler. Crash! His bomb burst some-where over the parapet. At once, far more promptly than one would have thought possible, a roar of fire, ten or twenty rifles, burst out from the Fascist parapet. They had been waiting for us after all. Momentarily you could see every sandbag in the lurid light. Men too far back were flinging their bombs and some of them were falling short of the parapet. Every loophole seemed to be spouting jets of flame. It is always hateful to be shot at in the dark – every rifle-flash seems to be pointed straight at yourself – but it was the bombs that were the worst. You cannot conceive the horror of these things till you have seen one burst close to you in darkness; in the daytime there is only the crash of the explosion, in the darkness there is the blinding red glare as well. I had flung myself down at the first volley. All this while I was lying on my side in the greasy mud, wrestling savagely with the pin of a bomb. The damned thing would not come out. Finally I realised that I was twisting it in the wrong direction. I got the pin out, rose to my knees, hurled the bomb, and threw myself down again. The bomb burst over to the right, outside the parapet; fright had spoiled my aim. Just at this moment another bomb burst right in front of me, so close that I could feel the heat of the explosion. I flattened myself out and dug my face into the mud so hard that I hurt my neck and thought that I was wounded. Through the din I heard an English voice behind me say quietly: 'I'm hit.' The bomb had, in fact, wounded several people round about me without touching myself. I rose to my knees and flung my second bomb. I forget where that one went.

The Fascists were firing, our people behind were firing, and I was very conscious of being in the middle. I felt the blast of a shot and realised that a man was firing from immediately behind me. I stood up and shouted at him: 'Don't shoot at me, you bloody fool!' At this moment I saw that Ben-jamin, 10 or 15 yards to my right, was motioning to me with his arm. I ran across to him. It meant crossing the line of spouting loopholes, and as I went I clapped my left hand over my cheek; an idiotic gesture – as though one's hand could stop a bullet! – but I had a horror of being hit in the face. Benjamin was kneeling on one knee with a pleased, devilish sort of expres-sion on his face and firing carefully at the rifle-flashes with his automatic pistol. Jorge had dropped wounded at the first volley and was somewhere out of sight. I knelt beside Benjamin, pulled the pin out of my third bomb and flung it. Ah! No doubt about it that time. The bomb crashed inside the parapet, at the corner, just by the machine-gun nest.

The Fascist fire seemed to have slackened very suddenly. Benjamin leapt to his feet and shouted: 'Forward! Charge!' We dashed up the short steep slope on which the parapet stood. I say 'dashed'; 'lumbered' would be a better word; the fact is that you can't move fast when you are sodden and mudded from head to foot and weighted down with a heavy rifle and bayonet and 150 cartridges. I took it for granted that there would be a Fascist waiting for me at the top. If he fired at that range he could not miss me, and yet somehow I never expected him to fire, only to try for me with his bayonet. I seemed to feel in advance the sensation of our bayonets crossing, and I wondered whether his arm would be stronger than mine. However, there was no Fascist waiting. With a vague feeling of relief I found that it was a low parapet and the sandbags gave a good foothold. As a rule they are difficult to get over. Everything inside was smashed to pieces, beams flung all over the place, and great shards of uralite littered everywhere. Our bombs had wrecked all the huts and dugouts. And still there was not a soul visible. I thought they would be lurking somewhere underground, and shouted in English (I could not think of any Spanish at the moment): 'Come on out of it! Surrender!' No answer. Then a man, a shadowy figure in the half-light, skipped over the roof of one of the ruined huts and dashed away to the left. I started after him, prodding my bayonet ineffectually into the darkness. As I rounded the corner of the hut I saw a man – I don't know whether or not it was the same man as I had seen before – fleeing up the communication trench that led to the other Fascist position. I must have been very close to him, for I could see him clearly. He was bareheaded and seemed to have nothing on except a blanket which he was clutching round his shoulders. If I had fired I could have blown him to pieces. But for fear of shooting one another we had been ordered to use only bayonets once we were inside the parapet, and in any case I never even thought of firing. Instead, my mind leapt backwards twenty years, to our boxing instructor at school, showing me in vivid pantomime how he had bayoneted a Turk at the Dardanelles. I gripped my rifle by the small of the butt and lunged at the man's back. He was just out of my reach. Another lunge: still out of reach. And for a little distance we proceeded like this, he rushing up the trench and I after him on the ground above, prodding at his shoulder-blades and never quite getting there – a comic memory for me to look back upon, though I suppose it seemed less comic to him.

On 27 April 1937 the old Basque capital of Guernica was set ablaze by an aerial attack, led by the German Luftwaffe Condor Legion. This was the first concentrated aerial attack on civilians, and the first operational use by the Nazis of the Blitzkreig. *Reports by the legendary correspondent George Lowther Steer gave rise to widespread shock and outrage, and inspired Picasso's iconic painting of the atrocity. Steer had travelled with a party of journalists to the town and they had witnessed the German Stukas diving on it from their car just a few miles away. The Reuters correspondent composed a sonnet on the spot. Steer's reports lost him his contract with the pro-Nationalist* Times *of London.* **Noel Monks** *of the* Daily Express, *who had been travelling separately, describes how he saw the bombing, and later returned to Guernica to see for himself.*

We were about 18 miles east of Guernica when Anton pulled to the side of the road, jammed on the brakes and started shouting. He pointed wildly ahead, and my heart shot into my mouth when I looked. Over the tops of some hills appeared a flock of planes. A dozen or so bombers were flying high. But down much lower, seeming just to skim the treetops, were six Heinkel 52 fighters. The bombers flew on towards Guernica, but the Heinkels, out for random plunder, spotted our car, and, wheeling like a flock of homing pigeons, they lined up the road – and our car.

Anton and I flung ourselves into a bomb hole, 20 yards to the side of the road. It was half-filled with water, and we sprawled in mud. We half-knelt, half-stood, with our heads buried in the muddy side of the crater.

After one good look at the Heinkels, I didn't look up again until they had gone. That seemed hours later, but it was probably less than twenty minutes. The planes made several runs along the road. Machine-gun bullets plopped into the mud ahead, behind, all around us. I began to shiver from sheer fright. Only the day before Steer, an old hand now, had 'briefed' me about being strafed. 'Lie still and as flat as you can. But don't get up and start running, or you'll be bowled over for certain.'

When the Heinkels departed, out of ammunition I presumed, Anton and I ran back to our car. Near by a military car was burning fiercely. All we could do was drag two riddled bodies to the side of the road. I was trembling all over now, in the grip of the first real fear I'd ever experienced. On occasions I'd been scared before – as when I'd crashed into the sea in the *Cutty Sark* – but here on the road to Guernica I was in a bad state of jitters indeed. Then suddenly the quaking passed and I felt exhilarated. These were the days in foreign reporting when personal experiences were copy, for there hadn't been a war for eighteen years, long enough for those who went through the last one to forget, and for a generation and a half who knew nothing of war to be interested. We used to call them 'I' stories, and when the Spanish war ended in 1939 we were as heartily sick of writing them as the public must have been of reading them.

Later that evening, Monks went to see Guernica for himself.

In the good 'I' tradition of the day, I was the first correspondent to reach Guernica, and was immediately pressed into service by some Basque soldiers collecting charred bodies that the flames had passed over. Some of the soldiers were sobbing like children. There were flames and smoke and grit, and the smell of burning human flesh was nauseating. Houses were collapsing into the inferno.

In the *plaza*, surrounded almost by a wall of fire, were about a hundred refugees. They were wailing and weeping and rocking to and fro. One middle-aged man spoke English.

He told me: 'At four, before the market closed, many aeroplanes came. They dropped bombs. Some came low and shot bullets into the streets. Father Aronategui was wonderful. He prayed with the people in the *plaza* while the bombs fell.' The man had no idea who I was, as far as I know. He was telling me what had happened to Guernica.

Most of Guernica's streets began or ended at the *plaza*. It was impossible to go down many of them, because they were walls of flame. Debris was piled high. I could see shadowy forms, some large, some just ashes. I moved round to the back of the *plaza* among survivors. They had the same story to tell, aeroplanes, bullets, bombs, fire.

Within twenty-four hours, when the grim story was told to the world,

Franco was going to brand these shocked, homeless people as liars. So-called British experts were going to come to Guernica, weeks afterwards, when the smell of burnt human flesh had been replaced by petrol dumped here and there among the ruins by Mola's men, and deliver pompous judgements: 'Guernica was set on fire wilfully by the Reds.'

No government official had accompanied me to Guernica. I wandered round the place at will. I drove back to Bilbao and had to waken the cable operator – it was nearly two in the morning – to send my message. Censorship had been lifted completely. The man who sent my despatch couldn't read English. If the 'Reds' had destroyed Guernica and hundreds of their fellow Basques, I could have blown the whole story for all they knew – as I certainly would have done. I told the facts about the bombing of Guernica in my message and described the terrible scenes I'd witnessed.

The only things left standing were a church, a sacred tree, symbol of the Basque people, and, just outside the town, a small munitions factory. There hadn't been a single anti-aircraft gun in the town. It had been mainly a fire raid. Steer and Holme picked up some dud incendiary bombs. They were branded with the German eagle. Some were handed to British agents and positively identified.

A sight that haunted me for weeks was the charred bodies of several women and children huddled together in what had been the cellar of a house. It had been a *refugio*. Franco's British apologists were going to proclaim that these people had been locked in the cellar by their own men while the house was dynamited and set alight.

The Chinese Revolution

Throughout the inter-war years, China was in the grip of war, civil war and indiscriminate violence against its civilians. Widespread popular reaction against foreign interference was exacerbated by the terms of the Paris peace conference, which reinforced the position of Japan in Shantung and fed Japanese imperial ambitions. Workers, students and intellectuals came together to form a Nationalist (Kuomintang) party dedicated to eliminating the warlords and unifying China against its enemies. At first Chiang Kai-shek, who had taken command of the Kuomintang in 1926, was happy to work with the nascent Communist party, but by April 1927 he decided that he could manage without them and they were ruthlessly purged. By moving around and building support in rural areas, the Communists survived repeated Kuomintang campaigns, until, in 1934, they decided to abandon their southern bases and embarked on their legendary 'Long March' of 4,000 miles to Yenan, in north-west China. There they established their stronghold. It was during the march that Mao Zedong (Tse-tung) emerged as leader.

__Hsiao Ch'ien__, one of China's best-known writers, was born in a Peking slum in 1910, and was orphaned by the time he was ten. By 1925 he had already worked in a publishing house and had become politically involved – taking part in demonstrations against both British and Japanese imperialism. In his autobiography, Traveller without a Map, *he describes the birth of a revolutionary.*

I spent that winter vacation with Zhong Yiyan, a radical Cantonese schoolmate. His home was in Qinghe, near Peking. His father, who had studied in England, was chief engineer of the nearby woollen textile factory. They had a very large compound with a vegetable garden at one end and a fish-pond at the other. They also kept twenty beehives and a beautiful flower garden. Yiyan's father was affable and full of good humour. While tending his bees, he would discuss with me from behind his apiarist's veil the question of how to liberate China. He thought the answer was education and heavy industry. I know now that the old man was trying to induce me to study something practical. After getting no response, he suddenly cast a sidelong glance at me and asked pointblank, 'Bing Qian [for that was my name then], what do you want to be when you grow up?'

I'd never thought about that before. 'I want to be a revolutionary!' I blurted out. At this, Yiyan's father laughed and laughed. He said I had no idea of what that meant. And to tell the truth, I didn't.

But I was soon to find out.

Peking was at that time under the rule of Zhang Zuolin, a warlord based in Manchuria whom the Western press called 'The Old Marshal'. He was so terrified of being inundated by a Red tide that he even banned *Master Ma's Introduction to Grammar*, a nineteenth-century textbook by Ma Jianzhong, because he thought Master Ma might be a cover for Mr Marx.

Zhang had three different police branches under his control: the regular police, a Public Security Corps, and a secret Detective Corps with special responsibility for tracking down Reds. Little did I realise that the father of one of my classmates, Peng, was head of the last group. His specific responsibility was to expose Reds in the classroom.

One day, at dusk, I was playing with some friends making caves by Sand Dune Pond. Just as a group of bats swooped down over our heads, a boy suddenly ran up to me. Dragging me behind the handball court, he whispered, 'Bing Qian, something awful – they're coming to arrest you.'

'But what for?' I asked, my hands on my hips.

In fact I didn't really understand the word 'arrest'. But we used it to mean 'you lose' when we played hide-and-seek, so I guessed it must mean something unpleasant.

Later someone told me on the sly that the detectives had already chosen their informer, my classmate Peng. Although in his teens, he was short, and scrawny as a chicken. But we were usually friendly with each other. I couldn't believe it, so I sought him out and asked him,

'Would you ever do anything to hurt me?'

He smiled quite calmly and shook his head. That was enough for me.

The next Saturday, when I was all alone on the playground reading my books, Peng suddenly ran up to me.

'Bing Qian, there's a telephone call for you in the porter's lounge.'

Weekends were the worst time for a homeless child like me. A little warmth was just what my soul ached for, so I went there quite unsuspectingly.

But there was no call for me, and the old doorman was nowhere to be seen, either. Instead there were two plainclothes policemen with fierce faces.

'Now Mr Hsiao, come with us and have a cup of tea,' they said, smiling contemptuously.

Peng had disappeared.

'I don't know you,' I said.

'Come on!' One of them grabbed my arm and the other pushed me out. I remember it as if it were yesterday: one with a goatee beard wore a short, grey, padded jacket and had bound his legs with silk; the other wore a black long gown and dark glasses – he was missing an eye. Struggle as I might, I was unable to escape from their rough hands.

They dragged me on to a tram, and that night I found myself locked in a room with sixteen or seventeen others, squatting with them on a *kang* not 6 feet wide. No talking was allowed. My belt and even my shoelaces had been taken from me, lest I attempt suicide. I used my shoes for a pillow, like all the other prisoners.

Who could sleep on a night like that? My heart was pounding wildly and I had no idea what might happen to me.

The guards talked loudly the whole night long, warming themselves at the stove. Some talked of the prostitutes they'd visited during the daytime, others of their luck at *yabao*, the game of gambling with dice under a dish. From their conversation I also learned how much they had got for catching each of us: 5 silver yuan.

This detention centre was in Baofang Lane, quite near the city's pork market, where pigs were butchered before daybreak. I listened to them shrieking and imagined the butchers (half naked, I was once told) attacking the poor animals with their sharp knives. I had eaten pork many times, but this was the first time I felt sympathy for the pigs.

Come dawn and at the blast of a whistle all seventeen of us had to get up. Half an hour was allowed for the latrine, after which we all silently squatted back down on the *kang* again for the rest of the day.

I discovered that there was a nine-year-old boy among us political prisoners. He smiled at me and soon we were friends. For talking to him I got a whipping, but on the sly we managed to play the finger-guessing game of 'stone, scissors, paper' anyway.

> *To the West, the nature of the Red Army, the Chinese Soviet and the true story behind the Long March was a mystery. Communists were under a death sentence, and in Nanking there was a well-established espionage network. It was believed that no one could enter Red territory and emerge alive. In June 1936, however, an American journalist called* **Edgar Snow** *seized the opportunity to cross the lines, reach the Communist capital, and meet Mao just at the point when Mao was prepared to go on record. He spent four months taking down Mao's life as a revolutionary, before emerging from the blockaded area in October. In* Red Star Over China, *he describes their meeting.*

I met Mao soon after my arrival: a gaunt, rather Lincolnesque figure, above average height for a Chinese, somewhat stooped, with a head of thick black hair grown very long, and with large, searching eyes, a high-bridged nose and prominent cheekbones. My fleeting impression was of an intellectual face of great shrewdness, but I had no opportunity to verify this for several days. Next time I saw him, Mao was walking hatless along the street at dusk, talking with two young peasants and gesticulating earnestly. I did not recognise him until he was pointed out to me – moving along unconcernedly with the rest of the strollers, despite the $250,000 which Nanking had hung over his head.

I could have written a book about Mao Tse-tung. I talked with him many nights, on a wide range of subjects, and I heard dozens of stories about him from soldiers and Communists. My written interviews with him totalled about twenty thousand words. He told me of his childhood and youth, how he became a leader in the Kuomintang and the Nationalist revolution, why he became a Communist, and how the Red Army grew. He described the Long March to the north-west and wrote a classical poem about it for me. He told me stories of many other famous Reds, from Chu Teh down to the youth who carried on his shoulders for over 6,000 miles the two iron despatch boxes that held the archives of the Soviet government ...

Mao had the reputation of a charmed life. He had been repeatedly pronounced dead by his enemies, only to return to the news columns a few days later, as active as ever. The Kuomintang had also officially 'killed' and buried Chu Teh many times, assisted by occasional corroborations from clairvoyant missionaries. Numerous deaths of the two famous men, nevertheless, did not prevent them from being involved in many spectacular exploits, including the Long March. Mao was indeed in one of his periods of newspaper demise when I visited Red China, but I found him quite substantially alive. There were good reasons why people said that he had a charmed life, however; although he had been in scores of battles, was once captured by enemy troops and escaped, and had the world's highest reward on his head, during all these years he had never once been wounded ...

Mao seemed to me a very interesting and complex man. He had the simplicity and naturalness of the Chinese peasant, with a lively sense of humour and a love of rustic laughter. His laughter was even active on the subject of himself and the shortcomings of the Soviets – a boyish sort of laughter which never in the least shook his inner faith in his purpose. He was plain-speaking and plain-living, and some people might have considered him rather coarse and vulgar. Yet he combined curious qualities of naïvety with incisive wit and worldly sophistication.

I think my first impression – dominantly one of native shrewdness – was probably correct. And yet Mao was an accomplished scholar of classical Chinese, an omnivorous reader, a deep student of philosophy and history, a good speaker, a man with an unusual memory and extraordinary powers of concentration, an able writer, careless in his personal habits and appearance but astonishingly meticulous about details of duty, a man of tireless energy, and a military and political strategist of considerable genius. It was interesting that many Japanese regarded him as the ablest Chinese strategist alive ...

I found him surprisingly well informed on current world politics. Even on the Long March, it seems, the Reds received news broadcasts by radio, and in the north-west they published their own newspapers. Mao was exceptionally well read in world history and had a realistic conception of European social and political conditions. He was very interested in the Labour party of England, and questioned me intensely about its present policies, soon exhausting all my information. It seemed to me that he found it difficult fully to understand why, in a country where workers were enfranchised, there was still no workers' government. I was afraid my answers did not satisfy him. He expressed profound contempt for Ramsay MacDonald, whom he designated as a *han-chien* – an arch-traitor of the British people.

His opinion of President Roosevelt was rather interesting. He believed him to be anti-fascist, and thought China could co-operate with such a man. He asked innumerable questions about the New Deal, and Roosevelt's foreign policy. The questioning showed a remarkably clear conception of the objectives of both. He regarded Mussolini and Hitler as mountebanks, but considered Mussolini intellectually a much abler man, a real Machiavellian, with a knowledge of history, while Hitler was a mere will-less puppet of the reactionary capitalists.

In the meantime, the enemy without, Japan, had occupied Manchuria in 1931, and in 1935 the neighbouring province of Jehol. In 1936 the Kuomintang and the Communists combined to form a united front against Japan, and Japan responded in 1937 with a full-scale invasion of China. After battling round Shanghai through much of the summer, the Japanese imperial army finally attacked the Chinese capital of Nanking, entering the old city on 13 December. There followed one of the worst orgies of violence against a civilian population ever witnessed in the twentieth century. At least two hundred thousand people were murdered and mutilated as the Japanese ran amok. The Japanese denied the truth of the atrocities for many years, and critical first-hand reports were suppressed by Tokyo until well after the defeat of Japan in 1945. Only twenty-two outsiders remained to record what happened – most journalists wisely retreated.

A secret despatch to the fleeing Nationalist government proved as accurate as it was graphic.

The slaughter committed by the Japanese outside the city and in the various districts neighbouring Nanking was even more savage and cruel than that which occurred within the city. Refugees fleeing from all over, wounded and sick soldiers, and family members of the military men died in even greater numbers and under even more cruel circumstances.

As the Kuomintang troops had already seized control of every sort of boat available in order to save their own lives, the refugees from Nanking who were trapped on the banks of the river could do nothing but gaze helplessly across the Yangtze. On 13 December, the sounds of gunfire emanating from within the city caused a stir among the refugees gathered along the river as they came to realise that the Japanese had already occupied the city. The situation along the river became extremely chaotic. Those with even a little strength left, whether they were routed soldiers or fleeing refugees, used every last bit of energy to put up one last fight. In a desperate attempt to flee across the river, some people went to houses and shops and removed wooden doors, planks of wood, bathtubs, long benches, logs and even old, rotten pieces of wood to serve as makeshift flotation devices. There were too many people and too few adequate implements. In the end, only a small number of people were lucky enough to cross the river successfully, while the majority were left behind in an entirely hopeless situation.

On the afternoon of 14 December, the Japanese troops suddenly threw open Yijiang gate and charged forward from the city towards Zhongshan wharf and Xiaguan station. Wielding machine guns and rifles, they recklessly fired upon the refugees and indiscriminately tossed grenades into the crowds. Panic-stricken, angry and in despair, thousands upon thousands of refugees were toppled. Some refugees who were still able to put up a struggle and were unwilling to allow themselves to be killed by the Japanese tossed themselves in the river and committed suicide. In the end, those left standing on the banks of the river were forced into the water by the Japanese and drowned *en masse*. After a short while, tens of thousands of people had lost their lives under the murderous blades of the Japanese soldiers.

On 16 December, more than five thousand people who had taken refuge in the Overseas Chinese Centre (now 81 North Zhongshan Road) were bound together in groups and transported on large trucks to Xiaguan station to be killed. The corpses were disposed of in the river.

There were various places along the river where the killings occurred on a larger scale. These areas included Straw Sandals gorge, Swallow cliff and Goddess of Mercy gate. Prior to the occupation of Nanking, those unable to escape to far-off areas scattered in groups to the outskirts of town. Moreover, those fleeing from the front lines (amongst whom were a large number of wounded and sick soldiers) increasingly attempted to squeeze into the suburban districts and the area along the Yangtze river. For a short while, those without the means to cross the river organised themselves into a refugee village in order to maintain some semblance of order necessary for their survival. But soon after the Japanese forces occupied Nanking, they began to scour the countryside. They rounded up and bound large numbers of refugees, about fifty thousand in total, who were detained for several days without provision of food or drink. A large number of the sick and wounded starved or froze to death. Finally, those who survived the ordeal were driven to Straw Sandals gorge where they were brutally slaughtered.

Something of the length to which the imperial command went to cover up the atrocities is given by the following short telegram despatch sent by the **Manchester Guardian** *correspondent at the end of 1937. It was intercepted successfully, and on 17 January 1938 the Japanese foreign minister issued a personal order that it should not be sent. It emerged at the war crimes tribunal held by the Allies nearly ten years after the event.*

Extra Message

Since return to Shanghai a few days ago I investigated reported atrocities committed by Japanese army in Nanking and elsewhere. Verbal accounts from reliable eyewitnesses and letters from individuals whose credibility is beyond question afford convincing proof that Japanese army behaved and is continuing to behave in a fashion reminiscent of Attila and his Huns. Not less than three hundred thousand Chinese civilians slaughtered, many cases in cold blood, robbery, rape, including children of tender years, and indiscriminate brutality towards civilians continues to be reported from areas where actual hostilities ceased weeks ago. Deep shame which better type of Japanese civilian here feel – reprehensible conduct of Japanese troops elsewhere heightened by series of local incidents where Japanese soldiers ran amok in Shanghai itself. Today's *North China Daily News* reports a particularly revolting case where a drunken Japanese soldier, unable to obtain women and drink he demanded, shot and killed three Chinese women over sixty and wounded several other harmless civilians. [Intercept and translation 2 January 1938.]

THE WORLD AT WAR 1939–45

War came to Europe, and then to the world, in September 1939. Two global conflicts were precipitated, first by the German invasion of Poland in September 1939, and secondly by the Japanese aerial attack on the American naval base at Pearl Harbor in December 1941. Within this frame there were at least five distinct regional wars, and within them numerous civil wars – in Yugoslavia, Italy, Greece and France. Even in the Low Countries and the Baltic states there were elements of an internal conflict.

War had become industrialised on a vast scale: the number of civilian dead and wounded hugely outweighed those among the uniformed military services. Empires were brought down – or at least given a firm push towards their demise. They included those of Britain, France, the Netherlands, Belgium and Portugal. A whole race, the Jews of Europe, was faced with extermination through the ruthless employment of industrial technologies used to mass-produce motor cars. And mainland hostilities in Asia were halted only by the dropping of nuclear weapons, as humankind discovered the ultimate method of encompassing its own annihilation.

Opening Salvos

In Britain it was as if the peace, fractious, poor and miserable as it had been for many, had been just a pause. The country, with its colonies, dependencies and dominions, was once again at war. The Second World War would be almost half as long again as the First. This time, too, civilians were in the front line, and their mood and sensibilities were of crucial importance.

One of the key sources for how the British people lived during this period and what they actually thought and felt, was the Mass Observation Project. It had been initiated at the end of 1936 by a turbulent amateur anthropologist, Tom Harrisson. During the abdication crisis of that year, in which Edward VIII gave up his throne for the love of Wallis Simpson, an American divorcee, the newspapers were constantly citing the opinions of the British public. Harrisson believed that neither the government nor the newspapers had any idea what the British people really thought, and thus the Mass Observation Project – a ramshackle and triumphantly unscientific affair – was born. Men and women throughout the land volunteered to record their thoughts and impressions, and by the time war broke out it had achieved a remarkably wide coverage of national life.

This is how J. R. Frier, a student aged nineteen; Muriel Green, an eighteen-year-old garage assistant, and Nella Last, a forty-nine-year-old housewife who joined the Women's Voluntary Service, received the news that the country was again at war.

Sunday, 3 September: About 9 a.m. it was announced that the prime minister would speak at 11.15 after the time limit for the German answer had elapsed. No one here had any doubt that it would be war. We all went on with household work till 11.15, and had our fears confirmed. The speech was accepted as the inevitable conclusion. But the air-raid warning which followed was totally unexpected. There were doubts as to whether it really was a warning. Mother was very flustered – several women in the neighbourhood fainted, I learned afterwards, and many ran into the road immediately. Some remarks – 'Don't go to the shelter till you hear the guns fire' – 'The balloons aren't even up yet' – 'The swine, he must have sent his planes over before the time limit was up.' When the All Clear sounded, there were more doubts as to whether it might not be another Take Cover signal. Within a minute everyone was at the gateways again; the women talking quickly to each other in nervous voices. More talk about Hitler and revolutions in Germany. 'Hitler's going to leave the Poles and start on us now' – 'Huh, if he can get here!' Discussion on whether warning was real or only a practice. Tempers were frayed, and irritated by petty things, such as an extra-loud note from the wireless. Much indignation when it was learned that warning had been given because of a single machine, afterwards recognised as friendly.

Most peculiar thing experienced today was desire for something to happen – to see aeroplanes coming over, and see defences in action. I don't really want to see bombs dropping and people killed, but somehow, as we are at war, I want it to buck up and start. At this rate, it will carry on for God knows how long.

Sunday, 3 September: Customer tells us of declaration of war. Feeling of hopelessness followed by annoyance at same. Think through friends who will eventually be called up. Decide to think of them as killed off and then it will not be such a blow if they are, and will be great joy if at the end they are not.

Spend the afternoon preparing for blackout. Stick brown paper over back door glass panel, etc. Bring out Public Information Leaflets and ARP [Air-Raid Precautions] book and read through the lot. Decide bathroom to be refuge room in air raid because it is downstairs and has only one small 18 square inch window, and has outside walls 18 inches thick. It already has most things in ARP book: washing things, disinfectant, bandages, etc. We take in a tin of Smiths potato crisps, three bottles of lemonade, several packets of chocolate from business stock, and some old magazines to read.

During the afternoon a friend from next village comes to see us. Says he has volunteered for the navy for the duration, as he is twenty-one and says he would far sooner drown than sit in a trench for days on end.

Sunday, 3 September: Bedtime. Well, we know the worst. Whether it was a kind of incredulous stubbornness or a faith in my old astrological friend who was right in the last crisis when he said, 'No war,' I never thought it would come. Looking back I think it was akin to a belief in a fairy's wand which was going to be waved.

I'm a self-reliant kind of person, but today I've longed for a close woman friend – for the first time in my life. When I heard Mr Chamberlain's voice, so slow and solemn, I seemed to see Southsea prom the July before the last crisis. The fleet came into Portsmouth from Weymouth and there were hundreds of extra ratings walking up and down. There was a sameness about them that was not due to their clothes alone, and it puzzled me, till I found out. It was the look on their faces – a slightly brooding, faraway look. They all had it – even the jolly-looking boys – and I felt I wanted to rush up and ask them what they could see that I could not. And now I know.

The wind got up and brought rain, but on the Walney shore men and boys worked filling sandbags. I could tell by the dazed look on many faces that I had not been alone in my belief that 'something' would turn up to prevent war. The boys brought a friend in and insisted on me joining in a game, but I could not keep it up. I've tried deep breathing, relaxing, knitting and more aspirins than I can remember, but all I can see are those boys with their look of 'beyond'.

My younger boy will go in just over a week. His friend who has no mother and is like another son will go soon – he is twenty-six. My elder boy is at Sunlight House in Manchester – a landmark. As a tax inspector he is at present in a 'reserved occupation' [i.e. not liable for conscription].

By May 1940 the German Wehrmacht had broken through in France. Neutral Netherlands had been invaded, and partly flooded. The Germans had pushed through the Ardennes to encircle the fortifications of the Maginot Line. Though the game seemed up, many brave French soldiers and airmen continued to fight. They included the literary air ace and pioneer of *long-distance airmail, **Antoine de Saint-Exupéry**, who was sent on a low-level reconnaissance flight to Arras, now surrounded by German tank parks, from which his chances of returning alive were two to one against.*

The adventure of war. Major Alias had thought it necessary to say to me one day, 'Take it easy, now!'

Take what easy, Major Alias? The fighters came down on you like lightning. Having spotted you from 1,500 feet above you, they take their time. They weave, they orient themselves, take careful aim. You know nothing of this. You are the mouse lying in the shadow of the bird of prey. The mouse fancies that it is alive. It goes on frisking in the wheat. But already it is the prisoner of the retina of the hawk, glued tighter to that retina than to any glue, for the hawk will never leave it now.

And thus you, continuing to pilot, to daydream, to scan the earth, have already been flung outside the dimension of time because of a tiny black dot on the retina of a man.

The nine planes of the German fighter group will drop like plummets in their own good time. They are in no hurry. At 550 miles an hour they will fire their prodigious harpoon that never misses its prey. A bombing squadron possesses enough fire power to offer a chance for defence; but a reconnaissance crew, alone in the wide sky, has no chance against the seventy-two machine-guns that first make themselves known to it by the luminous spray of their bullets. At the very instant when you first learn of its existence, the fighter, having spat forth its venom like a cobra, is already neutral and inaccessible, swaying to and fro overhead. Thus the cobra sways, sends forth its lightning, and resumes its rhythmical swaying.

Each machine-gun fires fourteen hundred bullets a minute. And when the fighter group has vanished, still nothing has changed. The faces themselves have not changed. They begin to change now that the sky is empty and peace has returned. The fighter has become a mere impartial onlooker when, from the severed carotid in the neck of the reconnaissance pilot, the first jets of blood spurt forth. When from the hood of the starboard engine the hesitant leak of the first tongue of flame rises out of the furnace fire. And the cobra has returned to its folds when the venom strikes the heart and the first muscle of the face twitches. The fighter group does not kill. It sows death. Death sprouts after it has passed.

Take what easy, Major Alias? When we flew over those fighters I had no decision to make. I might as well not have known they were there. If they had been overhead, I should never have known it.

Take what easy? The sky is empty.

*In Flanders, the French army began to crumble as it pulled back towards Dunkirk with the British. Among them was a staff officer, **Marc Bloch**. This great historian had served as an officer in the Great War and volunteered to serve again in 1939. He was evacuated from Dunkirk, but returned to France within weeks, taught history, organised resistance in eastern France, and was captured and executed by the Gestapo ten days after the Allied landings on D-Day in June 1944. In* Strange Defeat, *a harsh analysis of French military failure, he describes the moment that his section of the army collapsed.*

The army, as such, having ceased to exist, I had no staff duties to perform. But I still had a 'cure of souls'. True, I no longer commanded a fuel depot, nor yet a detachment of mobile tanks. But I had worked for too long with these fine fellows to feel that I was justified in concentrating attention on my own affairs until I had done something to assure their future which – in this instance – meant their embarkation. For no one was concerned to look further ahead than that. The one thought in everybody's mind was to get clear of this damned stretch of coast before the enemy should smash through our last defences; to escape captivity by the sole road open to us – the sea. A sort of escape-hysteria had got hold of this mob of men. They were to all intents and purposes unarmed, and, from where they stood, packed together on the beaches, they could watch the English ahead of them already putting out to sea. I spent most of 30 May in trying to get my men's names on to the official evacuation lists. I went first to Bray-les-Dunes, which was chock-a-block with a disorderly crowd of soldiers searching for their units, and with lorries. Any man who happened to come along turned himself into a driver, only, very often, to abandon his chance vehicle after a few hundred yards. Once more I appointed myself traffic-control officer, and tried, without much success, to get some kind of efficiency into the unfortunate military police who were clustered in ridiculous groups at every crossroads. A little later I might have been seen at the Perroquet café on the Belgian frontier, which, for a few hours, served as a temporary headquarters for the zone commander. From there I went to Malo-les-Bains, where I found most of the 'Q' branch personnel. I spent that night bivouacking on the dunes. Our period of rest was punctuated by German shells. Fortunately, the enemy gunners, nothing if not methodical, concentrated on a point just to the left of the Malo-Terminus Hotel. The first salvos claimed a number of victims. Thereafter the place was scrupulously avoided. If anyone had to pass near it, he did so at the run. Had the shooting been less accurate, what a scene of massacre there would have been in that sandy dormitory of ours among the sea grasses!

Early next day I was assured that my men would be got on board. How could I have known that a bomb would sink their ship? Still, most of them, though not all, alas, were fished out of the water. I was free at last to think about myself. Our former second-in-command, who was still in charge, showed no very great eagerness to get his subordinates away before he himself was safe. He did, however, give me permission to make what arrangements I could. The phrase sounded ominous. Did it mean that I was to pull a fast one on some other unfortunate? Luckily, early that afternoon, the commander of the Cavalry Corps was kind enough to furnish me and two of my friends with an official movement order. Nothing now remained but to find the ship to which we had been detailed.

As the result of a bungled message, the three of us were forced to go right through Dunkirk on two separate occasions, first from east to west, and then again in the reverse direction. I have a very vivid memory of the ruined town with its shells of buildings half-visible through drifting smoke, and its clutter, not of bodies but of human debris, in the streets. I can still hear the incredible din which, like the orchestral finale of an opera, provided an accompaniment to the last few minutes which we spent on the coast of Flanders – the crashing of bombs, the bursting of shells, the rat-tat-tat of machine-guns, the noise of anti-aircraft batteries, and, as a kind of figured bass, the persistent rattle of our own little naval pompom. But it is not the dangers and horrors of that day which have stuck most firmly in my memory. What comes back with especial clearness is our slow movement away from the jetty. A marvellous summer night shed its magic on the waters. The sky was pure gold, the sea a mirror, and the black, rank smoke, pouring from the burning refinery, made so lovely a pattern above the low shoreline that one was cheated into forgetting its tragic origin. Even the name painted on the stern of our vessel (*Royal Daffodil*) was like something out of an Indian fairy tale. All things, as we slipped away, seemed to be in a conspiracy to accentuate the overwhelming and purely selfish feelings of relief which filled my mind as I thought of the prisoner's fate which I had so narrowly escaped.

> *The story of the Dunkirk armada, the huge fleet of naval and civilian vessels that crossed the Channel to rescue the British Expeditionary Force and their allies from the French beaches, is one of defeat turned into victory. One of the smaller vessels to set out from the English south coast was the yacht* Sundowner, *owned and skippered by* **Commander C. H. Lightoller,** *RNR retired. He was the most senior officer to survive the* Titanic *disaster in 1912. On 1 June 1940 he approached the beaches.*

Half-way across we avoided a floating mine by a narrow margin, but having no firearms of any description – not even a tin hat – we had to leave its destruction to someone better equipped. A few minutes later we had our first introduction to enemy aircraft, three fighters flying high. Before they could be offensive, a British destroyer – *Worcester*, I think – overhauled us and drove them off. At 2.25 p.m. we sighted and closed the 25-foot motor cruiser *Westerly*; broken down and badly on fire. As the crew of two (plus three naval ratings she had picked up in Dunkirk) wished to abandon ship – and quickly – I went alongside and took them aboard, giving them the additional pleasure of again facing the hell they had only just left.

We made the fairway buoy to the Roads shortly after the sinking of a French transport with severe loss of life. Steaming slowly through the wreckage we entered the Roads. For some time now we had been subject to sporadic bombing and machine-gun fire, but as the *Sundowner* is exceptionally and extremely quick on the helm, by waiting till the last moment and putting the helm hard over – my son at the wheel – we easily avoided every attack, though sometimes near-lifted out of the water.

It had been my intention to go right on to the beaches, where my second son, Second Lieutenant R. T. Lightoller, had been evacuated some forty-eight hours previously; but those of the *Westerly* informed me that the troops were all away, so I headed up for Dunkirk piers. By now dive bombers seemed to be eternally dropping out of the cloud of enemy aircraft overhead. Within half a mile of the pierheads a two-funnelled grey-painted transport had overhauled and was just passing us to port when two salvos were dropped in quick succession right along her port side. For a few moments she was hidden in smoke and I certainly thought they had got her. Then she reappeared, still gaily heading for the piers and entered just ahead of us.

The difficulty of taking troops on board from the quay high above us was obvious, so I went alongside a destroyer (*Worcester* again, I think) where they were already embarking. I got hold of her captain and told him I could take about a hundred (though the most I had ever had on board was twenty-one). He, after consultation with the military CO, told me to carry on and get the troops aboard. I may say here that before leaving Cubitt's yacht basin, we had worked all night stripping her down of everything movable, masts included, that would tend to lighten her and make for more room.

My son, as previously arranged, was to pack the men in and use every available inch of space – which I'll say he carried out to some purpose. On deck I detailed a naval rating to tally the troops aboard. At fifty I called below, 'How are you getting on?' getting the cheery reply, 'Oh, plenty of room yet.' At seventy-five my son admitted they were getting pretty tight – all equipment and arms being left on deck.

I now started to pack them on deck, having passed word below for every man to lie down and keep down; the same applied on deck. By the time we had fifty on deck I could feel her getting distinctly tender, so took no more. Actually we had exactly a hundred and thirty on board, including three *Sundowners* and five *Westerlys*.

During the whole embarkation we had quite a lot of attention from enemy planes, but derived an amazing degree of comfort from the fact that the *Worcester*'s AA guns kept up an everlasting bark overhead.

Casting off and backing out we entered the Roads again; there it was continuous and unmitigated hell. The troops were just splendid and of their own initiative detailed look-outs ahead, astern and abeam for inquisitive planes, as my attention was pretty wholly occupied watching the steering and giving orders to Roger at the wheel. Any time an aircraft seemed inclined to try its hand on us, one of the look-outs would just call quietly, 'Look out for this bloke, skipper,' at the same time pointing. One bomber that had been particularly offensive, itself came under the notice of one of our fighters and suddenly plunged vertically into the sea just about 50 yards astern of us. It was the only time any man ever raised his voice above a conversational tone, but as that big black bomber hit the water they raised an echoing cheer.

My youngest son, Pilot Officer H. B. Lightoller (lost at the outbreak of war in the first raid on Wilhelmshaven), flew a Blenheim and had at different times given me a whole lot of useful information about attack, defence and evasive tactics (at which he was apparently particularly good) and I attribute in a great measure our success in getting across without a single casualty to his unwitting help.

On one occasion an enemy machine came up astern at about a hundred feet with the obvious intention of raking our decks. He was coming down in a gliding dive and I knew that he must elevate some 10 to 15 degrees before his guns would bear. Telling my son 'Stand by,' I waited till, as near as I could judge, he was just on the point of pulling up, and then 'Hard a-port.' (She turns 180 degrees in exactly her own length.) This threw his aim completely off. He banked and tried again. Then 'Hard a-starboard,' with the same result. After a third attempt he gave it up in disgust. Had I had a machine-gun of any sort, he was a sitter – in fact, there were at least three that I am confident we could have accounted for during the trip.

Not the least of our difficulties was contending with the wash of fast craft, such as destroyers and transports. In every instance I had to stop completely, take the way off the ship and head the heavy wash. The MC being where it was, to have taken one of these seas on either the quarter or beam would have at once put paid to our otherwise successful cruise. The effect of the consequent plunging on the troops below, in a stinking atmosphere with all ports and skylights closed, can well be imagined. They were literally packed like the proverbial sardines, even one in the bath and another on the WC, so that all the poor devils could do was sit and be sick. Added were the remnants of bully beef and biscuits. So that after discharging our cargo in Ramsgate at 10 p.m., there lay before the three of us a nice clearing-up job.

For many in the British army, denuded of heavy weapons and equipment in the hasty exit from France at Dunkirk, the routine of basic training took the form immortalised in **Henry Reed**'s *ironical poem 'Naming of Parts'.*

Today we have naming of parts. Yesterday,
We had daily cleaning. And tomorrow morning,
We shall have what to do after firing. But today,
Today we have naming of parts. Japonica
Glistens like coral in all of the neighbouring gardens,
    And today we have naming of parts.

This is the lower sling swivel. And this
Is the upper sling swivel, whose use you will see,
When you are given your slings. And this is the piling swivel,
Which in your case you have not got. The branches
Hold in the gardens their silent, eloquent gestures,
    Which in our case we have not got.

This is the safety catch, which is always released
With an easy flick of the thumb. And please do not let me
See anyone using his finger. You can do it quite easy
If you have any strength in your thumb. The blossoms
Are fragile and motionless, never letting anyone see
    Any of them using their finger.

And this you can see is the bolt. The purpose of this
Is to open the breech, as you see. We can slide it
Rapidly backwards and forwards: we call this
Easing the spring. And rapidly backwards and forwards
The early bees are assaulting and fumbling the flowers:
    They call it easing the Spring.

They call it easing the Spring: it is perfectly easy
If you have any strength in your thumb: like the bolt,
And the breech, and the cocking-piece, and the point of balance,
Which in our case we have not got; and the almond-blossom
Silent in all of the gardens and the bees going backwards and
    forwards,
    For today we have naming of parts.

The Battle of Britain and the Blitz

With the fall of France – the Germans entered Paris on 14 June 1940 – the battle of Britain could not be far away. In a speech to the House of Commons on 4 June, the prime minister Winston Churchill had declared: 'We shall defend our island, whatever the cost may be. We shall fight on the beaches, we shall fight on the landing-grounds, we shall fight in the fields and in the streets, we shall fight in the hills. We shall never surrender!' In the event, none of those battles ever took place: the battle of Britain took place in the air. No one can pinpoint the precise date on which it began, nor when it ended, for it had no official end, but by mid-July the RAF Fighter Command was fighting off the Luftwaffe as they attacked British convoys and bombed British ports, factories and airfields in preparation for an invasion. Who actually won in terms of blows inflicted is still disputed, but in this case, unusually, it was not a matter of who won, but who did not lose. For the Royal Air Force, which ensured that Britain would not be invaded, it was a defining moment.

__Geoffrey Wellum__ had joined the RAF from school the summer before. He flew a Spitfire from the beginning of the battle, sometime in midsummer, to its ragged end in the deep autumn. Finding his notebooks years later, he recorded the fear and excitement of one-to-one aerial combat.

No amount of training can prepare you for mortal combat. One has to realise before take-off that in order to have any chance of surviving and coming through you must remember a simple, straightforward golden rule: Never, but never fly straight and level for more than twenty seconds. If you do, you'll die ...

Off to port a squadron of Hurricanes is climbing all it knows in the same general direction as ourselves. As we gain height we draw slowly ahead of them. There is another gaggle of aircraft further off over the Thames estuary and coming in from the north. They also look like Hurricanes but I report them to Brian nevertheless.

Looks like the big build-up for a real party and a half. Our side seems to be throwing everything in and so, presumably, must the Germans be. This action is going to be a big one, no doubt about it. The controller reports another large formation of Huns building up over Gris Nez and starting to come across but he doesn't go into how many. Perhaps he thinks we've enough on our plate as it is. Where do all these bloody Germans come from? There seems to be no end to them.

'Gannic, this is Sapper. You are getting close now. Should soon see them slightly off to your starboard.'

'Yes, I can see them, Sapper. OK, Gannic. Tally-ho! Many bandits ahead level. Watch out for snappers and don't all rush at once. There's plenty for everybody.'

A great mass of German aeroplanes. Little chatter on the R/T. It's quite obvious what's required. For what we are about to receive.

Within seconds we are in among them, split up and each man for himself and fighting his own private battle. Things moving terribly quickly. There seem to be literally hundreds of aeroplanes with everybody shooting at everybody else. If we can split the Hun formations, well, at least that will be something.

For some odd reason I am taken by surprise at the sheer size of this battle in this truly tremendous arena. Wherever I look the sky is full of a mix of aircraft and the ferocity of our attack is almost frightening.

The bombers, Heinkels mainly in this batch, are in rigid formation and a milling mass of small gnat-like fighters battle it out around them. I try to latch on to a vic* of three Heinkels slightly on their own. They are away from their main formation but, before I can get near enough, a pair of 109s come in at me from the port beam. I see them in good time, turn into them and pass underneath. They go by overhead, pretty close, and as I look up at them I can see oil streaks on the bellies of their fuselages. They have yellow noses.

---

*A V-shaped formation of three or more aircraft; the word derives from an early phonetic alphabet.

Another 109. Bastard. I reverse the turn and try to get on to him but he is going too fast and I miss out. Some tracer goes over the top of my hood, not all that close but I have to break. I don't even see who took a pot at me. I must be difficult to hit as I throw the Spit about, never still for a second. What on earth is going on? There is great confusion and I am in the middle of an almighty bloody mix up and I haven't even fired my guns yet. Obviously I came bounding into the middle of this lot without bothering to think exactly where on earth I was going or who I was going to have a shot at. A bit immature that; not very bright at all.

But half a moment. There's a thing, all is not lost, a couple of Junkers 88s flying very tight together about half a mile distant and a fraction below. I've got my eye on you, you buggers. Just you hold on a bit mateys and I'll have your guts for garters. Even as I watch they drop their bombs and start a slow turn away ...

Throttle open, dive under the fighters, a quick burst and away. Come on then, let's get it over with. Ease the stick forward, feed on more power and down we go. A quick look around. Clear behind, but there is so much going on who can tell?

OK, now watch the target. Speed building up too quickly. Ease the throttle back slightly. The 109s still haven't seen me. I begin to swallow hard and my left knee begins to tremble for some bloody stupid reason. I'm getting excited again, although tensed up. Wish I was the cold calculating type with steely blue eyes.

There's no time to consider anything but those 88s. Astern of the bombers. They come towards me at an astonishing speed; too fast. Shit! Sight on. Oh, damn, I'm still miles too fast. Bloody hell! Overtaking like a rocket, open fire. The guns going, trembling Spitfire, smell of compressed air or cordite or something. Hold it a fraction longer; hits on the left-hand one, lots of them. Christ, Geoff, you're going to ram him. Stick forward, a thump. Either you've hit him or it's slipstream. Hope it's slipstream. Blimey, we're going vertically towards the ground. This is rather off-putting, but I think it's all right. You didn't hit him; you broke away a bit late and hit the slipstream. Strewth, that all happened quickly; bloody close as well.

Pull up and start to climb for another go. The sky is still full of aeroplanes. This is one hell of a battle, everybody mixing it. Each man for himself. I find myself just a little off to one side as I clamber for height and I have an uninterrupted view. It is magnificent and yet appalling. No fewer than six parachutes float lazily towards the ground. Friend or foe it doesn't matter, at least they're out of it.

'Never in the field of human conflict', said Churchill famously, 'was so much owed by so many to so few.' The most famous literary member of the 'few' who fought the battle of Britain was **Richard Hillary**. *An Oxford man, something of a dandy, and by his own definition 'one of the last of the long-haired boys', he was badly burned in the battle and lucky to survive. He recalls the day he met his nemesis over the Channel.*

At about 12,000 feet we came up through the clouds: I looked down and saw them spread out below me like layers of whipped cream. The sun was brilliant and made it difficult to see even the next plane when turning. I was peering anxiously ahead, for the controller had given us warning of at least fifty enemy fighters approaching very high. When we did first sight them, nobody shouted, as I think we all saw them at the same moment. They must have been 500 to 1,000 feet above us and coming straight on like a swarm of locusts. I remember cursing and going automatically into line astern: the next moment we were in among them and it was each man for himself. As soon as they saw us they spread out and dived, and the next ten minutes was a blur of twisting machines and tracer bullets. One Messerschmitt went down in a sheet of flame on my right, and a Spitfire hurtled past in a half-roll; I was weaving and turning in a desperate attempt to gain height, with the machine practically hanging on the airscrew. Then, just below me and to my left, I saw what I had been praying for – a Messerschmitt climbing and away from the sun. I closed in to 200 yards and from slightly to one side gave him a two-second burst; fabric ripped off the wing and black smoke poured from the engine, but he did not go down. Like a fool, I did not break away, but put in another three-second burst. Red flames shot upwards and he spiralled out of sight. At that moment I felt a terrific explosion which knocked the control stick from my hand, and the whole machine quivered like a stricken animal. In a second, the cockpit was a mass of flames: instinctively, I reached up to open the hood. It would not move. I tore off my straps and managed to force it back; but this took time, and when I dropped back into the seat and reached for the stick in an effort to turn the plane on its back, the heat was so intense that I could feel myself going. I remember a second of sharp agony, remember thinking 'So this is it!' and putting both hands to my eyes. Then I passed out.

When I regained consciousness I was free of the machine and falling rapidly. I pulled the rip-cord of my parachute and checked my descent with a jerk. Looking down, I saw that my left trouser leg was burnt off, that I was going to fall into the sea and that the English coast was deplorably far away. About 20 feet above the water, I attempted to undo my parachute, failed, and flopped into the sea with it billowing round me. I was told later that the machine went into a spin at about 25,000 feet and that at 10,000 feet I fell out – unconscious. This may well have been so, for I discovered later a large cut on the top of my head, presumably collected while bumping round inside.

The water was not unwarm and I was pleasantly surprised to find that my life-jacket kept me afloat. I looked at my watch: it was not there. Then, for the first time, I noticed how burnt my hands were: down to the wrist, the skin was dead white and hung in shreds: I felt faintly sick from the smell of burnt flesh. By closing one eye I could see my lips, jutting out like motor tyres. The side of my parachute harness was cutting into me particularly painfully, so that I guessed my right hip was burnt. I made a further attempt to undo the harness, but owing to the pain of my hands, soon desisted. Instead, I lay back and reviewed my position: I was a long way from land; my hands were burnt, and so, judging from the pain of the sun, was my face; it was unlikely that anyone on shore had seen me come down and even more unlikely that a ship would come by; I could float for possibly four hours in my Mae West. I began to feel that I had perhaps been premature in considering myself lucky to have escaped from the machine. After about half an hour my teeth started chattering, and to quiet them I kept up a regular tuneless chant, varying it from time to time with calls for help. There can be few more futile pastimes than yelling for help alone in the North Sea, with a solitary seagull for company, yet it gave me a certain melancholy satisfaction ...

It was to the Margate lifeboat that I owed my rescue. Watchers on the coast had seen me come down, and for three hours they had been searching for me. Owing to wrong directions, they were just giving up and turning back for land when ironically enough one of them saw my parachute. They were then 15 miles east of Margate.

While in the water I had been numb and had felt very little pain. Now that I began to thaw out, the agony was such that I could have cried out. The good fellows made me as comfortable as possible, put up some sort of awning to keep the sun from my face, and phoned through for a doctor. It seemed to me to take an eternity to reach shore. I was put into an ambulance and driven rapidly to hospital. Through all this I was quite conscious, though unable to see. At the hospital they cut off my uniform, I gave the requisite information to a nurse about my next of kin, and then, to my infinite relief, felt a hypodermic syringe pushed into my arm.

Hillary became one of the 'guinea pigs' – a group of badly burned patients whose faces were rebuilt by the plastic surgeon Archibald McIndoe. As soon as he had recovered sufficiently to use his hands, he returned to operational flying and was killed in a night raid on 7 January 1943. His book, The Last Enemy, *is one of the great classics of the war.*

*In the autumn of 1940 the Luftwaffe switched to heavy bombing raids, mostly at night. It marked the beginning of the Blitz on London and other major cities. This is **Frank Edwards**'s account of a raid that took place on 25 September, as recorded for Mass Observation.*

What a night, what a life! At 8.10 the sirens sounded heralding the nightly blitz. Guns started banging away and we went down our cellar. After about half an hour a bomb dropped uncomfortably close and the whole house seemed to shake. Fifteen minutes later there was the most terrific explosion I have yet heard, and the whole house felt as though it lifted right up. Dust blew all over the place and a little later we could smell burning. We went upstairs and had a careful look round everywhere in case there might be any incendiaries but such was not the case. However, we found that the blast had blown several panes of glass out of the front of the house and one or two out of the back.

AA guns were banging away, one moment sounding as though they were outside the front door, and a few seconds later a bit further away. Then very close again, and so on. And so it went on all through the night until six o'clock this morning when the sirens sounded the welcome All Clear.

Thursday, 26 September: At six o'clock this morning it was sufficiently light to see that most of the other houses in our end of the road had also lost their windows, but the houses on the opposite side were OK. It later transpired that these houses had lost their back windows whilst we had lost the front ones.

We had to walk down the road, but despite the terrific explosion we could not see any property missing, but we knew something must have gone not far away. When I set off, two hours later, to catch the bus for the office, I turned into the main road which runs at the end of our road, and what a sight met my eyes. Most of the houses had lost all the glass out of their windows and all the shops were in a like condition. Piles of glass lay in the front gardens of the houses, but in the case of the shops, mostly it had been swept into piles in the gutter by the ARP services.

Outside a confectioner and tobacconist's lock-up shop on the pavement were showcards, boxes of cigarettes, packets of sweets, packets of chocolate etc. Next to that everything from a chemist's window had been blown out, including the shelves. An off-licence was in a similar state, and so on. The district looked properly devastated. Little groups of people stood about talking of the damage etc.

When I returned home in the evening this looked like a town of wooden windows and doors although wood wasn't the only material used for repairs, for from what I could see of it every possible substance available had been pressed into service. This damage had all been caused by the blast from a landmine which had been dropped on houses in a road a good half-mile from this house, and it was around there that much structural damage was caused.

Right at the beginning of the war, the British Special Intelligence Service, the SIS, was evacuated from London to Bletchley Park. Among its number was **Fred Winterbotham**, *who had served as a fighter pilot in the First World War and been taken prisoner. He took charge of the secure distribution of signals intelligence that later became known as Ultra, and once the boffins of Bletchley had actually obtained one of Hitler's latest Enigma machines they had at least a chance of cracking the code. Fred Winterbotham describes how the miracle happened.*

It was, I think, generally accepted that of our own backroom boys 'Dilly' Knox was the mastermind behind the Enigma affair. He was quite young, tall, with a rather gangling figure, unruly black hair, his eyes, behind glasses, some miles away in thought. Like Mitchell, the designer of the Spitfire fighter aeroplane which tipped the scales in our favour during the battle of Britain, who worked himself to his death at the moment of his triumph, Knox too, knowing he was a sick man, pushed himself to the utmost to overcome the problems of Enigma variations (introduced by the Germans to further complicate their ciphers between 1940 and 1942). He, too, died with his job completed. J. H. Tiltman, another brilliant brain, had been borrowed from the army. He was tall and dark with a short, clipped, military moustache, and his regimental tartan trousers eventually gave way to green corduroy slacks which were thought slightly way-out in 1939. Oliver Strachey was an individualist, tall though a little stooped, with greying hair, broad forehead; his eyes, behind his glasses, always had a smile in them, as if he found life intensely amusing, except when our billeter used to stand at the foot of the stairs on Saturday mornings collecting our cheques. Oliver was also extremely musical. I believe he played several instruments, but he most enjoyed playing duets with Benjamin Britten on the grand piano in his rather untidy London flat. Then there was 'Josh' Cooper whom I saw fairly often, as he was primarily concerned with Air Force matters. He was another brilliant mathematician. Still in his thirties, he had to use powerful glasses which often seemed to get in the way of his straight black hair. Dick Pritchard, young, tall, clean-shaven, rather round of face, with a quiet voice, could talk on any subject with witty penetration. He, too, was deeply musical. It struck me at the time how often the art of undoing other people's ciphers was closely allied to a brain which could excel in both mathematics and music. It was rather frightening playing one's evening bridge with these men. It all came easily to them and the conversation was ever interesting. I could well have spent longer in our country retreat than I did, but it soon became apparent that the phoney war would last over the winter of 1939–40, so I took my small staff back to London in order to be near the Air Ministry. I missed the professorial atmosphere of Bletchley.

It is no longer a secret that the backroom boys of Bletchley used the new science of electronics to help them solve the puzzle of Enigma. I am not of the computer age nor do I attempt to understand them, but early in 1940 I was ushered with great solemnity to the shrine where stood a bronze-coloured column surmounted by a larger circular bronze-coloured face, like some eastern goddess who was destined to become the oracle of Bletchley, at least when she felt like it. She was an awesome piece of magic. We were, of course, all wondering whether the great experiment could really become operational, and if so, would it be in time for the hot war which we now felt was bound to break out in the spring? Hitler had given us six months' respite. Each day had, I think, been used to the full by every branch of the nation's defences. We all knew it was too little, too late, but at least in this one vital concept the possibilities were prodigiously exciting, for we had in our hands the very enciphering machine the Germans would be using in their wartime communications.

It must have been about the end of February 1940 that the Luftwaffe, the German Air Force, had evidently received enough Enigma machines to train their operators sufficiently well for them to start putting some practice messages on the air. The signals were quite short but must have contained the ingredients the bronze goddess had been waiting for. Menzies had given instructions that any successful results were to be sent immediately to him, and it was just as the bitter cold days of that frozen winter were giving way to the first days of April sunshine that the oracle of Bletchley spoke and Menzies handed me four little slips of paper, each with a short Luftwaffe message dealing with personnel postings to units. From the intelligence point of view they were of little value, except as a small bit of administrative inventory, but to the backroom boys at Bletchley Park and to Menzies, and indeed to me, they were like the magic in the pot of gold at the end of the rainbow.

The miracle had arrived.

*For **Theodora Fitzgibbon** the Blitz proved an educational experience in all the schools of life. She had been living in Paris before the war, mixing with the likes of Picasso and Cocteau, and escaped by bicycle as the Nazis invaded France. In Blitz-charred London she moved in bohemian circles and in her eloquent memoir,* With Love, *recalls the first big firebombing of the City towards the end of 1940.*

It was towards the end of this same Christmas week that the great fire and bombing raid on the City of London took place, when the Guildhall, eight beautiful Wren churches, Guy's Hospital and hundreds of office buildings were hit, but as it was on Sunday, the latter were mercifully empty. Fire watchers saw twenty-eight incendiary bombs fall on the roof of St Paul's Cathedral, and bounce off the dome. One was blazing, and miraculously fell outwards, where it was extinguished. Indeed, amidst the wall of flame and smoke the only clear sky was around the cathedral. Londoners with a new-found love of their city watched its survival from rooftops both near and far away. With tears running down their cheeks, they said in one voice:

'The old church stood it ...'

A few days later a landmine was dropped on Old Church Street in Chelsea.

We soon left, and went towards the remains of Chelsea Old Church to see if we could help. The nurses' home of the Cheyne Hospital for Children had the top floor blown off: a neat nurse's bedroom, the ceiling light still shining, looked like a stage set. A warden perilously climbed up the bombed staircase and switched it off, although there was a flaming gas main burning around the corner which floodlit the entire area. The church was nothing but an immense heap of timber and stone, flames licking through it; a large vaulted tomb with a stone urn on top rose up undamaged in the front. The New Café Lombard and all the large and small houses at that end of Old Church Street had been flung together into a giant mountain of shale-like destruction, all lit by the fires and the gas main. Under that fantastic mountain were people, some still alive. Heavy stones were flung aside like pebbles: the local grocer of the street, Mr Cremonesi, put his hand down through a space and felt warm flesh. A naked unhurt woman was pulled up. An old lady appeared, staggering, from the far side of the mountain, having been flung at least 30 yards and then covered with glass, wood and bricks, from which she had extricated herself. She seemed unhurt. A curious rattling sound like a time bomb made us cautious: a battered tin was moving on a piece of stick. Below, the young woman had forced it through the bricks to attract attention. She was rescued by a war reserve policeman. A sixteen-year-old girl, pinned, only her head showing, talked to a rescue worker: she was freed, but died several hours later.

Young and old brought buckets of water to supply stirrup pumps to douse the fires. The dust was like a great fog. Charred papers and smouldering wood choked the helpers. Still the raid continued with whining bombs, cracking, thudding guns, droning aeroplanes, both German and our own night fighters. Huge chandeliers of flares hanging in the sky like Roman candles illuminated the bombers' targets. Our hands were cut and bleeding, and when I saw the blood on Peter's hands I felt suddenly sick and faint. He led me down to the Embankment. Although the day had been warm, a breeze came off the river and it was chill. He held me close to warm me. Several wardens, police and onlookers were there talking. Two landmines had been parachuted down on the church, which was why the usual whining sound was absent. All the fire-watchers at my post had been killed except Arthur Mallett who had previously been chased by the dustbin lid. One of the mines had landed beside him and the other fire-watchers.

'For Christ's sake, run!' he had cried.

He had run so fast he couldn't stop in time to turn the corner into Old Church Street with the others.

'Bugger this, right ho, I'll carry straight on,' he had said to himself. He'd crouched behind a small iron post, seconds before the second mine landed, which also detonated the first one.

'Blimey,' he said laconically, 'that lot's gone.' All he had lost was the trouser on his right leg. Now he wanted a cup of tea, and to find his sister, so over the mountain he went, and met her half-way in that pitiful no man's land.

The Thames was at low tide, factories in flames opposite, as we smoked our cigarettes leaning over the wall near the steps leading down to the river. Bombs were dropping all round, but we were too exhausted to bother.

The Battlefield Extends

Throughout the early months of 1941 the progress of the war in the Mediterranean was one of steady advance by the Axis armies through the Balkans and Greece, and tactical withdrawal and defeat for the Allies.

On the other side of the world, on 7 December that year, the Japanese bombed Pearl Harbor in Hawaii, thus bringing the United States fully into the war. The aim of the Japanese – to extend their power in the Pacific by crippling the US fleet and taking advantage of the already weakened colonial powers – backfired. America brought all its industrial muscle to bear on churning out ships, aircraft and armaments, and Japan achieved for the Allies what Winston Churchill had failed to achieve – the full-blooded backing of arguably the most powerful nation in the world. The price was high: the Americans lost 19 ships, 149 planes, 1,178 wounded and 2,403 dead.

*   ***Senator Daniel K. Inouye*** *was a high-school student when Pearl Harbor was attacked. This is his account of it.*

The family was up by 6.30 that morning, as we usually were on Sunday, to dress and have a leisurely breakfast before setting out for nine o'clock services at church. Of course anyone who has some memory of that shattering day can tell you precisely what he was doing at the moment when he suddenly realised that an era was ending, that the long and comfortable days of peace were gone, and that America and all her people had been abruptly confronted with their most deadly challenge since the founding of the Republic.

As soon as I finished brushing my teeth and pulled on my trousers, I automatically clicked on the little radio that stood on the shelf above my bed. I remember that I was buttoning my shirt and looking out the window – it would be a magnificent day; already the sun had burned off the morning haze and glowed bright in a blue sky – when the hum of the warming set gave way to a frenzied voice. 'This is no test,' the voice cried out. 'Pearl Harbor is being bombed by the Japanese! I repeat: this is not a test or a manoeuvre! Japanese war planes are attacking Oahu!'

'Papa!' I called, then froze into immobility, my fingers clutching that button. I could feel blood hammering against my temple, and behind it the unspoken protest, like a prayer – It's not true! It is a test, or a mistake! It can't be true! – but somewhere in the core of my being I knew that all my world was crumbling as I stood motionless in that little bedroom and listened to the disembodied voice of doom.

Now my father was standing in the doorway listening, caught by that special horror instantly sensed by Americans of Japanese descent as the nightmare began to unfold. There was a kind of agony on his face, and my brothers and sister, who had pushed up behind him, stopped where they were and watched him as the announcer shouted on:

'... not a test. This is the real thing! Pearl Harbor has been hit and now we have a report that Hickam Field and Schofield Barracks have been bombed, too. We can see the Japanese planes ...'

'Come outside!' my father said to me, and I plunged through the door after him. As my brothers John and Bob started out, too, he turned and told them: 'Stay with your mother!'

We stood in the warm sunshine on the south side of the house and stared out towards Pearl Harbor. Black puffs of anti-aircraft smoke littered the pale sky, trailing away in a soft breeze, and we knew beyond any wild hope that this was no test, for practice rounds of anti-aircraft, which we had seen a hundred times, were fleecy white. And now the dirty grey smoke of a great fire billowed up over Pearl and obscured the mountains and the horizon, and if we listened attentively we could hear the soft crrrump of the bombs amid the hysterical chatter of the ack-ack.

And then we saw the planes. They came zooming up out of that sea of grey smoke, flying north towards where we stood and climbing into the bluest part of the sky, and they came in twos and threes, in neat formations, and if it hadn't been for that red ball on their wings, the rising sun of the Japanese empire, you could easily believe that they were Americans, flying over in precise military salute ...

It was past 8.30 – the war was little more than half an hour old – when I reported in at the aid station, two classrooms in the Lunalilo Elementary School. I had gained the first six years of my education in this building and before the day was out it would be half-destroyed by our own anti-aircraft shells which had failed to explode in the air. Even now confusion was in command, shouting people pushing by each other as they rushed for litters and medical supplies.

Somewhere a radio voice droned on, now and then peaking with shrill excitement, and it was in one such outburst that I learned how the *Arizona* had exploded in the harbour. Many other vessels were severely hit.

And then, at 9 a.m., the Japanese came back. The second wave of bombers swooped around from the west and the anti-aircraft guns began thundering again. Mostly the planes hammered at military installations – Pearl, Hickam, Wheeler Field – and it was our own ack-ack that did the deadly damage in the civilian sectors. Shells, apparently fired without timed fuses, and finding no target in the sky, exploded on impact with the ground. Many came crashing into a three-by-five-block area of crowded McCully, the first only moments after the Japanese planes reappeared. It hit just three blocks from the aid station and the explosion rattled the windows. I grabbed a litter and rounded up a couple of fellows I knew.

'Where're we going?' one yelled at me.

'Where the trouble is! Follow me!'

In a small house on the corner of Hauoli and Algaroba Streets we found our first casualties. The shell had sliced through the house. It had blown the front out and the tokens of a lifetime – dishes, clothing, a child's bed – were strewn pathetically into the street.

I was propelled by sheerest instinct. Some small corner of my mind worried about how I'd react to what lay in that carnage – there would be no textbook cuts and bruises, and the blood would be real blood – and then I plunged in, stumbling over the debris, kicking up clouds of dust and calling, frantically calling, to anyone who might be alive in there. There was no answer. The survivors had already fled and the one who remained would never speak again. I found her half-buried in the rubble, one of

America's first civilian dead of the Second World War. One woman, all but decapitated by a piece of shrapnel, died within moments. Another, who had fallen dead at the congested corner of King and McCully, still clutched the stumps where her legs had been. And all at once it was as though I had stepped out of my skin; I moved like an automaton, hardly conscious of what I was doing and totally oblivious of myself. I felt nothing. I did what I had been taught to do and it was only later, when those first awful hours had become part of our history, that I sickened and shuddered as the ghastly images of war flashed again and again in my mind's eye, as they do to this day.

By 1942, the focus of the fighting had shifted to the Western Desert of Egypt and Libya. In May, the German Afrika Korps, under Field Marshal Erwin Rommel, began an offensive aimed at pushing the British forces into Egypt, and by 21 June he had seized Tobruk and taken some thirty-five thousand British prisoners of war. In July the British 8th Army checked Rommel's advance in the first battle of El Alamein. This duel in the desert was, because of the emptiness of the terrain and the lack of civilians – not unlike a battle at sea, and in **Keith Douglas**, *the British had a remarkable chronicler. Douglas, an accomplished poet and artist, fought at El Alamein as a tank commander and wrote his remarkable account,* Alamein to Zem-Zem, *almost immediately afterwards. He was killed in Normandy, three days after the D-Day landings.*

Here he describes the opening phases of the El Alamein campaign, Churchill's 'end of the beginning' for the Allies.

'There they are!' cried the infantryman suddenly. A few yards from the left of the tank, two German soldiers were climbing out of a pit, grinning sheepishly as though they had been caught out in a game of hide-and-seek. In their pit lay a Spandau machine-gun with its perforated jacket. So much, I thought with relief, for the machine-gun nest. But men now arose all round us. We were in a maze of pits. Evan flung down the Besa machine-gun, cried impatiently, 'Lend us your revolver, sir,' and snatching it from my hand, dismounted. He rushed up and down calling 'Out of it, come on out of it, you bastards,' etc. The infantry officer and I joined in this chorus, and rushed from trench to trench; I picked up a rifle from one of the trenches and aimed it threateningly, although I soon discovered that the safety catch was stuck and it would not fire. The figures of soldiers continued to arise from the earth as though dragons' teeth had been sown there. I tried to get the prisoners into a body by gesticulating with my useless rifle. To hurry a man up, I pointed a rifle at him, but he cowered to the ground, like a puppy being scolded, evidently thinking I was going to shoot him on the spot. I felt very embarrassed, and lowered the rifle: he shot away after his comrades as though at the start of a race. I began to shout: 'Raus, raus, raus,' with great enthusiasm at the occupants of some trenches further back, who were craning their necks at us in an undecided way. Evan unluckily discouraged them by blazing off at them with a Spandau which he had picked up, and some high explosive began to land near the tank, which was following us about like a tame animal. Evan now found a man shamming dead in the bottom of a pit and was firing at his heels with my revolver, swearing and cursing at him. Another German lay on the ground on his back, occasionally lifting his head and body off the ground as far as the waist, with his arms stretched stiffly above his head and his face expressive of strenuous effort, like a man in a gymnasium. His companions gesticulated towards him and pointed at their heads, so that I thought he had been shot in the head. But when I looked more closely, I could see no wound, and he told me he was ill. Two of them assisted him away.

From the weapon pits, which were crawling with flies, we loaded the back of the tank with Spandaus, rifles, Luger pistols, Dienstgläser, the lightweight German binoculars, British tinned rations and the flat round German tins of chocolate.

As the main body of the prisoners was marched away under an infantry guard, the high explosive began to land closer to us. I did not feel inclined to attack the further position single-handed, so I moved the tank back and tacked it on to the column of prisoners. The mortar stopped firing at us, and some of the infantry climbed on to the tank to ride back. I reported over the air that we had taken some prisoners.

'Nuts five, how many prisoners?' asked what I presumed to be Andrew's voice. 'Nuts five wait. Off.' I said, counting, 'Nuts five about figures four zero. Over.' 'Bloody good. Most excellent.' Apparently it was the colonel talking. 'Now I want you to send these chaps back to our Niner' – he meant the brigadier – 'so that you'll get the credit for this.' This was unfortunately more than my conscience would stand. I felt that all the work had been done by Evan and the infantry officer, and said so. This was a bad thing to say to Piccadilly Jim, because it showed him that I did not agree with him about snatching little gobbets of glory for the regiment whenever possible. The infantry were in another brigade, as Piccadilly Jim knew. Evan said: 'You were a bloody fool to say that, sir. You've as good as thrown away an MC.' I said shortly that if I had, it was an undeserved one.

The reaction on me of all this was an overpowering feeling of insignificance. I went over to the infantry officers who were searching the prisoners and said: 'You did most of the dirty work, so you'd better take them back to your brigade.' The one who had ridden on my tank replied: 'Yes, we had orders to,' in such a supercilious way that I almost decided to insist on my right to escort them after all. The man with a bad head was lying groaning on the ground. He clutched his head and waved it from side to side. I think perhaps he had ostitis: the pain made him roll about and kick his legs like a baby.

The turret, after the removal of the Besa, and our leaping in and out of it, was in utter confusion. During our struggles with the machine-gun the bottom of an ammunition box had dropped out, and the belt of it was coiled everywhere. The empty belt fired from the biscuit box mounting had fallen in whorls on top of this. The microphones, spare headphones, gunner's headphones and all their respective flexes were inextricably entwined among the belts. Empty cartridge and shell cases littered the floor. On the surface of this morass of metal reposed the Besa itself, and an inverted tin of Kraft cheese, which had melted in the sunlight. I rescued a microphone and a pair of headphones, and got permission to retire and reorganise. On my way back I was to call at the colonel's tank. This I duly did, but my ears were singing so loudly that I could scarcely hear his kind words. As soon as the tank moved away from the prisoners, we were again fired on by a mortar, which followed us as we moved back, dropping shells consistently a few yards behind us. We brewed up in dead ground to the enemy behind a ridge; the mortar continued to search this ground with fire, but never got nearer than 30 yards, and that only with one shot.

The War in Italy

During 1943 the war shifted slowly to the northern shores of the Mediterranean. On 17 August, Sicily was taken after hard fighting by the British and the Americans: the old Mafia chieftains were restored to their fiefdoms and ninety thousand Italian troops were allowed to escape across the Straits of Messina. By this time the king of Italy, Victor Emmanuel III, had forced the resignation of Mussolini, who was promptly arrested. The new prime minister, Marshal Badoglio, just as promptly sent representatives to agree an armistice with Allied representatives in Lisbon. Negotiations were kept secret for as long as possible, but as soon as Italy's surrender was announced, German troops already in the country became an army of occupation, while Badoglio's government looked to the Allies to protect Italy from the Germans.

The Allied landings on the Italian mainland in Calabria and at Salerno took place in September, Naples fell in October and Rome the following June, but every Allied offensive was hard won, and the Italians themselves became embroiled in an increasingly vindictive civil war. Two great classics of western literature, If This is a Man *by Primo Levi and* Catch 22 *by Joseph Heller, were both born of the Italian campaign, and they are matched by a torrent of reportage and memoirs of high quality. One of the most recent is* **Professor Michael Howard**'s *description of his blooding as platoon commander in the Coldstream Guards.*

We spent that night and the following day in the southern suburbs of Salerno. I slept in a barn, the first time I had a roof over my head since leaving England – and the following night we passed through the dead streets of the city to take up positions in steep vineyards immediately to the north. We relieved 46th Division, which was side-slipping leftwards on to the Sorrento peninsula. They had obviously had a very bad time. The unit we relieved was nervous and insubordinate, and the young platoon commander only maintained control with difficulty. 'If you don't do what you are told I'll shoot you!' he hissed in exasperation – and sounded as if he meant it. Next morning we saw why they were so unhappy. We were out of sight of the enemy, but not out of range of their mortars. Their bombs came crashing down with a frequency that made it unwise to stir for long from the very inadequate slit-trenches scraped out on the terraced hillside. Not for the last time I wondered whether we ourselves used our mortars with the skill displayed by the Germans. Our companies further up the hill were even more exposed and suffered heavy losses. There was a grim contrast between the danger of our situation and the spectacular beauty of the bay of Salerno spread out below us: the deep, deep blue sea and clear blue sky framed by vines laden with bunches of grapes, like a third-rate stage set.

That night I was again sent out on a reconnaissance patrol, and again performed indifferently. I quickly became aware of how poorly I had been trained to move quietly at night. The two enormous guardsmen I took with me had not been trained at all. We blundered around the steep mountain paths in bright moonlight, alarmingly conspicuous on the paths and horribly noisy off them. Eventually we approached a farm where dogs began to bark and nervous German sentries opened up with machine-gun fire. Although we were still far short of our objective, I saw no way of reaching it and every prospect of getting horribly lost in the attempt, and so turned back with such information as we had. Next morning I reported it to the suave, desert-booted, silk-scarved brigade intelligence officer – a Balliol man, as it turned out – who kindly said that I had told him exactly what he needed to know and gave me breakfast in the battle-scarred but still comfortable villa which brigade HQ occupied at the foot of the hill. Then I returned up the mountain path to learn from Alan what was expected from us next.

It seemed quite a lot. That night 46th Division would attack on our left to open a way across the Sorrento peninsula towards Naples. We would support them with an attack to pin the Germans down on our front. Since this was a feint, only one company would be deployed – ours – but with heavy artillery support. Our objective was a small hill – the 'Pimple' – beyond the large hospital that dominated the town. Securing it would straighten our own lines and give us a view over the valley below. Little opposition, said Alan in an alarmingly deadpan voice, was to be expected.

This all sounded simple enough, though I would be lying if I pretended that I looked forward to it with anything except rather sick apprehension. In practice the whole affair proved so wonderfully illustrative of Clausewitz's 'friction of war' that it is worth describing in some detail.

First we had to find our way to the starting-point, which meant leaving our scattered slit-trenches after dark, still under spasmodic mortar-fire, shaking out into single file, and moving in the correct order over steep mountain paths to line up along the perimeter wall of the hospital. That took far longer than expected. The files lost one another, the platoons somehow got into the wrong order. We eventually arrived at the start-line long after H-hour, almost too late to catch up with the artillery barrage. Two out of my three sections had disappeared altogether, and turned up only as the attack began. From the dark hill facing us, streams of tracer bullets were already zipping over the low wall behind which we eventually formed up. Once again I had an absurd sense of *déjà vu*. This was just another B movie, and I was playing the David Niven role as the gallant platoon commander. All right, I thought, if I was cast as David Niven I had better behave like David Niven; so I hissed 'Right – over with me!'

Everything thereafter became so confused that it is hard to make any coherent narrative out of it. We stumbled down the slope, dodging under the fixed lines of enemy fire, and began to climb the opposite hill. The first obstacle was a terrace-wall about 6 feet high, up which the faithful Johanson pushed me. There were flashes and ear-splitting detonations as the Germans lobbed down grenades. Fire was coming from a dark patch of trees in front, into which we plunged, firing blindly. There were only four or five men still with me and I roared abusively, summoning the others. Once the wood was clear, we pushed on shouting like madmen and shooting at the dim figures we saw scuttling away ahead. By the time we reached the summit, the hill seemed clear. My training clicked in: as the rest of the platoon came up, I disposed them in good positions of all-round defence, our firepower considerably increased by the capture of half a dozen Spandaus and a good quantity of grenades. About four of my men had been wounded, one of them, alas, my precious Johanson. More had somehow, by accident or intent, 'got lost' – this happens quite often in battle – but turned up in time to share the triumph. Alan came chugging up the hill, understandably delighted, and spoke kind words. I had done all right.

There was no time to relax. Almost at once the Germans started shelling us with great vigour, and we sheltered gratefully in their trenches. (One of the many military virtues of the Germans we did not share was that when they dug trenches they dug them very fast and very deep.) Shortly afterwards, our own guns opened up an enormous barrage. The hills behind Salerno rumbled and flashed and shells whined swiftly over us like lost souls. Moan, moan, moan, they wept, and up the valley we heard the crump of their explosions. For ten minutes or so they fired unopposed; then three immense crashes on the hospital signalled the German reply. Our own hill rocked under a stunning double punch from heavy guns, and we heard the German shells mingling their whines with ours in the air above us. I was caught in the open by one such burst. As the hill shook, I fell into my slit-trench and tried to burrow deeper into the ground while the shell-fragments above me buzzed in strange circles, like malicious insects. One seemed literally to circle above me as if waiting for its chance to strike. I lay there for an hour or more, watching the pale moon shining through a bare tree above me and listening to the howls and groans and screechings in the air in this monstrous witches' sabbath.

We stood to at dawn. In the first grey hints of light we buried the German dead. These were the first corpses I had handled: shrunken pathetic dolls lying stiff and twisted, with glazed blue eyes. Not one could have been over twenty, and some were little more than children. With horrible carelessness we shovelled them into their own trenches and piled on the earth. The scene still remains etched on my mind: the hunched, urgent diggers, the sprawling corpses with their dead eyes in a cold dawn light that drained all colour from the scene, leaving only mournful blacks and greys. When we had finished, we stuck their rifles and helmets above the graves and scuttled quickly back under cover. It was a scene worthy of Goya.

At the beginning of October 1943, as the American Fifth Army reached the outskirts of Naples, the people rose up and the German occupation forces withdrew. The city was in chaos, many people were on the brink of starvation, and some street children did indeed starve. The Allied Control Commission attempted some semblance of order, but it was largely a futile exercise. A young British army intelligence officer called **Norman Lewis**, *who arrived in Naples with the Fifth Army on 6 October, found himself involved in trying to administer the city and wrote an immortal memoir of his time there,* Naples 44. *It was a time when life was cheap and sex, though rampant, observed certain rituals.*

The sexual attitudes of Neapolitans never fail to produce new surprises. Today Prince A, now well known to us all and an enthusiastic informant from our first days at the Riviera di Chiaia, visited us with his sister, whom we met for the first time. The prince is the absentee landlord of a vast estate somewhere in the south, and owns a nearby palace stacked with family portraits and Chinese antiques. He is the head of what is regarded as the second or third noble family of southern Italy. The prince is about thirty years of age, and his sister could be twenty-four. Both are remarkably alike in appearance: thin, with extremely pale skin and cold, patrician expressions bordering on severity. The purpose of the visit was to enquire if we could arrange for the sister to enter an army brothel. We explained that there was no such institution in the British army. 'A pity,' the prince said. Both of them speak excellent English, learned from an English governess.

'Ah well, Luisa, I suppose if it can't be, it can't be.' They thanked us with polite calm, and departed.

Last week a section member was invited by a female contact to visit the Naples cemetery with her on the coming Sunday afternoon. Informants have to be cultivated in small ways whenever possible, and he was quite prepared to indulge a whim of this kind, in the belief that he would be escorting his friend on a visit to a family tomb, expecting to buy a bunch of chrysanthemums from the stall at the gate. However, hardly were they inside when the lady dragged him behind a tombstone, and then – despite the cold – lay down and pulled up her skirts. He noticed that the cemetery contained a number of other couples in vigorous activity in broad daylight. 'There were more people above ground than under it,' he said. It turned out that the cemetery is the lovers' lane of Naples, and custom is such that one becomes invisible as soon as one passes through the gates. If a visitor runs into anyone he knows neither a sign nor a glance can be exchanged, nor does one recognise any friend encountered on the 133 bus which goes to the cemetery. I have learned that to suggest to a lady a Sunday-afternoon ride on a 133 bus is tantamount to solicitation for immoral purposes.

In recognition of his medical interests in civilian life, Parkinson deals with the doctors of Naples. One of his most valuable contacts is Professore Placella, whose speciality is the restoration of virginity. He boasts that his replacement hymen is much better than the original, and that – costing only 10,000 lire – it takes the most vigorous husband up to three nights to demolish it.

In March 1944, even greater destruction engulfed the city when Vesuvius erupted. The eruption itself was more catastrophic than that which buried Pompeii in AD 79. Norman Lewis witnessed it, and the Italian journalist **Curzio Malaparte** *was caught up in a terrifying stampede as villages on the forward slopes were overtaken by burning lava.*

The uproar was terrific, sometimes assuming the proportions of a riot. Lost in that fearsome crowd, which swept them now this way, now that, as it surged to and fro, turning them round and buffeting them like the gale in Dante's hell, the American soldiers looked as if they too were possessed by a primeval terror and fury. Their faces were begrimed with sweat and ashes, their uniforms were in rags. Now they too were humbled. No longer were they free men, no longer were they proud conquerors. They were conquered wretches, victims of the blind fury of nature. They too were seared to the depths of their souls by the fire that was consuming the sky and the earth.

From time to time a hollow, muffled rumbling, which spread through the secret recesses of the earth, shook the pavement beneath our feet and made the houses rock. A hoarse, deep, gurgling voice rose from the wells and from the mouths of the sewers. The fountains exhaled sulphurous vapours or threw up jets of boiling mud. That subterranean rumbling, that deep voice, that boiling mud caused a sudden efflux of people from their lairs in the bowels of the earth. For during those melancholy years the wretched populace, in order to escape the merciless air raids, had made their homes in the winding tunnels of the ancient Angevin aqueduct which runs beneath the streets of Naples. This aqueduct, say the archaeologists, was excavated by the first inhabitants of the city, who were Greeks or Phoenicians, or by the Pelasgians, those mysterious men who came from the sea. There is an allusion to the Angevin aqueduct and its strange population in Boccaccio's tale of Andreuccio de Perugia. These unhappy creatures were emerging from their filthy hell-holes, from the dark caves, the underground passages, the wells and the mouths of the sewers. Each one carried on his shoulders his wretched chattels, or, like a modern Aeneas, his aged father, or his young children, or the *pecuriello*, the paschal lamb, which at Eastertide (it was actually Holy Week) brings joy to even the meanest Neapolitan home, and is sacred, because it is the image of Christ ...

Those crowds of mud-stained, spectral beings who were everywhere emerging from beneath the ground, that seething mob which was rushing like a river in flood towards the low-lying parts of the city, and the brawls, the yells, the tears, the oaths, the songs, the panic, the sudden stampedes, and the ferocious struggles that would break out in the vicinity of a chapel, a fountain, a cross or a baker's shop, created a frightful, stupendous chaos of sound, which filled the city and was overflowing on to the sea-front, into Via Partenope, Via Caracciolo, the Riviera di Chiaia, and the streets and squares that front the sea between the Granili and Mergellina. It was as if the people in their despair looked to the sea alone for salvation, as if they expected that the waves would quench the flames which were devouring the land, or that the marvellous compassion of the Virgin or St Januarius would enable them to walk on the waters and escape.

But when they reached the sea-front, where they were greeted by the fearsome spectacle of Vesuvius, red-hot, with streams of lava winding their way down its slopes, and the blazing villages (the blast from the prodigious conflagration spread as far as the island of Capri, which could be seen drifting on the horizon, and the snow-covered mountains of Cilento), the crowd dropped to their knees; and at the sight of the sea, which was covered with a horrible green and yellow film like the mottled hide of some loathsome reptile, they called upon heaven to help them, uttering loud wails, bestial yells and savage oaths. Many, spurred on by the curses and the frightful abuse of the infuriated, envious populace, plunged into the waves, hoping that they would provide a foothold, and were ignominiously drowned.

Meanwhile, in January 1944, Allied troops had landed at Anzio, south of Rome, and began slowly to fight their way north. The year from June 1943 to June 1944 was one of the most disastrous in Italian history. Mussolini was restored to a semblance of power under German protection as puppet ruler of northern Italy, so that when Badoglio agreed terms of surrender with the Allies, his authority held only for the southern provinces. The civil war, which broke out between Fascists, Republicans and Communists, all aiming to snatch political advantage from military defeat, was small-scale at first but none the less vicious, and it quickly spread. Soon the woods and hills of the rather wild no man's land north of Rome were full of partisans, deserters, escaped prisoners of war and members of the civilian population trying to avoid conscription.

*For much of the winter of 1943 the young **Eric Newby** was on the run in German-occupied northern Italy. He had been taken prisoner the year before while on a sabotage operation in Sicily, but, following Badoglio's armistice in September, had escaped from his prison camp in Parma. His experiences, often very funny, are described in* Love and War in the Apennines, *an engaging memoir by a master story-teller – full of bizarre personal detail, most of it self-deprecating. He had his strangest encounter of all when, while working – or rather sleeping – in the Zanonis' fields, he came face to face with the enemy.*

I woke to find a German soldier standing over me. At first, with the sun behind him he was as indistinct as the peaks had become, but then he swam into focus. He was an officer and he was wearing summer battle-dress and a soft cap with a long narrow peak. He had a pistol but it was still in its holster on his belt and he seemed to have forgotten that he was armed because he made no effort to draw it. Across one shoulder and hanging down over one hip in a very unmilitary way he wore a large old-fashioned civilian haversack, as if he was a member of a weekend rambling club, rather than a soldier, and in one hand he held a large, professional-looking butterfly net. He was a tall, thin, pale young man of about twenty-five with mild eyes and he appeared as surprised to see me as I was to see him, but much less alarmed than I was, virtually immobilised, lying on my back without my boots and socks on.

'*Buon giorno,*' he said, courteously. His accent sounded rather like mine must, I thought. '*Che bella giornata.*'

At least up to now he seemed to have assumed that I was an Italian, but as soon as I opened my mouth he would know I wasn't. Perhaps I ought to try and push him over the cliff, after all he was standing with his back to it; but I knew that I wouldn't. It seemed awful even to think of murdering someone who had simply wished me good day and remarked on what a beautiful one it was, let alone actually doing it. If ever there was going to be an appropriate time to go on stage in the part of the mute from Genoa which I had often rehearsed but never played, this was it. I didn't answer.

'*Da dove viene, lei?*' he asked.

I just continued to look at him. I suppose I should have been making strangled noises and pointing down my throat to emphasise my muteness, but just as I couldn't bring myself to assail him, I couldn't do this either. It seemed too ridiculous. But he was not to be put off. He removed his haversack, put down his butterfly net, sat down opposite me in the hollow and said:

'*Lei, non è Italiano.*'

It was not a question. It was a statement of fact which did not require an answer. I decided to abandon my absurd act.

'*Si, sono Italiano.*'

He looked at me, studying me carefully: my face, my clothes and my boots which, after my accent, were my biggest give-away, although they were very battered now.

'I think that you are English,' he said, finally, in English. 'English, or from one of your colonies. You cannot be an English deserter; you are on the wrong side of the battle front. You do not look like a parachutist or a saboteur. You must be a prisoner of war. That is so, is it not?'

I said nothing.

'Do not be afraid,' he went on. 'I will not tell anyone that I have met you, I have no intention of spoiling such a splendid day either for you or for myself. They are too rare. I have only this one day of free time and it was extremely difficult to organise the transport to get here. I am anxious to collect specimens, but specimens with wings. I give you my word that no one will ever hear from me that I have seen you or your companions if you have any.'

In the face of such courtesy it was useless to dissemble and it would have been downright uncouth to do so.

'Yes, I am English,' I said, but it was a sacrifice to admit it. I felt as if I was pledging my freedom.

He offered me his hand. He was close enough to do so without moving. It felt strangely soft when I grasped it in my own calloused and roughened one and it looked unnaturally clean when he withdrew it.

'*Oberleutnant* Frick. Education Officer. And may I have the pleasure of your name, also?'

'Eric Newby,' I said. 'I'm a lieutenant in the infantry, or rather I was until I was put in the bag.' I could see no point in telling him that I had been in SBS, not that he was likely to have heard of it. In fact I was expressly forbidden, as all prisoners were, to give anything but my name, rank and number to the enemy.

'Excuse me? In the bag?'

'Until I was captured. It's an expression.'

He laughed slightly pedantically, but it was quite a pleasant sound. I expected him to ask me when and where I had been captured and was prepared to say Sicily, 1943, rather than 1942, which would have led to all sorts of complications; but he was more interested in the expression I had used.

'Excellent. In the bag, you say. I shall remember that. I have little opportunity now to learn colloquial English. With me it would be more appropriate to say 'in the net', or, 'in the bottle'; but, at least no one has put you in a prison bottle, which is what I have to do with my captives.'

Although I don't think he intended it to be, I found this rather creepy, but then I was not a butterfly hunter. His English was very good, if perhaps a little stilted. I only wished that I could speak Italian a quarter as well.

He must have noticed the look of slight distaste on my face because the next thing he said was, 'Don't worry, the poison is only crushed laurel leaves, a very old way, nothing modern from IG Farben.'

Now he began delving in his haversack and brought out two bottles, wrapped in brown paper which, at first, I thought must contain the laurel with which he used to knock out his butterflies when he caught them; but, in fact, they contained beer, and he offered me one of them.

'It is really excellent beer,' he said. 'Or, at least, I find it so. To my taste Italian beer is not at all good. This is from Munich. Not easy to get now unfortunately. Permit me to open it for you.'

It was cool and delicious. I asked him where he had come from.

'From Salsomaggiore, in the foothills,' he said. 'It is a spa and like all spas it is very melancholy, or at least I find them so, although we Germans are supposed to like melancholy places. It is the feeling that no one who has ever visited them has been quite well, and never will be again, that I find disagreeable. Now it is a headquarters. My job there is to give lectures on Italian culture, particularly the culture of the Renaissance, to groups of officers and any of the men who are interested. It is scarcely arduous because so few of them are.

'I must confess', he went on, 'that there are some aspects of my countrymen's character that I cannot pretend to understand. I do not speak disloyally to make you feel more friendly to me because, no doubt, you, also, do not always understand your own people, but surely only Germany would employ a professor of entomology from Göttingen with only one lung, whose only interest is lepidoptera, to give lectures on Renaissance painting and architecture to soldiers who are engaged in destroying these things as hard as they are able. Do you not think it strange?'

'I wouldn't say that,' I said. 'I'm sure we do the same sort of thing and, if we don't, I'm sure the Americans do.'

'Really,' he said. 'You surprise me. You would not say that it is strange?

'The intention is, of course,' he continued, 'to make us popular with the inhabitants, but that is something we can never be. For instance, I came to that village down there by car. I suggested to the driver that he might like to accompany me up here; but he is not interested in the countryside or lepidoptera. Besides he told me that there is a regulation against leaving military vehicles unattended. I did not ask him to accompany me because I wanted his company but because I knew that he would not enjoy himself in that village, or any other. When we arrived at it no one would speak to us. There was scarcely anyone to speak to anyway, which was very strange because it is a Sunday. They must have thought I had come to make some kind of investigation. It might have been better if we had not been wearing guns; but it is a regulation.'

I could visualise the state of panic the village must have been thrown into by their arrival, with young men running from the houses and the *stalle* and up the mountainsides, like hunted hares.

'It is not pleasant to be disliked,' he said, 'and it is very unpleasant to be German and to know that one is hated, because one is German and, because, collectively, we are wrong in what we are doing. That is why I hate this war, or one of the reasons. And of course, because of this, we shall lose it. We must. We have to.'

'It's going to take you a long time to lose it at this rate,' I said. 'Everything seems to be going very slowly.'

'It may seem so to you,' he said. 'But it won't be here, in Italy, that we shall be beaten. We shall hold you here, at least through this winter and perhaps we could hold you through next summer, but I do not think there will be a next summer. What is going on in Russia is more than flesh and blood can stand. We are on the retreat from Smolensk; we are retreating to the Dnieper. According to people who have just come from there we are losing more men every day than we have lost here in the Italian peninsula in an entire month. And what are you doing?' he asked.

I told him that I was on my way south towards the front. There seemed no point in telling him that I was living here. Also I was ashamed.

'If you take the advice of an enemy,' he said, 'you will try to pass the winter here, in these mountains. By the time you get to the battle front it will be very, very cold and very, very difficult to pass through it. Until a few days ago we all thought we would be retiring beyond the Po; but now the winter line is going to be far south of Rome. It has already been given a name. They call it the *Winterstellung*.'

'Tell me one thing,' I said. 'Where have we got to now. I never hear any news.'

'You have Termoli and Foggia on the east coast, which means that you will now be able to use bombers in close support and you have Naples; but take my advice and wait for the spring.'

I asked him where he had learned his English. He told me that he had spent several summer vacations in England before the war.

'I liked England,' he said. 'And the English. You do not work hard but you have the good sense not to be interested in politics. I liked very much your way of life.'

He got to his feet.

'Lieutenant,' he said, 'it has given me great pleasure to have met you. Good luck to you and, perhaps, though I do not think it probable, we shall meet again after the war at Göttingen, or London.'

'Or Philippi,' I felt like saying, but didn't.

'Now if you would be so kind,' he said, 'please give me the empty bottle as I cannot obtain more of this beer without handing the bottles back. Bottles are in short supply.'

The last I saw of him was running across the open downs with his net unfurled, in the direction from which I had come, making curious little sweeps and lunges as he pursued his prey, a tall, thin, rather ungainly figure with only one lung. I was sorry to see him go.

*The air war over Italy was one-sided – for the most part the Allies had total air superiority and Italy would have been bombed out of the war even if her land forces had not been defeated. The antics of the Allied Tactical Air Force became the subject of one of the great satires of the Second World War, **Joseph Heller**'s Catch-22. Heller served with the ATAF and many of his descriptions are caricatures of real-life experience. The phrase 'Catch 22' has, of course, become part of the language. The anti-hero, Bombardier Yossarian, tries to get out of flying operations by pleading clinical insanity – but in trying to get out of flying in bombers (which was as risky as being an infantryman in the First World War) he demonstrated that he was in fact completely sane. That meant sane enough to fly – the 'Catch-22' of the written (or unwritten) flying manual for the US Air Force.*

Actually, it was not Captain Black but Sergeant Knight who triggered the solemn panic of Bologna, slipping silently off the truck for two extra flak suits as soon as he learned the target and signalling the start of the grim procession back into the parachute tent that degenerated into a frantic stampede finally before all the extra flak suits were gone.

'Hey, what's going on?' Kid Sampson asked nervously. 'Bologna can't be that rough, can it?'

Nately, sitting trance-like on the floor of the truck, held his grave young face in both hands and did not answer him.

It was Sergeant Knight and the cruel series of postponements, for just as they were climbing up into their planes that first morning, along came a jeep with the news that it was raining in Bologna and that the mission would be delayed. It was raining in Pianosa too by the time they returned to the squadron, and they had the rest of that day to stare woodenly at the bomb line on the map under the awning of the intelligence tent and ruminate hypnotically on the fact that there was no escape. The evidence was there vividly in the narrow red ribbon tacked across the mainland: the ground forces in Italy were pinned down 42 insurmountable miles south of the target and could not possibly capture the city in time. Nothing could save the men in Pianosa from the mission to Bologna. They were trapped.

Their only hope was that it would never stop raining, and they had no hope because they all knew it would. When it did stop raining in Pianosa, it rained in Bologna. When it stopped raining in Bologna, it began again in Pianosa. If there was no rain at all, there were freakish, inexplicable phenomena like the epidemic of diarrhoea or the bomb line that moved. Four times during the first six days they were assembled and briefed and then sent back. Once, they took off and were flying in formation when the control tower summoned them down. The more it rained, the worse they suffered. The worse they suffered, the more they prayed that it would continue raining. All through the night, men looked at the sky and were saddened by the stars. All through the day, they looked at the bomb line on the big, wobbling easel map of Italy that blew over in the wind and was dragged in under the awning of the intelligence tent every time the rain began. The bomb line was a scarlet band of narrow satin ribbon that delineated the forwardmost position of the Allied ground forces in every sector of the Italian mainland.

The morning after Hungry Joe's fist fight with Huple's cat, the rain stopped falling in both places. The landing strip began to dry. It would take a full twenty-four hours to harden; but the sky remained cloudless. The resentments incubating in each man hatched into hatred. First they hated the infantrymen on the mainland because they had failed to capture Bologna. Then they began to hate the bomb line itself. For hours they stared relentlessly at the scarlet ribbon on the map and hated it because it would not move up high enough to encompass the city. When night fell, they congregated in the darkness with flashlights, continuing their macabre vigil at the bomb line in brooding entreaty as though hoping to move the ribbon up by the collective weight of their sullen prayers.

'I really can't believe it,' Clevinger exclaimed to Yossarian in a voice rising and falling in protest and wonder. 'It's a complete reversion to primitive superstition. They're confusing cause and effect. It makes as much sense as knocking on wood or crossing your fingers. They really believe that we wouldn't have to fly that mission tomorrow if someone would only tiptoe up to the map in the middle of the night and move the bomb line over Bologna. Can you imagine? You and I must be the only rational ones left.'

In the middle of the night Yossarian knocked on wood, crossed his fingers, and tiptoed out of his tent to move the bomb line up over Bologna.

D-day and After

By summer 1943 German troops were in retreat. Defeat at El Alamein and
Stalingrad put the Germans on the defensive for the first time since 1939;
the Allied invasion of Italy presented a major threat in the south, and a sus-
tained bombing campaign paved the way for an Anglo-American invasion of
northern Europe. Many British and American troops were withdrawn from
Italy to prepare for the amphibious landings in Normandy which eventually
came on 6 June 1944 – the largest operation of its kind in history. It was a
close-run thing, particularly for the Americans on the right flank, hemmed
in by cliffs on what had been code-named Omaha beach. They were nearly
driven back to the sea as the Germans dug in above and inside the cliffs.

Among those who landed with the British 3rd Division on Sword Beach
*was a young artillery officer, **Norman Scarfe**. In Assault Division he tells*
the story of the initial landing. His record is unusual for the highly personal
quality of the writing: Scarfe was still with his division at Bremen when the
fighting ended almost a year later.

Our terrific barrage and bombardment 'lifted' on ahead as our infantry
assaulted the beach defences: and just as the East Yorks and the South
Lancs felt the relief of the solid sands under their feet, the Germans were
emerging from the solid and comfortably furnished underground shelters, which seem to have given them good protection from everything
but shock. Within a few minutes the enemy was applying the fire of rifle,
machine-gun, mortar and field gun to *Queen* Beach, particularly to *Red*,
opposite the *Cod* strong-point. The South Lancs on the right had severe
casualties in A Company, Major Harward, the company commander,

being mortally wounded, and one of his subalterns, Allen, killed breaching the beach wire. They sent C Company left to assist the East Yorks in the reduction of *Cod*, while Lieutenant R. W. Pearce MC took command of A Company and directed it right towards Lion-sur-Mer. On this beach the gapping teams had opened four exits at the end of an hour, despite heavy casualties in men and tanks.

On *Red* Beach C Company of the South Lancs were engaging the active *Cod*, when the HQ and remaining companies of the South Lancs landed almost on the strong-point. B Company went in to help them, and Major Harrison, their commander, was killed immediately. So was Bell-Walker, who assumed command and led an attack on a pillbox. Battalion HQ moved up towards the sand dunes near an 88-millimetre position, and the battalion commander, Lieutenant-Colonel R. P. H. Burbury, was killed by a sniper's bullet as he directed this assault.

The *Red* Beach gapping teams suffered crippling enemy fire, lost most of their tanks and were nearly all reduced to clearance by hand. Their first two exits became blocked by damaged tanks. They managed to open one gap with lateral communications after an hour and a half, and two more within the next quarter of an hour. No mines were found on the beach itself, though the exits and strips behind the dunes and beside the streets were thickly inlaid with them.

The obstacle-clearing teams fared worse. Their work was more formidable even than they had expected; their first discovery was that every ramp-type obstacle and a number of the stakes, steel hedgehogs and concrete tetrahedra were armed with a Tellermine or Anti-Aircraft shell with push-igniter to operate against the first craft that fouled them. The situation was aggravated by the high tide and swell. By the time the unarmoured element of the obstacle-clearing teams got ashore the seaward ramps stood in 6–8 feet of water and were about to be submerged. Enemy small arms were still active and mortar-fire was coming down. Men on *Red* Beach were swimming in an effort to remove the mines and shells, and a number were dislodged and dropped to the bottom. Then, as more LCT ran ashore, it became impossible to work at the deep obstacles. Fortunately it had become evident that the obstacles were not preventing the discharge of craft and that some of the mines were failing to detonate.

During these early tasks on the beach the casualties to the flails, AVs, RE and bulldozers amounted to 50 per cent of the machines, 5 Assault Regiment, RE, suffered heavy casualties amongst their officers, and 629 Field Squadron lost nearly 20 per cent of their men, some of whom were drowned. From among the division's own engineers, 246 Field Company, affiliated as usual to 8 Brigade, landed one assault demolition team with each of the assault companies of infantry and a mine-clearance team with each of the four reserve companies of those two battalions. It was one of the platoons of 246 Field Company, landing at five minutes past eight, that made the first exit off White Beach with a borrowed armoured bulldozer, before proceeding, according to plan, to search and clear and mark a forward route to Hermanville. The East Yorks, supported by the surviving tanks of B Squadron of 13th/18th Hussars, and the South Lancs supported by the survivors of A Squadron, both accompanied by their affiliated FOOs of the 76th Field Regiment and with one FOO of the 33rd Field Regiment, had begun the advance inland.

The hinterland was not hard to defend. It is quite easy to visualise, especially easy for those who saw it then: the wind was very fresh, and, blowing the clouds fast across the sky, it uncovered the sun at intervals throughout the day. The effect was that the prepared, sensitive minds of the men were exposed to a series of flashlight photographs that were developed on the spot and printed indelibly.

Ernie Pyle, veteran American war correspondent, who had been with the US armies in North Africa and Italy, arrived the following day on Omaha beach. He shared the hardships of the soldiers throughout, and wrote so empathically of the plight of 'GI Joe' that servicemen and their families wrote to him by the thousand seeking his advice on anything from grand strategy to mundane matters of survival in the field. This is a part of his first despatch from Normandy, on 12 June 1944.

Normandy beachhead: Due to a last-minute alteration in the arrangements, I didn't arrive on the beachhead until the morning after D-day, after our first wave of assault troops had hit the shore.

By the time we got here the beaches had been taken and the fighting had moved a couple of miles inland. All that remained on the beach was some sniping and artillery fire, and the occasional startling blast of a mine geysering brown sand into the air. That plus a gigantic and pitiful litter of wreckage along miles of shoreline.

Submerged tanks and overturned boats and burnt trucks and shell-shattered jeeps and sad little personal belongings were strewn all over these bitter sands. That plus the bodies of soldiers lying in rows covered with blankets, the toes of their shoes sticking up in a line as though on drill. And other bodies, uncollected, still sprawling grotesquely in the sand or half-hidden by the high grass beyond the beach. That plus an intense, grim determination of work-weary men to get this chaotic beach organ-ised and get all the vital supplies and the reinforcements moving more rapidly over it from the stacked-up ships standing in droves out to sea.

Now that it is over it seems to me a pure miracle that we ever took the beach at all. For some of our units it was easy, but in this special sector where I am now our troops faced such odds that our getting ashore was like my whipping Joe Louis down to a pulp.

In this column I want to tell you what the opening of the Second Front in this one sector entailed, so that you can know and appreciate and for ever be humbly grateful to those both dead and alive who did it for you.

Ashore, facing us, were more enemy troops than we had in our assault waves. The advantages were all theirs, the disadvantages all ours. The Germans were dug into positions that they had been working on for months, although these were not yet all complete. A 100-foot bluff a couple of hundred yards back from the beach had great concrete gun emplacements built right into the hilltop. These opened to the sides instead of to the front, thus making it very hard for naval fire from the sea to reach them. They could shoot parallel with the beach and cover every foot of it for miles with artillery fire.

Then they had hidden machine-gun nests on the forward slopes, with crossfire taking in every inch of the beach. These nests were connected by networks of trenches, so that the German gunners could move about without exposing themselves.

Throughout the length of the beach, running zigzag a couple of hundred yards back from the shoreline, was an immense V-shaped ditch 15 feet deep. Nothing could cross it, not even men on foot, until fills had been made. And in other places at the far end of the beach, where the ground is flatter, they had great concrete walls. These were blasted by our naval gunfire or by explosives set by hand after we got ashore.

Our only exits from the beach were several swales or valleys, each about 100 yards wide. The Germans made the most of these funnel-like traps, sowing them with buried mines. They contained, also, barbed-wire entanglements with mines attached, hidden ditches, and machine-guns firing from the slopes.

This is what was on the shore. But our men had to go through a maze nearly as deadly as this before they even got ashore. Underwater obstacles were terrific. The Germans had whole fields of evil devices under the water to catch our boats. Even now, several days after the landing, we have cleared only channels through them and cannot yet approach the whole length of the beach with our ships. Even now some ship or boat hits one of these mines every day and is knocked out of commission.

The Germans had masses of those great six-pronged spiders, made of railroad iron and standing shoulder-high, just beneath the surface of the water for our landing craft to run into. They also had huge logs buried in the sand, pointing upward and outward, their tops just below the water. Attached to these logs were mines.

In addition to these obstacles they had floating mines offshore, land-mines buried in the sand of the beach, and more mines in chequerboard rows in the tall grass beyond the sand. And the enemy had four men on shore for every three men we had approaching the shore.

And yet we got on.

On 6 June 1944, British, American and Canadian troops carried out the biggest amphibious landing in history on the beaches of Normandy. **Ernest Hemingway**, *already a literary as well as journalistic legend, shared the experience of landing on Juno Beach with US infantry. His despatch, published a month later in* Collier's Magazine *is among his most celebrated.*

No one remembers the date of the Battle of Shiloh. But the day we took Fox Green beach was the sixth of June, and the wind was blowing hard out of the northwest. As we moved in toward land in the gray early light, the 36-foot coffin-shaped steel boats took solid green sheets of water that fell on the helmeted heads of the troops packed shoulder to shoulder in the stiff, awkward, uncomfortable, lonely companionship of men going to a battle. There were cases of TNT, with rubber-tube life preservers wrapped around them to float them in the surf, stacked forward in the steel well of the LCV(P), and there were piles of bazookas and boxes of bazooka rockets encased in waterproof coverings that reminded you of the transparent raincoats college girls wear.

All this equipment, too, had the rubber-tube life preservers strapped and tied on, and the men wore these same gray rubber tubes strapped under their armpits.

As the boat rose to a sea, the green water turned white and came slamming in over the men, the guns and the cases of explosives. Ahead you could see the coast of France. The gray booms and derrick-forested bulks of the attack transports were behind now, and, over all the sea, boats were crawling forward toward France.

As the LCV(P) rose to the crest of a wave, you saw the line of low, silhouetted cruisers and the two big battlewagons lying broadside to the shore. You saw the heat-bright flashes of their guns and the brown smoke that pushed out against the wind and then blew away.

'What's your course, coxswain?' Lieutenant (jg) Robert Anderson of Roanoke, Virginia, shouted from the stern.

'Two-twenty, sir,' the coxswain, Frank Currier of Saugus, Massachusetts, answered. He was a thin-faced, freckled boy with his eyes fixed on the compass.

'Then steer two-twenty, damn it!' Anderson said. 'Don't steer all over the whole damn' ocean!'

'I'm steering two-twenty, sir,' the coxswain said patiently.

'Well steer it, then,' Andy said. He was nervous, but the boat crew, who were making their first landing under fire, knew this officer had taken LCV(P)s in to the African landing, Sicily and Salerno, and they had confidence in him.

'Don't steer into that LCT,' Andy shouted, as we roared by the ugly steel hull of a tank landing craft, her vehicles sea-lashed, her troops huddling out of the spray.

'I'm steering two-twenty,' the coxswain said.

'That doesn't mean you have to run into everything on the ocean,' Andy said. He was a handsome, hollow-cheeked boy with a lot of style and a sort of easy petulance. 'Mr Hemingway, will you please see if you can see what that flag is over there, with your glasses?'

I got my old miniature Zeiss glasses out of an inside pocket, where they were wrapped in a woolen sock with some tissue to clean them, and focused them on the flag. I made the flag out just before a wave drenched the glasses.

'It's green.'

'Then we are in the mine-swept channel,' Andy said. 'That's all right. Coxswain, what's the matter with you? Can't you steer two-twenty?'

I was trying to dry my glasses, but it was hopeless the way the spray was coming in, so I wrapped them up for a try later on and watched the battleship *Texas* shelling the shore. She was just off on our right now and firing over us as we moved in toward the French coast, which was showing clearer all the time on what was, or was not, a course of 220 degrees, depending on whether you believed Andy or Currier the coxswain.

The low cliffs were broke by valleys. There was a town with a church spire in one of them. There was a wood that came down to the sea. There was a house on the right of one of the beaches. On all the headlands, the gorse was burning, but the northwest wind held the smoke close to the ground.

*On 20 July 1944, a small group of dedicated anti-Nazis carried out a plan to kill Hitler. The July Bomb Plot, as it became known, was a failure – partly because the meeting at which it happened did not take place underground as originally planned, but in a wooden hut, so that much of the blast was dissipated, and partly because Count von Stauffenberg, who carried it out, was hampered by having only one hand and could therefore trigger only one bomb rather than the planned two. The orgy of terror that followed is well known though there was little or nothing in the way of written evidence against the plotters. Most people had long been too frightened to commit anything to paper, and in the wake of the plot anything there had been was destroyed. The exception was the remarkable 'Missie' (**Marie Vassiltchikov**), born in 1917 in Petrograd (St Petersburg), whose family had left Russia in 1919. Although never a German citizen, her knowledge of five languages ensured*

that she found work in Berlin, first with the Broadcasting Association, and
later with the information department of the Ministry of Foreign Affairs.
She was close to many of the conspirators, in particular Adam Trott, and
was therefore in considerable danger herself following the failure of the plot.
Missie's only concession to this was to write her diary in a personal short-
hand. Following a rumour that von Stauffenberg's wife and four children had
been murdered, she records going in search of Adam.

I went down to Adam's room. I found him with one of his assistants, who
soon left. Adam threw himself down on a sofa and, pointing to his neck,
said 'I'm in it up to here.' He looked dreadful. We talked in whispers. The
sight of him made me unhappier still. I told him so. He said yes, but to me
it was merely as if I had lost the favourite tree in my orchard, whereas for
him it's everything he had hoped for that was gone. The intercom rang:
our boss, Dr Six, wanted to see him. We agreed to meet in the evening. I left
a note with his secretary, saying I would wait for his phone call.

When I went over to Maria Gersdorff, I told her how anxious I was
about Adam. 'But why?' she asked. 'He knew Stauffenberg only slightly,
didn't he? No. I'm certain he is not deeply involved!' – 'No,' I said, 'not
really involved at all.'

Adam rang and we agreed to meet at Aga Fürstenberg's after six. I then
went over to the Adlon, where I was meeting Loremarie Schönburg and
Aga. The latter was furious because, when she met Hasso Etzdorf in the
street, he turned his back on her. I assume he, too, is deeply compromised.
We assembled at Aga's and had tea on the lawn. Tony Saurma and Georgie
Pappenheim were there too. Then Adam joined us. He had been with Dr
Six, trying to put him off the scent. He looked like death. I drove back with
him to his house and sat on the balcony in the sun while he changed. An
air-raid alarm sounded; it had the irritating effect of a swarm of bees, no
more. When Adam reappeared, we sat outside and he told me about some
of it:

Stauffenberg, he said, was a wonderful man, not only brilliantly intelligent but also with exceptional vitality and drive. He was one of the few
plotters frequently admitted to Hitler's presence. He had been to Supreme
Headquarters with his bomb twice before but each time there had been
some hitch or else Himmler or Goering or some of the others whom he

wanted to kill together with Hitler had stayed away from the meeting at the last moment. The third time he was summoned, he had told his fellow conspirators that he would go ahead with it, whatever the circumstances. The strain was getting too much for him and no wonder. If only it had been somebody who could fire a gun, the attempt might have succeeded. But Stauffenberg was too badly disabled ... He had lost in him, Adam said, his closest friend. He seemed completely crushed.

Adam himself had spent the whole day of the 20th at the AA in the Wilhelmstrasse, waiting for the military take-over. He said he knew he would be arrested, he was too deeply compromised. I did not ask him to what extent. He was sending away his maid; she had witnessed too many meetings in this house and, if questioned, might talk. He feared that Helldorf, too, might break down under torture.

On 18 August, Adam Trott and the other convicted conspirators were hanged – or rather slowly strangled, as piano wire was used instead of rope to prolong the agony. The executions were filmed on Hitler's instructions, while the executioner, who was famous for his macabre humour, cracked obscene jokes.

In August Paris was liberated. One of the first correspondents to enter the city, with Le Clerc's Free French, was **Alan Moorehead**, *who found no sooner than he had arrived that the fighting was far from over. One of the most accomplished reporters of the war, Moorehead told his story of it in* Eclipse, *a brilliant and sober memoir written immediately afterwards when the memory was fresh.*

We walked a hundred yards down the street to the Boulevard Montparnasse, and all the celebration was there cut off with the same abruptness with which a cliff falls into the sea. Out beyond the corner of the Boulevard Montparnasse there was simply empty space; first the wide empty crossroads, then the empty gardens, then the sinister façade of the Senate buildings, where the enemy snipers were holding out. Every few minutes a fusillade of shots came out of one of the upper windows, and they smacked sharply against the walls of the houses looking on to the gardens. Occasionally one of the French tanks drawn up under the trees spat out a stream of tracers that ran like fireworks up the face of the Senate. Here on this side was the wild rejoicing; there on that side the empty space and the war. There was no liaison between these two scenes; they might have been separate sets at a movie studio. But occasionally some unknowing cyclist or perhaps a woman hurrying home from her shopping would walk out into the empty space. At once the gendarmes and the Resistance boys blew madly on their whistles. Frantically they beckoned the trespassers back into the cover of the walls. Then for a little there would be nothing but the empty space again, and the bursts of machine-gun fire.

It was the same wherever you turned. Along all the streets where the army had penetrated the snipers had drawn back, and the people had rushed into the open to express their joy. Then when you got to the head of the column the crowds and the exultation died away together. People crept from door to door along the walls, furtively and silently. Odd shots burst down from the rooftops.

This was the high moment in the lives of the boys of the Forces Françaises Intérieures, the *maquis* of the streets, the youths who had plotted in the secret cellars against the Germans through all these years. Now they were out in the open, shooting with their hoarded arms. Many of them were half-mad with passionate excitement. They had long since passed the stage where they recognised any risk at all. At this tense crisis of their revolution they had seized every workable car from the city garages, and now they were careering hectically through the streets, five or ten men to a car, all armed, trying to draw the fire of the snipers on the rooftops.

For a full week before we had arrived, this street fighting had been going on. Already three-quarters of Paris had fallen to the Resistance movement. The whole city had been secretly divided into resistance zones, little underground cells that might be in a garage or a back-street hotel.

As an accredited war correspondent, Moorehead was under military orders – which of course he was bound to break as he sought a decent bed and a spot of civilisation. When he reached the Ritz, he found that the major celebrity reporter, one of the biggest egos of the trade (and sadly too often imitated), had beaten him to liberating the bar.

It seemed sensible to disobey orders and head for somewhere comfortable like the Ritz. As we turned back into the Place Vendôme it even began to seem possible that we were going to liberate the place. With precision and great aplomb the staff booked us in: perhaps we can waive the usual formality of seeing your identity card. Will you go up to your rooms now or have dinner at once?

It was a little galling to find Ernest Hemingway sitting in the dining room over a bottle of Heidsieck. At that time he was acting as the commander of a company of *maquis* who had fought their way in through Versailles. He had liberated the Ritz just an hour before.

Through that night there was spasmodic gunfire in the northern suburbs, but in the morning Paris was calm again, de Gaulle had arrived and every able-bodied Parisian in the centre of the city was hurrying to the Champs-Élysées. The people had now settled into their exhilaration. They had composed themselves for pleasure, just as previously they had had to compose themselves for the misery of the arrival of the Germans. In June 1940 they had rushed for their homes; now they rushed into the streets. Both moves were spontaneous, subjective, unpremeditated.

The last time the Champs-Élysées had filled with a crowd like this was on 14 July 1939, for the Bastille celebrations, during that last summer of peace when people, despairing of the future, were determined to seize what pleasure they could. And now the colours were the same, the immense tricolour floating from the Arc, the girls with flowers in their hair, the red, white and blue dresses, the flags hanging from the window boxes. They stood in the same places under the trees on either side of the road, in all the windows and the balconies, and they perched like flies on the housetops. Some things were missing from that other day: Daladier with his cabinet on the wooden stand in front of the Café Coupole, the diplomats, the top hats and the ceremonial dress. But the real difference lay in the intangible emotion of the people, this sense of utter relief. It had the glow and freshness of an adolescent love affair.

As Robert Capa noted, 'The liberation of Paris was the most unforgettable day in the world. The most unforgettable day plus seven was also the bluest. The food was gone, the champagne was gone, and the girls had returned to their homes.' Only 25 miles away the war was still going on, and at Verdun the Germans were still advancing. General Patton was on the offensive and had crossed the river Saar into Germany.

On 13 February 1945, the RAF and US Air Force bombed Dresden, setting off a firestorm which killed between one and two hundred thousand people and destroyed the ancient city. The main targets and victims were civilian, the main purpose being to undermine German morale. Among a group of American prisoners of war brought to the city was **Kurt Vonnegut, Jr.** *He had sought shelter in a huge meat safe in the slaughterhouse that became his prison. The memory of the raid never left him. In his writings he would only produce his recollections in fragments. This he did most brilliantly in his magic-realist novella* Slaughterhouse-Five, *in which he told his story through his* alter ego, Billy Pilgrim.

Billy was down in the meat locker on the night that Dresden was destroyed. There were sounds like giant footsteps above. Those were sticks of high-explosive bombs. The giants walked and walked. The meat locker was a very safe shelter. All that happened down there was an occasional shower of calcimine. The Americans and four of their guards and a few dressed carcasses were down there, and nobody else. The rest of the guards had, before the raid began, gone to the comforts of their own homes in Dresden. They were all being killed with their families.

So it goes.

The girls that Billy had seen naked were all being killed, too, in a much shallower shelter in another part of the stockyards.

So it goes.

A guard would go to the head of the stairs every so often to see what it was like outside, then he would come down and whisper to the other guards. There was a firestorm out there. Dresden was one big flame. The one flame ate everything organic, everything that would burn.

It wasn't safe to come out of the shelter until noon the next day. When the Americans and their guards did come out, the sky was black with smoke. The sun was an angry little pinhead. Dresden was like the moon now, nothing but minerals. The stones were hot. Everybody else in the neighbourhood was dead.

So it goes ...

'Dresden was destroyed on the night of 13 February 1945,' Billy Pilgrim began. 'We came out of our shelter the next day.' He told Montana about the four guards who, in their astonishment and grief, resembled a barber-shop quartet. He told her about the stockyards with all the fence posts gone, with roofs and windows gone – told her about seeming little logs lying around. These were people who had been caught in the firestorm. So it goes.

Billy told her what had happened to the buildings that used to form cliffs around the stockyards. They had collapsed. Their wood had been consumed, and their stones had crashed down, had tumbled against one another until they locked at last in low and graceful curves.

'It was like the moon,' said Billy Pilgrim.

The guards told the Americans to form in ranks of four, which they did. Then they had them march back to the hog barn which had been their home. Its walls still stood, but its windows and roof were gone, and there was nothing inside but ashes and dollops of melted glass. It was realised then that there was no food or water, and that the survivors, if they were going to continue to survive, were going to have to climb over curve after curve on the face of the moon.

Which they did.

The curves were smooth only when seen from a distance. The people climbing them learned that they were treacherous, jagged things – hot to the touch, often unstable – eager, should certain important rocks be disturbed, to tumble some more, to form lower, more solid curves.

Nobody talked much as the expedition crossed the moon. There was nothing appropriate to say. One thing was clear: absolutely everybody in the city was supposed to be dead, regardless of what they were, and that anybody that moved in it represented a flaw in the design. There were to be no moon men at all.

American fighter planes came in under the smoke to see if anything was moving. They saw Billy and the rest moving down there. The planes sprayed them with machine-gun bullets, but the bullets missed. Then they saw some other people moving down by the riverside and they shot at them. They hit some of them. So it goes.

The idea was to hasten the end of the war.

Billy's story ended very curiously in a suburb untouched by fire and explosions. The guards and the Americans came at nightfall to an inn which was open for business. There was candlelight. There were fires in three fireplaces downstairs. There were empty tables and chairs waiting for anyone who might come, and empty beds with covers turned down upstairs.

There was a blind innkeeper and his sighted wife, who was the cook, and their two young daughters, who worked as waitresses and maids. This family knew that Dresden was gone. Those with eyes had seen it burn and burn, understood that they were on the edge of a desert now. Still – they had opened for business, had polished the glasses and wound the clocks and stirred the fires, and waited and waited to see who would come.

There was no great flow of refugees from Dresden. The clocks ticked on, the fires crackled, the translucent candles dripped. And then there was a knock on the door, and in came four guards and one hundred American prisoners of war.

The innkeeper asked the guards if they had come from the city.

'Yes.'

'Are there more people coming?'

And the guards said that, on the difficult route they had chosen, they had not seen another living soul.

*Above the ground **Victor Klemperer** witnessed the bombing – and survived. He was a Jew, a respected academic who had been saved by his marriage to a Christian wife who resisted heavy official pressure to divorce him. Remarkably, especially for a Jew, he managed to keep a detailed journal, in which he writes of 'living in fear of Auschwitz'. Of the 1,265 Jews living in Dresden in the summer of 1941, fewer than two hundred were still in the city in February 1945. The bombing came just as those that remained were about to be stripped of their protected status and deported. Here, written down a week or so later, are extracts from Klemperer's entries for 13 and 14 February – a torrent of powerful images.*

Outside it was bright as day. Fires were blazing at Pirnaischer Platz, on Marschallstrasse, and somewhere on or over the Elbe. The ground was covered with broken glass. A terrible strong wind was blowing. Natural or a firestorm? Probably both. In the stairwell of 1 Zeughausstrasse the window frames had been blown in and lay on the steps, partly obstructing them. Broken glass in our rooms upstairs. In the hallway and on the side facing the Elbe, windows blown in, in the bedroom only one; windows also broken in the kitchen, blackout torn in half. Light did not work, no water. We could see big fires on the other side of the Elbe and on Marschallstrasse. Frau Cohn said, in her room furniture had been shifted by the blast. We placed a candle on the table, drank a little cold coffee, ate a little, groped our way over the broken glass, lay down in bed. It was after midnight – we had come upstairs at eleven. I thought: just sleep, we're alive, tonight we'll have peace and quiet, now just put your mind at rest! As she lay down, Eva said: 'But there's glass in my bed!' I heard her stand up, clear away the glass, then I was already asleep. After a while, it must have been after one o'clock, Eva said: 'Air raid warning.' 'I didn't hear anything.' 'Definitely. It wasn't loud, they're going round with hand sirens, there's no electricity.' We stood up. Frau Stühler called at our door: 'Air raid warning.' Eva knocked at Frau Cohn's door – we have heard nothing more of either – and we hurried downstairs. The street was as bright as day and almost empty, fires were burning, the storm was blowing as before. As usual there was a steel-helmeted sentry in front of the wall between the two Zeughausstrasse houses (the wall of the former synagogue with the barracks behind it). In passing I asked him whether there was a warning. 'Yes.' Eva was two steps ahead of me. We came to the entrance hall of No. 3. At that moment a big explosion near by. I knelt, pressing myself up against the wall, close to the courtyard door. When I looked up, Eva had disappeared. I thought she was in our cellar. It was quiet; I ran across the yard to our Jews' cellar. The door was wide open. A group of people cowered whimpering to the right of the door, I knelt on the left, close to the window. I called out several times to Eva. No reply. Big explosions. Again the window in the wall opposite burst open, again it was bright as day, again water was pumped. Then an explosion at the window close to me. Something hard and glowing hot struck the right side of my face. I put my hand up, it was covered in blood, I felt for my eye, it was still there. A group of Russians – where had they come from? – pushed out of the door. I jumped over to them. I had the rucksack on my back, the grey bag with our manuscripts and Eva's jewellery in my hand, my old hat had fallen off. I stumbled and fell. A Russian lifted me up. To the side there was a vaulting, God knows of what already half-destroyed cellar. We crowded in. It was hot. The Russians ran on in some other direction, I with them. Now we stood in an open passageway, heads down, crowded together. In front of me lay a large unrecognisable open space, in the middle of it an enormous crater. Bangs, as light as day, explosions. I had no thoughts, I was not even afraid, I was simply tremendously exhausted, I think I was expecting the end. After a moment I scrambled over some vaulting or a step or a parapet into the open air, threw myself into the crater, lay flat on the ground for a while, then clambered up one side of the crater, over the edge into a telephone kiosk. Someone called out: 'This way, Herr Klemperer!' In the demolished little lavatory building close by stood Eisenmann Sr, little Schorschi in his arms. 'I don't know where my wife is.' 'I don't know where my wife and the other children are.' 'It's getting too hot, the wooden panelling is burning ... over there, the hall of the Reich Bank building!' We ran into a hall, it was surrounded by flames, but looked solid. There seemed to be no more bombs exploding here, but all around everything was ablaze. I could not make out any details; I saw only flames everywhere, heard the noise of the fire and the storm, felt terribly exhausted inside. After a while Eisenmann said: 'We must get down to the Elbe, we'll get through.' ...

The burning went on and on. To the right and left of me the way was still blocked (all the time I thought: to have an accident now would be wretched). Some tower glowed dark red, the tall building with the turret on Pirnaischer Platz seemed about to fall – but I did not see it collapse – the ministry on the other side burned silvery bright. It grew lighter, and I saw a stream of people on the road by the Elbe. But I did not yet have the courage to go down. Finally, probably at about seven, the terrace – the terrace forbidden to Jews – was by now somewhat empty, I walked past the shell of the still burning Belvedere and came to the terrace wall. A number of people were sitting there. After a minute someone called out to me: Eva was sitting unharmed on the suitcase wearing her fur coat. We greeted one another very warmly, and we were completely indifferent to the loss of our belongings, and remain so even now. At the critical moment, someone had literally pulled Eva out of the entrance hall of No. 3 Zeughausstrasse and into the Aryan cellar, she had got out to the street through the cellar window, had seen both Nos. 1 and 3 completely alight, had been in the cellar of the Albertinum for a while, then reached the Elbe through the smoke, had spent the rest of the night partly looking for me ... had in addition observed the destruction of the Thamm building (thus of all our furniture), and partly sitting in a cellar under the Belvedere. Once, as she was searching, she had wanted to light a cigarette and had had no matches; something was glowing on the ground, she wanted to use it – it was a burning corpse. On the whole, Eva had kept her head much better than I, observed much more calmly and gone her own way, even though pieces of wood from a window had struck her head as she was climbing out. (Fortunately the skull was thick and she was unharmed.) The difference: she acted and observed, I followed my instincts, other people, and saw nothing at all. So now it was Wednesday morning, 14 February, and our lives were saved and we were together.

The War in Russia

In August 1939, just before his invasion of Poland, Hitler concluded a non-aggression pact with his old ideological enemy, the Soviet Union. In spite of British and French guarantees of protection, Poland was defeated in a few weeks, and as tides of refugees tried to escape the German advance, Soviet tanks rolled in to seize eastern Poland – as agreed in a secret clause of the treaty. After only twenty-one years of independence, Poland was once again to be partitioned.

Then, in June 1941, following defeat in the battle of Britain, Hitler turned his forces on Russia. Operation Barbarossa brought more than two million service men and women into the theatre of war on both sides – the scale of the operation is still scarcely credible – and by late summer the German advance had reached the approaches to Leningrad and Moscow. For all the planning and preparation of the invasion, the Germans, like Napoleon's Grande Armée in 1812 before, were entirely unprepared for the onslaught of winter on the Russian steppe.

***George Grossjohann**, a Wehrmacht officer who served in four different campaigns – in Poland, Ukraine, Russia and France – did most of his fighting in Russia and Romania between 1941 and 1944. In his memoir* Five Years, Four Fronts *he describes how the triumphant German advance was brought to an abrupt halt.*

The first Russian winter for us came in the early weeks of December, which made it incredibly difficult to construct a continuous front. Instead of using shovels, we had to use explosives to excavate bunkers and trenches. Since the Mius positions were way up front, we could only work on improving them at night. Almost every evening, we had to retake the positions under construction from the Russians, who settled in them as soon as the pioneers stopped working at dawn.

We did not possess a continuous front throughout almost the whole winter of 1941–2. The abundant snowfalls which meanwhile had come also made it impossible for the Russians to penetrate between the geographically disparate villages. My company was deployed in Gribovka, one of those solitary Russian villages directly on the west bank of the Mius. In this icy cold we had the saying, 'He who is thrown out of his village is lost.'

On 11 December 1941, Germany declared war on the United States. When I heard this on my Volksempfänger radio receiver in my cottage in Gribovka, I immediately thought of our little *Oberst* [Colonel] Newiger and his sombre prognosis after the campaign in the west. Indeed, all the world powers had entered the war, and, with the exception of Japan, unfortunately all were against us! ...

My Russian, or more precisely Ukrainian, hosts were as nice and friendly as the French had been during my time in Normandy. I was always given a sofa covered with black wax-coated sheet cloth to sleep on, while the whole family retired to sleep on the giant stove. Unfortunately, my sofa was so full of bugs that in the morning I always looked as if I had measles. My hosts, who seemed to be completely immune to bedbugs, were always greatly amused when I got up in the morning swollen from stings and bites. But their harmless glee in my misfortune was certainly not ill intended.

*In the late autumn of 1942 General von Paulus's 6th Army, which had been racing to seize the southern oilfields, began laying siege to Stalingrad on the Volga. As winter again drew on, the Soviets effected a double en- circlement, besieging the besiegers, who were a force over a quarter of a million strong. In the city itself fighting was at close quarters. The Russians, led by the determined General Chuikov, never lost their toehold on the west bank of the river, and more than ten thousand civilians survived the worst of the fighting. The writer and journalist **Vasily Grossman**, a Russian Jew and the author of some of the best reportage of the conflict, wangled his way across the Volga into Chuikov's headquarters in December 1942 – when the outcome of the siege was far from certain.*

When one enters a bunker and the underground quarters of officers and soldiers, one feels again an ardent wish to retain for ever in one's memory the remarkable traits of this unique life. The lamps and the chimney made from artillery shell cases, cups made of brass shell bases standing on tables near crystal glasses. Next to an anti-tank grenade sits a china ashtray on which is written 'Wife, don't make your husband angry.' There is a huge dull electric bulb in the commander-in-chief's bunker, and a smile from Chuikov, who says: 'Yes, and a chandelier. Aren't we living in a city?' And this volume of Shakespeare in General Gurov's underground office ... All these samovars and gramophones, blue family sugar bowls and round mirrors in wooden frames on the clay walls of basements. All this everyday life, with peaceful household things rescued from the burning buildings.

Journeying across the front to Stalingrad, Grossman had been impressed by the simple resourcefulness of the Russian infantryman in his forward positions – he seemed to need much less for survival in the snow than the German soldier.

At the front line out in the steppe, winter. A hole covered with a groundsheet. A stove made from a helmet. A chimney from a brass shell. The fuel consists of tall weeds. On the march, one soldier carries an armful of tall weeds, another one a handful of chips, the third one a shell, the fourth one a stove.

On 16 December 1942 the Volga froze. This meant that trucks could be driven across the ice to bring food to the besieged who were facing starvation.

All those who, for a hundred days, held on to the Volga crossing and crossed the dark grey icy river, looked into the eyes of a quick, pitiless death. One day someone will sing a song about those who are now asleep on the Volga's bed ...

At night, we could walk upon the Volga. The ice was two days old and did not bend any longer beneath our feet. The moon lit the network of paths, uncountable tracks of sledges. A liaison soldier was walking in front of us, quickly and confidently as if he'd spent half of his life walking on these intermingling paths. Suddenly the ice started cracking. The liaison soldier came to a wide ice clearing, stopped and said: 'Aha! We must have taken the wrong path. We should have stayed to the right.' Liaison men always utter this sort of consoling phrase, no matter where they take you.

Barges smashed by shells have frozen into the ice. There's a bluish glistening of ice-covered hawsers. Sterns rise steeply up, so do the bows of sunken motor boats.

Fighting is still going on in the factories … Guns fire with hollow bangs, rumblings, and the explosions of shells resound drily and clearly. Often, bursts of machine-gun and sub-machine-gun fire can be heard distinctly. This music is fearfully similar to the peaceful work of the plant, like riveting or steam hammers beating steel bars, and flattening them. It is as if liquid steel and slag pouring into a mould are lighting the fresh ice on the Volga with a pink, quick glow.

The sun rises and illuminates the edges of large holes made by heavy bombs. The depths of these frightening holes are always in a gloomy penumbra. The sun is afraid to touch them …

The sun shines over hundreds of railway tracks where tanker wagons are lying like killed horses, with their bellies torn open; where hundreds of freight carriages are jammed one on top of another, blasted there by the force of an explosion, and crowded around cold locomotives like a panic-stricken herd huddling around its leaders.

*By mid-1943 the German armies were retreating along a huge front. That autumn, **Guy Sajer**, a young soldier with the elite Grosse Deutschland Division, found himself on a desperate and interminable march towards the river Dnieper, outside Kiev. They reached Konotop where they hoped to find refuge, but instead found themselves surrounded, their only hope (as their captain, Wesreidau, saw it) a 'swift and brutal breakthrough' to the west.*

I was sick of the whole thing. My stomach was turning over and I felt cold. I looked for Hals or some other friend, but couldn't see any familiar faces. They must all have been sent to a different position. For me, they had become almost like relatives, and their absence weighed on me. I felt very much alone among these mutilated men with their raging fevers, trying to find some excuse for hope and encouragement. I myself began to daydream about a soft bed with silk covers, imitating the veteran, who liked to dream aloud about beds like that, which he himself had never known.

Even before the war, he'd been an unfortunate and unhappy man, but he knew how to dream. Sometimes, as his bony body lay stretched out on the hard ground, he smiled in a way which suggested such a powerful sense of well-being that I am sure, in those moments at least, he was unaware of the harshness of his situation, and that his dream was more powerful than reality. I myself was not yet that well trained, and my dreams could not obliterate the feverish vice which gripped my temples.

Straight ahead, to the west, the smoke had climbed so high it blotted out the sky, and the distant horizon was ringed with fire. What substance could be feeding such a huge conflagration?

Companies of men black with dust and soot were pouring back, on the run. It seemed that our first contact with the Russians had not been in our favour. The retreating troops left a certain number of wounded with us, but no one knew what to do with them. The medical teams, which at best were inadequate, had already packed up and gone, or were about to leave. The wounded men were left lying in the street where they had been put down, trying to staunch the flood of their own blood, which was often pouring from several wounds at once. Everyone tried to help as much as possible, but we were capable only of ludicrous gestures. The most extraordinary scenes unfolded in front of our incredulous eyes. As we were sponging off a fellow who'd passed out, a fat *gefreiter* [lance corporal] came to help us, explaining that he'd just dropped a fellow with a smashed knee. 'He was making too much noise, and I couldn't stand it. Give me someone who's knocked out, any time.'

For the moment, our stretch of cleared street was not under bombardment. The battle was raging directly ahead, as well as to the north-west and south-west. Directly to the north, the Russian artillery was raking over the ruins like a monstrous plough. However, as a few of the retreating men huddled beside us trying to catch their breath, the Russian fire shifted, and began to sweep through our position like a giant scythe. Our officers' orders were drowned by the shouts of the men, and the uproar of a frantic stampede for shelter.

Our jostling and cries for help and screams of panic were finally obliterated by explosions. Everyone who was able to had run off the street. The slightest protuberance offered some hope of survival, as a wall of fire passed over the two thousand troops concentrated on that spot. The wounded, abandoned in the open, lay writhing in the dust. Through the uproar, we could hear the sound of disarticulated bodies falling back to the ground in broken pieces. As at Belgorod, the earth shook, and everything trembled and grew dim, as the whole landscape suddenly became mobile. The filthy hands of ill and wounded men resigned to death scratched the ground for one last time, and the lined faces of veterans who believed they had already seen everything were transformed by desperate, imploring panic. Quite near us, behind a heap of tiles, a Russian shell scored a bull's-eye, exploding in the midst of eleven men who had huddled together like children caught in a sudden rain. The Russian shell landed in the precise centre of their trembling group, mixing flesh and bones and tiles in a torrent of blood.

Chance, which continued to favour me, had driven me along with three companions to the shelter of a staircase in a roofless house. The building was hit on all sides during the bombardment, and the cellar filled with broken beams and other debris. However, thanks to our extraordinary helmets, our heads survived intact. When the thunder stopped for a moment and we heard the screams of the newly wounded, we looked outside. The horror of what we saw was so overwhelming that we fell back, as if paralysed, on to the shaky stairs.

'God help us,' someone shouted. 'There's nothing but blood.'

'We've got to get away from here,' screamed another voice, in a tone close to madness.

He ran outside, and we followed him. The air was filled with bestial cries. Everyone who'd been lucky enough to survive was falling back to the west, where, as always, safety lay, and now the front, and the gap through which we would try to escape. Anyone who could still stand was helped. The wounded grabbed at the men running past. Two haggard soldiers in front of me were dragging a third man through the dust, probably a friend who was nearly dead. How long had they pulled him along like that, and how long would it take them to dump him?

I can no longer tell how long our stampede lasted, through the anonymous ruins and thick smoke and roaring guns. The Russians were firing at us from all sides, at close range, with 50-millimetre guns. We staggered on carrying the wounded as best we could.

In complete disorder, we came to a railroad track strewn with the burnt-out wreckage of a train, and a few Russian corpses. We trampled over them with a kind of fierce delight, taking our revenge for their artillery and their 50-millimetre fire. The tracks ran through a kind of trench. We galloped down it, passing a second train as still and broken as the first. Some of our vehicles seemed to be parked there too, surrounded by a crowd of soldiers and several *Panzermänner* [tank troops]. We ran right into a group of officers. Wesreidau, who had stayed with us throughout, was one of them. We were given a few minutes' rest, and everyone dropped where he stood. To the south-west, the din seemed to have increased tenfold, and made my head swim.

Then we received a fresh blow. Wesreidau and two of his aides ran through the groups of exhausted men.

'Get up! Get moving! We've got to push on now! The division has broken through. If you don't hurry, we'll be caught in the trap, so get the hell up! We're the last ones left.' ...

We fought our way through the fires of hell, losing almost half of our remaining men, as we pushed for more than nine hours, from shell-hole to shell-hole, along the famous and tragic Konotop-Kiev road, past burnt-out tanks and piles of hundreds of shrivelled corpses.

The War in Europe Ends

Across the battlefields of Europe in 1945 many were taken by surprise by the end of the war. Hundreds of prisoners of war were marched back from camps in Poland before the advancing Russian armies. They joined a flood of hundreds of thousands of refugees – some ten million Germans would leave the Baltic lands and the marches of eastern Europe in the aftermath of defeat.

Fey von Hassell's father, Germany's former ambassador to Rome, had battled against Hitler since before the war began, and once it had started, became the chief political adviser to the main group of military officers opposed to the Nazis. He was finally implicated in the July 1944 bomb plot, and admitted his involvement under Gestapo interrogation.

The executions and imprisonments that followed the bomb plot were not restricted to those directly involved. Fey, as von Hassell's daughter, was arrested by the SS at her Italian husband's villa near Venice, and was taken to Innsbruck with her two sons. The boys were literally wrenched from her and then vanished – neither she nor anyone else in the family would know where they were for almost a year. She herself was moved from camp to camp, often on the march, occasionally imprisoned, and always in imminent fear of execution. Even a month before the war officially ended, and while the remnants of the Reich were in flames, the SS was still issuing orders on behalf of Himmler for the execution of prisoners likely to fall into Allied hands. Fey and her fellows owed their survival to a Briton, Captain Sigismund Payne Best, who had banded them together and used his influence with one of the chief SS guards, Edgar Stiller, to save their lives. They finally crossed into Italian South Tyrol, where one of their number, Colonel von Bonin, made contact with an old friend now serving in the German Southern Army.

This extract from A Mother's War *describes a moment of terror just outside Villabassa.*

Somehow, during that long afternoon, I could sense that the guards' attitude towards us was changing. They realised that we were becoming more powerful, and hence they became more friendly. They talked openly about their longing to return home, free from the harsh glare of their superiors. They speculated along with the rest of us about what would happen next. They knew that they could no longer be compelled to take part in atrocities that had made them old beyond their years. Their eyes took on renewed vitality; they even began to laugh and joke with us. Strange as it may seem, in such a desperate situation, with their ravaged country on the brink of defeat, I had the impression that those men were happy for the first time in a long while.

Only later was I to find out what was happening while we remained cooped up in that bus. [Colonel von] Bonin and [Dr Wilhelm] Flügge had, during the long journey over the mountains, overheard a conversation among the SS sergeants in the front. After a quick glance around, they had assumed that their tired prisoners were asleep. Instead, Bonin and Flügge were slumped over, only feigning sleep, and so had heard these words: 'What are we going to do about those who still have to be liquidated? Well, we were ordered to put the bomb under the bus either just before or just after the ——'

Although neither of the two could make out the rest of that phrase, they had heard enough to realise that something had to be done urgently. Bonin knew that the headquarters of the German Southern Army had to be somewhere near by. The army commander, General Heinrich von Vietinghoff, was a friend of his from his days on the General Staff. If only they could contact the general, perhaps he could help. They had said nothing to the rest of us for fear that we might panic.

When Bonin and Flügge reached the centre of Villabassa, they saw on the other side of the road a group of German officers standing and talking. One was a general. Bonin looked, and then looked again. His eyes had not deceived him! There across the road was General von Vietinghoff himself! Astonished and excited, he rushed over and hugged the general, whispering in his ear that urgent help was needed.

Vietinghoff grasped immediately the main elements of the colonel's surprising story – that there was a strange collection of important hostages sitting in buses just outside the town who were, at any moment, going to be blown up by the SS. The general promised to take 'appropriate measures'. A delicate ceasefire had just been negotiated with the Allies, and on no account would he allow the slaughter of innocent civilians under his jurisdiction. Then, without another word, Vietinghoff was driven off.

Bonin and Flügge quickly discovered that our SS commanders were at the Hotel Bachmann, really a small country inn in the main square of the village. So they went straight to the place themselves, where they found Bader, Stiller and several other SS stuffing themselves with sausages and beer. Bader was apparently incensed to see his two 'prisoners' walk in the door, but after a strained pause, he turned back to his food. Bonin and Flügge ordered a coffee and settled down at another table.

About an hour went by, with our two companions wondering what, if anything, General von Vietinghoff would do to help. Then suddenly the door burst open, and in walked a Wehrmacht major with pistol at the ready and a squad of soldiers behind him. He shouted at the astonished SS men, who had no time to react. Bader went into a rage, but the major told him to shut up and to hand over all weapons. One of the SS, who had pulled out a pistol, was arrested and taken away. After a dressing down by the major, the others were let free, except for Stiller, who, thinking it would be safer, elected to remain at the inn with Bonin. The latter apparently agreed, because Stiller, unlike Bader, had always shown at least a grudging sympathy towards us and had been particularly friendly with Captain Payne Best. All this happened in the space of a few minutes. When the air had cleared, Bonin, Flügge and the Wehrmacht officer sat down, satisfied, and ordered themselves something to drink.

In the meantime, the rest of us were still stuck in the bus, getting hungrier, thirstier and more impatient by the minute. It was already late afternoon. Although we had absolutely no idea of the danger we had been in, we were worried about our two companions and wondered what had happened to the SS commanders. The young guards were also becoming restless and nervous. Incredibly enough, we eventually persuaded them to let some of us walk down to Villabassa, while they remained watching the bus!

As we made our way in the beating rain towards the village, a convoy of German army trucks hurtled past. Soldiers were leaning out, shouting at everyone they saw, 'There's peace, there's peace! We're going home!' Although we had been expecting it for so long, it came as a shock. Maybe that was why Bader had not returned.

We pressed on towards the village in great excitement, easily finding the Bachmann, where the others were eating and celebrating. Captain Payne Best was already there with another Wehrmacht officer who had been with us, General Georg Thomas. They, too, had evidently had the same idea and persuaded their guards to let them go. Best was talking with Major Werner Alvensleben, the officer who had just disarmed the SS. For the first time, we ordered drinks like ordinary people.

I had a long talk with Alvensleben, who I discovered knew my family. I had once even stayed on his family's estate with my parents! Moreover, this Alvensleben turned out to be the brother of the SD man in Udine who had refused to help me when I had been arrested at Brazzà. When I asked him about this brother, the major said bitterly, 'Let's not talk about him. As you can imagine, he's the black sheep of the family! He has always been a Nazi, and I only hope for his sake that he doesn't make it through the end of the war.'

Alvensleben said that he and his ten or so soldiers would remain in charge of us, but as protectors rather than as warders. These were the orders of General von Vietinghoff. The Wehrmacht was worried that Bader and his band of SS men, who were still in the vicinity of Villabassa, might make a last determined attempt to carry out the order to liquidate us.

The most urgent problem was to arrange sleeping quarters for our large group. The town was already crowded with German soldiers and refugees, and the hotel was full. After negotiations with some town officials, the older people, like the Blums and the Thyssens, were put into the local parish priest's house; others were quartered in different private houses. Now that we were known as ex-prisoners of the SS, it was easier to persuade people to take us in. For lack of anywhere else, we younger women were to sleep on mattresses on the floor of the hotel. Much better than sleeping in the buses for yet another night! At around seven o'clock the hotel staff brought in some delicious hot food, and the traditional soup: Tyrolean *Knödel* [dumplings]. It was the first good food that we had had since Schönberg!

During the evening, groups of excited soldiers on their way home kept coming into the hotel. Some insisted that the war was not yet over, shouting, 'Churchill and the Americans are going to join us in an attack on the Russians. We must throw them out of our country. You will see, now we'll go against the Russians!' I think they already knew that it was not going to happen. But imagining what the Russians were doing to their wives, mothers and daughters, they were desperate. Besides everything else, this pathetic ranting brought home to me the criminality of Hitler and the Nazis against the Germans themselves.

René Cutforth endured three years as a prisoner of war. He was captured in North Africa, and was shipped from Italy into Germany, where he spent nearly two years in Offlag 12B near Coblenz on the Rhine. There the escape attempts stopped, and Cutforth began to feel that he was 'going round the bend' after the RAF bombed the nearby railway and smashed a lavatory window, revealing a highly obscene and very stark portrait of Hitler on the gallows. The punishment parade that followed starred the commandant and an officer known as 'the man who died at Stalingrad'. Cutforth was finally turned loose as British aircraft attacked his prison train.

The war ended for us by a stream. Two men from the camp heard a rustle in the bushes across the water and looked up to see a tank on the other side nose its way to the edge. Its gun came hard round on them but immediately a head popped up through the turret.

'Who are you?' it said.

'British prisoners of war.'

'Got any Krauts over there?'

'Yes, prison officers and guards.'

'Well, send them over.'

That was the last we saw of the commandant, Hauptmann [Captain] Foerster, and the man who died at Stalingrad – up to their chins in cold water, stepping gingerly into captivity.

The Americans had come and gone in a flash. They stayed about half an hour. After sending their tanks through all the barbed wire and shooting up the prison camp guards, they had released about 250,000 slave-labour prisoners in the area and twenty thousand POWs and then they zoomed on down the road.

'Sorry, boys. We've got to go. Got a date with the Ruskies just a few blocks up.' What they left behind was in fact total chaos.

I shall always see the end of the war not as VE Day in London or even my return to England but as Hermann Goering Strasse in Lollar at seven o'clock that night.

Huge bonfires were lit from end to end of the street and fed on the good solid furniture dragged from the citizens' houses. The Hermann Goering Strasse was lined with ornate silvered lamp-standards, very solid, and with cross-pieces to put the ladders on for repairs. The lamps were out, but from each cross-piece dangled a nasty corpse – they were the camp commandants, commandants of the Russian women's slave-labour camp, the Polish women's slave-labour camp, the Russian prisoner of war camp and all their officers and head guards. Between the bonfires the over-stuffed mattresses of the German rich had been dragged into the street and on these in the red light the rescued Russian and Polish girls, stark naked, were giving of their best to all comers in a sort of frenzy of giving rather than a frenzy of sex. In the side streets the comrades and the Poles, already armed with guns, were exchanging rapid fire from windows and from behind pillar boxes. Corpses littered the H.G. Strasse. A great ring of Russians at one end of the street had pushed into the middle a soldier in a singlet with a great round shaven head lolling like an imbecile's. He was dancing like a genius whilst in deepest bass and shrill falsetto and with a complicated pattern of handclapping, all of them concentrated intensely on giving him the music for the ballet called 'The End of the War'.

The other end of the street was Polish, and here a manic figure with rapt face and streaming hair had claimed as his loot a huge grand piano. It was chocked up on an island in the middle of the street, and there all night among the bonfires below the corpses, the mad Pole played on.

Cutforth did not go home to England. Confinement for three years in POW cages had persuaded him it was safer to walk on the wild side.

In the spring of 1945 I was sitting on a ration box under a piece of corrugated iron jammed across the angle of two ruined walls, all that was left of a customs shed on an airport in East Germany. I don't know the name of the place – I don't think I ever did. I'd been sitting there for about a week. The Canadian paratroopers who ran the place sent me enormous meals of eggs and bacon and beans and bread and tea about six times a day. I fell on each new dixieful like a ravening wolf. My stomach wasn't hungry, but I was. Partly because I had just finished three years as a prisoner of war, but mainly for some deeper-seated reason which I didn't care to examine. Eating seemed to me to be the only activity that was safe to get involved in. Everything else seemed to lead backwards or forwards. Backwards to my life before the war which I wanted no part of – I disowned it – or forwards into the sheer irrelevance of life in the British army and a future of name, rank and unit, orders, conversation in the mess, and finally no doubt the imbecilities of economic competition in civilian England. A trap. Life was a series of traps. Childhood first, trapped in a family. Then a meaningless school. Then the irrelevant rituals of social behaviour, trapped in a job. Then the army, and then, as if to underline the lesson once and for all, the prison camp I had got out of ten days before. The lesson was not lost. That was going to be the lot. No more traps for me, and in case anyone insisted on confronting me with one, I had, tucked into the waistband of my old khaki battledress trousers, a heavy Mauser pistol and ten of its great savage slugs. I was wearing one of those American Air Force jackets with a fur collar which I'd stolen from a delousing dump (how rich the Yanks were). I had about a foot of beard and very long dirty hair and I still wore my old desert boots although the soles were flapping away from the uppers. I must have looked like a tough proposition: in fact, though, as I sat there in the early summer sunshine I'd reverted to a technique of my childhood when confronted by a strange hostile dog. I had believed that if I stayed very still it might go away.

Three or four of the paratroopers came across to eat their elevenses out of the wind in my shelter. They'd brought another great dixieful for me and as I was wolfing it down, one of them began shaking his head from side to side and kept this up for a long time.

'I don't get it,' he finally said, since I took no notice.

'What.'

'You've been sitting here now for a week and before that you were wandering around loose in occupied Germany. What is keeping you? Why the hell don't you go home?'

'Don't want home,' I said.

'Well, what I have to tell you is this, Bud,' the paratrooper said, 'and it's straight up. The station commander thinks you're a nut. "I can't have that nut living in this shelter," he said. "One day some general will look in on us and raise hell about him." '

'When he does, I'll leave,' I said.

'Oh yes, you'll leave for the nuthouse with a posse of psychologists, or there is another thing. You're a deserter,' he said. It had never crossed my mind.

'Oh hell, I am through with the war,' I said.

'Yes, but is the war through with you? Now look, you see that dirty old kite over there? The old Dakota? Now that takes off in half an hour. It lands in England four hours later. That's what it's there for, picking up fellows like you on the loose – for one reason or another. All you do is go and sit in it. Well, I have to go. Been nice knowing you. Give it a thought, fellow.'

I gave it a thought for twenty-five minutes, then I walked over and climbed into the Dakota with all my worldly possessions and five packs of Camel cigarettes. There were a dozen other men on the plane, all very dirty and most of them asleep. Nobody talked much and at three o'clock in the afternoon, we came down on a runway in a field full of buttercups in Oxfordshire. I had been away four years. It was England all right. There was that special kind of early summer light calming down the romantic distances, and turning the hedgerows into dark blue mists.

With the Allied advance into Germany came the discovery of the camps. Patrick Gordon-Walker, later a Labour MP and cabinet minister, was one of the first British officers into the concentration camp at Bergen-Belsen

*near Hanover, which was liberated on 12 April 1945. It was not an exter-
mination camp as such, but it might as well have been. Jewish prisoners were
neglected and allowed to starve. And typhus was rife.*

We had only a handful of men so far, and the SS stayed there that night.
The first night of liberty, many hundreds of people died of joy.

Next day some men of the Yeomanry arrived. The people crowded
around them kissing their hands and feet – and dying from weakness.
Corpses in every state of decay were lying around, piled up on top of each
other in heaps. There were corpses in the compound in flocks. People were
falling dead all around, people who were walking skeletons. One woman
came up to a soldier who was guarding the milk store and doling the milk
out to children, and begged for milk for her baby. The man took the baby
and saw that it had been dead for days, black in the face and shrivelled
up. The woman went on begging for milk. So he poured some on the dead
lips. The mother then started to croon with joy and carried the baby off in
triumph. She stumbled and fell dead in a few yards. I have this story and
some others on records spoken by the men who saw them ...

I went into the typhus ward, packed thick with people lying in dirty
rags of blankets on the floor, groaning and moaning. By the door sat an
English Tommy talking to the people and cheering them up. They couldn't
understand what he said, and he was continually ladling milk out of a
cauldron. I collected together some women who could speak English and
German and began to make records. An amazing thing is the number who
managed to keep themselves clean and neat. All of them said that in a day
or two more, they would have gone under from hunger and weakness.

There are three main classes in the camp: the healthy, who have
managed to keep themselves decent, but nearly all of these had typhus;
then there were the sick, who were more or less cared for by their friends;
then there was the vast underworld that had lost all self-respect, crawling
around in rags, living in abominable squalor, defecating in the compound,
often mad or half-mad. By the other prisoners they are called Mussulmen.
It is these who are still dying like flies. They can hardly walk on their legs.
Thousands still of these cannot be saved, and if they were, they would be
in lunatic asylums for the short remainder of their pitiful lives.

*Among those who died of typhus in Belsen was **Anne Frank**. She was the daughter of German-Jewish parents who had moved to Amsterdam in 1933 to escape the encroaching anti-Semitism in Germany. Holland did not prove a safe haven for long. In May 1940 the Nazis occupied Belgium and the Netherlands, and in July 1942, increasingly fearful for their safety, the family went into hiding. Anne was thirteen. For the next two years she kept a remarkable diary until, in August 1944, the eight fugitives in the 'Secret Annexe'* were betrayed, along with their protectors. Anne was taken first to Auschwitz, and, at the end of October, to Belsen. It is thought that she died in February or March 1945, just a month or two before the liberation.*

Anne's diary took the form of letters to her friend Kitty. It was in November 1942 that Mr Dussel became the eighth person to take up residence in the Annexe. He brought grim news from the outside world, little of which had reached those already in hiding.

Mr Dussel has told us much about the outside world we've missed for so long. He had sad news. Countless friends and acquaintances have been taken off to a dreadful fate. Night after night, green and grey military vehicles cruise the streets. They knock on every door, asking whether any Jews live there. If so, the whole family is immediately taken away. If not, they proceed to the next house. It's impossible to escape their clutches unless you go into hiding. They often go around with lists, knocking only on those doors where they know there's a big haul to be made. They frequently offer a bounty, so much per head. It's like the slave hunts of the olden days. I don't mean to make light of this; it's much too tragic for that. In the evenings when it's dark, I often see long lines of good, innocent people, accompanied by crying children, walking on and on, ordered about by a handful of men who bully and beat them until they nearly drop. No one is spared. The sick, the elderly, children, babies and pregnant women – all are marched to their death.

We're so fortunate here, away from the turmoil. We wouldn't have to give a moment's thought to all this suffering if it weren't for the fact that we're so worried about those we hold dear, whom we can no longer help. I

---

* The Secret Annexe has since become a museum and national memorial to the victims of the Holocaust.

feel wicked sleeping in a warm bed, while somewhere out there my dearest friends are dropping from exhaustion or being knocked to the ground.

I get frightened myself when I think of close friends who are now at the mercy of the cruellest monsters ever to stalk the earth.

And all because they're Jews.

In Poland, five years of Nazi and Soviet occupation had been, from the outset, exceptionally ferocious. The SS and the Gestapo had free rein in many towns, including Warsaw, where the Jews were herded into ghettos. Those that did not starve were later marked down for extermination in camps built on Polish soil. Non-Jews found themselves fodder for slave labour and deportation.

*In April and May 1943, the survivors of the Warsaw ghetto staged an uprising against the Nazis. It was suppressed, and sixty thousand Jews were murdered in the aftermath. The Italian journalist **Curzio Malaparte**, that disaffected supporter of Mussolini, was sent by an Italian paper to cover the fighting on the Eastern Front and used his accreditation in the Fascist cause to visit Warsaw before the rising. The Nazi authorities even allowed him to enter the 'forbidden' walled zone of the ghetto, where disease was already at work.*

Jewish policemen stood in pairs at the street crossings with the Star of David stamped in red on their yellow armlets; they stood motionless and impassive amid the incessant traffic of sledges pulled by troikas of boys, baby carriages, hand carts loaded with furniture, heaps of rags, old iron, and all sorts of miserable junk. From time to time groups of people gathered at street corners, stamped their feet on the frozen snow and clapped their open hands on their shoulders; they stood close with their arms round one another – ten, twenty, thirty of them, in order to give each other a little warmth. The squalid little Nalewki, Przyrynek and Zakroczymska street cafés were crowded with old, bearded men, standing pressed together, silent, perhaps like animals giving each other warmth and courage. When we appeared on the threshold those who were near the door drew back in fear; I heard some frightened screams, some groans; then silence fell again, broken only by panting breaths, the silence of animals already resigned to death. All gazed at the Black Guard who followed me. All gazed at his angel's face, a face that all recognised, that all had seen a hundred times shining amid the olive trees near the gates of Jericho, of Sodom, of Jerusalem. The face of an angel announcing God's wrath. Then I smiled, I said, '*Prosze pana* (I beg your pardon),' and I was aware that those words to them were a wonderful present. I said '*Prosze pana*' smiling, and all around me I saw smiles of wonder, of joy and of gratitude, coming to life on those faces the colour of soiled paper. I said '*Prosze pana*' and I smiled.

Squads of young men went through the streets picking up the dead bodies; they went into the halls, climbed the stairs and found their way into the rooms. They were young gravediggers, mostly, students from Berlin, Munich and Vienna, some deported from Belgium, Holland, France and Romania. Many of them had once been rich and happy; they had lived in beautiful homes; they had grown up amid fine furniture, old pictures, books, musical instruments, valuable silver and delicate china; and now, their clothes in tatters, they laboriously dragged feet wrapped in rags through the slush. They spoke French, Czech, Romanian and the mellow Viennese German; they were cultured young men trained in the best universities of Europe – ragged, hungry, devoured by vermin, still sore from the blows, the insults and the suffering that they had endured in concentration camps and during the awful trek from Vienna, from Berlin, from Munich, from Paris, from Prague, from Bucharest to the ghetto of Warsaw. But there was a wonderful light in their faces, a youthful determination to help one another, to relieve the measureless misery of their people; there was gentle and resolute challenge in their gaze. I lingered to watch them during their work of mercy, and in a low voice I said in French: '*Un jour vous serez libres, vous serez heureux et libres*' (Some day you will be free, some day you will be happy and free), and the young gravediggers lifted their faces and looked at me smiling. Then they turned their eyes slowly on the Black Guard who followed me like a shadow; they gazed fixedly upon the cruel-faced and handsome Angel, the death-warning Angel of the Scriptures, and they bent over the dead bodies stretched out on the pavements – they bent over, bringing their own happy smiles close to the bluish faces of the dead. They lifted the dead gently as if they were lifting wooden statues, and they placed them on carts drawn by teams of ragged and wan youths; the outlines of the corpses remained in the snow with those horrible and mysterious yellowish stains that corpses leave on everything that comes into contact with them. Packs of bony dogs ran sniffing after these funeral processions; and flocks of ragged boys, their faces marked with hunger, lack of sleep and fear, scoured the snow picking up rags, pieces of paper, empty tins, potato peelings – all that precious refuse that is always left by hunger, poverty and death.

Sometimes I heard within the houses soft singing and monotonous wailing that broke off as soon as I appeared on the threshold. An indescribable stench of filth, wet clothing and dead flesh filled the air in the squalid rooms in which pitiful throngs of old people, women and children lived heaped like prisoners in a crowded jail, some sitting on the floor, some leaning against the walls, some stretched out on bundles of straw and paper. On the beds lay the sick, the dying and the dead. Everyone suddenly became silent, staring at me, staring at the Angel who followed me. A few went on silently chewing some miserable morsel. Others, mostly young people with wan faces, with blank eyes that the lenses of spectacles made larger, were gathered around the window, reading. That too was a means of cheating the debasing expectancy of death. Occasionally, when we appeared, someone would rise from the ground, turn away from the wall or leave a group of his companions and come to meet us slowly, saying softly in German: 'Let's go.'

On 1 August 1944, Tadeusz Komorowski led another rising in Warsaw, naïvely hoping that the advancing Russians would support the Poles. He little realised that Russian policy was to leave them to their fate. The rebels' quarter was set on fire and their community crushed by the Germans, while the Red Army waited on the banks of the Vistula.

One of the survivors of the ghetto, and the rising, was **Wladyslaw Szpilman***, known to the world today simply as 'the pianist' after his memoir of salvation was made into an Oscar-winning film. Here he describes the end of the ghetto and the torching of Warsaw on Hitler's specific order.*

I was alone: alone not just in a single building or even a single part of a city, but alone in a whole city that only two months ago had had a population of a million and a half and was one of the richer cities of Europe. It now consisted of the chimneys of burnt-out buildings pointing to the sky, and whatever walls the bombing had spared: a city of rubble and ashes under which the centuries-old culture of my people and the bodies of hundreds of thousands of murdered victims lay buried, rotting in the warmth of these late autumn days and filling the air with a dreadful stench.

People visited the ruins only by day, riff-raff from outside the city furtively slinking about with shovels over their shoulders, scattering through the cellars in search of loot. One of them chose my own ruined home. He mustn't find me here; no one was to know of my presence. When he came up the stairs and was only two floors below me, I roared in a savage, threatening voice, 'What's going on? Get out! Rrraus!'

He shot away like a startled rat: the last of the wretched, a man scared off by the voice of the last poor devil left alive here.

Szpilman fled from house to house, but towards the end of the German occupation he suddenly found his hideout occupied by a German rear party.

A tall, elegant German officer was leaning against the kitchen dresser, his arms crossed over his chest.

'What are you doing here?' he repeated. 'Don't you know the staff of the Warsaw fortress commando unit is moving into this building any time now?'

I slumped on the chair by the larder door. With the certainty of a sleepwalker, I suddenly felt that my strength would fail me if I tried to escape this new trap. I sat there groaning and gazing dully at the officer. It was some time before I stammered, with difficulty, 'Do what you like to me. I'm not moving from here.'

'I've no intention of doing anything to you!' The officer shrugged his shoulders. 'What do you do for a living?'

'I'm a pianist.'

He looked at me more closely, and with obvious suspicion. Then his glance fell on the door leading from the kitchen to the other rooms. An idea seemed to have struck him.

'Come with me, will you?'

We went into the next room, which had obviously been the dining room, and then into the room beyond it, where a piano stood by the wall. The officer pointed to the instrument.

'Play something!'

Hadn't it occurred to him that the sound of the piano would instantly attract all the SS men in the vicinity? I looked enquiringly at him and did not move. He obviously sensed my fears, since he added reassuringly, 'It's all right, you can play. If anyone comes, you hide in the larder and I'll say it was me trying the instrument out.'

When I placed my fingers on the keyboard they shook. So this time, for a change, I had to buy my life by playing the piano! I hadn't practised for two and a half years, my fingers were stiff and covered with a thick layer of dirt, and I had not cut my nails since the fire in the building where I was hiding. Moreover, the piano was in a room without any window panes, so its action was swollen by the damp and resisted the pressure of the keys.

I played Chopin's Nocturne in C sharp minor. The glassy, tinkling sound of the untuned strings rang through the empty flat and the stairway, floated through the ruins of the villa on the other side of the street and returned as a muted, melancholy echo. When I had finished, the silence seemed even gloomier and more eerie than before. A cat mewed in a street somewhere. I heard a shot down below outside the building – a harsh, loud German noise.

The officer looked at me in silence. After a while he sighed, and muttered, 'All the same, you shouldn't stay here. I'll take you out of the city, to a village. You'll be safer there.'

I shook my head. 'I can't leave this place,' I said firmly.

Only now did he seem to understand my real reason for hiding among the ruins. He started nervously.

'You're Jewish?' he asked.

'Yes.'

He had been standing with his arms crossed over his chest; he now unfolded them and sat down in the armchair by the piano, as if this discovery called for lengthy reflection.

'Yes, well,' he murmured, 'in that case I see you really can't leave.'

He appeared to be deep in thought again for some time, and then turned to me with another question. 'Where are you hiding?'

'In the attic.'

'Show me what it's like up there.'

We went upstairs. He inspected the attic with a careful and expert eye.

In so doing he discovered something I had not yet noticed: a kind of extra floor above it, a loft made of boards under the roof valley and directly above the entrance to the attic itself. At first glance you hardly noticed it because the light was so dim there. The officer said he thought I should hide in this loft, and he helped me look for a ladder in the flats below. Once I was up in the loft I must pull the ladder up after me.

When we had discussed this plan and put it into action, he asked if I had anything to eat.

'No,' I said. After all, he had taken me unawares while I was searching for supplies.

'Well, never mind,' he added hastily, as if ashamed in retrospect of his surprise attack. 'I'll bring you some food.'

Only now did I venture a question of my own. I simply could not restrain myself any longer. 'Are you German?'

He flushed, and almost shouted his answer in agitation, as if my question had been an insult. 'Yes, I am! And ashamed of it, after everything that's been happening.'

Abruptly, he shook hands with me and left.

Three days passed before he reappeared. It was evening, and pitch-dark, when I heard a whisper under my loft. 'Hello, are you there?'

'Yes, I'm here,' I replied.

Soon afterwards something heavy landed beside me. Through the paper, I felt several loaves and something soft, which later turned out to be jam wrapped in greaseproof paper. I quickly put the package to one side and called, 'Wait a moment!'

The voice in the dark sounded impatient. 'What is it? Hurry up. The guards saw me come in here, and I mustn't stay long.'

'Where are the Soviet troops?'

'They're already in Warsaw, in Praga on the other side of the Vistula. Just hang on a few more weeks – the war will be over by spring at the latest.'

The voice fell silent. I did not know if the officer was still there, or if he had gone. But suddenly he spoke again, 'You must hang on, do you hear?' His voice sounded harsh, almost as if he were giving an order, convincing me of his unyielding belief that the war would end well for us. Only then did I hear the quiet sound of the attic door closing.

Szpilman's rescuer was **Wilm Hosenfeld***. Here is Hosenfeld's diary entry for Sunday, 11 August 1944.*

The Führer is to issue a decree that Warsaw is to be razed to the ground. A start has been made already. All the streets liberated in the uprising are being destroyed by fire. The inhabitants have to leave the city, and are going westward in crowds of many thousands. If the news of this decree is true then it's clear to me that we have lost Warsaw, and with it Poland and the war itself. We are giving up a place we held for five years, extending it and telling the world it was a forfeit of war. Monstrous methods were used here. We acted as if we were the masters and would never go away. Now we can't help seeing that all is lost, we're destroying our own work, everything of which the civil administration was so proud – it saw its great cultural tasks as being here and wanted to prove their necessity to the world. Our policy in the east is bankrupt, and we are erecting a final memorial to it with the destruction of Warsaw.

Primo Levi*, by profession a research chemist, arrived at Auschwitz in 1944 – which, as he said later with truthful irony, was 'a piece of good fortune': the German war machine was by then so overstretched that those who could work were not immediately murdered. Levi was born in Turin in 1919 in a large family apartment where he lived all his life except for the time he spent as a partisan in the mountains, then at Auschwitz and finally on the perilous journey home. Sephardic Jews by descent, his family had been in Italy for more than three and a half centuries at the point when Mussolini, under pressure from Hitler, declared them to be aliens and outcasts.*

He was taken to Auschwitz after being captured in the winter of 1943 in northern Italy. By his own confession Levi had not been a very effective member of the resistance, but of Auschwitz he would be the master chronicler. Here, taken from his memoir If This Is a Man, *he describes the moment when he is tattooed with his prisoner inmate number.*

Häftling:* I have learnt that I am *Häftling.* My number is 174517; we have been baptised, we will carry the tattoo on our left arm until we die.

The operation was slightly painful and extraordinarily rapid: they

---

* Prisoner.

placed us all in a row, and one by one, according to the alphabetical order of our names, we filed past a skilful official, armed with a sort of pointed tool with a very short needle. It seems that this is the real, true initiation: only by 'showing one's number' can one get bread and soup. Several days passed, and not a few cuffs and punches, before we became used to showing our number promptly enough not to disorder the daily operation of food distribution; weeks and months were needed to learn its sound in the German language. And for many days, while the habits of freedom still led me to look for the time on my wristwatch, my new name ironically appeared instead, a number tattooed in bluish characters under the skin.

Only much later, and slowly, a few of us learned something of the funereal science of the numbers of Auschwitz, which epitomise the stages of destruction of European Judaism. To the old hands of the camp, the numbers told everything: the period of entry into the camp, the convoy of which one formed a part, and consequently the nationality. Everyone will treat with respect the numbers from 30,000 to 80,000: there are only a few hundred left and they represented the few survivals from the Polish ghettos. It is as well to watch out in commercial dealings with a 116,000 or a 117,000: they now number only about forty, but they represent the Greeks of Salonika, so take care they do not pull the wool over your eyes. As for the High Numbers, they carry an essentially comic air about them, like the words 'freshman' or 'conscript' in ordinary life. The typical High Number is a corpulent, docile and stupid fellow: he can be convinced that leather shoes are distributed at the infirmary to all those with delicate feet, and can be persuaded to run there and leave his bowl of soup 'in your custody'; you can sell him a spoon for three rations of bread; you can send him to the most ferocious of the Kapos to ask him (as happened to me!) if it is true that his is the *Kartoffelschalenkommando*, the 'Potato Peeling Command', and if one can be enrolled in it.

In fact, the whole process of introduction to what was for us a new order took place in a grotesque and sarcastic manner. When the tattooing operation was finished, they shut us in a vacant hut. The bunks are made, but we are severely forbidden to touch or sit on them: so we wander around aimlessly for half the day in the limited space available, still tormented by the parching thirst of the journey. Then the door opens and a boy in a striped suit comes in, with a fairly civilised air, small, thin and blond. He speaks French and we throng around him with a flood of questions which till now we had asked each other in vain.

But he does not speak willingly; no one here speaks willingly. We are new, we have nothing and we know nothing; why waste time on us? He reluctantly explains to us that all the others are out at work and will come back in the evening. He has come out of the infirmary this morning and is exempt from work for today. I asked him (with an ingenuousness that only a few days later already seemed incredible to me) if at least they would give us back our toothbrushes. He did not laugh, but with his face animated by fierce contempt, he threw at me '*Vous n'êtes pas à la maison.*' And it is this refrain that we hear repeated by everyone. You are not at home, this is not a sanatorium, the only exit is by way of the Chimney. (What did it mean? Soon we were all to learn what it meant.)

And it was in fact so. Driven by thirst, I eyed a fine icicle outside the window, within hand's reach. I opened the window and broke off the icicle but at once a large, heavy guard prowling outside brutally snatched it away from me. '*Warum?*' I asked him in my poor German. '*Hier ist kein warum* (There is no why here)', he replied, pushing me inside with a shove.

The explanation is repugnant but simple: in this place everything is forbidden, not for hidden reasons, but because the camp has been created for that purpose. If one wants to live one must learn this quickly and well:

No Sacred Face will help thee here! it's not
A Serchio bathing-party ...

Hour after hour, this first long day of limbo draws to its end. While the sun sets in a tumult of fierce, blood-red clouds, they finally make us come out of the hut. Will they give us something to drink? No, they place us in line again, they lead us to a huge square which takes up the centre of the camp and they arrange us meticulously in squads. Then nothing happens for another hour: it seems that we are waiting for someone.

Martha Gellhorn, *an American foreign correspondent who had made her name in the theatres of war, was in the concentration camp of Dachau when* *the Nazi surrender ended the Second World War in Europe. Her testimony speaks for itself.*

Behind the barbed wire and the electric fence, the skeletons sat in the sun and searched themselves for lice. They have no age and no faces; they all look alike and like nothing you will ever see if you are lucky. We crossed the wide, crowded, dusty compound between the prison barracks and went to the hospital. In the hall sat more of the skeletons, and from them came the smell of disease and death. They watched us but did not move; no expression shows on a face that is only yellowish, stubby skin, stretched across bone. What had been a man dragged himself into the doctor's office; he was a Pole and he was about 6 feet tall and he weighed less than a hundred pounds and he wore a striped prison shirt, a pair of unlaced boots and a blanket which he tried to hold around his legs. His eyes were large and strange and stood out from his face, and his jawbone seemed to be cutting through his skin. He had come to Dachau from Buchenwald on the last death transport. There were fifty boxcars of his dead travelling companions still on the siding outside the camp, and for the last three days the American army had forced Dachau civilians to bury these dead. When this transport had arrived, the German guards locked the men, women and children in the boxcars and there they slowly died of hunger and thirst and suffocation. They screamed and they tried to fight their way out; from time to time, the guards fired into the cars to stop the noise.

This man had survived; he was found under a pile of dead. Now he stood on the bones that were his legs and talked and suddenly he wept. 'Everyone is dead,' he said, and the face that was not a face twisted with pain or sorrow or horror. 'No one is left. Everyone is dead. I cannot help myself. Here I am and I am finished and cannot help myself. Everyone is dead.'

The Polish doctor who had been a prisoner here for five years said, 'In four weeks, you will be a young man again. You will be fine.'

Perhaps his body will live and take strength, but one cannot believe that his eyes will ever be like other people's eyes.

The doctor spoke with great detachment about the things he had watched in this hospital. He had watched them and there was nothing he could do to stop them. The prisoners talked in the same way – quietly, with

The Wright Brothers make the first powered flight at Kitty Hawk, North Carolina, on 17 December 1903. (© *CORBIS*)

The suffragette Emily Wilding Davison is fatally injured when she runs on to the course at the Epsom Derby in 1913. (*Hulton Archive/Getty Images*)

Archduke Franz Ferdinand and his wife approach their car on a visit to Sarajevo on 28 June 1914. Moments later they are assassinated, an event which precipitated the First World War. (*Hulton Archive/Getty Images*)

Ernest Shackleton's ship, the *Endurance*, trapped in pack-ice in 1915, putting paid to his attempt to cross the whole of the Antarctic continent. (© *Frank Hurley/Royal Geographic Society 2005*)

British soldiers going 'over the top', September 1918. (*Hulton Archive/Getty Images; stereograph by H. D. Girdwood*)

The funeral procession of Italian-born film actor Rudolph Valentino coming up Broadway, New York, on 1 September 1926 (*Hulton Archive/Getty Images*)

Crowds gather in Wall Street, New York, on 24 October 1929, as news of the collapse of the financial market spreads through the city. (*Hulton Archive/Getty Images*)

The burning of the Reichstag in Berlin on 27 February 1933, a pivotal event in the establishment of Nazi Germany. (*akg-images*)

A man bows into the wind in the tempest that devastated Oklahoma and New Mexico on 14 April 1935, recorded by Woody Guthrie in 'The Great Dust Storm'. (© *CORBIS*)

Hiroshima in ruins after the dropping of the atom bomb on 6 August 1945. (*Time & Life Pictures/Getty Images; photograph by Bernard Hoffman*)

The people of Budapest demonstrate against the Soviet-backed Hungarian regime, 1956. The Soviets crushed the revolt. (*Time & Life Pictures/Getty Images; photograph by Michael Rougier*)

The Mint 400 Bikers Race, 1971, across the Mojave Desert, Nevada, reported on in high-energy style by Hunter S. Thompson. (*Time & Life Pictures/Getty Images; photograph by Bill Eppridge*)

Communist Khmer Rouge soldiers drive through Phnom Penh, Cambodia, during their takeover in April 1975. (*AFP/Getty Images*)

Chinese army tanks in Tiananmen Square, Beijing, in June 1989. (*AP/PA Photos; photograph by Jeff Widener*)

Members of the Afghan Mujahedin guerrilla group in 1989. (*Getty Images; photograph by David Stewart-Smith*)

The iconic 110-storey Twin Towers of the World Trade Center, 11 September 2001. (*AP/ PA Photos; photograph by Marty Lederhandler*)

a strange little smile as if they apologised for talking of such loathsome things to someone who lived in a real world and could hardly be expected to understand Dachau.

'The Germans made here some unusual experiments,' the doctor said. 'They wished to see how long an aviator could go without oxygen, how high in the sky he could go. So they had a closed car from which they pumped the oxygen. It is a quick death,' he said. 'It does not take more than fifteen minutes, but it is a hard death. They killed not so many people, only eight hundred in that experiment. It was found that no one can live above 36,000 feet altitude without oxygen.'

'Whom did they choose for this experiment?' I asked.

'Any prisoner', he said, 'so long as he was healthy. They picked the strongest. The mortality was a hundred per cent, of course.'

'It is very interesting, is it not?' said another Polish doctor.

We did not look at each other. I do not know how to explain it, but aside from the terrible anger you feel, you are ashamed. You are ashamed for mankind ...

In Dachau if a prisoner was found with a cigarette butt in his pocket he received twenty-five to fifty lashes with a bullwhip. If he failed to stand at attention with his hat off, 6 feet away from any SS trooper who happened to pass, he had his hands tied behind his back and he was hung by his bound hands from a hook on the wall for an hour. If he did any other little thing which displeased the jailers he was put in a box. The box is the size of a telephone booth. It is so constructed that being in it alone a man cannot sit down, or kneel down, or of course lie down. It was usual to put four men in it together. Here they stood for three days and nights without food or water or any form of sanitation. Afterwards they went back to the sixteen-hour day of labour and the diet of water soup and a slice of bread like soft grey cement.

What had killed most of them was hunger; starvation was simply routine. A man worked those incredible hours on that diet and lived in such overcrowding as cannot be imagined, the bodies packed into airless barracks, and woke each morning weaker, waiting for his death. It is not known how many people died in this camp in the twelve years of its existence, but at least forty-five thousand are known to have died in the last three years. Last February and March, two thousand were killed in the gas chamber, because, though they were too weak to work, they did not have the grace to die; so it was arranged for them.

The gas chamber is part of the crematorium. The crematorium is a brick building outside the camp compound, standing in a grove of pine trees. A Polish priest had attached himself to us and as we walked there he said, 'I started to die twice of starvation but I was very lucky. I got a job as a mason when we were building this crematorium, so I received a little more food, and that way I did not die.' Then he said, 'Have you seen our chapel, Madame?' I said I had not, and my guide said I could not; it was within the zone where the two thousand typhus cases were more or less isolated. 'It is a pity,' the priest said. 'We finally got a chapel and we had Holy Mass there almost every Sunday. There are very beautiful murals. The man who painted them died of hunger two months ago.'

Now we were at the crematorium. 'You will put a handkerchief over your nose,' the guide said. There, suddenly, but never to be believed, were the bodies of the dead. They were everywhere. There were piles of them inside the oven room, but the SS had not had time to burn them. They were piled outside the door and alongside the building. They were all naked, and behind the crematorium the ragged clothing of the dead was neatly stacked, shirts, jackets, trousers, shoes, awaiting sterilisation and further use. The clothing was handled with order, but the bodies were dumped like garbage, rotting in the sun, yellow and nothing but bones, bones grown huge because there was no flesh to cover them, hideous, terrible, agonising bones, and the unendurable smell of death.

We have all seen a great deal now; we have seen too many wars and too much violent dying; we have seen hospitals, bloody and messy as butchers' shops; we have seen the dead like bundles lying on all the roads of half the earth. But nowhere was there anything like this. Nothing about war was ever as insanely wicked as these starved and outraged, naked, nameless dead. Behind one pile of dead lay the clothed healthy bodies of the German soldiers who had been found in this camp. They were shot at once when the American army entered. And for the first time anywhere one could look at a dead man with gladness ...

I have not talked about how it was the day the American army arrived, though the prisoners told me. In their joy to be free, and longing to see their friends who had come at last, many prisoners rushed to the fence and died electrocuted. There were those who died cheering, because that effort of happiness was more than their bodies could endure. There were those who died because now they had food, and they ate before they could be stopped, and it killed them. I do not know words to describe the men who have survived this horror for years, three years, five years, ten years, and whose minds are as clear and unafraid as the day they entered.

I was in Dachau when the German armies surrendered unconditionally to the Allies. The same half-naked skeleton who had been dug out of the death train shuffled back into the doctor's office. He said something in Polish; his voice was no stronger than a whisper. The Polish doctor clapped his hands gently and said, 'Bravo.' I asked what they were talking about.

'The war is over,' the doctor said. 'Germany is defeated.'

We sat in that room, in that accursed cemetery prison, and no one had anything more to say. Still, Dachau seemed to me the most suitable place in Europe to hear the news of victory. For surely this war was made to abolish Dachau, and all the other places like Dachau, and everything that Dachau stood for, and to abolish it for ever.

The War in Asia and the Pacific

Japan, having entered the global war with its pre-emptive strike on Pearl Harbor in December 1941, swiftly followed it up with a strike from land and sea on Singapore, forcing the British to surrender their base there on 15 February 1942. This signalled the beginning of the end of the British empire as a real power in Asia. Some 130,000 British and Commonwealth soldiers were taken prisoner at Singapore and many of them ended up working on the Burma railway – the 'railway of death' – which was being built by the Japanese through Thailand (Siam). Two out of three POWs died. Jeffrey English describes the work routine on the railway in May 1943.

The work here was again on a rock cutting, about a mile from the camp and reached through the usual little track of churned-up mud. The shifts changed over down at the cutting, not back at camp, and so the men were paraded at 7 a.m. to be counted, and then had to march down to commence work at 8 a.m. The party coming off duty had to march back to the camp, and did not arrive until some time after 8.30 a.m. But that did not mean ten and a half hours for food and sleep. On five days a week rations had to be collected from the river, which involved going out at 1.30 p.m. and getting back between 5 p.m. and 6 p.m.

At our previous camp the ration parties had been drawn from the semi-sick, but here all men not bedded down had to go on the working parties to the cutting, and so the afternoon ration parties had to be found from the now off-duty night shift. A man would work or be going to and from work for the best part of fourteen hours, do a four-hour ration fatigue, and have only six hours out of twenty-four for feeding, cleaning himself up and sleeping.

For the first week or so, when we still had over three hundred 'fit' in the combined Anglo-Australian camp, each individual only got two ration fatigues a week. It would have been even less, but of course one half of our three hundred were on the day shift, and only the other half were on the unhappy night shift.

On three pints of rice a day, all this, of course, was impossible and flesh and blood could not stand the strain; and in addition to the overwork we had dysentery and other diseases spreading at a frightening pace. As the numbers of 'fit' men dwindled, the burden carried by the remainder consequently grew, until after only a few weeks the fitter men were doing all five ration fatigues a week as well as working the night shift in the cutting, and only having two days a week of real rest. As they gradually cracked up, more unfortunates, just past the crisis of their exhaustion or illnesses but in no way fully recovered, would be forced out in their place, lasting in their turn perhaps three or four days before they themselves had to be replaced by yet others not quite so ill.

Just as this gruelling programme put that at our previous camp in the shade, so did the new Nip Engineers make the last lot look like gentlemen. There, they had generally beaten only those whom they caught flagging or who had somehow provoked their precariously balanced ill humour; but here they beat up indiscriminately, beating every man in a gang if they wanted it to go faster, and two of them in particular were simply bloodthirsty sadists.

They were known to us as 'Musso' and 'The Bull', and they seemed to compete amongst themselves as to who could cause the most hurt. They were both on the night shift, and both would come on duty with a rope's end strapped to the wrist. These they plied liberally, and they also carried a split-ended bamboo apiece, whilst Musso in particular would lash out with anything which came handy, such as a shovel. Every morning two or three men would come back to camp with blood clotted on their faces and shoulders or matted in their hair, whilst others would return with puffy scarlet faces but no eyelashes or eyebrows, these having been burnt off where they'd had a naked acetylene flare waved slowly across the eyes – a favourite trick of another Nip known to us as 'Snowdrop'.

They drove the men on, not just to make them work, but as a cruel master drives a beast of burden to force it on to further efforts greater than it can manage; and one would see half a dozen men staggering along with an 18-foot tree trunk, or rolling an outsize boulder to the edge of the cutting, with the Nip running alongside lashing out at them or kicking their knees and shins and ankles to keep them going.

Frequently men fainted, and to make sure that they weren't shamming, the Nip would kick them in the stomach, ribs or groin. If the man still didn't move, the favourite trick was to roll him over face downwards, and then jump up and down on the backs of his knees, so as to grind the kneecaps themselves into the loose gravel. If he fell on his side, a variation was to stand on the side of his face and then wriggle about, grinding and tearing his undercheek in the gravel: and as a way of telling a faked faint from a real one, both of these methods are, believe me, highly efficacious.

On one occasion a man was beaten up so badly by the Nips that they thought he wouldn't live, and so they got four prisoners and told them to bury him under a heap of rocks. The prisoners observed that he wasn't yet dead, but the Nips indicated that that didn't matter – they could bury him alive. It was only after a great deal of persuasion by a spunky Australian officer (who naturally took a personal bashing for his trouble, but didn't let that deter him) that the Nips eventually changed their minds and let the man be carried back to camp. He was carried on a stretcher, and came round later, but the beating had sent him almost off his head; he disappeared into the jungle and we couldn't find him for two days. On the third day he crept in for food; but he was now quite mental and became a gibbering idiot at the mere sight of a Nip. Had we bedded him down in a hospital tent, he could very well have simply popped off again; and so we found him a job in the cookhouse where he would be working with others, and he worked there for a shaky fortnight before he packed it in and died.

*The Japanese advanced to the borders of India, where they were turned back by the 14th Army, under General 'Uncle Bill' Slim. It took pride in its sobriquet 'the forgotten army', and was predominantly Asian rather than British. It was the only Allied force to defeat the Japanese on land. In the closing months of the campaign **George MacDonald Fraser**, who later became the author of the famous Flashman chronicles, joined the Border regiment in Slim's army for this, the last land campaign in World War II, helping to* *capture a vital strong-point in Japanese territory, hold it against counter-attack, and then spearhead the final assault in which the Japanese armies were, to quote General Slim, 'torn apart'. MacDonald Fraser's memoir* Quartered Safe Out Here *is a masterpiece in miniature: as Melvyn Bragg said, 'The sense of front-line danger is palpable.'*

Winston Churchill has said that there is nothing more exhilarating than being shot at and not being hit. Each to his taste; I wouldn't call it exhilarating, quite, but it does bring a reaction beyond mere relief; satisfaction, I think. The first time it happened to me I didn't even realise it, at first. We were patrolling, four of us, less than a mile out from the perimeter, scouting for any sign of impending counter-attack on Meiktila, and had just turned back; all round there was dusty plain and dry paddy stretching away into the haze, with here and there a grove of trees in the distance and patches of scrub. Corporal Little had paused to scan with his binoculars, and I was crossing the crest of a little bund [embankment] when there was a sharp pfft! in the air above me, followed a little later by a distant crack. If the others had reacted quickly, I'd have done the same, but Little simply squatted down, and the other two looked round before following suit; there was no sudden hitting of the deck or cries of alarm. Little just said: 'Gidoon, Jock,' and continued his scan.

'Somewheres ower theer,' called Forster.

'Aye,' said Little, and lowered his glasses. 'Bloody miles off. Lal [Little] bastard. Awoy, then, let's git on.'

That was all. No second shot, and not a thing to be seen, but their lack of interest, let alone concern, nonplussed me until I reflected that the shot had come from a long way off, that the chance of its hitting had been negligible, and there was nothing to be done about it anyway: searching in the general direction of the sniper would have been futile and risky. Had it been at closer range, that would have been different; as it was, Little's job was to reconnoitre and report.

*The writer **J. G. Ballard** and his family were living in Shanghai when the war broke out. They were interned by the Japanese in Lunghua prison, where the regime was much less brutal than that of the POW camps. The thirteen-year-old Ballard even experienced a peculiar kind of freedom.*

I thrived in Lunghua, and made the most of my years there, in the school report parlance of my childhood. My impression is that, during the first year of internment, life in the camp was tolerable for my parents and most of the other adults. There were very few rows between the internees, despite the cramped space, malaria mosquitoes and meagre rations. Children went regularly to school, and there were packed programmes of sporting and social events, language classes and lectures. All this may have been a necessary illusion, but for a while it worked, and sustained everyone's morale.

Hopes were still high that the war would soon be over, and by the end of 1943 the eventual defeat of Germany seemed almost certain. The commandant, Hyashi, was a civilised man who did his best to meet the internees' demands. Almost a caricature short-sighted Japanese with a toothbrush moustache, spectacles and slightly popping eyes, he would cycle around Lunghua on a tandem bicycle with his small son, also in glasses, sitting on the rear saddle. He would smile at the noisy British children, a feral tribe if there was one, and struck up close relationships with members of the camp committee. Among the documents Mrs Braidwood sent me was a letter which Hyashi wrote to her husband some time after he had been dismissed as commandant, in which he describes (in English) his horse rides around Shanghai and sends his warm regards. After the war my father flew down to the war-crimes trials in Hong Kong and testified as a witness for Hyashi, who was later acquitted and released.

I also made friendships of a kind with several of the young Japanese guards. When they were off duty I would visit them in the staff bungalows 50 yards from G Block, and they would allow me to sit in their hot tubs and then wear their kendo armour. After handing me a duelling sword, a fearsome weapon of long wooden segments loosely strung together, they would encourage me to fence with them. Each bout would last twenty seconds and involved me being repeatedly struck about the helmet and face mask, which I could scarcely see through, every dizzying blow being greeted with friendly cheers from the watching Japanese. They too were bored, only a few years older than me, and had little hope of seeing their families again soon, if ever. I knew they could be viciously brutal, especially when acting under the orders of their NCOs, but individually they were easygoing and likeable. Their military formality and never-surrender ethos were of course very impressive to a thirteen-year-old looking for heroes to worship.

The bloodiest fighting for the Philippine archipelago took place during the first and last American offensives, at Guadalcanal in the Solomon Islands, and at Iwo Jima, the most costly battlefield in American military history. Before Guadalcanal, the Japanese troops had not once tasted defeat, and, convinced they were invincible, they were aiming at the beaches of the last surviving Allied power in the Pacific, Australia. By August 1942 it was also believed that the Japanese were building an airfield on Guadalcanal. The Americans took it in a fast landing operation, though the Japanese counter-attacked repeatedly in September. Here the writer and historian **William Manchester** *describes the initial landing attack, in which he took part.*

The palms on the beach were bent seaward, curtseying towards Tulagi, but inland they stood tall and straight. Because the soap company needed the ground beneath them kept clear for harvesting the coconuts, the marines had a clear run to the crushed-coral airstrip, which was swiftly taken and named Henderson Field after a corps pilot who had died in the battle of Midway. Repair sheds, hangars and revetments were already finished. Obviously the enemy had expected to use the field within a week at the latest. The scoop was that the Japanese liked to fight in the dark, so Vandegrift expected a counter-attack that first night. He was very vulner- able on Red Beach. Equipment had piled up alarmingly. When a Bougainville coastwatcher had radioed, 'Twenty-four torpedo bombers headed yours,' sailors manhandling the crates had had to dive for shelter. Luckily the bombardiers from Rabaul were wildly inaccurate, merely inflicting minor damage on one US destroyer. But the only disturbance on the canal after darkness was from land crabs, screeching tropical birds and a stamped-ing herd of wild pigs. Men whispered hopefully to one another that now, with the beachhead secure, GIs would relieve them, letting them return to the bars of Wellington. They studied the unfamiliar stars in the sky and dreamed their wistful dreams.

Across Ironbottom Sound the situation was very different. There the marines were encountering their first real combat. Tulagi, Gavutu and

Tanambogo were honeycombed with caves and the leathernecks were taking casualties. Hand grenades were almost useless; the enemy tossed them back. Merritt Edson's Raiders (1st Raider Battalion) had forty-seven killed; the Marine Parachutists, eighty-four dead. It is a myth – inspired by the Iwo Jima flag-raising – that every World War II marine carried an American flag in his pack, but somebody on tiny Tanambogo had one of them, and for several hours the island resembled a nineteenth-century battlefield, with the Stars and Stripes snapping angrily over one end of Tanambogo and the Rising Sun over the other. After a noisy charge a marine sergeant pulled down the Nip banner, and dynamiters sealed the caves one by one. That should have given the enemy's commanders pause – nothing like that had happened to them before – but their rear echelon was as over-confident as ours was fearful. Rabaul reassured Tokyo; the chief of the naval general staff donned his dress uniform and appeared at Hirohito's summer villa at Nikko to inform the emperor that there was no cause for worry. One banzai attack, he predicted, would drive the marines into the sea. That Friday night four waves of crack Nip troops hit the Raider lines on Tulagi with mortars, grenades and machine-guns. A handful of attackers made it through the lines to the old British residency but were killed back there when they were discovered hiding under the veranda. At dawn Pfc John Ahrens, an Able Company BAR man, was found covered with blood. He had been shot twice in the chest and bayoneted three times. Around him were the corpses of a Nip officer, a Nip sergeant and thirteen Nip infantrymen. His huge company commander, Lewis W. Walt, picked up the dying youth and held him in his arms. Ahrens said, 'Captain, they tried to come over me last night, but I don't think they made it.' Walt said softly, 'They didn't, Johnny. They didn't.'

> *In these closing stages of the war the Japanese command increasingly called on the suicide pilots of the Kamikaze – the 'divine wind'.* **Michael Moyni-han**, *serving in the British Pacific Fleet, witnessed a wave of suicide attacks at uncomfortably close range.*

Out of a clear evening sky Japanese Kamikazes swooped for the second time in five days on heavy units of the British Pacific Fleet ... The first two to penetrate the fighter and flak screen made for the same ship, an aircraft carrier. Both hit the flight deck and both by some lucky chance plunged from there into the sea, blazing wrecks. A Kamikaze attack is unlike anything one has known in the western war. At the back of one's mind continually is the thought of the pilots, fanatical, cold-blooded, whose last ambition is that death might also be glory. They wear, we are told, some kind of ceremonial uniform.

Of the death dive of a third Kamikaze I had a breathtaking view from the admiral's bridge. Its approach was signalled as usual by the gun flashes of battleship, carrier, cruiser, destroyer, and the growing rash of smoke puffs against the clear sky. The Zeke was flying low and we could see it now speeding on a level course across the fleet, ringed round, pursued, by the bursting shells. It seemed to bear a charmed life, cutting unscathed through the murderous hail of flak. Less than a mile from us we saw it turn aft of another carrier. It was approaching its kill. The air all around was smudged and clamorous with the bursting shells, joined now by the sharper points of pom-poms firing from the carrier's decks.

The Jap climbed suddenly and dived. It was all a matter of seconds. He came up the centre of the flight deck, accurate as a homing plane, and abruptly all was lost in a confusion of smoke and flame. The whole superstructure of the ship vanished behind billows of jet-black smoke shot through by flames as the tanks of aircraft ranged on the deck exploded.

It seemed at the time that the ship was doomed, that nothing could survive that inferno. But within half an hour the flames were extinguished and the smoke had drifted and dispersed in the sunlight. Through glasses we could see the armour-plated deck of the carrier swarming with activity. The island was blackened and a hole gaped at its base, but the damage seemed negligible for all that chaos of smoke and flame. When a few weeks ago this carrier was hit by a Kamikaze, planes were taking off again within seven minutes.

Outside Japan, it was generally believed that Kamikaze pilots were willing and fanatical volunteers. In fact many were university students who were either drafted or forced to volunteer. Far from being cold-blooded, they were the elite in the Japanese imperial world; some were scholars and a few were poets.

Here is one of the last poems of the Kamikaze **Hayashi Tadao**, *together*

with his last letter to his mother, dated 30 May 1945. He was shot down by
an American fighter plane two days after the Allies had issued the Potsdam
Declaration laying down the terms on which Japan would be allowed to
surrender.

My plane
Earlier today it tried to take off
Turned sharply to the left
It twisted, twisted sharply
At that time, I thought to myself
It is all right with me to die now
If one must go, it is better to go quickly
It has been such a long day of struggle and pain.

Mother, you often talked about how we would live together in Kyoto after
my graduation from the university ... Kyoto is really a very peaceful and
plebeian city. You and I – it is the best place to live together, while continuing to learn. Mother, there is no hope of living together now that we are
swept in the torrents of the world. How are you going to live? What from
the past can you use for moral support for your life? What moral strength
can you depend on to continue to live? My ageing mother to whom I
cannot offer my love. I cannot bear the thought of you – my poor mother.

On 6 August 1945, an American B-29 Flying Fortress dropped the first
atom bomb released in anger on Hiroshima. **Colonel Paul Tibbets** *was the*
pilot.

We started our take-off on time which was somewhere about 2.45, I think,
and the aeroplane went on down the runway. It was loaded quite heavily
but it responded exactly as I had anticipated it would. I had flown this
aeroplane the same way before and there was no problem and there was
nothing different this night in the way we went. We arrived over the initial
point and started in on the bomb run which had about eleven minutes to
go, rather a long type of run for a bomb but on the other hand we felt we
needed this extra time in straight and level flight to stabilise the air speed
of the aeroplane, to get everything right down to the last-minute detail.
As I indicated earlier the problem after the release of the bomb is not to

proceed forward but to turn away. As soon as the weight had left the aeroplane I immediately went into this steep turn and we tried then to place distance between ourselves and the point of impact. In this particular case that bomb took fifty-three seconds from the time it left the aeroplane until it exploded and this gave us adequate time of course to make the turn. We had just made the turn and rolled out on level flight when it seemed like somebody had grabbed a hold of my aeroplane and given it a real hard shaking because this was the shock wave that had come up. Now after we had been hit by a second shock wave not quite so strong as the first one I decided we'll turn around and go back and take a look. The day was clear when we dropped that bomb, it was a clear sunshiny day and the visibility was unrestricted. As we came back around again facing the direction of Hiroshima we saw this cloud coming up. The cloud by this time, now two minutes old, was up at our altitude. We were 33,000 feet at this time and the cloud was up there and continuing to go right on up in a boiling fashion, as if it was rolling and boiling. The surface was nothing but a black boiling, like a barrel of tar. Where before there had been a city with distinctive houses, buildings and everything that you could see from our altitude, now you couldn't see anything except a black boiling debris down below.

The bomb killed eighty thousand people – a quarter of the population of Hiroshima. **Dr Michihiko Hachiya**, *director of the Communications Hospital, was one of the survivors.*

The hour was early; the morning still, warm and beautiful. Shimmering leaves, reflecting sunlight from a cloudless sky, made a pleasant contrast with shadows in my garden as I gazed absently through wide-flung doors opening to the south.

Clad in drawers and undershirt, I was sprawled on the living room floor exhausted because I had just spent a sleepless night on duty as an air warden in my hospital.

Suddenly, a strong flash of light startled me – and then another. So well does one recall little things that I remember vividly how a stone lantern in the garden became brilliantly lit and I debated whether this light was caused by a magnesium flare or sparks from a passing trolley.

Garden shadows disappeared. The view where a moment before it had been so bright and sunny was now dark and hazy. Through swirling dust I could barely discern a wooden column that had supported one corner of my house. It was leaning crazily and the roof sagged dangerously.

Moving instinctively, I tried to escape, but rubble and fallen timbers barred the way. By picking my way cautiously I managed to reach the *roka* [an outside hallway] and stepped down into my garden. A profound weakness overcame me, so I stopped to regain my strength. To my surprise I discovered that I was completely naked. How odd! Where were my drawers and undershirt?

All over the right side of my body I was cut and bleeding. A large splinter was protruding from a mangled wound in my thigh, and something warm trickled into my mouth. My cheek was torn, I discovered as I felt it gingerly, with the lower lip laid wide open. Embedded in my neck was a sizeable fragment of glass which I matter-of-factly dislodged, and with the detachment of one stunned and shocked I studied it and my bloodstained hand.

Where was my wife?

Suddenly thoroughly alarmed, I began to yell for her: 'Yaeko-san! Yaeko-san! Where are you?' Blood began to spurt. Had my carotid artery been cut? Would I bleed to death? Frightened and irrational, I called out again, 'It's a 500-ton bomb! Yaeko-san, where are you? A 500-ton bomb has fallen!'

Yaeko-san, pale and frightened, her clothes torn and bloodstained, emerged from the ruins of our house holding her elbow. Seeing her, I was reassured. My own panic assuaged, I tried to re-assure her.

'We'll be all right,' I exclaimed. 'Only let's get out of here as fast as we can.'

She nodded, and I motioned for her to follow me.

It was all a nightmare. We started out, but after twenty or thirty steps I had to stop. My breath became short, my heart pounded and my legs gave way under me. An overpowering thirst seized me and I begged Yaeko-san to find me some water. But there was no water to be found. After a little my strength somewhat returned and we were able to go on.

I was still naked, and although I did not feel the least bit of shame, I was disturbed to realise that modesty had deserted me. On rounding a corner we came upon a soldier standing idly in the street. He had a towel draped across his shoulder, and I asked if he would give it to me to cover my nakedness. The soldier surrendered the towel quite willingly but said not a word. A little later I lost the towel, and Yaeko-san took off her apron and tied it around my loins.

Our progress towards the hospital was interminably slow, until finally, my legs, stiff from drying blood, refused to carry me further. The strength, even the will, to go on deserted me, so I told my wife, who was almost as badly hurt as I, to go on alone. This she objected to, but there was no choice. She had to go ahead and try to find someone to come back for me.

Yaeko-san looked into my face for a moment, and then, without saying a word, turned away and began running towards the hospital. Once, she looked back and waved and in a moment she was swallowed up in the gloom. It was quite dark now, and with my wife gone, a feeling of dreadful loneliness overcame me.

I must have gone out of my head lying there in the road because the next thing I recall was discovering that the clot on my thigh had been dislodged and blood was again spurting from the wound.

I pressed my hand to the bleeding area and after a while the bleeding stopped and I felt better.

In time I came to an open space where the houses had been removed to make a fire lane. Through the dim light I could make out ahead of me the hazy outlines of the Communications Bureau's big concrete building, and beyond it the hospital. My spirits rose because I knew that now someone would find me; and if I should die, at least my body would be found. I paused to rest. Gradually things around me came into focus. There were the shadowy forms of people, some of whom looked like walking ghosts. Others moved as though in pain, like scarecrows, their arms held out from their bodies with forearms and hands dangling. These people puzzled me until I suddenly realised that they had been burned and were holding their arms out to prevent the painful friction of raw surfaces rubbing together. A naked woman carrying a naked baby came into view. I averted my gaze. Perhaps they had been in the bath. But then I saw a naked man, and it occurred to me that, like myself, some strange thing had deprived them of their clothes. An old woman lay near me with an expression of suffering on her face; but she made no sound. Indeed, one thing was common to everyone I saw – complete silence.

All who could were moving in the direction of the hospital. I joined in the dismal parade when my strength was somewhat recovered, and at last reached the gates of the Communications Bureau.

In the last days the young **J. G. Ballard** *witnessed the American Air Force close to, exactly as did his counterpart in the novel* Empire of the Sun. *Suddenly there appeared in the skies the B-29 Flying Fortresses and the P-51 Mustangs, the Cadillacs of the skies.*

In the last days of August, I was on the roof of F Block when a B-29 flew towards the camp at a height of about 800 feet. Its bomb doors were open, and for a few seconds I assumed that we were about to be attacked. A line of canisters fell from the bomb bays, parachutes flared and the first American relief supplies floated towards us. A stampede followed, as everyone helped to drag the canisters back to their blocks. Each one was a cargo of treasure, but a sensible rationing system saw that every family received its fair share. There were tins of Spam and Klim, cartons of Lucky Strike cigarettes, cans of jam and huge bars of chocolate. I remember vividly our first meal on our little card table, and the extraordinary taste of animal fat, sugar, jam and chocolate. The vast lazy planes that floated overhead were emissaries from another world. The camp came alive again, as the internees found a new purpose in their lives. Everyone hoarded and guarded their new supplies, listening out for the sound of American engines, quick to point out the smallest unfairness.

Tired of all this, and revived by the Spam and chocolate, I decided to walk to Shanghai. I had spent years staring at the apartment houses of the French Concession, and I was eager to see Amherst Avenue again. Without telling my parents, I set off for the fence behind the old shower blocks. Confident that I could walk the 5 miles to the western suburbs of Shanghai, I stepped through the wire.

WINDS OF CHANGE

Prologue: the Nuclear Test at Bikini Atoll

*The second half of the twentieth century has been dominated, in many ways, by the flexing of nuclear muscles. In 1946, as if in a hurry to confirm its unique position as a nuclear power, the United States proceeded to demonstrate its nuclear capabilities with two tests in the Pacific. The site chosen was Bikini Atoll – several tiny islands surrounding a lagoon in which seventy-three target vessels had been moored. The Bikini islanders were moved, not without protest, to Rongerik, and the flesh-and-blood element of the test was represented, according to journalist **James Cameron**, by a few goats and one or two brown-spotted pigs. The name of the bombing aircraft was Dave's Dream and the bomb itself bore a portrait of Rita Hayworth and the name Gilda. This is Cameron's description of the dropping of the first bomb.*

At seven in the morning the first aircraft appeared, a flying boat wheeling in wide circuits, droning round at 3,000, until abruptly it tired of it and streaked back to the south-east.

The loudspeaker system began a raucous confused chatter, indiscriminate radiophone conversations between ships and planes, filling the air with a backstage buzz of orders and counter-orders. Somewhere about in the roof of the sky already hung the bomb, suspended in the rack of the B-29 Dave's Dream, which had taken off according to plan at Ray Hour. Ray Hour was the moment of the bomber's take off. Even the moments of the day had new and special names. How Hour was the planned moment of the drop. Mike Hour was to be the actual moment of the drop, according to how many dry runs the bombardier needed to get the crimson spot of the *Nevada* trued up in his bombsight.

As the day began to grow one felt the sky filling with aircraft of all kinds, seen and unseen, manned and unmanned, bombers and flying boats and spotters, pilotless drones from the carrier *Shangri La* and – because by now this operation had achieved in America an importance momentarily even greater than the World Series – a bomberful of public relations officers and broadcasters from the radio networks. Then high above, just fleetingly visible as a twinkling speck when the sun caught it, the B-29 began its experimental cast over the target, 18 miles away square on the starboard beam. Far too lofty and distant to be heard, the bomber flirted for a second like a mote in the sunlight and was lost.

Over the radio, suddenly came the announcement: broadcast transmission began.

'Listen, world – this is Crossroads.'

It was dramatic, you could not deny it was intensely dramatic, a *coup de théâtre*. 'Listen, world ...'

Then soon after eight we caught the voice of the bomb-aimer in our loudspeakers. We heard the chant, tinny and remote as an old gramophone in another world: 'Skylight here. First simulated bomb release; stand by. Mark: first simulated bomb release. First practice run; stand by.'

At 8.51: 'This is a live run. Mark: coming up on 35 miles off target, 35 miles. Mark: adjust goggles. Stand by.'

At 8.58 he said: 'Eighteen miles.'

In two minutes, for good or ill, the thing would be falling through the empty air, its controlling drogue tight like a drumhead; two bullets face to face, twin charges of plutonium to rush headlong to the uproarious embrace, the critical mass, the meeting of ultimate release.

The loudspeaker said: 'Bomb gone. Bomb gone. Bomb gone.'

I had on my goggle-mask, so black and deep it was like staring into velvet; behind that opacity all things vanished, sea, and ships and sunlight. At the bomb-aimer's words I began to count. Then I found I was counting too fast; I made an effort to slow down. I felt the sweat dripping down my back and I was glad I had no clothes on. I felt that the time between the beginning and end of the bomb's fall was far too much. I had no consciousness of calculation, I felt that in the nature of things expectancy does not endure so long without anticlimax. When my counting had reached fifty-five the bomb went off.

It is difficult to say what one had foreseen. However keenly you wait for the stage revolver-shot it is always louder than you expect; however long you wait for an atom bomb it is presumably a little less than you feared.

In that first fine edge of a second it might have been a sudden star, low down on the horizon. Then it grew and swelled and became bright, and brighter; it pierced the goggles and struck the eye as a crucible does, and in that moment it was beyond every doubt there ever was an atom bomb, and nothing else.

It was a spheroid, then an uprising wavering thing like a half-filled balloon, then a climbing unsteady dome like a mosque in a dream. It looked as though it were throbbing. I tore off my goggles and the globe had become a column, still rising, a gentle peach-colour against the sky, and from 18 miles I could see a curtain of water settling like rain back into the lagoon. Somehow I found it not impossible to believe that the thing had produced a hundred million centigrade degrees of heat, ten times that of the surface of the sun, that this was the answer of the little men in pince-nez to 10,000 tons of TNT; yet it was beautiful, in its monstrous way; a writhing lovely mass. Then, just as I remembered the sound of the explosion, it finished its journey and arrived.

It was not a bang, it was a rumble, not overloud, but it thudded into all the corners of the morning like a great door slammed in the deepest hollows of the sea. Beside me a heavy wire stay unexpectedly quivered like a cello string for a moment, then stopped.

Now, standing up unsteadily from the sea, was the famous Mushroom. In seven minutes fifteen seconds our ship's trigonometry gave it 23,000 feet in height and 11,600 feet in diameter. It climbed like a fungus; it looked like a towering mound of firm cream shot with veins and rivers of wandering red; it mounted tirelessly through the clouds as though it were made of denser, solider stuff, as no doubt it was. The only similes that came to mind were banal: a sundae, red ink in a pot of distemper. From behind me I heard a frenetic ticking of typewriters; very soon I found I was fumbling with my own. The reportage had begun. Many of us will never live it down.

The Soviet Union responded with its first nuclear bomb in 1949 and a rapid build-up of nuclear arsenals followed. Fear of annihilation led to an extended

'Cold War' between the US and Russia, punctuated with moments of high tension, as in the Cuban missile crisis of 1962 when Nikita Khrushchev, the Soviet leader, and President Kennedy came to the brink of war. By then the nuclear capabilities of both countries were sufficient to obliterate the world in its entirety. It was not until 1969 that talks began on strategic arms limitation (SALT).

New Horizons, Revolutions and Independence

For many people the hardship of the Second World War fed a fierce impulse for change that frequently challenged social inequality.

*On 1 December 1955, **Rosa Parks** sat on a seat at the front of a bus in Montgomery, Alabama. As a result of the bus segregation policies in the city, African Americans were supposed to sit at the back, and, according to Rosa Parks, 'Nothing angered black people more than bus segregation.' A year after the incident she describes, the US Supreme Court ruled that bus segregation was illegal.*

When I got off from work that evening of 1 December, I went to Court Square as usual to catch the Cleveland Avenue bus home. I didn't look to see who was driving when I got on, and by the time I recognised him, I had already paid my fare. It was the same driver who had put me off the bus back in 1943, twelve years earlier. He was still tall and heavy, with red, rough-looking skin. And he was still mean-looking. I didn't know if he had been on that route before – they switched the drivers around sometimes. I do know that most of the time if I saw him on a bus, I wouldn't get on it.

I saw a vacant seat in the middle section of the bus and took it. I didn't even question why there was a vacant seat even though there were quite a few people standing in the back. If I had thought about it at all, I would probably have figured maybe someone saw me get on and did not take the seat but left it vacant for me. There was a man sitting next to the window and two women across the aisle.

The next stop was the Empire Theater, and some whites got on. They filled up the white seats, and one man was left standing. The driver looked back and noticed the man standing. Then he looked back at us. He said, 'Let me have those front seats,' because they were the front seats of the black section. Didn't anybody move. We just sat right where we were, the four of us. Then he spoke a second time: 'Y'all better make it light on yourselves and let me have those seats.'

The man in the window seat next to me stood up, and I moved to let him pass by me, and then I looked across the aisle and saw that the two women were also standing. I moved over to the window seat. I could not see how standing up was going to 'make it light' for me. The more we gave in and complied, the worse they treated us.

I thought back to the time when I used to sit up all night and didn't sleep, and my grandfather would have his gun right by the fireplace, or if he had his one-horse wagon going anywhere, he always had his gun in the back of the wagon. People always say that I didn't give up my seat because I was tired, but that isn't true. I was not tired physically, or no more tired than I usually was at the end of a working day. I was not old, although some people have an image of me as being old then. I was forty-two. No, the only tired I was, was tired of giving in.

The driver of the bus saw me still sitting there, and he asked was I going to stand up. I said, 'No.' He said, 'Well, I'm going to have you arrested.' Then I said, 'You may do that.' These were the only words we said to each other. I didn't even know his name, which was James Blake, until we were in court together. He got out of the bus and stayed outside for a few minutes, waiting for the police.

As I sat there, I tried not to think about what might happen. I knew that anything was possible. I could be manhandled or beaten. I could be arrested. People have asked me if it occurred to me then that I could be the test case the NAACP had been looking for. I did not think about that at all. In fact if I had let myself think too deeply about what might happen to me, I might have got off the bus. But I chose to remain.

Meanwhile there were people getting off the bus and asking for transfers, so that began to loosen up the crowd, especially in the back of the bus. Not everyone got off, but everybody was very quiet. What conversation there was, was in low tones; no one was talking out loud. It would have been quite interesting to have seen the whole bus empty out. Or if the other three had stayed where they were, because if they'd had to arrest four of us instead of one, then that would have given me a little support. But it didn't matter. I never thought hard of them at all and never even bothered to criticise them.

Eventually two policemen came. They got on the bus, and one of them asked me why I didn't stand up. I asked him, 'Why do you all push us around?' He said to me, and I quote him exactly, 'I don't know, but the law is the law and you're under arrest.'

The history of disease goes hand in hand with a history of sometimes miraculous cures. Polio, which has now been virtually eradicated from the developed world, was still claiming victims in the 1950s. **Patrick Cockburn,** *who comes from what might be called a dynasty of journalists, was a victim of the last major polio outbreak in northern Europe, which happened in Cork, in Ireland, in 1956. He has since reported from the Balkans, the Middle East and Iraq, and few journalists can match him for physical courage, insight and mental as well as physical determination. In* The Broken Boy *he looks back at the effects of polio on him and on the city.*

It soon became apparent that almost everybody in Cork alive at the time had been affected by the epidemic either because one of their relatives had got it or because they had been evacuated as children to other parts of Ireland. Donal O'Donovan, a civil servant working for the county medical officer of health, compiled a weekly register of people with notifiable infections, including polio. He noticed a strange aspect of the disease: 'The thing I remember most about the epidemic in Cork is that about ninety-five per cent of the cases occurred in the more well-to-do suburbs like Douglas and Bishopstown.' He realised – as few did in Cork at the time – that the poorer parts of the city were being spared.

It took me a long time to get better – or as well as I was ever going to get. At first I was in a wheelchair, wore a hard plastic waistcoat and only gradually began to walk using wooden crutches and a calliper on one leg. Kitty would push me into Youghal on my red-and-white tricycle and later back up a steep hill by a disused quarry filled with gorse. In the kitchen I rode around and around the table on my tricycle, swatting the flies hovering over it with a rolled-up newspaper. My right leg was not strong enough to push the pedal down so I had to use a hand to push my knee down to keep the tricycle moving. Emotionally I was more like a four- or five-year-old in my dependence on others and, with the egotism of a small child, I expected everybody to have nothing to do except look after me.

I am not sure how others perceived me. My cousin Shirley, whom I would have met in Myrtle Grove the day I fell ill if she had not gone for a walk with her nanny, spent the rest of the autumn confined to the grounds of the house. 'I was dreadfully upset when I saw you again,' she said. 'You were wearing callipers and my father carried you into the house and put you down on a sofa in the library.'

Doctors believed that for two years after the illness it was possible through exercise to revive damaged muscles. Three times a week a hired car arrived at Brook Lodge and I lay down flat in the back seat. I became bored watching the tops of trees and buildings week after week from my prone position as we travelled the 30 miles to Cork. I would prod the driver in the back to encourage him to drive fast over hump-backed bridges so for an instant I had the satisfying sensation that the car had taken off before it bumped back on to the road. Once the driver turned to me in irritation and said: 'I think you are the most spoiled boy I have ever met.' In Cork we drove to City Hall, the large grey building by the Lee, where Pauline Kent, my physiotherapist, had a small cramped room upstairs. 'You try to find if there is a flicker of movement against gravity by the muscles,' she said. 'If there is you exercise these muscles to develop them and to stop the joints seizing up.'

Pauline was energetic, able, short-tempered and overworked. She found Dr Saunders patronising and unhelpful about her work. Once when he visited her, she snappishly asked: 'Why do I have to waste time walking a hundred yards to use a telephone and I don't even have a minute spare to go to the lavatory?' I liked her because she liked me and built up my determination to walk again. After a few months Pauline persuaded the Corporation to take over an old Turkish baths, a red-brick building in Cork's South Mall. I used to swim slowly in the pool with my legs trailing uselessly behind me.

One of the most unlikely best-sellers of the 1960s, and one whose legacy has been amplified by time, was a slim volume called Silent Spring. *In it*

Rachel Carson alerted the world, and America in particular, to the damage caused to domestic and wild life by the indiscriminate use of pesticides, herbicides, animal growth hormones and fertilisers. Following its serialisation in the New Yorker in June and July 1962, a huge counter-attack was organised by the giants of the chemical industry – what Peter Matthiessen called 'an ugly campaign to reduce a brave scientist's protest to a matter of public relations'. It backfired. The book was a runaway success and is still regarded as the cornerstone of the new environmentalism. Carson died two years later at the age of fifty-six. Here she describes the effect of two relatively new chemicals, dieldrin and heptachlor, on fields in Hardin County, Texas.

Dead birds found in the treated areas had absorbed or swallowed the poisons used against the fire ants, a fact clearly shown by chemical analysis of their tissues. (The only bird surviving in any numbers was the house sparrow, which in other areas too has given some evidence that it may be relatively immune.) On a tract in Alabama treated in 1959 half of the birds were killed. Species that live on the ground or frequent low vegetation suffered 100 per cent mortality. Even a year after treatment, a spring die-off of songbirds occurred and much good nesting territory lay silent and unoccupied. In Texas, dead blackbirds, dickcissels and meadowlarks were found at the nests, and many nests were deserted. When specimens of dead birds from Texas, Louisiana, Alabama, Georgia and Florida were sent to the Fish and Wildlife Service for analysis, more than 90 per cent were found to contain residues of dieldrin or a form of heptachlor, in amounts up to 38 parts per million.

Woodcocks, which winter in Louisiana but breed in the north, now carry the taint of the fire ant poisons in their bodies. The source of this contamination is clear. Woodcocks feed heavily on earthworms, which they probe for with their long bills. Surviving worms in Louisiana were found to have as much as 20 parts per million of heptachlor in their tissues six to ten months after treatment of the area. A year later they had up to 10 parts per million. The consequences of the sub-lethal poisoning of the woodcock are now seen in a marked decline in the proportion of young birds to adults, first observed in the season after fire ant treatments began.

Some of the most upsetting news for southern sportsmen concerned the bobwhite quail. This bird, a ground nester and forager, was all but eliminated on treated areas. In Alabama, for example, biologists of the Alabama Co-operative Wildlife Research Unit conducted a preliminary census of the quail population in a 3,600-acre area that was scheduled for treatment. Thirteen resident coveys – 121 quail – ranged over the area. Two weeks after treatment only dead quail could be found. All specimens sent to the Fish and Wildlife Service for analysis were found to contain insecticides in amounts sufficient to cause their death. The Alabama findings were duplicated in Texas, where a 2,500-acre area treated with heptachlor lost all of its quail. Along with the quail went 90 per cent of the songbirds. Again, analysis revealed the presence of heptachlor in the tissues of dead birds.

In addition to quail, wild turkeys were seriously reduced by the fire ant programme. Although eighty turkeys had been counted on an area in Wilcox County, Alabama, before heptachlor was applied, none could be found the summer after treatment – none, that is, except a clutch of unhatched eggs and one dead poult. The wild turkeys may have suffered the same fate as their domestic brethren, for turkeys on farms in the area treated with chemicals also produced few young. Few eggs hatched and almost no young survived. This did not happen on nearby untreated areas.

If the Cold War was one of the factors dominating the post-war world, the other was the retreat, whether forced or not, from empire. In the cases of Italy and Japan, for example, defeat accelerated the break-up of their empires and colonies, but even for those countries on the winning side the impulse of their colonial dependencies towards independence and self- government was, for the most part, overwhelming.

On the stroke of midnight on 14/15 August 1947 India was granted independence by the British, and divided into India and Pakistan. The partition was overseen by the last British viceroy of India, Lord Mountbatten. As Franz Fanon wrote in The Wretched of the Earth *(1961), 'National liberation, national renaissance, the restoration of nationhood to the people, commonwealth: whatever may be the headings used on the new formula introduced, decolonisation is always a violent phenomenon.' India was no exception. Independence precipitated the flight of millions of Muslims into the new state of Pakistan, while Hindus fled in the other direction*

– migrations on a scale unparalleled in world history in time of peace. More than a million died during partition.

*The Punjab was divided between the two new states. The British administrator **Penderel Moon**, who was critical of Mountbatten's policy, wrote, in his memoir* Divide and Quit, *a dramatic account of travelling through the Punjab in August 1947, the month in which it was divided by the British.*

Day by day news from the Punjab seemed to get worse. Owing to censorship, reports were vague, but the disorder was clearly growing and spreading. I decided to curtail my stay in Simla. I wrote to Gurmani saying that I hoped to be back in Bahawalpur by the evening of the 25th. Many people told me that driving across East Punjab would be dangerous, especially with two Muslim servants. But it was infinitely safer than going by train. There was, in fact, no danger at all except possibly if one had a breakdown, and even then military patrols on the Grand Trunk Road would have afforded protection. I am glad to say that my servants neither showed nor, I think, felt the slightest alarm – indeed my bearer insisted that we should go by Amritsar, which was considered the more risky route, in order that we might pass through Jullundur, his native town. He rightly foresaw that this would be his last opportunity of seeing it.

The rains had been particularly heavy and great pools and sheets of water were standing in the fields and village tracks. I could not imagine how, in these conditions, the Boundary Force could hope to move about and keep order in the countryside. With their wheeled transport they would get bogged down immediately. Cavalry was the only answer, and there was no cavalry. So far as I could make out, the villages of the Eastern Punjab were just being allowed to run amok as they pleased. From the Grand Trunk Road, particularly on the stretch from Ambala to Ludhiana, murderous-looking gangs of Sikhs, armed with guns and spears, could be seen prowling about or standing under the trees, often within 50 yards of the road itself. Military patrols in jeeps and trucks were passing up and down the road, yet taking not the slightest notice of these gangs, as though they were natural and normal features of the countryside. This was not at all my idea of how things should be done. I felt that gangs such as these should not be tolerated for one instant, but mercilessly shot down wherever they were seen.

The towns were all under curfew and had a curiously derelict appearance. At Ludhiana not a soul was visible and there was no sign of life at all, except two donkeys copulating in the middle of the road just near the clock tower. At Jullundur a few people were stirring, but many of the houses looked as though they had been plundered and the streets were strewn with litter. I asked my bearer whether he would like us to turn aside to have a look at his house, but seeing the condition of the town he shook his head and said, 'No; it's all been destroyed.'

At Amritsar we had to stop for petrol, our tank being almost empty. I thought I might have to try to obtain some from the deputy commissioner as all the petrol pumps seemed to be closed. However, at last we found one that was functioning. The Sikh serving it recognised me and was very obliging, but also very talkative. He was full of some alleged massacre of Sikhs by a Muslim battalion on the border, just beyond Atari. When I asked him about the massacres of Muslims by Sikhs that had occurred in the Amritsar district, he disclaimed all knowledge of them.

At Wagah, midway between Amritsar and Lahore, we had to cross the newly established frontier between India and Pakistan, but there were as yet no formalities and we drove across without, I think, even being stopped. Lahore was not burning as briskly as it had been ten days earlier and seemed generally in rather better shape, but all the shops in the Mall were still closed.

We stopped the night in Lahore and pushed on the next morning down the Multan road. There were no armed bands roaming about the countryside as there were on the Indian side of the frontier and we struck nothing unusual till we had gone about 70 miles and reached Okara. Stopping at the outskirts of the town to get some petrol I was surprised to see Daultana, one of the ministers of the newly formed West Punjab government, sitting not far from the pump, surrounded by a group of men. It seemed a strange place to find a minister. He came up to me and exchanged a few words and explained that there had been an 'incident' at Okara and he had come to enquire into it.

Ten miles further on, as we rounded a bend in the road after crossing a canal, we almost ran into a bullock-cart, stranded in the middle of the road with the bullocks unyoked and standing to one side. We had to stop practically dead and then pull right over on to the side of the road, as the cart entirely blocked the metalled portion. As we did so, I noticed a man lying under the cart, and then two police constables suddenly appeared – they had been standing on the far side of the cart – and signalled us on. I felt a bit mystified and, looking back, saw one of the constables with his rifle raised to his shoulder aiming at the man under the cart. There was a crack – and the poor fellow was presumably finished off. This was to me a novel form of summary justice on the high road.

Along the outskirts of the town of Montgomery the road was completely blocked for about a mile by a string of bullock-carts laden with goods and chattels and paraphernalia of all kinds and halted under a fine avenue of trees. We had to get right off the road and drive along in the fields. Most of the men with the carts were Sikhs, but only low-caste Mazhabis or Labanas and not at all well-to-do. They were trekking towards India and had halted in the shade during the afternoon heat or perhaps even for the night. Some of them were pulling large chunks of bark off the trees to serve as fuel. We were getting back again on to the road near the end of the column and I had alighted from the car to direct the driver over some rough ground, when someone recognised me as a former deputy commissioner of Multan and I was immediately surrounded by a throng of rather piteous-looking people clamouring for protection. I couldn't at first make out what from, as their column seemed in fairly good order; but they insisted that they were being looted and then, looking along the column on the side facing Montgomery, I saw that groups of men were helping themselves to bundles and packages from the carts and walking off across the fields towards the town carrying them on their heads. A few police constables were standing around, but doing nothing to prevent this. The Sikh refugees said that there were some military encamped on the other side of the town and begged me to go and ask them to give protection. I felt compelled to do so, but my efforts were entirely fruitless. I spent a long time searching for the military encampment, which was several miles away, only to find it empty except for one sepoy who said the troops had all gone out – he didn't know where.

The desire of Jews for a homeland of their own had formed the main thrust of the Zionist agenda since the late nineteenth century. It had been agreed in principle at the first Zionist Congress in 1896, and in 1917, in the Balfour

Declaration, the British committed themselves to creating a Jewish homeland in Palestine – the Israel of biblical times. The Holocaust in Germany gave tragic impetus to the need for such a homeland, and in 1947 the British, who had been entrusted with the administration of the old League of Nations mandate of Palestine at the end of the First World War, and now found themselves reviled by both Jews and Palestinians, handed the problem over to the newly formed United Nations to solve. In November of that year the UN proposed the division of Palestine into two states, one for the Arabs and one for the Jews, and the following May the British withdrew and the State of Israel became a reality. Journalist **James Cameron** *was in Tel Aviv for the event.*

In Rothschild Boulevard in the middle of Tel Aviv stood the Museum Hall, a building as undistinguished as all others in the town; it had once been the home of Meir Dizengoff, first mayor of Tel Aviv. It was to be undistinguished no longer.

Outside the hall was drawn up a guard of honour of cadets from the Jewish Officers' School. A strong detachment of Haganah military police meticulously scrutinised the credentials of every soul entering up the steps from the Boulevard. In the steaming heat of that afternoon the atmosphere of crisis was almost tangibly neurotic. The Yishuv had waited six hundred generations for this day; Jewry had trod a long hard road from Babylon and pharaoh's Egypt and the desert and the ghettos of the world; what had seemed endless was now at last to have an end. The moment could not and must not be wrecked now by a chance intruding enemy. Security was tense. Every arrival passed the cordons of guards who were men from Berlin and London and Cracow and South Africa and Iraq and Egypt, from the death camps of Germany and Poland, from the farms of Galilee. No museum had ever been harder to enter.

The hall was crowded to suffocation, the heat magnified by the film-camera lights, the shadows broken by the flashbulbs. Above it all, against the blue and white hangings, looked down the portrait of the sombre-bearded Viennese journalist Theodor Herzl, who had dreamed it all how long ago? Just over fifty years.

Below the portrait of Herzl sat the eleven of the National Administration and the secretary. At the centre table sat the fourteen members of the National Council. Around them in a semicircle were the rabbis, mayors, elders of the Yishuv, officers of the Haganah command, councillors, fund-raisers, the Zionist General Council. But from Jerusalem none could come, nor from Haifa and the north. Tel Aviv was still an enclave in a hostile land.

At exactly four o'clock David Ben-Gurion, wearing a necktie for the only time in living memory, rapped his gavel on the table. The whole hall rose to its feet. The Philharmonic Orchestra concealed upstairs drew up its bows – but they were too late, already the crowd was singing the 'Hatikvah'.

It faded out, and Ben-Gurion said: 'The land of Israel was the birthplace of the Jewish people. Here their spiritual, religious and national identity was formed. In their exile from the land of Israel the Jews remained faithful to it in all the countries of their dispersal, never ceasing to hope and pray for the restoration of their national freedom.'

His white woolly halo danced, his face glistened in the heat, his eloquence mounted to a Hebraic fervour; he was speaking for Joshua and David, Nehemiah and Ezra the Writer, for the fugitives from the crusaders and Saladin and Spain, for the survivors of Dachau and Ravensbrück, for the sabra Yishuv who had drained the Hulah swamps, the founders of Rehovot, the builders of Tel Aviv itself, for the immigrant bus-drivers and the waiters in the cafés of Dizengoff Square, and those who were yet to come.

'Therefore by virtue of the natural and historic right of the Jewish people to be a nation as other nations, and of the resolution of the General Assembly of the United Nations, we hereby proclaim the establishment of the Jewish nation in Palestine, to be called the Medinat Yisrael: the State of Israel.'

It was far from over; he had now to read the articles arising from the declaration, the setting-up of provisional authorities, the principles of 'social and political equality of all citizens distinguishing not between religions, races or sexes, providing freedom of religion, conscience, education, language and culture, the safeguarding of the Holy Places of all faiths.

'We appeal to the United Nations for help to the Jewish people in building their state, and to admit Israel into the family of nations. We offer only peace and friendship to all neighbouring states and people ...'

And finally: 'With trust in God, we set our hand to this declaration, at this session of the Provisional State Council, on the soil of the Homeland, in the city of Tel Aviv, on this Sabbath eve, the fifth of Iyar 5708, the fourteenth day of May 1948.'

It had taken exactly thirty-two minutes. Plus, of course, two thousand years.

In 1953, Josef Stalin died. Europe was by then in the depths of the Cold War – a war fought out for the most part in a world of spies, subversion and political posturing. In both Europe and Asia, Russia sought to dominate the countries it had liberated, while at home the tight party dictatorship initiated by Lenin in the wake of the revolution (and imposed by the use, in his own words, of 'merciless mass terror'), had become, under Stalin, even more brutal, capricious and paranoid. Of the terror of 1930–2 Nikolai Bukharin, whom Lenin had once described as 'the favourite of the party', said: 'We were conducting a mass annihilation of completely defenceless men, together with their wives and children.'

*One of the key weapons in Stalin's armoury was the vast string of prison work-camps across the tundra and into Siberia known as the Gulag Archipelago, and its most famous inmate – and chronicler – was **Alexander Solzhenitsyn**. Here he describes the odds on a successful escape in the closing years of Stalin's rule.*

To defend yourself in that savage world was impossible. To go on strike was suicide. To go on hunger strikes was useless.

And as for dying, there would always be time.

So what was left for the prisoner? To break out! To go and change one's fate!

Chekhov used to say that if a prisoner was not a philosopher who could get along equally well in all possible circumstances (or let us put it this way: who could retire into himself) then he could not but wish to escape and he *ought* to wish to.

He could not but wish to! That was the imperative of a free soul. True, the natives of the archipelago were far from being like that. They were much more submissive than that. But even among them there were always those who thought about escape or who were just about to. The continual escapes in one or another place, even those that did not succeed, were a true proof that the energy of the *zeks* had not yet been lost.

Here is a camp compound. It is well guarded; the fence is strong and the inner cordon area is reliable and the watchtowers are set out correctly – every spot is open to view and open to fire. But all of a sudden you grow sick to death of the thought that you are condemned to die right here on this bit of fenced-off land. So why not try your luck? Why not burst out and change your fate? This impulse is particularly strong at the beginning of your term of imprisonment, in the first year, and it is not even deliberate. In that first year when, generally speaking, the prisoner's entire future and whole prison personality are being decided. Later on this impulse weakens somehow; there is no longer the conviction that it is more important for you to be *out there*, and all the threads binding you to the outer world weaken, and the cauterising of the soul is transformed into decay, and the human being settles into camp harness.

During all the years of the camps, there were evidently quite a few escapes. Here are some statistics accidentally come by: in the month of March 1930 alone 1,328 persons escaped from imprisonment in the Russian republic of the Soviet Union. (And how inaudible and soundless this was in our society.)

With the enormous development of the archipelago after 1937, particularly during the war years, when battle-fit infantrymen were rounded up and sent to the front, it became even more difficult to provide proper escort, and not even the evil notion of self-guarding could solve all the problems of the chiefs. So they relied on certain invisible chains which kept the natives reliably in their place.

The strongest of these chains was the prisoners' universal submission and total surrender to their situation as slaves. Almost to a man, both the 58s [prisoners held under article 58] and the non-political offenders were hard-working family people capable of manifesting valour only in lawful ways, on the orders of and the approval of the higher-ups. Even when they had been imprisoned for five and ten years they could not imagine that singly – or, God forbid, collectively – they might rise up for their liberty since they saw arrayed against them the state (*their own* state), the NKVD, the police, the guards and the police dogs. And even if you were fortunate enough to escape unscathed, how could you live afterwards on a false passport, with a false name, when documents were checked at every intersection, when suspicious eyes followed passers-by from behind every gateway?

Another chain was *the death factory* – camp starvation. Although it was precisely this starvation that at times drove the despairing to wander through the taiga in the hope of finding more food than there was in camp, yet it was this starvation that also weakened them so that they had no strength for a long flight, and because of this it was impossible to save up a stock of food for the journey.

And there was another chain too – the threat of a new term. A political prisoner was given a new tenner for an escape attempt under that same article 58 (and gradually it proved best to give article 58–14 – Counter-Revolutionary Sabotage).

Another thing restraining the *zeks* was not the compound but the privilege of going without escort. The ones guarded the least, who enjoyed the small privilege of going to work and back without a bayonet at their backs, or once in a while dropping into the free settlement, highly prized their advantages. And after an escape these were taken away.

The geography of the archipelago was also a solid obstacle to escape attempts – those endless expanses of snow or sandy desert, tundra, taiga.

The hostility of the surrounding population, encouraged by the authorities, became the principal hindrance to escapes. The authorities were not stingy about rewarding the captors. (This was an additional form of political indoctrination.) And the nationalities inhabiting the areas around the gulag gradually came to assume that the capture of a fugitive meant a holiday, enrichment, that it was like a good hunt or like finding a small gold nugget.

But the desperate heart sometimes did not weigh things. It saw: the river was flowing and a log was floating down it – and one jump! We'll float on down. Vyacheslav Bezrodny from the Olchan camp, barely released from the hospital, still utterly weak, escaped down the Indigirka river on two logs fastened together – to the Arctic Ocean! Where was he going? And what was he hoping for? In the end he was not so much caught as picked up on the open sea and returned over the winter road to Olchan to that very same hospital.

It is not possible to say of everyone who didn't return to camp on his own, who was not brought in half-alive, or who was not brought in dead, that he had escaped. Perhaps he had only exchanged an involuntary and long-drawn-out death in camp for the free death of a beast in the taiga.

The *quiet* escapes were usually more fortunate in their results. Some of them were surprisingly successful. But we rarely hear of these happy stories; *those who broke out* do not give interviews; they have changed their names, and they are in hiding. Kuzikov-Skachinsky, who escaped successfully in 1942, tells the story now only because he was caught in 1959 – after seventeen years.

And we have learned of the successful escape of Zinaida Yakovlevna Povalyayeva because in the end it fell through. She got her term because she had stayed on as a teacher in her school during the German occupation. But she was not immediately arrested when the Soviet armies arrived, and before her arrest she was married to a pilot. Then she was arrested and sent to Mine No. 8 at Vorkuta. Through some Chinese working in the kitchen she established communication with freedom and with her husband. He was employed in civil aviation and arranged a trip to Vorkuta for himself. On an appointed day Zina went to the bath in the work zone, where she shed her camp clothing and released her hair, which had been curled the night before, from under her headscarf. Her husband was waiting for her in the work sector. There were security officers on duty at the river ferry, but they paid no attention to a girl with curly hair who was arm in arm with a flier. They flew out on a plane. Zina spent one year living on false papers. But she couldn't resist the desire to see her mother again – and her mother was under surveillance. At her new interrogation she managed to convince them she had escaped in a coal car. And they never did find out about her husband's participation.

1956 was a year of unrest and violence for those under Soviet control, and for some who weren't. In April, Russian leaders Nikita Khrushchev and Nikolai Bulganin visited Britain: during their stay a Royal Naval frogman disappeared while diving in Portsmouth harbour and his headless body was recovered over a year later. In June, workers and soldiers in Poland rioted against the Communist government and the presence of Soviet officers in the armed forces. The Soviet response was a massive build-up of armed forces on the border.

Then, in October 1956, in Budapest, capital of Hungary, the anti-Communists rose up to overthrow the puppet regime of Moscow, and, after days of street fighting and reprisals, nearly succeeded. The Soviet forces were about to pull out but, realising that the West would not go to war on Hungary's behalf and was in any case distracted by what was to become the Suez crisis (Anglo-French landings in Egypt began on 5 November), they redoubled their efforts and brutally crushed the revolt.

Victor Zorza *of the* Guardian, *an émigré himself, describes the scene on the Hungarian border with Austria at Nickelsdorf on 28 October.*

The Austrian border guards at Nickelsdorf raised the barrier for a Hungarian rebel leader's car to go through. He had come across to arrange for the passage of medical and food supplies to Hungary. The journalists quickly followed him. We stayed in no man's land and ran to the Hungarian frontier post.

Could we go on from here? No, we could not. We beseeched the rebel who seemed to be in charge. The other rebels beseeched us.

Finally out of the hubbub a clear Hungarian voice rang out. The man was giving a statement to the world press; a German gave a translation. The Hungarian said that his people wanted to live in peace and friendship with all countries, that they regretted the unfriendliness and hostility of the past.

A girl, the only one in the crowd of rebels, took up the tale. 'Today is my seventeenth birthday,' she said, a little bashfully, with just a hint of pride in her voice. Seventeen, and she was one of the rebels who were defying the massive might of the Soviet army. Seventeen, and she had just come from the town of Győr, 60 or so kilometres from the frontier, where, someone else told us, eighty members of the security police had been 'liquidated' by the workers; where, she announced proudly, 'we put up a ladder against the Russian memorial, threw a noose round the red star on top of it, and pulled it down.'

She was seventeen, but the Budapest youths who had attacked Russian tanks with their bare hands were younger. Many were now dead. 'What is your estimate of our casualties?' she asked. 'Estimates vary from two hundred to ———' Perhaps the journalist who was replying was going to say ten thousand, a figure that has been mentioned in some reports.

But the girl's question had been purely rhetorical. 'I must tell you that the dead must be counted not in hundreds, but in many, many thousands,' she said. 'What is the feeling of the Hungarian people about the sacrifice they are making?' another journalist asked. 'They believe that by thus drawing the attention of the world to what is happening they will compel the Russians to get out,' she said, and without pausing, asked: 'And what is the feeling of the British people?' We all hesitated. No one was anxious to reply.

Haltingly one of the reporters began to frame an answer. 'First, amazement.' Then a pause. 'Second – admiration.' Then quickly, desperately, as if he wanted to withdraw each word as soon as he had uttered it: 'And a great feeling of guilt.' The girl came back like a flash: 'There is much to be guilty for.'

In South Africa, long independent, the policy of apartheid – the separation of races – was imposed with the full panoply of a police state. It began soon after the war with the election, in 1948, of the Afrikaner National Party which was committed to white dominance. Rioting in Johannesburg in 1950 resulted in the prime minister, D. F. Malan, being given dictatorial powers to reinforce the policy. But as more and more African countries gained their independence, unrest in South Africa increased. Black activists organised demonstrations to burn pass books, the hated symbol of the apartheid regime, and in March 1960, at Sharpeville, the South African police hit back – and with lethal force. **Humphrey Taylor** *reported the carnage for* Drum *magazine.*

We went into Sharpeville the back way, around lunchtime last Monday, driving along behind a big grey police car and three Saracen armoured cars ...

There were crowds in the streets as we approached the police station. There were plenty of police, too, well armed.

A constable shoved the butt of his rifle against my windshield. Another pointed his rifle at my chest. Another leaned into the car, shouting: 'Have you got a permit to be in this location?'

I said no, whereupon he bellowed: 'Then get out, get out, get out! or I will arrest you on the spot. Understand?'

He had a police gun in his holster and a black pistol tucked into his belt. We decided to go around the other side of the police station, where we parked in a big field.

We could see a couple of the Saracens, their tops poking starkly above the heads of the crowd, just over 100 yards away from us. This was about seven minutes before the police opened fire.

The crowd seemed to be loosely gathered around them and on the fringes people were walking in and out. The kids were playing. In all there were about three thousand people. They seemed amiable.

I said to Ian Berry, *Drum*'s chief photographer: 'This is going to go on all day.' He replied: 'Let's hang on for a bit.'

Suddenly there was a sharp report from the direction of the police station.

'That's a shot,' Berry said.

There were shrill cries of *Izwe Lethu* – women's voices, I thought. The cries came from the police station and I could see a small section of the crowd swirl around the Saracens. Hands went up in the Africanist salute.

Then the shooting started. We heard the chatter of a machine-gun, then another, then another.

'Here it comes,' said Berry. He leapt out of the car with two cameras and crouched in the grass, taking pictures.

The first rush was on us, then past.

There were hundreds of women, some of them laughing. They must have thought that the police were firing blanks.

One woman was hit about 10 yards from our car. Her companion, a young man, went back when she fell. He thought she had stumbled.

Then he turned her over and saw that her chest had been shot away. He looked at the blood on his hand and said: 'My God, she's gone!'

Hundreds of kids were running, too. One little boy had on an old black coat which he held up behind his head, thinking perhaps that it might save him from the bullets. Some of the children, hardly as tall as the grass, were leaping like rabbits. Some of them were shot, too.

Still the shooting went on. One of the policemen was standing on top of a Saracen, and it looked as though he was firing his Sten gun into the crowd. He was swinging it around in a wide arc from his hip as though he were panning a movie camera. Two other police officers were on the truck with him, and it looked as though they were firing pistols ...

The police have claimed they were in desperate danger because the crowd was stoning them. Yet only three policemen were reported to have been hit by stones – and more than two hundred Africans were shot down.

The police also have said that the crowd was armed with 'ferocious weapons' which littered the compound after they fled.

I saw no weapons, although I looked very carefully, and afterwards studied the photographs of the death scene. While I was there I saw only shoes, hats and a few bicycles left among the bodies.

It seemed to me that tough stuff was behind the killings at Sharpeville. The crowd gave me no reason to feel scared, though I moved among them without any distinguishing mark to protect me, quite obvious with my white skin.

I think the police were scared, though, and I think the crowd knew it.

That final shrill cry from the women before the shooting started certainly sounded much more like a jeer than a battle-cry. And the first Africans who fled past me after the shooting started were still laughing.

*The champion of the anti-apartheid struggle, in which he was to be the ultimate survivor and winner, was **Nelson Mandela**. In 1964 he and his colleagues were tried for sabotage and insurrection against the state. As leader of the African National Congress he was expected to be given the death penalty. Here, in his powerful autobiography* Long Walk to Freedom, *he describes the last day of the trial on 12 June.*

I waved hello to Winnie and my mother. It was heartening to see them there; my mother had journeyed all the way from the Transkei. It must be a very odd sensation to come to a courtroom to see whether or not your son will be sentenced to death. Though I suspect my mother did not understand all that was going on, her support never wavered. Winnie was equally stalwart, and her strength gave me strength.

The registrar called out the case: 'The state against Nelson Mandela and others.' Before sentence was passed, there were two pleas in mitigation.

One was delivered by Harold Hanson and the other by the author Alan Paton, who was also national president of the Liberal party. Hanson spoke eloquently, saying that a nation's grievances cannot be suppressed, that people will always find a way to give voice to those grievances. 'It was not their aims which had been criminal,' said Hanson, 'only the means to which they had resorted.' Hanson said the judge would do well to recall that his own people, the Afrikaners, had struggled violently for their freedom.

Though Paton did not himself support violence, he said the accused had had only two alternatives: 'to bow their heads and submit, or to resist by force'. The defendants should receive clemency, he said, otherwise the future of South Africa would be bleak.

But de Wet did not seem to be listening to either man. He neither looked up nor took any notes while they spoke. He seemed absorbed in his own thoughts. He had obviously already decided; he was merely waiting for the moment to reveal his decision.

He nodded for us to rise. I tried to catch his eye, but he was not even looking in our direction. His eyes were focused on the middle distance. His face was very pale, and he was breathing heavily. We looked at each other and seemed to know: it would be death, otherwise why was this normally calm man so nervous? And then he began to speak:

'I have heard a great deal during the course of this case about the grievances of the non-European population. The accused have told me and their counsel have told me that the accused, who were all leaders of the non-European population, were motivated entirely by a desire to ameliorate these grievances. I am by no means convinced that the motives of the accused were as altruistic as they wish the court to believe. People who organise a revolution usually take over the government and personal ambition cannot be excluded as a motive.'

De Wet paused for a moment as if to catch his breath. His voice, which was muted before, was now barely audible:

'The function of this court, as is the function of the court in any other country, is to enforce law and order and to enforce the laws of the state within which it functions. The crime of which the accused have been convicted, that is the main crime, the crime of conspiracy, is in essence one of high treason. The state has decided not to charge the crime in this form. Bearing this in mind and giving the matter very serious consideration I have decided not to impose the supreme penalty which in a case like this would usually be the proper penalty for the crime, but consistent with my duty that is the only leniency which I can show. The sentence in the case of all the accused will be one of life imprisonment.'

We looked at each other and smiled. There had been a great collective gasp in the courtroom when de Wet announced that he was not sentencing us to death. But there was consternation among some spectators because they had been unable to hear de Wet's sentence. Dennis Goldberg's wife called to him, 'Dennis, what is it?'

'Life!' he yelled back, grinning. 'Life! To live!'

I turned and smiled broadly to the gallery, searching out Winnie's face and that of my mother, but it was extremely confused in the court, with people shouting, police pushing the crowd this way and that. I could not see them. I flashed the thumbs-up ANC salute as many of the spectators were dashing outside to tell the crowd the verdict. Our police guardians began to hustle us out of the dock and towards the door leading underground, but although I looked again for Winnie's face, I was not able to see her before I ducked through the door leading to the cells below.

Youth, Sex and Violence

In October 1960 the Crown brought a prosecution against Penguin Books for planning to publish an unexpurgated text of D. H. Lawrence's Lady Chatterley's Lover, *which it deemed an obscene publication under British law. The action, which was brought thirty years after Lawrence's death, proved to be a turning-point in Britain's laws on censorship. The prosecution was opened by **Mervyn Griffith-Jones**, the Crown counsel. His speech is a classic mirror of the times – times past, as it turned out.*

Let me emphasise it on behalf of the prosecution: do not approach this matter in any priggish, high-minded, super-correct, mid-Victorian manner. Look at it as we all of us, I hope, look at things today, and then, to go back and requote the words of Mr Justice Devlin, 'You will have to say, is this book to be tolerated or not?', in the sense that it must tend, or may tend, to deprave and corrupt. Members of the jury, when you have seen this book, making all such allowances in favour of it as you can, the prosecution will invite you to say that it does tend, certainly that it may tend, to induce lustful thoughts in the minds of those who read it. It goes further, you may think. It sets upon a pedestal promiscuous and adulterous intercourse. It commends, and indeed it sets out to commend, sensuality almost as a virtue. It encourages, and indeed even advocates, coarseness and vulgarity of thought and of language. You may think that it must tend to deprave the minds certainly of some and you may think many of the persons who are likely to buy it at the price of 3s 6d and read it, with two hundred thousand copies already printed and ready for release.

You may think that one of the ways in which you can test this book, and test it from the most liberal outlook, is to ask yourselves the question, when you have read it through, would you approve of your young sons, young daughters – because girls can read as well as boys – reading this book. Is it a book that you would have lying around in your own house? Is it a book that you would even wish your wife or your servants to read?

Let me at once – because not for one moment do I wish to overstate this case – let me at once concede that D. H. Lawrence is a well-recognised and indeed great writer. Let me at once concede, but perhaps not to so great an extent, that there may be some literary merit in this book. I put it no higher. Certainly let me concede that some of his books have great literary merit. All that I concede. But, again, you have – have you not? – to judge this book, balancing the extent of the obscenity (if you so find it is obscene) against any interests of literature, art and so on, and you have to say in the end, balancing the whole thing, the one against the other: is its publication proved to be justified for the public good?

And so we come, members of the jury, to the book itself. And you must forgive me if I have occupied too much of your time in preliminaries. The book has been passed to you. It is a book about – if I may summarise it in literally a word almost – Lady Chatterley, who is a young woman whose husband was wounded in the First World War. They were married at the beginning of the war; he comes back wounded so that he is crippled and paralysed from the waist downwards and unable to have any sexual inter-course. Members of the jury, other views may be put before you; I invite you to say that, in effect, the book is a book describing how that woman, deprived of sex from her husband, satisfies her sexual desires – a sex-starved girl – how she satisfies that starvation with a particularly sensual man who happens to be her husband's gamekeeper. And you have the episodes of sexual intercourse. There are, I think, described in all thirteen throughout the course of this book. You will see that they are described in the greatest detail, save perhaps for the first. You may think that this book, if its descriptions had been confined to the first occasion on which sexual intercourse is described, would be a very much better book than it is. But twelve of them certainly are described in detail leaving nothing to the imagination. The curtain is never drawn. One follows them not only into the bedroom but into bed and one remains with them there.

At the beginning of November 1960, the jury threw out the case against Penguin, *and publication of* Lady Chatterley *went ahead. It sold by the tens of thousands. The* **Guardian** *welcomed the verdict, but not the book's code of ethics.*

The jury's verdict on *Lady Chatterley's Lover* is a triumph of common sense – and the more pleasing because it was unexpected.

We shall never know, of course, precisely what the jury thought. They could acquit on either of two grounds – that the book was simply not obscene, or that, even if it was, its literary and other merits nevertheless justified its publication as being for the public good. As ordinary men and women, with their feet well planted on the ground and with the judge's injunction not to get lost 'in the higher realms of literature, education, sociology and ethics' in their ears, they would be likely to look at the straightforward question of obscenity. In hearing the defence evidence they may have wondered at the inconsistencies in what the 'experts' said in support of the book (inconsistencies some of which the judge mentioned in his summing-up). But they may have wondered still more at the prosecution's theme that the book put promiscuity on a pedestal and that it contained only 'padding' between bouts of sexual intercourse. These charges were too exaggerated to survive a reading of the book.

Physical love plays an important part in the book. It is the chief theme – though there is an important secondary theme in the sterility, ugliness and inhumanity of life in a Midland mining community and in a society devoted to money-making. The theme of physical love calls for detailed description of sexual acts. These are what make the book controversial. But their purpose is an honest one. It is to show the redeeming power of that love and the importance of tenderness. D. H. Lawrence emphasises that where harshness or brutality exist a couple cannot come to a full and harmonious relationship together. Mellors (the gamekeeper) is shown from an early stage as warm and kind, and where he is passionate he is 'wholesome'. That is the key to his influence over Lady Chatterley. To the judge's question whether there is 'any spark of affection' until late in the book the answer is 'yes'. The compassion of Mellors for the wretchedness of Lady Chatterley is what brings them together at first.

Mellors and Lady Chatterley are nevertheless in an immoral

relationship. Here some of the defence witnesses were vulnerable – especially the four Church of England clergy who courageously came forward to give evidence. Yet there is a valid answer to the charge of immorality. It is, first, that the Chatterleys' marriage had already withered from within. The wife had sought to hold together her companionship with a husband half-paralysed and half-mad, but her efforts did not avail. Secondly, she herself is changed by Mellors from frustration and physical decline to being vitally alive. Thirdly, their relationship becomes a dedicated one – and, contrary to the prosecution's view, with a real hope of ultimate and lasting marriage. (That plainly lies behind the concluding letter.) Fourthly, as one of the clergy said, this is a novel and not a tract. Novels deal with life as it is.

> *Sexual intercourse began*
>   *In nineteen sixty-three*
> *(Which was rather late for me)–*
> *Between the Lady Chatterley ban*
>   *And the Beatles' first LP.*

*So wrote Philip Larkin. The Beatles' first LP, too, came along in 1963 – and suddenly the sixties became the swinging sixties. When the Fab Four hit America on 7 February 1964, **Tom Wolfe** was in New York to see them.*

By 6.30 a.m. yesterday, half the kids from South Orange, NJ to Seaford LI, were already up with their transistors plugged in their skulls. It was like a civil defence network or something. You could turn anywhere on the dial, WMCA, WCBS, WINS, almost any place, and get the bulletins: 'It's B-Day! Six-thirty a.m.! The Beatles left London thirty minutes ago! They're thirty minutes out over the Atlantic Ocean! Heading for New York!'

By 1 p.m. about four thousand kids had finished school and come skipping and screaming into the international terminal at Kennedy Airport. It took 110 police to herd them. At 1.20 p.m., the Beatles' jet arrived from London.

The Beatles left the plane and headed for customs inspection and everybody got their first live look at the Beatles' hairstyle, which is a mop effect that covers the forehead, some of the ears and most of the back of the neck. To get a better look, the kids came plunging down the observation deck, and some of them already had their combs out, raking their hair down over their foreheads as they ran.

Then they were crowding around the plate-glass windows overlooking the customs section, stomping on the floor in unison, some of them beating time by bouncing off the windows.

The Beatles – George Harrison, twenty; John Lennon, twenty-three; Ringo Starr, twenty-three; and Paul McCartney, twenty-one – are all short, slight kids from Liverpool who wear four-button coats, stovepipe pants, ankle-high black boots with Cuban heels. And droll looks on their faces. Their name is a play on the word 'beat'.

They went into a small room for a press conference, while some of the girls tried to throw themselves over a retaining wall.

Somebody motioned to the screaming crowds outside. 'Aren't you embarrassed by all this lunacy?'

'No,' said John Lennon. 'It's crazy.'

'What do you think of Beethoven?'

'He's crazy,' said Lennon. 'Especially the poems. Lovely writer.'

In the two years in which they have risen from a Liverpool rock-and-roll dive group to the hottest performers in the record business, they had seen much of this wildness before. What really got them were the American teenage car sorties.

The Beatles left the airport in four Cadillac limousines, one Beatle to a limousine, heading for the Plaza Hotel in Manhattan. The first sortie came almost immediately. Five kids in a powder blue Ford overtook the caravan on the expressway, and as they passed each Beatle, one guy hung out the back window and waved a red blanket.

A white convertible came up second, with the word BEETLES scratched on both sides in the dust. A police car was close behind that one with the siren going and the alarm light rolling, but the kids, a girl at the wheel and two guys in the back seat, waved at each Beatle before pulling over to the exit with the cops gesturing at them.

In the second limousine, Brian Sommerville, the Beatles' press agent, said to one of the Beatles, George Harrison: 'Did you see that, George?'

Harrison looked at the convertible with its emblem in the dust and said, 'They misspelled Beatles.'

But the third sortie succeeded all the way. A good-looking brunette, who said her name was Caroline Reynolds, of New Canaan, Connecticut, and Wellesley College, had paid a cab driver $10 to follow the caravan all the way into town. She cruised by each Beatle, smiling faintly, and finally caught up with George Harrison's limousine at a light at Third Avenue and 63rd Street.

'How does one go about meeting a Beatle?' she said out of the window.

'One says hello,' said Harrison out of the window.

'Hello!' she said. 'Eight more will be down from Wellesley.' Then the light changed and the caravan was off again.

At the Plaza Hotel, there were police everywhere. The Plaza, on Central Park South just off Fifth Avenue, is one of the most sedate hotels in New York. The Plaza was petrified. The Plaza accepted the Beatles' reservations months ago, before knowing it was a rock-and-roll group that attracts teenage riots.

About five hundred teenagers, most of them girls, had shown up at the Plaza. The police herded most of them behind barricades in the square between the hotel and the avenue. Every entrance to the hotel was guarded. The screams started as soon as the first limousine came into view.

The Beatles jumped out fast at the Fifth Avenue entrance. The teenagers had all been kept at bay. Old ladies ran up and touched the Beatles on their arms and backs as they ran up the stairs.

After they got to the Plaza the Beatles rested up for a round of television appearances (the Ed Sullivan Show, Sunday), recordings (Capitol Records), concerts (Carnegie Hall, Wednesday) and a tour (Washington, Miami). The kids were still hanging around the Plaza hours after they went inside.

One group of girls asked everybody who came out, 'Did you see the Beatles? Did you touch them?'

A policeman came up, and one of them yelled, 'He touched a Beatle! I saw him!'

The girls jumped on the cop's arms and back, but it wasn't a mob assault. There were goony smiles all over their faces.

Throughout 1968 student demonstrations against capitalism, against the Vietnam War (see p. 291ff.), against authoritarian educational policies, rocked Europe and America. King was assassinated in April, Soviet tanks rolled into Czechoslovakia in August, bringing an end to the Prague Spring. **Hans Koning** *describes the rioting in Paris on the night of 10 May.*

The Quartier Latin on the left bank of the Seine is a marvellously thick soup of college buildings, France's more famous middle schools, parks, cafés, boulevards and little streets: perfect headquarters for a new French revolution. There is nothing like that in American cities. I remember sitting in a Paris Left Bank café on the evening of 10 May which was going to be the Night of the Barricades: the night of 10 May to 11 May was to turn the tide against the police and put the students well-nigh in control of that part of the city. Before it had got really dark, there was already a wild excitement in the air. You could almost taste it; it affected everyone. Waiters distractedly put coffees and drinks down and didn't bother to check the money. As the evening wore on, tourist types and older people from other areas looked around, got their things together, and left in a hurry. But don't think that there was fear in the air, that people felt threatened. There was elation, not worry.

Some future rightist French government may bulldoze the Latin Quarter into wide-open spaces with scattered glass-and-concrete high rises – just as in the nineteenth century Baron Haussmann got rid of all the narrow workmen's streets and alleyways for Louis Napoleon and replaced them by the star pattern of the great boulevards, each one as straight as the path of a cannonball. When I got back to Paris in 1970, I found that the city had already asphalted over the paving stones of many streets and squares. The cobblestoned touristy charm had gone, but no future students would have paving stones to hand to heave at the cops.

The fighting of the 10–11 May night was astounding. It was astounding to watch the students being unafraid of police with tear gas and CS gas, concussion grenades, nightsticks, pistols, helmets, visors, shields, grenade rifles and the famous leaded capes. It was equally astounding to find their courage 'rewarded', so to speak, by sympathy and even admiration not only from the radio reporters of the independent radio stations (Europe One and Radio Luxembourg) but also from the public at large. The fight was so unequal, the police so brutal that you had to be a very determined Law and Order person to feel sympathy for the authorities.

The students had made three demands: that the police get out of the Sorbonne, that the university be reopened and that the arrested students and other demonstrators be released. They decided to try to enforce their case not 'by writing letters to the papers' but by protest marches. That night, with the police barring their way wherever they went, they built their barricades where they found themselves stuck, in the rue Saint-Jacques, the rue Gay-Lussac, and some other narrower streets south of the Panthéon. They dug in. It was the police, the CRS and the Gardes Mobiles from the army who attacked.

Through the night various professors, famous scientists and men of letters appealed (often on the radio) for the police to let up. When a statement of the Sorbonne rector blamed the students for not negotiating, Radio Luxembourg put an almost immediate student reaction on the air, repeating the three basic demands and inviting Rector Roche to answer them. The only answer was a repeat of Roche's original statement. When dawn came, the last barricades fell to the police, and the remaining young men, and some young women, were dragged, often clubbed, into the police vans. An unknown number was taken to the hospital by volunteers who had to fight the police to get through.

It was a cold morning. The streets were littered with stones, with debris of all sorts, burned-out cars, shoes and lost pieces of clothing. A restless crowd of young people, probably mostly students too, filled the streets. It looked as if the police had won, but actually they had lost. The mood of the city and the country had turned against them.

In 1969 British troops were drafted on to the streets of the towns and villages of Northern Ireland. Initially their task was to protect the Catholic minority after a year and a half of increasingly violent civil rights protests. Within months a new version of the Irish Republican Army, the IRA, was formed – the Provisionals. With their political arm, 'Provisional' Sinn Fein, they called for a fully independent Ireland, including the detachment of the six counties of Northern Ireland from British rule. Armed confrontation ensued, bringing the introduction of internment without trial, and on 30 January 1972, in Londonderry, British paratroopers fired on a civil rights march, killing thirteen civilians. 'Bloody Sunday', as it became known, was followed by IRA calls for a general strike and, on 2 February, by the torching of the British embassy in Dublin. The British army maintained that it came under fire from the crowd, while the IRA saw it as a premeditated massacre of innocent people. **Simon Winchester** *was there, and reported in the* Guardian.

The tragic and inevitable doomsday situation which has been universally forecast for Northern Ireland arrived in Londonderry yesterday afternoon when soldiers firing into a large crowd of civil rights demonstrators, shot and killed thirteen civilians.

Seventeen more people, including a woman, were injured by gunfire and another woman was seriously injured after being knocked down by a speeding armoured car.

The army reported two military casualties and said that their soldiers had arrested between fifty and sixty people, who had been allegedly involved in the illegal protest march.

After the shooting, which lasted for about twenty-five minutes in and around the Rossville Flats area of Bogside, the streets had all the appearance of the aftermath of Sharpeville. Where, only moments before, thousands of men and women had been milling around, drifting slowly towards a protest meeting to be held at Free Derry Corner, there was only a handful of bleeding bodies, some lying still, others still moving with pain, on the white concrete of the square.

The army's official explanation for the killing was that their troops had fired in response to a number of snipers who had opened up on them from below the flats. But those of us at the meeting heard only one shot before the soldiers opened up with their high-velocity rifles.

And while it is impossible to be absolutely sure, one came away with the firm impression, reinforced by dozens of eyewitnesses, that the soldiers, men of the 1st Battalion The Parachute regiment, flown in specially from Belfast, may have fired needlessly into the huge crowd.

Miss Bernadette Devlin said it was 'bloody cold blooded murder'. Mr John Hume said it was 'another Sharpeville', and he demanded the immediate withdrawal of all these 'uniformed murderers'. Mr Michael Canavan of the Derry Citizens' Central Council said: 'It was impossible to say who fired first. Personally I am sure it was the army, but it doesn't really matter. What was so terrible and so tragic was that the soldiers fired into a huge crowd of people, and fired indiscriminately at that. The death toll must show us that their firing was indiscriminate.'

The death toll at 7.30 p.m., three hours after the shooting, was said to be twelve, all men, and all said to be in their mid-twenties. A thirteenth victim was reported later.

*In 1964 **Ryszard Kapuscinski** was appointed by the Polish Press Agency as its only foreign correspondent, with responsibility for fifty countries. By the time he returned to Poland ten years later, he had survived twenty-seven coups and revolutions in Africa, Asia and Latin America – experiences which he recorded in* The Soccer War. *His later adventures included the war in Angola, the revolution in Iran and a journey across the dying Soviet empire in 1989. His reporting was touched with an extraordinary sense of romance, of magic realism, and seems particularly suited to the 'soccer war' itself, which was waged with bloody ferocity in 1969 between Honduras and El Salvador.*

Luis Suarez said there was going to be a war, and I believed whatever Luis said. We were staying together in Mexico. Luis was giving me a lesson in Latin America: what it is and how to understand it. He could foresee many events. In his time he had predicted the fall of Goulart in Brazil, the fall of Bosch in the Dominican Republic and of Jimenez in Venezuela. Long before the return of Perón he believed that the old *caudillo* would again become president of Argentina; he foretold the sudden death of the Haitian dictator François Duvalier at a time when everybody said Papa Doc had many years left. Luis knew how to pick his way through Latin politics, in which amateurs like me got bogged down and blundered helplessly with each step.

This time Luis announced his belief that there would be a war after putting down the newspaper in which he had read a report on the soccer match between the Honduran and Salvadoran national teams. The two countries were playing for the right to take part in the 1970 World Cup in Mexico.

The first match was held on Sunday 8 June 1969, in the Honduran capital, Tegucigalpa.

Nobody in the world paid any attention.

The Salvadoran team arrived in Tegucigalpa on Saturday and spent a sleepless night in their hotel. The team could not sleep because it was the target of psychological warfare waged by the Honduran fans. A swarm of people encircled the hotel. The crowd threw stones at the windows and beat sheets of tin and empty barrels with sticks. They set off one string of firecrackers after another. They leaned on the horns of cars parked in front of the hotel. The fans whistled, screamed and sent up hostile chants. This went on all night. The idea was that a sleepy, edgy, exhausted team would be bound to lose. In Latin America these are common practices.

The next day Honduras defeated the sleepless El Salvador squad one–nil.

Eighteen-year-old Amelia Bolanios was sitting in front of the television in El Salvador when the Honduran striker Roberto Cardona scored the winning goal in the final minute. She got up and ran to the desk which contained her father's pistol in a drawer. She then shot herself in the heart. 'The young girl could not bear to see her fatherland brought to its knees,' wrote the Salvadoran newspaper *El Nacional* the next day. The whole capital took part in the televised funeral of Amelia Bolanios. An army honour guard marched with a flag at the head of the procession. The president of the republic and his ministers walked behind the flag-draped coffin. Behind the government came the Salvadoran soccer eleven who, booed, laughed at and spat on at the Tegucigalpa airport, had returned to El Salvador on a special flight that morning.

But the return match of the series took place in San Salvador, the beautifully named Flor Blanca stadium, a week later. This time it was the Honduran team that spent a sleepless night. The screaming crowd of fans broke all the windows in the hotel and threw rotten eggs, dead rats and stinking rags inside. The players were taken to the match in armoured cars of the 1st Salvadoran Mechanised Division – which saved them from revenge and bloodshed at the hands of the mob that lined the route, holding up portraits of the national heroine Amelia Bolanios.

The army surrounded the ground. On the pitch stood a cordon of soldiers from a crack regiment of the Guardia Nacional, armed with submachine-guns. During the playing of the Honduran national anthem the crowd roared and whistled. Next, instead of the Honduran flag – which had been burnt before the eyes of the spectators, driving them mad with joy – the hosts ran a dirty, tattered dishrag up the flag-pole. Under such conditions the players from Tegucigalpa did not, understandably, have their minds on the game. They had their minds on getting out alive. 'We're awfully lucky that we lost,' said the visiting coach, Mario Griffin, with relief.

El Salvador prevailed, three–nil.

The same armoured cars carried the Honduran team straight from the playing field to the airport. A worse fate awaited the visiting fans. Kicked and beaten, they fled towards the border. Two of them died. Scores landed in hospital. One hundred and fifty of the visitors' cars were burned. The border between the two states was closed a few hours later.

Luis read about all of this in the newspaper and said that there was going to be a war. He had been a reporter for a long time and he knew his beat.

In Latin America, he said, the border between soccer and politics is vague. There is a long list of governments that have fallen or been overthrown after the defeat of the national team. Players on the losing team are denounced in the press as traitors. When Brazil won the World Cup in Mexico, an exiled Brazilian colleague of mine was heartbroken: 'The military right wing', he said, 'can be assured of at least five more years of peaceful rule.' On the way to the title, Brazil beat England. In an article with the headline 'Jesus Defends Brazil' the Rio de Janeiro paper *Jornal dos Sportes* explained the victory thus: 'Whenever the ball flew towards our goal and a score seemed inevitable, Jesus reached his foot out of the clouds and cleared the ball.' Drawings accompanied the article, illustrating the supernatural intervention.

'Houston, Tranquillity Base here. The Eagle *has landed.' On 21 July 1969, three American astronauts landed on the moon. Less than ten years since President John F. Kennedy had promised to do just that,* **Neil Armstrong** *put down the fragile little landing craft. This is his memory of that moment.*

It took us somewhat longer to emerge from *Eagle* than we had anticipated but the delay was not, as my wife and perhaps some others have half-jokingly suggested, to give me time to think about what to say when I actually stepped out on to the moon. I had thought about that a little before the flight, mainly because so many people had made such a big point of it. I had also thought about it a little on the way to the moon, but not much. It wasn't until after landing that I made up my mind what to say: 'That's one small step for a man, one giant leap for mankind.' Beyond those words I don't recall any particular emotion or feeling other than a little caution, a desire to be sure it was safe to put my weight on that surface outside *Eagle*'s footpad ...

The most dramatic recollections I have now are the sights themselves, those magnificent visual images. They go far beyond any other visual experiences I've had in my life. Of all the spectacular views we had, the most impressive to me was on the way towards the moon when we flew through its shadow. We were still thousands of miles away but close enough so that the moon almost filled our circular window. It was eclipsing the sun, from our position, and the corona of the sun was visible around the limb of the moon as a gigantic lens-shaped or saucer-shaped light stretching out to several lunar diameters. It was magnificent, but the moon itself was even more so. We were in its shadow so there was no part of it illuminated by the sun. It was illuminated only by the earth, by earthshine. It made the moon appear blue-grey and the entire scene looked decidedly three-dimensional.

I was really aware, visually aware, that the moon was in fact a sphere, not a disc. It seemed almost as if it were showing us its roundness, its similarity in shape to our earth, in a sort of welcome. I was sure then that it would be a hospitable host. It had been awaiting its first visitors for a long time.

The Vietnam War

The war in Vietnam, which was to occupy the United States for a decade and a half during the 1960s and early 1970s, had its roots in the post-war dissolution of Europe's colonial empire. The Japanese had occupied French Indo-China in 1941, and on their surrender in 1945, a communist regime had seized power in North Vietnam. The French regained control of southern Vietnam but withdrew after their defeat by the communists in 1954. Vietnam was then partitioned, with a pro-Western government established in the south. Before long, the communists in the north were sending guerrillas across the border to destabilise the Saigon government.

During the early sixties President Kennedy provided military advice to South Vietnam, and in 1965 President Johnson committed growing numbers of American ground forces to the defence of the country. The cost to the US was immense and fruitless. Saigon fell to the communists in the early summer of 1975 by which time the Americans had suffered 58,200 killed and over three hundred thousand wounded. It was America's first great military failure: it scarred a generation and marked American politics for the rest of the twentieth century and beyond. It also reshaped journalism and reportage – and not just in the United States.

*One of the most celebrated single pieces about Americans fighting in Vietnam was written by a British journalist, **Nicholas Tomalin**. 'The General Goes Zapping Charlie Cong' was defined by Tom Wolfe as a prime example of 'new journalism', where journalists hijacked the skills of the novelist to increase the dramatic tension of the subject.*

After a light lunch last Wednesday, General James F. Hollingsworth, of Big

Red One, took off in his personal helicopter and killed more Vietnamese than all the troops he commanded.

The story of the general's feat begins in the divisional office at Ki-Na, 20 miles north of Saigon, where a Medical Corps colonel is telling me that when they collect enemy casualties they find themselves with more than four injured civilians for every wounded Viet Cong – unavoidable in this kind of war.

The general strides in, pins two medals for outstanding gallantry to the chest of one of the colonel's combat doctors. Then he strides off again to his helicopter, and spreads out a polythene-covered map to explain our afternoon's trip.

The general has a big, real American face, reminiscent of every movie general you have seen. He comes from Texas, and is forty-eight. His present rank is brigadier general, assistant division commander, 1st Infantry Division, United States Army (which is what the big red figure one on his shoulder flash means).

'Our mission today', says the general, 'is to push those goddam VCs right off Routes 13 and 16. Now you see Routes 13 and 16 running north from Saigon towards the town of Phuoc Vinh, where we keep our artillery. When we got here first we prettied up those roads, and cleared Charlie Cong right out so we could run supplies up.

'I guess we've been hither and thither with all our operations since, an' the ol' VC he's reckoned he could creep back. He's been puttin' out propaganda he's goin' to interdict our right of passage along those routes. So this day we aim to zap him, and zap him, and zap him again till we've zapped him right back where he came from. Yes, sir. Let's go.'

The general's UH-18 helicopter carries two pilots, two 60-calibre machine-gunners, and his aide, Dennis Gillman, an apple-cheeked sub-altern from California. It also carries the general's own M-16 carbine (hanging on a strut), two dozen smoke-bombs, and a couple of CS anti-personnel gas bombs, each as big as a small dustbin. Just beside the general is a radio console where he can tune in on orders issued by battalion commanders flying helicopters just beneath him, and company commanders in helicopters just below them.

Under this interlacing of helicopters lies the apparently peaceful landscape beside Routes 13 and 16, filled with farmhouses and peasants hoeing rice and paddy fields.

So far today, things haven't gone too well. Companies Alpha, Bravo and Charlie have assaulted a suspected Viet Cong HQ, found a few tunnels but no enemy.

The general sits at the helicopter's open door, knees apart, his shiny black toecaps jutting out into space, rolls a filter-tip cigarette to and fro in his teeth, and thinks.

'Put me down at Battalion HQ,' he calls to the pilot.

'There's sniper fire reported on choppers in that area, general.'

'Goddam the snipers, just put me down.'

Battalion HQ at the moment is a defoliated area of 4 acres packed with tents, personnel carriers, helicopters and milling GIs. We settle into the smell of crushed grass. The general leaps out and strides through his troops.

'Why, general, excuse us, we didn't expect you here,' says a sweating major.

'You killed any 'Cong yet?'

'Well no, general, I guess he's just too scared of us today. Down the road a piece we've hit trouble, a bulldozer's fallen through a bridge, and trucks coming through a village knocked the canopy off a Buddhist pagoda. Saigon radioed us to repair that temple before proceeding – in the way of civic action, general. That put us back an hour ...'

'Yeah. Well, major, you spread out your perimeter here a bit, then get to killin' VC's will you?'

Back through the crushed grass to the helicopter.

'I don't know how you think about war. The way I see it, I'm just like any other company boss, gingering up the boys all the time, except I don't make money. I just kill people, and save lives.'

In the air the general chews two more filter-tips and looks increasingly forlorn. No action on Route 16, and another Big Red One general has got his helicopter in to inspect the collapsed bridge before ours.

'Swing us back along again,' says the general.

'Reports of fire on choppers ahead, sir. Smoke flare near spot. Strike coming in.'

'Go find that smoke.'

A plume of white rises in the midst of dense tropical forest, with a Bird Dog spotter plane in attendance. Route 16 is to the right; beyond it a large settlement of red-tiled houses.

'Strike coming in, sir.'

Two F105 jets appear over the horizon in formation, split, then one passes over the smoke, dropping a trail of silver, fish-shaped canisters. After four seconds' silence, light orange fire explodes in patches along an area 50 yards wide by three-quarters of a mile long. Napalm.

The trees and bushes burn, pouring dark oily smoke into the sky. The second plane dives and fire covers the entire strip of dense forest.

'Aaaaah,' cries the general. 'Nice. Nice. Very neat. Come in low, let's see who's left down there.'

'How do you know for sure the Viet Cong snipers were in that strip you burned?'

'We don't. The smoke position was a guess. That's why we zap the whole forest.'

'But what if there was someone, a civilian, walking through there?'

'Aw come, son, you think there's folks just sniffing flowers in tropical vegetation like that? With a big operation on hereabouts? Anyone left down there, he's Charlie Cong all right.'

I point at a paddy field full of peasants less than half a mile away.

'That's different, son. We know they're genuine.'

The pilot shouts: 'General, half-right, two running for that bush.'

'I see them. Down, down, goddam you.'

In one movement he yanks his M-16 off the hanger, slams in a clip of cartridges and leans right out of the door, hanging on his seatbelt to fire one long burst in the general direction of the bush.

'General, there's a hole, maybe a bunker, down there.'

'Smoke-bomb, circle, shift it.'

'But general, how do you know those aren't just frightened peasants?'

'Running? Like that? Don't give me a pain. The clips, the clips, where in hell are the cartridges in this ship?'

The aide drops a smoke canister, the general finds his ammunition and the starboard machine-gunner fires rapid bursts into the bush, his tracers bouncing up off the ground round it.

We turn clockwise in ever tighter, lower circles, everyone firing. A shower of spent cartridge cases leaps from the general's carbine to drop, lukewarm, on my arm.

'I ... WANT ... YOU ... TO ... SHOOT ... RIGHT ... UP ... THE ... ASS ... OF ... THAT ... HOLE ... GUNNER.'

Fourth time round the tracers flow right inside the tiny sandbagged opening, tearing the bags, filling it with sand and smoke.

The general falls back off his seatbelt into his chair, suddenly relaxed, and lets out an oddly feminine, gentle laugh. 'That's it,' he says, and turns to me, squeezing his thumb and finger into the sign of a French chef's ecstasy.

Another celebrated piece of New Journalism in Vietnam reporting was **Michael Herr**'s Dispatches, *a sustained piece of reportage by a brilliant writer, often imitated since but never surpassed. Here he describes the mantrap that was the marine command post and airstrip at Khe Sanh.*

He was a tall blond from Michigan, probably about twenty, although it was never easy to guess the ages of marines at Khe Sanh since nothing like youth ever lasted in their faces for very long. It was the eyes: because they were always either strained or blazed-out or simply blank, they never had anything to do with what the rest of the face was doing, and it gave everyone the look of extreme fatigue or even a glancing madness. (And age. If you take one of those platoon photographs from the Civil War and cover everything but the eyes, there is no difference between a man of fifty and a boy of thirteen.) This marine, for example, was always smiling. It was the kind of smile that verged on the high giggles, but his eyes showed neither amusement nor embarrassment nor nervousness. It was a little insane, but it was mostly esoteric in the way that so many marines under twenty-five became esoterics after a few months in 1 Corps. On that young, nondescript face the smile seemed to come out of some old knowledge, and it said, 'I'll tell you why I'm smiling, but it will make you crazy.'

He had tattooed the name MARLENE on his upper arm, and up on his helmet there was the name JUDY, and he said, 'Yeah, well, Judy knows all about Marlene. That's cool, there's no sweat there.' On the back of his flak jacket he had once written, 'Yea, though I walk through the Valley of the

Shadow of Death I shall fear no Evil, because I'm the meanest mother-fucker in the Valley,' but he had tried later, without much success, to scrub it off because, he explained, every damn dude in the DMZ had that written on their flak jackets. And he'd smile.

He was smiling on this last morning of his tour. His gear was straight, his papers in order, his duffel packed, and he was going through all of the last-minute business of going home, the back-slapping and goosing; the joshing with the Old Man ('Come on, you know you're gonna miss this place.' 'Yes, sir. Oh wow!'); the exchanging of addresses; the old, frag-mented reminiscences blurted out of awkward silences. He had a few joints left, wrapped up in a plastic bag (he hadn't smoked them, because, like most marines at Khe Sanh, he'd expected a ground attack, and he didn't want to be stoned when it came), and he gave these to his best friend, or, rather, his best surviving friend. His oldest friend had been blown away in January, on the same day that the ammo dump had been hit. He had always wondered whether Gunny, the company gunnery sergeant, had known about all the smoking. After three wars Gunny probably didn't care much; besides, they all knew that Gunny was into some pretty cool shit himself. When he dropped by the bunker they said goodbye, and then there wasn't anything to do with the morning but to run in and out of the bunker for a look at the sky, coming back in every time to say that it really ought to clear enough by ten for the planes to get in. By noon, when the goodbyes and take-cares and get-a-little-for-me's had gone on for too long by hours, the sun started to show through the mist. He picked up his duffel and a small awol bag and started for the airstrip and the small, deep slit-trench on the edge of the strip.

Khe Sanh was a very bad place then, but the airstrip there was the worst place in the world. It was what Khe Sanh had instead of a V-ring, the exact, predictable object of the mortars and rockets hidden in the surrounding hills, the sure target of the big Russian and Chinese guns lodged in the side of CoRoc Ridge, 11 kilometres away across the Laotian border. There was nothing random about the shelling there, and no one wanted anything to do with it. If the wind was right, you could hear the NVA 0.50-calibres starting far up the valley whenever a plane made its approach to the strip, and the first incoming artillery would precede the landings by seconds. If you were waiting there to be taken out, there was nothing you could do but curl up in the trench and try to make yourself small, and if you were coming in on the plane, there was nothing you could do, nothing at all ...

On this last morning, the young marine caught a ride from his company position that dropped him off 50 metres from the strip. As he moved on foot he heard the distant sound of the C-123 coming in, and that was all he heard. There was hardly more than a 100-foot ceiling, scary, bearing down on him. Except for the approaching engines, everything was still. If there had been something more, just one incoming round, he might have been all right, but in that silence the sound of his own feet moving over the dirt was terrifying to him. He later said that this was what made him stop. He dropped his duffel and looked around. He watched the plane, his plane, as it touched down, and then he ran leaping over some discarded sandbags by the road. He lay out flat and listened as the plane switched loads and took off, listened until there was nothing left to listen to. Not a single round had come in.

Back at the bunker there was some surprise at his return, but no one said anything. Anyone can miss a plane. Gunny slapped him on the back and wished him a better trip the next time out. That afternoon he rode in a jeep that took him all the way to Charlie Med, the medical detachment for Khe Sanh that had been set up insanely close to the strip, but he never got himself past the sandbagging outside of the triage room.

> *Saigon fell on 30 April 1975. The Americans scrambled as many of their own people as they could out of the country, lifting the last by helicopter from roofs of hotels and compounds. **James Fenton**, one of the great reporter-poets, describes what happened when the new rulers arrived.*

By now there was chaos on the streets. The trucks which had passed us in one direction as we were coming out of Saigon appeared to have returned. Clearly nobody knew where to go. There was gunfire at the crossroads just ahead, and I think that we all felt, having lost our car, in great danger. We were saved by a taximan who dumped a load of customers and offered to take us back for 4,000 piastres. I would have paid whatever I had. We got into the car, put our heads down, and sped back to the city centre.

In the Reuters office I was writing an account of what I had just seen when Barron* came in again.

'I don't know what's happening,' he said, 'I've just seen a tank with the flag of the National Liberation Front.' I went to the door and looked out to the left, in the direction of Thieu's palace, and saw the tank. Without thinking, I ran after it and flagged it down just as it turned towards the palace gates. The tank slowed down and a North Vietnamese soldier in green jumped off the back and went at me with his gun, as if to hit me. In my confusion, I couldn't remember the NLF salute, or how to explain to the soldier that I wanted a ride. I tried everything – a salute, another salute, a clenched fist, a hitch-hiker's thumb. Finally (after, that is, a few extremely nervous seconds) I held out my hand to shake his. He took my hand abruptly and indicated the back of the tank. I remember worrying, as I climbed on, that I might touch something very hot. Then, as the soldiers told me to keep my head down, I idiotically produced my passport, which they dismissed scornfully. The tank speeded up, and rammed the left side of the palace gate. Wrought iron flew into the air, but the whole structure refused to give. I nearly fell off. The tank backed again, and I observed a man with a nervous smile opening the centre portion of the gate. We drove into the grounds of the palace, and fired a salute.

I had taken a ride on the first tank to reach the palace, but it was not until several weeks later that I realised this was the case: looking up from my crouching position at the back, I saw another vehicle in the grounds (which turned out to be a South Vietnamese tank). Damn, I thought, I was on the second; still, never mind. I wondered whether I was under arrest. I tried to talk to the soldiers, but I did not notice that some of them were captured troops of the South Vietnamese Army who had been co-opted in order to show the way. On the top of the tank was an open carton of Winston cigarettes, which struck me as odd. No doubt it had been thrown up from the looting crowd. I also remember noticing that another tank was passing behind us on the lawn. Its tracks crushed the verge of a flower bed, and I remember thinking: that was unnecessary. Also, I noticed an extraordinary number of dragonflies in the air.

---

* Brian Barron of the BBC.

I was very, very excited. The weight of the moment, the privilege of being a witness, impressed itself at once. Over and above my self-consciousness, and the trivial details which were made all the more interesting by the extraordinary nature of the event, there was the historical grandeur of the scene. Events in history are not supposed to look historical: no eye perceived a battlefield at a glance, no dying leader composed his followers around him in the neoclassical manner; many war photographs, even some of the great ones, are said to have been rearranged. The victors write, rewrite or retouch their history. Indeed in one Western account of these events, I noticed that the tank I have just described was meant to have knocked the palace gate to the ground 'like a wooden twig'. The man who opened the gate, a civilian guard, has in this account been subbed out. The guards themselves have fled. Nothing is allowed to interfere with the symmetry of the scene, or interrupt the conquest with wild, flailing arms.

And yet the North Vietnamese do not merely touch up history. They also enact it in the heroic manner. This was the first time I had seen their genius for imposing their style upon events, for acting in the manner of their propaganda. The spectacle was tremendous and, as one of their officers realised, not to be missed. He ran up to a British cameraman filming the arrival of the tanks, and begged him: 'You take film for us? You take film for us?' The tanks rolled on to the lawn, and formed automatically into a semicircle in front of the palace, firing a salute into the air as they did so. Soon the air became full of the sound of saluting guns. Beside the gate, sitting in a row on the lawn, was a group of soldiers, former members of the palace guard. They waved their hands above their heads in terror. An NLF soldier took his flag and, waving it above his head, ran into the palace. A few moments later, he emerged on the terrace, waving the flag round and round. Later still, there he was on the roof. The red and yellow stripes of the Saigon regime were lowered at last.

Jon Swain must have been one of the youngest reporters covering the conflict in Vietnam and Cambodia when both countries were taken over by communist insurgents. Having spent a part of his childhood growing up in Asia, Swain, the most fearless of newsmen, had a natural empathy with Cambodia and its people. In River of Time *he describes what happened to the*

Cambodians sheltering in the French embassy when the Khmer Rouge, led by Pol Pot, arrived in Phnom Penh in April 1975.

All this time, hundreds of Cambodians were sheltering in the embassy; Pran was one of them. Since our arrival, we had managed to keep him safely with us as one of the 'internationals'. We had also found shelter for some of the Cambodian journalists, interpreters and their families. But most were having to camp outdoors on the grass.

I awoke the next morning to find the Scottish team playing bridge in the garden. There was the usual wisecrack about British phlegm in a tight spot. The banter did not last long. Word spread that the Khmer Rouge were reclassifying the embassy as an international regroupment centre for foreigners only. Implicit in its loss of diplomatic status was that it was no longer protected foreign territory and the Khmer Rouge soldiers could enter, without warning, at any time, and force the Cambodians out at gunpoint.

The bridge game broke up in silence as Dyrac* came to tell the Cambodians they should leave in the interests of self- preservation ...

The news fell like a death sentence. Hundreds of Cambodians – as well as Vietnamese and Chinese who had lived their lives in Cambodia and regarded themselves as Cambodians – packed up a few belongings and prepared to leave. The odd thing was that so few of them expressed surprise at being ejected. They were numbed and resigned, and bleakly stared ahead. Here and there, some cried quietly. We shared our food with them and with heavy hearts watched them trudge towards the front gate – women, children, elderly people, friends. As they moved in a tattered column towards the Khmer Rouge soldiers waiting for them they did not look back – had they done so they would have seen many of us break down into tears. Suddenly it rained. It usually did at funerals ...

One Cambodian couple I knew gave away their seven-month-old baby which would never survive the long march into the countryside. I was too choked to look them in the face as they handed the boy to a Frenchwoman to be cared for. 'He is my only baby. He is a beautiful baby,' the wife sobbed, holding him in her arms for the last time and smothering his face with kisses of love and wet tears.

---

* Jean Dyrac, the French consul.

The French had already collected all our passports and at the Comité de la Ville's request were making lists of all the people in the embassy. We had to try to keep Pran with us. Sydney was insistent. Although his family was safely out of Cambodia, having been evacuated with the Americans, Pran had stayed to help Sydney cover the city's fall for the *New York Times*. Now it had all gone horribly wrong and Sydney felt overwhelming responsibility for his Cambodian assistant, reinforced by the fact that Pran, with his loyalty and quickness of mind, had saved all our lives.

We could think of only one solution: to forge a second British passport I had and give it to Pran as his own. Armed with this and a new identity, we imagined he could stay with us. That he looked Asian was not an insurmountable barrier, for he could perhaps pass himself off as a Nepalese holder of a British passport. There was a similarity of features. It was a chance but it might work.

There was no time to lose. Using a razor-blade, Al Rockoff scraped off my picture and replaced it with one of Pran. For glue, we used a gummy mixture of water and rice. More difficult was erasing my name. In the end we had to compromise: Pran became John Ancketill Brewer – my first three names. It was quite a mouthful to pronounce for a Briton, let alone a Cambodian turned Nepalese; he walked around the building repeating 'John Ancketill Brewer' until he was reasonably word perfect. Duly doctored, his British passport, number C352165, issued by the British embassy, Saigon, on 11 December 1973, was handed in to the consulate and we settled down to wait and hope.

A little while later, a group of solemn-faced embassy officials came to see us. Shaking their heads sadly, they gave back my passport, saying it was a good try but they had seen through the forgery immediately. They imagined the Khmer Rouge would too. What would Pran do in a confrontation? Would he be able to bluff it out? The next few hours were a nightmare as we agonised what to do. In the end Pran took the decision for us.

People were still leaving the city. We could see them toiling down the road outside, bedraggled and broken. But the numbers were dwindling. Pran decided the longer he was identified with foreigners in the embassy the tougher time he would have afterwards justifying himself to the Khmer Rouge. He would leave with the next batch of Cambodians who were even then packing their things in preparation for departure and try to make it across the border to Thailand ...

He had taught us what friendship meant and when his luck ran out we had nothing to give him except money and food. Our abandonment of him confirmed in me the belief that we journalists were in the end just privileged passengers in transit through Cambodia's landscape of hell. We were eyewitnesses to a great human tragedy none of us could comprehend. We had betrayed our Cambodian friends. We had been unable to save those who had saved us. We were protected simply because our skins were white. I felt ashamed.

The withdrawal of American combat troops from Vietnam in August 1972 coincided with a more domestic American drama, the Watergate affair. The cover-up of a break-in by Republican party henchmen into the Democratic party HQ led eventually to the fall of President Richard Nixon. **Bob Woodward** *and* **Carl Bernstein** *of the* Washington Post *were the heroes of the pack of sleuthing journalists digging into the affair. Unusually, they gave journalism a good name. Here they meet their prime source, Mark Felt, deputy head of the FBI, the legendary 'Deep Throat', whose guidance was to help them unseat a president.*

Woodward had a source in the Executive Branch who had access to information at CRP [Committee for the Re-election of the President, also known as CREEP] as well as at the White House. His identity was unknown to anyone else. He could be contacted only on very important occasions. Woodward had promised he would never identify him or his position to anyone. Further, he had agreed never to quote the man, even as an anonymous source. Their discussions would be only to confirm information that had been obtained elsewhere and to add some perspective.

In newspaper terminology, this meant the discussions were on 'deep background'. Woodward explained the arrangement to managing editor Howard Simons one day. He had taken to calling the source 'my friend', but Simons dubbed him 'Deep Throat', the title of a celebrated pornographic movie. The name stuck.

At first Woodward and Deep Throat had talked by telephone, but as the tensions of Watergate increased, Deep Throat's nervousness grew. He

didn't want to talk on the telephone, but had said they could meet somewhere on occasion.

Deep Throat didn't want to use the phone even to set up the meetings.
He suggested that Woodward open the drapes in his apartment as a signal.
Deep Throat could check each day; if the drapes were open, the two would
meet that night. But Woodward liked to let the sun in at times, and suggested another signal.

Several years earlier, Woodward had found a red cloth flag lying in the
street. Barely 1 foot square, it was attached to a stick, the type of warning
device used on the back of a truck carrying a projecting load. Woodward
had taken the flag back to his apartment and one of his friends had stuck
it into an old flower pot on the balcony. It had stayed there.

When Woodward had an urgent enquiry to make, he would move the
flower pot with the red flag to the rear of the balcony. During the day, Deep
Throat would check to see if the pot had been moved. If it had, he and
Woodward would meet at about 2 a.m. in a pre-designated underground
parking garage. Woodward would leave his sixth-floor apartment and
walk down the back stairs into an alley.

Walking and taking two or more taxis to the garage, he could be reasonably sure that no one had followed him. In the garage, the two could
talk for an hour or more without being seen. If taxis were hard to find, as
they often were late at night, it might take Woodward almost two hours to
get there on foot. On two occasions, a meeting had been set and the man
had not shown up – a depressing and frightening experience, as Woodward had waited for more than an hour, alone in an underground garage
in the middle of the night. Once he had thought he was being followed –
two well-dressed men had stayed behind him for five or six blocks, but he
had ducked into an alley and had not seen them again.

If Deep Throat wanted a meeting – which was rare – there was a different procedure. Each morning, Woodward would check page 20 of his *New
York Times*, delivered to his apartment house before 7 a.m. If a meeting
was requested, the page number would be circled and the hands of a clock
indicating the time of the rendezvous would appear in a lower corner of
the page. Woodward did not know how Deep Throat got to his paper.

The man's position in the Executive Branch was extremely sensitive.

He had never told Woodward anything that was incorrect. It was he who had advised Woodward on 19 June that Howard Hunt was definitely involved in Watergate. During the summer, he had told Woodward that the FBI badly wanted to know where the *Post* was getting its information. He thought Bernstein and Woodward might be followed, and cautioned them to take care when using their telephones. The White House, he had said at the last meeting, regarded the stakes in Watergate as much higher than anyone outside perceived. Even the FBI did not understand what was happening. The source had been deliberately vague about this, however, making veiled references to the CIA and national security which Woodward did not understand.

The day after the indictments were handed down, Woodward broke the rule about telephone contact. Deep Throat sounded nervous, but listened as the draft of a story was read to him. It said that federal investigators had received information from Nixon campaign workers that high officials of the Committee for the Re-election of the President had been involved in the funding of the Watergate operation.

'Too soft,' Deep Throat said. 'You can go much stronger.'

A Walk on the Wild Side

*Some of the best travel writing of the century has come from the pens of loners and mavericks. **W. H. Davies**, Welsh poet and itinerant, was arguably the first of the literary hobos, famous for his hymn to idleness in the poem 'Leisure':*

What is this life if, full of care,
We have no time to stop and stare.

Bored with life as an apprentice in Monmouth, he took off for the United States where he wandered the Mississippi in a houseboat, and jumped freight boxcars on the railroad. He described his life idling through the Midwest in The Autobiography of a Super-Tramp, *which came out in 1908. In it he anticipated the other great wandering minstrels and balladeers of remote America, down to Jack Kerouac, Hunter S. Thompson and Bob Dylan. Here he describes the art of free-riding the railroad, or boxcar jumping.*

Upon this we had several drinks, for I was so pleased at Brum's decision, that I ordered drink after drink with bewildering succession. Brum informed me of a freight train that was to leave the yards at midnight, on which we could beat our way to a small town on the borders of the hop country. Not knowing what to do with ourselves until that time arrived, we continued to drink until we were not in a fit condition for this hazardous undertaking – except we were fortunate to get an empty car, so as to lie down and sleep upon the journey. At last we made our way towards the yards, where we saw the men making up the train. We kept out of sight until that was done and then in the darkness Brum inspected one side of the train and I the other, in quest of an empty car. In vain we sought for that comfort. There was nothing to do but to ride the bumpers or the top of the car, exposed to the cold night air. We jumped the bumpers, the engine whistled twice, toot! toot! and we felt ourselves slowly moving out of the yards. Brum was on one car and I was on the next facing him. Never shall I forget the horrors of that ride. He had taken fast hold on the handlebar of his car, and I had done likewise with mine. We had been riding for some fifteen minutes, and the train was going at its full speed when, to my horror, I saw Brum lurch forward, and then quickly pull himself straight and erect. Several times he did this, and I shouted to him. It was no use, for the man was drunk and fighting against the overpowering effects, and it was a mystery to me how he kept his hold. At last he became motionless for so long that I knew the next time he lurched forward his weight of body must break his hold, and he would fall under the wheels and be cut to pieces. I worked myself carefully towards him and woke him. Although I had great difficulty in waking him, he swore that he was not asleep. I had scarcely done this when a lantern was shown from the top of the car, and a brakesman's voice hailed us. 'Hallo, where are you two going?' 'To the hop fields,' I answered. 'Well,' he sneered, 'I guess you won't get to them on this train, so jump off, at once. Jump! d'ye hear?' he cried, using a great oath, as he saw we were little inclined to obey. Brum was now wide awake. 'If you don't jump at once', shouted this irate brakesman, 'you will be thrown off.' 'To jump', said Brum quietly, 'will be sure death, and to be thrown off will mean no more.' 'Wait until I come back,' cried the brakesman, 'and we will see whether you ride this train or not,' on which he left us, making his way towards the caboose. 'Now', said Brum, 'when he returns we must be on the top of the car, for he will probably bring with him a coupling pin to strike us off the bumpers, making us fall under the wheels.' We quickly clambered on top and in a few minutes could see a light approaching us, moving along the top of the cars. We were now lying flat, so that he might not see us until he stood on the same car. He was very near to us, when we sprang to our feet, and unexpectedly gripped him, one on each side, and before he could recover from his first astonishment. In all my life I have never seen so much fear on a human face. He must have seen our half-drunken condition and at once gave up all hopes of mercy from such men, for he stood helpless, not knowing what to do. If he struggled it would mean the fall and death of the three, and did he remain helpless in our hands, it might mean being thrown from that height from a car going at the rate of 30 miles an hour. 'Now', said Brum to him, 'what is it to be? Shall we ride this train without interference, or shall we have a wrestling bout up here, when the first fall must be our last? Speak?' 'Boys,' said he, affecting a short laugh, 'you have the drop on me; you can ride.' We watched him making his way back to the caboose, which he entered, but every moment I expected to see him reappear assisted by others. It might have been that there was some friction among them, and that they would not ask assistance from one another. For instance, an engineer has to take orders from the conductor, but the former is as well paid, if not better, than the latter, and the most responsibility is on his shoulders, and this often makes ill blood between them. At any rate, American tramps know well that neither the engineer nor the fireman, his faithful attendant, will inform the conductor or brakesman of their presence on a train. Perhaps the man was ashamed of his ill-success, and did not care to own his defeat to the conductor and his fellow brakesmen; but whatever was the matter, we rode that train to its destination and without any more interference.

*An equally quixotic journey was later undertaken by **Hunter S. Thompson** and his attorney to Las Vegas in 1972. It was a trip in more ways than one, as Thompson entered the city with a veritable arsenal of drugs for what ultimately became a psychedelic odyssey in search of the American dream. It could be argued that* Fear and Loathing in Las Vegas *is more about style than content, but it is the model, the essence, of Gonzo journalism, and it infected action reporting from Vietnam to the present day. Here Thompson and the attorney witness the Mint Bikers Race – or was it the biker race of the Mint Gun Club? Anyway it was a pretty on-off affair.*

The racers were ready at dawn. Fine sunrise over the desert. Very tense. But the race didn't start until nine, so we had to kill about three long hours in the casino next to the pits, and that's where the trouble started.

The bar opened at seven. There was also a 'koffee & donut canteen' in the bunker, but those of us who had been up all night in places like the Circus-Circus were in no mood for coffee and doughnuts. We wanted strong drink. Our tempers were ugly and there were at least two hundred of us, so they opened the bar early. By 8.30 there were big crowds around the crap-tables. The place was full of noise and drunken shouting.

A bony, middle-aged hoodlum wearing a Harley-Davidson T-shirt boomed up to the bar and yelled: 'God damn! What day is this – Saturday?'

'More like Sunday,' somebody replied.

'Hah! That's a bitch, ain't it?' the H-D boomer shouted to nobody in particular. 'Last night I was out home in Long Beach and somebody said they were runnin' the Mint 400 today, so I says to my old lady, "Man, I'm goin'." ' He laughed. 'So she gives me a lot of crap about it, you know ... so I started slappin' her around and the next thing I knew two guys I never even seen before got me out on the sidewalk workin' me over. Jesus! They beat me stupid.'

He laughed again, talking into the crowd and not seeming to care who listened. 'Hell yes!' he continued. 'Then one of 'em says, "Where you going?" And I says, "Las Vegas, to the Mint 400." So they gave me 10 bucks and drove me down to the bus station ...' He paused. 'At least I think it was them ...

'Well, anyway, here I am. And I tell you that was one hell of a long night, man! Seven hours on that goddamn bus! But when I woke up it was dawn and here I was in downtown Vegas and for a minute I didn't know what the hell I was doin' here. All I could think was, "O Jesus, here we go again: Who's divorced me this time?" '

He accepted a cigarette from somebody in the crowd, still grinning as he lit up. 'But then I remembered, by God! I was here for the Mint 400 ... and, man, that's all I needed to know. I tell you it's wonderful to be here, man. I don't give a damn who wins or loses. It's just wonderful to be here with you people ...'

Nobody argued with him. We all understood. In some circles, the 'Mint 400' is a far, far better thing than the Super Bowl, the Kentucky Derby and the Lower Oakland Roller Derby Finals all rolled into one. This race attracts a very special breed, and our man in the Harley T-shirt was clearly one of them.

*

The correspondent from *Life* nodded sympathetically and screamed at the bartender: 'Senzaman wazzyneeds!'

'Fast up with it,' I croaked. 'Why not five?' I smacked the bar with my open, bleeding palm. 'Hell yes! Bring us ten!'

'I'll back it!' The *Life* man screamed. He was losing his grip on the bar, sinking slowly to his knees, but still speaking with definite authority: 'This is a magic moment in sport! It may never come again!' Then his voice seemed to break. 'I once did the Triple Crown,' he muttered. 'But it was nothing like this.'

The frog-eyed woman clawed feverishly at his belt. 'Stand up!' she pleaded. '*Please* stand up! You'd be a very handsome man if you'd just *stand* up!'

He laughed distractedly. 'Listen, madam,' he snapped. 'I'm damn near intolerably handsome down here where I am. You'd go *crazy* if I stood up!'

The woman kept pulling at him. She'd been mooning at his elbows for two hours, and now she was making her move. The man from *Life* wanted no part of it; he slumped deeper into his crouch.

I turned away. It was too horrible. We were, after all, the absolute cream of the national sporting press. And we were gathered here in Las Vegas for a very special assignment: to cover the Fourth Annual 'Mint 400' ... and when it comes to things like this, you don't fool around.

But now – even before the spectacle got under way – there were signs that we might be losing control of the situation. Here we were on this fine Nevada morning, this cool bright dawn on the desert, hunkered down at some greasy bar in a concrete blockhouse and gambling casino called the Mint Gun Club about 10 miles out of Vegas ... and with the race about to start, we were dangerously disorganised.

Outside, the lunatics were playing with their motorcycles, taping the headlights, topping off oil in the forks, last minute bolt-tightening (carburettor screws, manifold nuts etc.) ... and the first ten bikes blasted off on the stroke of nine. It was extremely exciting and we all went outside to watch. The flag went down and these ten poor buggers popped their clutches and zoomed into the first turn, all together, then somebody grabbed the lead (a 405 Husquvarna, as I recall), and a cheer went up as the rider screwed it on and disappeared in a cloud of dust.

'Well, that's that,' somebody said. 'They'll be back around in an hour or so. Let's go back to the bar.'

Some of the best reporters travel alone. **Linda Polman** *is a Dutch writer in the mould of Ryszard Kapuscinski and Graham Greene. Throughout the 1990s the United Nations was drafted into war zones, only to find itself unable to halt the murder and genocide. In 1995 Polman hung on in Somalia, then in what seemed like perpetual meltdown, after most other journalists left. That year too she went out among the refugees fleeing from Rwanda into Zaire, and witnessed the failure of the UN to instil order into the chaos of Haiti. Her report on Haiti has become a classic.*

While three-quarters of the population cannot read or write, most of the children in Haiti have not been to school for three years. The schools are closed because people can't spare the admission fees, so there's no money to pay the teachers. The Haitian-American Institute is a language school in Port-au-Prince. Its principal, an American woman, looks exhausted. She is drinking too much. With an unsteady hand she lights up another Comme Il Faut cigarette.

'Twenty years ago I taught Haitian children an English vocabulary which would allow them to study medicine or law in the States. After the coup against Aristide I gave a crash course in slang. Just in case the boat made it to Florida and they were picked up by the immigration service. I taught them to say things like "Yo, motherfucker, you sayin' I ain't American just 'cause I's a nigger?" They still had some hope then. Now, with the blockade, they haven't got a chance. So the Institute is closed. No more students.'

We are dining in Pétionville, the only place in the country where, with a little effort, you can imagine you're not in Haiti. There are discotheques and stores where you can buy cordless telephones and computers. True, the supermarkets are smelling mouldier every day and they no longer sell fresh or frozen products. But the tinned fancy pink salmon and the Beaujolais Nouveau are still on the shelves. And they say that the few hundred square metres that make up this suburb of Port-au-Prince are now home to a few dozen more millionaires than before the embargo.

Eating within sight of the hungry Haitians who have climbed the hill from the slums *là-bas* is, once again, not a success. The dinner is nerve-racking. We order spaghetti. I don't know the restaurant's real name, but the journalists call it Cindy's Place, after the prostitute who invariably manages to find us here. She hangs around the gate to the terrace until she sees someone she knows, then minces over to him, pulls up a chair and joins the meal. Her mini-skirted, high-heeled friends in the street jump out in front of the kerb-crawling cars. They are little girls dressed up in women's clothes. More and more of them are working the same patch, which leads to screaming rows. Potential clients let them parade in front of the headlights before they start negotiating a price for what they have seen. Apart from the clamour of the hookers, we have to endure the screaming of street children, who are after the leftovers from our plates, and keep out the cacophony produced by a perambulating combo playing old Beatles numbers. We collect some money just to shut them up.

Is our perception distorted by vexation, or are there really more cripples stumbling round than before? Every few minutes we seem to see somebody passing by with deformed limbs.

'People no longer get their broken arms and legs reset and put in plaster. They can't afford it,' says Dr Frantz Large. He sits grimly behind a plate of French fries at the next table. 'I don't see any more patients at my surgery because people know that I'm going to prescribe medicines they can't pay for, even if they're in stock. The hospital is almost empty for the same reason: you can lie in a bed for free, but you have to find and pay for medicines and bandages yourself. We still have a few nurses who push beds into the dry whenever it rains. The roof leaks, of course. Six months ago three shiploads of medical aid arrived. Nobody knows what happened to it. If you guys go looking for it, you'll probably find it costing a fortune up here in the drugstores of Pétionville, or maybe in the Dominican Republic.' Dr Large laughs a tired and humourless laugh.

THE AGE OF THE REPORTER

The Front Line

If Vietnam set a new style and agenda of journalism, the short campaign waged by the British to recover the Falkland Islands from Argentine occupation in 1982 reached back to a much earlier era. It was the last of the British imperial wars and was conducted by British forces alone, who allowed only male British reporters to accompany them. The remoteness was summed up by the BBC's **Brian Hanrahan**, *who describes in this piece the sorties of British Harrier fighters from the aircraft carrier* Hermes. *In it he utters the famous phrase 'I counted them all out, and I counted them all back', because, under the restrictions imposed by British military censorship, he was not allowed to give the actual number of planes involved. William Howard Russell had far more freedom of information when he reported the Charge of the Light Brigade at Balaclava, a century and a quarter before.*

At 6 pm on Saturday evening [1 May], ships of the Royal Navy went into action off the Falkland Islands. They bombarded the coast with their 4½-inch guns, a follow-up to the morning's bombing runs. As the ships moved in, Mirage fighters of the Argentine Air Force moved out to attack. The Sea Harriers, which had been continually patrolling overhead, swooped to intercept. The planes cartwheeled across the sky in a fierce dogfight. At the end two Argentine planes had been shot down; others were believed to have been damaged. Captain Lin Middleton of HMS *Hermes* said the British aircraft had all returned safely, their pilots uninjured. This was the end of a day in which the Task Force defences had been probed continually by Argentine aircraft. But until the naval bombardment started, each time the aircraft had turned away.

The naval Task Force had entered the exclusion zone around the Falklands at 7 a.m. Greenwich Mean Time in the morning. Within an hour, the air strike had begun. HMS *Hermes*, on its radar, tracked a Vulcan bomber in to shed its load of twenty-one 1,000-pound bombs across Stanley airport. The night was an ideal one for surprise: dark and overcast, no moon, just an occasional star breaking through the clouds. As the big bomber turned back to base, we monitored its radio codeword: the mission was successful.

A few hours after the Vulcan attack, it was *Hermes*'s turn. At dawn the navy's Sea Harriers took off, each carrying three 1,000-pound bombs. They wheeled in the sky before heading for the islands – at that stage just 90 miles away. Some of the planes went to create more havoc at Stanley, the others to a small airstrip called Goose Green, near Darwin, 120 miles to the west. There they found and bombed a number of grounded aircraft mixed in with decoys. At Stanley the planes went in low, in waves just seconds apart. They glimpsed the bomb craters left by the Vulcan and they left behind them more fire and destruction. The pilots said there had been smoke and dust everywhere, punctuated by the flash of explosions. They faced a barrage of return fire, heavy but apparently ineffective. I'm not allowed to say how many planes joined the raid, but I counted them all out, and I counted them all back. Their pilots were all unhurt, cheerful and jubilant, giving thumbs-up signs. One plane had a single bullet hole through the tail; it's already been repaired.

After studying the reconnaissance photographs, the admiral's staff pronounced both raids a success – aircraft had been damaged and the airfields cratered. The intention of the attack was threefold: to damage radar and missiles that could threaten the Harriers; to deny Stanley as a base to Argentine aircraft; and to cut off the Falklands by air, enforcing Britain's blockade of the islands. The bombing pattern was designed to strike only at the airport, not at the town which is several miles away. There were intended to be no civilian casualties. At the end of the day Rear-Admiral Sandy Woodward, the Task Force commander, said: 'We didn't want this fight. I'd hoped we could put it off, but we've shown our colours and it's been our day.'

In June 1982, Israeli forces invaded Lebanon and bombed Beirut. The country had already been in the grip of civil war for seven years. The Israeli aim was to crush the Palestinian Liberation Organisation, founded in 1967, which was using refugee camps as bases for launching terrorist attacks against Israel. There had been Palestinian refugee camps in Lebanon since 1948, and two of the more desperate and miserable of them were at Sabra and Chatila in the south of Beirut. On 16–17 September 1982 the Lebanese militia raided the camps and, under the eyes of the occupying Israeli forces near by, killed hundreds of Palestinian civilians, old men, women and children. **Robert Fisk** *of* The Times *was one of the first reporters to see the aftermath.*

They were everywhere, in the road, in laneways, in backyards and broken rooms, beneath crumpled masonry and across the top of garbage tips. The murderers – the Christian militiamen whom Israel had let into the camp to 'flush out terrorists' fourteen hours before – had only just left. In some cases the blood was still wet on the ground. When we had seen a hundred bodies, we stopped counting ...

Each corridor through the rubble produced more bodies. The patients at a Palestinian hospital simply disappeared after gunmen ordered the doctors to leave. There were signs of hastily dug mass graves. Perhaps a thousand people were butchered here, perhaps half that number again.

The full story of what happened in Chatila on Friday night and Saturday morning may never be known, for most of the witnesses are either dead or would never wish to reveal their guilt.

What is quite certain is that at six o'clock on Friday night, truckloads of gunmen in the uniform – and wearing the badges – of the right-wing Christian Falange militia and Major Saad Haddad's renegade army from southern Lebanon were seen by reporters entering the southern gate of the camp.

There were bonfires inside and the sound of heavy gunfire. Israeli troops and armour were standing round the perimeter of the camp and made no attempt to stop the gunmen – who have been their allies since their invasion of Lebanon – going in.

A spokesman for the Israeli foreign ministry was to say later that the militias had been sent into Chatila to hunt down some of the two thousand Palestinian 'terrorists' who the Israelis alleged were still in the camp. Correspondents were forbidden to enter.

What we found inside the camps at ten o'clock next morning did not quite beggar description, although it would perhaps be easier to retell in a work of fiction or in the cold prose of a medical report.

But the details should be told for – this being Lebanon – the facts will change over the coming weeks as militias and armies and governments blame each other for the horrors committed upon the Palestinian civilians.

Just inside the southern gates of the camp, there used to be a number of single-storey concrete-walled houses. When we walked across the muddy entrance of Chatila, we found that these buildings had all been dynamited to the ground. There were cartridge cases across the main road and clouds of flies swarmed across the rubble. Down a laneway to our right, not more than 50 yards from the entrance, there lay a pile of corpses.

There were more than a dozen of them, young men whose arms and legs had become entangled with each other in the agony of death. All had been shot at point-blank range through the right or left cheek, the bullet tearing away a line of flesh up to the ear and entering the brain. Some had vivid crimson scars down the left side of their throats. One had been castrated. Their eyes were open, and the flies had only begun to gather. The youngest was perhaps only twelve or thirteen years old.

On the other side of the main road, up a track through the rubble, we found the bodies of five women and several children. The women were middle-aged, and their corpses lay draped over a pile of rubble. One lay on her back, her dress torn open, and the head of a little girl emerging from behind her. The girl had short, dark curly hair and her eyes were staring at us and there was a frown on her face. She was dead.

Another child lay on the roadway like a discarded flower, her white dress stained with mud and dust. She could have been no more than three years old. The back of her head had been blown away by a bullet fired into her brain. One of the women also held a tiny baby to her body. The bullet that had passed through her breast had killed the baby too.

To the right of us there was what appeared to be a small barricade of concrete and mud. But as we approached it we found a human elbow visible on the surface. A large stone turned out to be part of a torso. It was as if the bodies had been bulldozed to the side of the laneway, as indeed they had. A bulldozer – its driver's seat empty – stood guiltily just down the road.

Beyond this rampart of earth and bodies there was a pile of what might have been sacks in front of a low redstone wall. We had to cross the barricade to reach it and tried hard not to step on the bodies buried beneath.

Below the low wall a line of young men and boys lay prostrated. They had been shot in the back against the wall in a ritual execution, and they lay, at once pathetic and terrible, where they had fallen. The execution wall and its huddle of corpses was somehow reminiscent of something seen before, and only afterwards did we realise how similar it all was to those old photographs of executions in occupied Europe during the Second World War. There may have been twelve or twenty bodies there. Some lay beneath others ...

Across Chatila came the disembodied voice of an Israeli officer broadcasting through a tannoy from atop an armoured personnel carrier. 'Stay off the streets,' he shouted. 'We are only looking for terrorists. Stay off the streets. We will shoot.'

An hour later, at Galerie Semaan – far from Chatila – someone did open fire at the soldiers and I threw myself into a ditch beside an Israeli major. The Israelis fired shoals of bullets into a ruined building beside the road, blowing pieces of it into the air like confetti. The major and I lay huddled in our ditch for fifteen minutes. He asked about Chatila and I told him all I had seen.

Then he said, 'I tell you this. The Haddad men were supposed to go in with us. We had to shoot two of them yesterday. We killed one and wounded another. Two more we took away. They were doing a bad thing. That is all I will tell you.' Was this at Chatila? I asked. Had he been there himself? He would say no more.

Then his young radio operator, who had been lying behind us in the mud, crawled up next to me. He was a young man. He pointed to his chest. 'We Israelis don't do that sort of thing,' he said. 'It was the Christians.'

In 1981 a new disease emerged. Gay men in San Francisco and New York began to die of a cancer called Kaposi's sarcoma – a cancer common in Africa but rare elsewhere. This was just one of the killer diseases caused by what became known as Aids (acquired immune deficiency syndrome). The American writer **Harold Brodkey** *was diagnosed with the disease in 1993. He wrote his own story in* This Wild Darkness: The Story of My Death. *This is how it begins.*

Spring 1993: I have Aids. I am surprised that I do. I have not been exposed since 1977, which is to say that my experiences, my adventures in homosexuality took place largely in the 1960s and 1970s, and back then I relied on time and abstinence to indicate my degree of freedom from infection and to protect others and myself.

At first, shadows and doubts of various kinds disturbed my sleep, but later I felt more certainty of safety. Before Aids was identified, I thought five years without noticeable infection would indicate that one was without disease. When Aids was first identified, five years was held to indicate safety. That changed. Twenty years now is considered a distance in time that might indicate safety, but a slight number of Aids cases are anomalous; that is, the delay in illness is not explicable within the assumed rules, even under the most careful, cynical investigation. It doesn't matter much. I have Aids. I have had *Pneumocystis carinii* pneumonia, which almost killed me. Unlikely or not, blood test, T-cell count, the fact that it was *Pneumocystis* means I have Aids and must die.

There it is. At the time I was told, I didn't even believe I had pneumonia. I thought it was literary exhaustion, and age, and bad flu-bronchitis – the death-urgency brought on by finishing a book, what I called the Venice book, *Profane Friendship*. When the piece of journalism I was working on, a piece about the Academy Awards for the *New Yorker*, was done and scheduled to go to press, I went to see my doctor, Barry Hartman. I wasn't so familiar with him yet that I could easily call him Barry. He was my new internist, a specialist in infectious diseases. He had taken over the practice of the doctor I'd had before. He looked at the X rays and at how thin I was and said it might be Aids and *Pneumocystis*, and I pooh-poohed him. Because of my wife, Ellen Schwamm, I agreed to the HIV test, but I refused to go to the hospital. And Barry said he might be wrong.

He said he would telephone with the test results. I said he shouldn't worry about it. I wasn't tense.

I went home, went to bed, took the general-spectrum antibiotic Barry had prescribed, and in bed went through the Academy Awards piece with the fact-checker on the phone. And I suffered with flu-bronchitis and fever but not with foreboding. I had some nervousness about the test, since you never know what surprises God has up his sleeve, destiny's sleeve. But not

much. It had been a very long time. I didn't even have that lapsed awareness one can get when sick, You goddamned fool, why did you stay up so
late? I didn't have that kind of contrition.

But by the next evening I was so much worse that I could not find a
balance point in the gusts of unpleasant sensation. I don't remember
feeling panicky, but I felt so sick I was uneasy about death (from illness, at
least) for the first time in my life. Ellen was treating me with an unyielding attention and a kind of sweetness, without any noticeable flicker of
independence or irony. She had never once been like that with me, even
sexually. You'd have to know her to know how rare any state other than
autonomy is for her. It was strange how the illness kept getting heavier
and more settled by the hour, with a kind of muffled rapidity. Again and
again, it thudded to a level of horrendousness, consolidated that, and then
thuddingly sank to a worse level still. Nothing was stopping the process of
strangulation. I kept putting on a front for Ellen, or trying to, until, in a
kind of extreme inward silence, nothing was working. The weird, choked
dizziness didn't moderate or waver; I found I could not breathe at all, even
sitting up.

I gave in. I said we'd better get to the hospital. The ambulance people
came, and I whispered to them that I could not walk or sit up. Or breathe.
They went down for a gurney [trolley] and oxygen. Breathing through a
tube in my nose and motionless and sheeted on a gurney, I was wheeled
through our apartment and into the elevator and across the lobby, past
the doorman, on to the sidewalk, into the air briefly, and then into the
ambulance. This is how my life ended. And my dying began.

*In 1980 the Iraqi forces of Saddam Hussein attacked Iran across the waters
of the Shatt al Arab, starting a war that would last eight years and cost
well over a million casualties. During that time Saddam was also battling
enemies, perceived and real, at home – and in particular waging war on the
Iraqi Kurds in campaigns that were tantamount to genocide. The Kurds in
the border region between Iraq and Iran were particularly vulnerable, and
in March 1988 Saddam's forces gassed Kurdish communities round the
village of Halabja. Men, women and children simply dropped in the streets.
Richard Beeston, who later became foreign editor of* The Times, *witnessed
the aftermath.*

Like figures unearthed in Pompeii, the victims of Halabja were killed so quickly that their corpses remained in suspended animation.

There was the plump baby whose face, frozen in a scream, stuck out from under the protective arm of a man, away from the open door of a house that he never reached.

Near by, a family of five who had been sitting in their garden eating lunch was cut down – the killer gas not even sparing the family cat, or the birds in the tree which littered the well-kept lawn.

Their neighbours had had the foresight to hide in an underground shelter. It became their mass grave, with ten men, women and children huddled together in the darkness, surrounded by their best carpets and the family's valuables.

The Iraqi bombers first struck last Wednesday, dropping the chemical agents relentlessly and leaving behind the groans of the mustard gas victims, the trail of refugees and the haunting waxwork figures frozen by the cyanide vapour.

Halabja was once a prosperous market town surrounded by green pasture on the shore of Dar Bandikhan Lake, overlooked on three sides by the snow-capped mountains of Kurdistan. But for the fifty thousand Kurdish farmers and shopkeepers, their proximity to the Iranian border turned the district into a battlefield which inflicted the worst punishment on the civilian population.

Mrs Jamila Abdullah, aged twenty-eight, a teacher in Halabja's primary school, said: 'It was about half-past six in the afternoon and the Iraqis had already left the town. I was at home when I heard the explosion and then smelt the bad smell.' She had the presence of mind to dowse her scarf with water and hold it to her face. But the other victims in a makeshift ward in the Iranian town of Bakhtaran, and those taken to Tehran for special treatment, were less fortunate. Nurses wearing black chadors went from bed to bed in the crowded Bakhtaran clinic, administering cream to women and children, most of them writhing in agony.

In one side-street of Halabja an entire neighbourhood in a 500-yard radius appeared to have been wiped out by a bomb containing cyanide. Dr Said Foroutan, a small and shy Revolutionary Guard with a neat uniform, darted from corpse to corpse taking photographs and notes. A specialist on the effects of chemical weapons, who during his time at the war front has probably had some of the most extensive first-hand experience in the world, he explained how the nerve gas and cyanide vapour killed their victims instantly, and how the sulphuric mustard gas left those it affected alive and in permanent agony.

The details were lost on one tearful Kurd, only one of ten residents to be seen in the town, as he picked his way through the bloated carcasses of livestock and the bodies of his former neighbours.

'I do not know where my children are,' said Mr Abdul Rahman, aged sixty, an employee of the town's mosque.

Iraq had had its revenge and the Kurds of Halabja, probably not for the last time, had paid the price.

In China, by the late 1970s, President Deng Xiaoping appeared to be inaugurating a new and more liberal era. This was a process that had begun with the visit of the US president Richard Nixon to China in 1972, and economic reforms and substantial foreign investment had followed. By the second half of the 1980s, however, there were student demonstrations in a number of cities, protesting against the lack of progress, and culminating in the mass rally of students and workers that took place in Tiananmen Square in Beijing in the summer of 1989. For six weeks the square was a giant peace camp, sometimes numbering as many as a million people – a beacon of hope for a new, democratic, China. At first the ageing Chinese leadership hesitated about what to do, fearing that if it ordered in local units of the People's Liberation Army, the soldiers might side with the protesters. Then rumours began to spread that units were to be brought in from distant garrisons in the provinces. Meanwhile messages were blared from a loudspeaker: 'Go home and save your life. You will fail. You are not behaving in the correct Chinese manner. This is not the West.' **John Simpson** *of the BBC, well known for his courage and his uncanny ability to be where history is being made, was there.*

That the army was coming was no longer rumour but fact and our translator heard that it would move in at one o'clock. It was half-past midnight. In the distance, above the noise of the crowd, I thought I could hear the sound of guns. I wanted to find a vantage point from which we could film, without being spotted by the army. But the tension that was bonding members of the crowd together did not have the same effect on the members of our small team. It was hot and noisy. We argued. We started shouting, and I headed off on my own.

I pushed through the crowds, immediately feeling better for being on my own. There were very few foreign journalists left in the square by now, and I felt especially conspicuous. But I also felt good. People grabbed my hand, thanking me for being with them. I gave them a V for Victory sign and was applauded by everyone around me. It was hard to define the mood. There was still a spirit of celebration, that they were out on the streets, defying the government, but the spirit was also giving way to a terrible foreboding. There was also something else. Something I hadn't seen before: a reckless ferocity of purpose.

I crossed back into the main part of Tiananmen Square, the village of student tents. There were sticks and cardboard and broken glass underfoot. The smells were familiar and strong – wood-smoke, urine and heavy disinfectant. A couple clung to each other, her head on his shoulder. I passed in front of them, but they didn't raise their eyes. A student asked me to sign his T-shirt, a craze from earlier days. He had thick glasses and a bad complexion, and he spoke English. 'It will be dangerous tonight,' he said. 'We are all very afraid here.'

I finished signing his shirt, at the back below the collar. He grabbed my hand and shook it excitedly. His grip was bony and clammy. I asked him what he thought would happen.

'We will all die.'

He straightened up and shook my hand again, and slipped away between the tents.

The camp was dark. There were a few students left; most of them had gathered in the centre of the square, around the Monument to the People's Heroes. I could hear their speeches and the occasional burst of singing – the 'Internationale', as always. Here, though, it was quiet. This was where the students had chosen to build their statue of the Goddess of Democracy, with her sightless eyes, her torch held in both hands. The symbol of all our aspirations, one of the student leaders called her: the fruit of our struggle. To me, she looked very fragile.

The speeches and the songs continued in the distance. Then suddenly they stopped. There was a violent grinding and a squealing sound – the familiar sound of an armoured personnel carrier. I heard screaming, and behind me, in the avenue, everyone started running. When I finally spotted the vehicle, I could see that it was making its way with speed down the side of the square. It seemed uncertain of its direction – one moment driving straight for the square, and then stopping, turning, stopping again, as if looking for a way to escape. There was a sudden angry roar, and I know it was because the vehicle had crushed someone under its tracks. It then turned in my direction – it was pointed at me – and I felt a different kind of panic. The action was starting and I was separated from my colleagues: it is an article of faith to stay with your camera crew in times of danger.

The vehicle carried on, careering back and forth. It must have knocked down six or seven people. By now it was on fire, having been hit repeatedly by Molotov cocktails. Somehow, though, it escaped and headed off to the west.

Then a second armoured personnel carrier came along Changan Avenue, alone and unsupported like the first. This time everyone turned and ran hard towards the vehicle, knowing that they, with their numbers and their petrol bombs, had the power to knock it out. They screamed with anger and hate as the vehicle swung randomly in different directions, threatening to knock people down as it made its way through the square. The Molotov cocktails arched above our heads, spinning over and over, exploding on the thin shell of armour that protected the men inside. Still the vehicle carried on, zigzagging, crossing the avenue, trying to find a way through the barricade. A pause, and it charged, head-on, straight into a block of concrete – and then stuck, its engine whirring wildly. A terrible shout of triumph came from the crowd: primitive and dark, its prey finally caught. The smell of petrol and burning metal and sweat was in the air, intoxicating and violent. Everyone around me was pushing and fighting to get to the vehicle. At first I resisted; then, close beside it, I saw the light of a camera, just where the crowd was starting to swarm. There were only three cameramen still filming in the entire square, and I knew that my colleague was the only one crazy enough to be that close. Now I was the one fighting, struggling to get through the crowd, pulling people back, pushing them out of my path, swearing, a big brutal Englishman stronger than any of them. I tore one man's shirt and punched another in the back. All around me the men seemed to be yelling at the sky, their faces lit up; the vehicle had caught fire. A man – his torso bare – climbed up the side of the vehicle and stood on top of it, his arms raised in victory, the noise of the mob welling up around him. They knew they had the vehicle's crew trapped inside. Someone started beating at the armoured glass with an iron bar.

I reached the cameraman and pulled hard at his arm to get his attention. He scarcely noticed me, amid the buffeting and the noise and the violence, and carried on filming. He and his sound recordist and the Chinese lighting man were a few feet from the vehicle: close enough to be killed if it exploded or if the soldiers came out shooting. But I couldn't make them step back, and so we stayed there, the four of us, the heat beating against our faces as people continued to pour petrol on the bonnet and roof and smashed at the doors and the armoured glass. What was it like inside? I imagined the soldiers half-crazed with the noise and the heat and the fear of being burned alive.

The screaming around me rose even louder: the handle of the door at the rear of the vehicle had turned a little, and the door began to open. A soldier pushed the barrel of a gun out, but it was snatched from his hands, and then everyone started grabbing his arms, pulling and wrenching until finally he came free, and then he was gone: I saw the arms of the mob, flailing, raised above their heads as they fought to get their blows in. He was dead within seconds, and his body was dragged away in triumph. A second soldier showed his head through the door and was then immediately pulled out by his hair and ears and the skin on his face. This soldier I could see: his eyes were rolling, and his mouth was open, and he was covered with blood where the skin had been ripped off. Only his eyes remained – white and clear – but then someone was trying to get them as well, and someone else began beating his skull until the skull came apart, and there was blood all over the ground, and his brains, and still they kept on beating and beating what was left.

Then the horrible sight passed away, and the ground was wet where he had been.

There was a third soldier inside. I could see his face in the light of the flames, and some of the crowd could too. They pulled him out, screaming, wild at having missed killing the other soldiers. It was his blood they wanted, I was certain, it was to feel the blood running over their hands. Their mouths were open and panting, like dogs, and their eyes were expressionless. They were shouting, the Chinese lighting man told me afterwards, that the soldier they were about to kill wasn't human, that he was just a thing, an object, which had to be destroyed. And all the time the noise and the heat and the stench of oil burning on hot metal beat at us, overwhelming our senses, deadening them.

Just as the third soldier was lifted out of the vehicle, almost fainting, an articulated bus rushed towards us stopping, with great skill, so that its rear door opened just beside the group with the soldier. The students had heard what was happening, and a group had raced the bus over to save whomever they could. The mob did not want to give up its prize. The students tried to drag the soldier on board, and the crowd held on to him, pulling him back. By some mischance the bus door started closing and it seemed that he must be killed.

I had seen people die in front of me before. But I had never seen three people die, one after the other, in this way. Once again the members of the crowd closed around the soldier, their arms raised over their heads to beat him to death. The bus and the safety it promised were so close. It seemed to me then that I couldn't look on any longer, a passive observer, watching another man's skin torn away or his head broken open, and do nothing. I saw the soldier's face, expressing only horror and pain as he sank under the blows of the people around him, and I started to move forward. The ferocity of the crowd had entered me, but I felt it was the crowd that was the animal, that it wasn't properly human. The soldier had sunk down to the ground, and a man was trying to break his skull with a half-brick, bringing it down with full force. I screamed obscenities at the man – stupid obscenities, as no one except my colleagues could have understood them – and threw myself at him, catching him with his arm up, poised for another blow. He looked at me blankly, and his thin arm went limp in my grasp. I stopped shouting. He relaxed his grip on the brick, and I threw it under the bus. It felt wet. A little room had been created around the soldier, and the student who had tried to rescue him before could now get to him. The rest of the mob hadn't given up, but the students were able to pull the soldier away and get him on to the bus by the other door. He was safe.

*On 10 November 1989 the Berlin Wall, which had divided the democratic West from the communist East of the city ever since the height of the Cold War in 1961, began to come down – literally pulled to pieces by hundreds of willing hands. It was a beacon of hope after a decade of relentless conflict, and marked a sharp acceleration in the collapse of Soviet/communist power in eastern Europe. By the end of 1991 the Soviet Union itself had fallen apart, and the Cold War was over. This report was from **Peter Millar** and **Richard Ellis** of the* Sunday Times.

More than one million Germans from East and West held the world's biggest non-stop party in Berlin yesterday, as their sober leaders tried in vain to dampen the euphoria by warning that a united Germany was not yet on the political agenda.

East Berliners poured into West Berlin to celebrate their liberty on free beer and wine, and late last night one twenty-four-year-old visitor from the East gave birth to a baby girl on one of the city's bustling streets, to the delight of the partying crowds.

The new life seemed symbolic. Berlin was itself a city reborn. The party clogged the streets as the barriers that divided Germany melted like the ice of the Cold War. Officials said well over a million people had passed the frontiers from East Germany into West Berlin and West Germany in a matter of hours.

After nightfall, as the party proved unstoppable, police shut off traffic from several main streets, and sealed off the wall at the Brandenburg gate to prevent demonstrators from dancing on it. West Berlin police said they were in constant touch with their East German colleagues on the other side of the wall.

Tension gave way to heated but good-natured banter between West Berliners and the normally sullen East German guards standing on the wall.

'I'm not here talking to you because I have to or because I've been told to,' one policeman said. 'I'm here because I want to [be].'

'What's your name, what's your name?' shouted the crowd.

'Call me Karl-Heinz,' he answered.

'Tell me, what will happen when there's no more use for the wall?' he was asked.

'Well, if it goes that far, I suppose we'll get to know each other.'

Along the Kurfürstendamm, tens of thousands of East and West Berliners linked their arms to sing songs celebrating their newly gained solidarity.

To the tune of 'Glory glory hallelujah', they chorused '*Berlin ist eine Stadt, Deutschland ist ein Land*' (Berlin is one city, Germany is one country). As they sang, people held up cigarette lighters, matches and candles and sparklers to demonstrate their feelings.

For the benefit of American television crews, there were songs even in English: 'We shall overcome' and 'This land is my land'.

Street poets regaled the crowds with jokes and verses that concentrated on the collapse of the Berlin Wall. 'Die Maur', as the wall is known in German, is in two, said one, but no longer is Berlin.

Sales of beer and champagne soared as East Berliners continued to come over to the West to join the festivities, and traffic in West Berlin was at a standstill ...

The first new border crossing point came into use just after dawn after a night of activity by workmen with bulldozers. East Berliners filed on foot from Bernauerstrasse into the West.

This had been the scene of some of the most dramatic and emotional events of August 1961 when the wall was built – East Berliners dropping from upper-storey windows while troops bricked up their front doors. Several died.

On Potsdamer Platz, once the Piccadilly Circus of the German empire and a hundred yards from the unmarked site of Hitler's bunker, the bulldozers were creating a crossing to be opened this morning.

Elsewhere, official teams were knocking down the wall to create eighteen new crossing points. At one new site, East Berlin engineers shook hands with their western counterparts through the gap they had created in the 6-inch-thick, steel-reinforced concrete.

Tourists watched in amazement, their cameras recording the historic moments. One American borrowed a hammer from a Berliner and told his wife: 'Get one of me hitting the wall, honey.'

Every small piece chipped off was seized as a souvenir. At one partly destroyed section near the Tiergarten, young West Berliners sold off chunks of the wall for DM10.

In the gift shops, newly printed T-shirts were selling well, the most popular bearing the slogan *'Der Letze macht das Licht aus!'* (the last one turns out the light).

On 11 February 1990, Nelson Mandela was released from prison – over a quarter of a century after his incarceration on Robben Island. In a speech on 2 February, F. W. de Klerk had stood before Parliament and laid the ground-work for a democratic South Africa. Mandela wrote: 'In a breathtaking moment, in one sweeping action, he had virtually normalised the situation ... Our world had changed overnight.' The first national, non-racial, one-person-one-vote election took place on 24 April 1994. It was won by the African National Congress (ANC) and Nelson Mandela, who had cast his vote for the first time in his life, became president.

Even as South Africa prepared for this historic event, the Rwandan capital Kigali, one of the most beautiful cities in the continent, went into meltdown. Civil war between the majority Hutus and the minority Tutsis resulted in genocide, with eight hundred thousand people, mainly Tutsis, killed – butchered, as Paul Rusesabagina put it in An Ordinary Man, *'by their friends, neighbours and countrymen'. The UN and the inter-national community, for the most part, either ran for refuge, or just stood by. The massacres triggered one of the biggest movements of refugees in modern African history.*

Paul Rusesabagina, *the son of a Hutu farmer and his Tutsi wife, was the manager of the main luxury hotel in the centre of Kigali. Heroically he kept his hotel open and with incredible courage turned it into a sanctuary, saving the lives of more than twelve hundred people and watching over the evacuation of his staff and guests, as well as his own family, before attempt-ing to save himself.*

We arrived in my hometown after a few hours. It was as deserted as the roads had been. This was where my friend Aloise had wanted us to take refuge – the place where the *mwami* had taken his cows for safety during wars of past centuries. But that old myth had been broken in the past few weeks. The genocide had come here, too. More than 150 people connected to the Seventh-Day Adventist Church had had the same idea as Aloise. These rural pastors and their families had come here thinking they would be protected at the college at Gitwe where I had attended school. They had all been slaughtered.

It occurred to me that if I had stayed with my earlier ambition to be a pastor, I might very well have been among them, and killed in the same classroom where I had learned to make letters.

Things were no better in the neighbouring town where my family had lived. In the commune house several dozen Tutsis had gathered under the protection of the local mayor, who had promised to shield them from the mobs of ordinary people who had taken up machetes against their neighbours. On 18 April an official had been called to a political meeting in the nearby city of Gitarama, and when he came back there was trouble. 'I am no longer the person you knew,' he allegedly said, and then put a handgun to the head of a friend of his, a man he had gone to school with and had known for more than twenty years. He shot his friend and then ordered an attack on the commune house. Those refugees who weren't killed immediately darted into the swamps and the hills, where they spent the next two months trying to hide from the bands of bar keepers, schoolteachers and housewives who had been told: 'Do your work.'

I went to the home of my elder brother Munyakayanza and found him sitting quietly in the front room with his wife. Seeing him alive made me want to cry with gratitude. We embraced, but I could feel that his muscles were tense. His eyes darted from my eyes to the places behind my shoulder. The area around his house was usually full of life, neighbours passing back and forth, children rolling bicycle rims with sticks, and teenagers playing tussling games, but now there was nobody. Not even any cooking fires were burning. It was totally quiet.

'Our neighbours have been killed by the militia,' he told me. He and his wife survived because they were Hutus. Now that the rebel army had driven out the militia it was not safe any more to be of this class. In fact, it could be a death sentence. Some rogue members of the RPF had begun to conduct reprisal killings in several parts of Rwanda. Around me I could see burned-out houses where people had been roasted alive within their own walls.

'Listen, brother,' Munyakayanza told me. 'Please leave this place. The houses, they have eyes. The trees have ears.'

I decoded his message. My presence here would be noticed and was a danger to both his family and mine. I quickly hugged him again and left. My wife started to cry, and I tried my best to comfort her, but it was impossible. We now headed towards my wife's hometown, the old Tutsi capital of Nyanza. Tatiana was so frightened she could barely speak, but we had to see, we had to go there, even though we already knew in our hearts what we would find.

Most of her family had been slain by their neighbours. Several of them had been buried in a shallow pit used for the maturing of bananas. Tatiana's mother had been one of the sweetest, kindest women I'd ever met. She had always shared food with her neighbours in times of trouble and was always available to help look after children in their parents' absence. She had been murdered along with her daughter-in-law and six grandchildren. The walls of her house had been knocked down. I could see some of its distinctive tiles already plastered into the walls of nearby houses. The looting had been quick and efficient.

I felt bright hatred surging up in my throat for the bastards that had done this. I am not a violent man, but if I had had a gun in that moment, and if somebody had pointed me to a convincing scapegoat, I would have murdered him without hesitation. I had saved more than a thousand people in the capital, but I could not save my own family. What a stupid and useless man I was!

I tasted, in that moment, the poison and self-hatred in my country's bloodstream, that irresistible fury against a ghost, the quenchless desire to make someone pay for an unrightable wrong. My father would have said that I had drunk from the water that was upstream from the lamb.

My wife and I crouched there in the remains of her mother's house, holding on to each other, and for the first time in many years, I wept.

Long after the Islamic revolution of 1979, Jane Austen brought a strange message of hope to one of the quieter corners of Tehran. From the autumn of 1995, every Thursday for nearly two years, an inspired teacher named **Azar**

Nafisi gathered together a group of her female students to read the Western classics. It was a highly dangerous undertaking: while fundamentalists seized the universities and morality squads staged arbitrary raids, seven young women removed their veils to talk about Scott Fitzgerald, Vladimir Nabokov, Henry James and – Jane Austen. Most were in love with Mr Darcy, whether in print or on film. A few were critical and took copious notes, which they filed to the authorities. Azar Nafisi eventually left Tehran for America and 'the green light that Gatsby once believed in', but before she went she was approached by one of the more censorious of her former students, who had briefly joined one of the militias.

I remember her. I remember that particular discussion of *Wuthering Heights*, because I remember how Miss Ruhi had unglued herself from her friend and followed me out of the classroom, pushing me almost into a corner of the hall. She leapt at me and spluttered out her indignation over the immorality of Catherine and Heathcliff. There was so much passion in her words – I had been taken aback. What was she talking about?

I was not about to put another novel on trial. I told her it was immoral to talk about a great novel in this manner, that characters were not vehicles for pedantic moral imperatives, that reading a novel was not an exercise in censure. She said something about other professors, their delicacy in censoring even the word wine out of the stories they taught, lest it offend the Islamic sensibilities of their students. Yes, I thought, and they have been stuck teaching *The Pearl*. I told her she could drop the class or take the matter to higher authorities, that this was the way it would be in my class and that I would continue to teach what I taught. I left her there in the darkened corner of that very long hallway. Though I saw her afterwards, in my mind I left her there for ever. And now she had excavated herself and polished up her image.

She had also objected to *Daisy Miller*: she found Daisy not only immoral but foolish and 'unreasonable'. But then, despite our differences and her obvious disapproval of the novels I taught, she had enrolled in my class again the following year. There were rumours that she was having an affair with one of the big shots in the Muslim Students' Association. Nassrin was always bringing these rumours to my attention, trying to prove how hypocritical 'these people' were.

She said now that she missed college. It didn't seem like much at the time, but later she noticed how much she missed it. She missed the films we watched together and the class discussions. 'Do you remember your Dear Jane Society?' I was puzzled – how did she know about that? It was a joke shared by me and a handful of my students. She said, 'I always wanted to be in on it. I always thought it would be a great deal of fun. I really liked Jane Austen – if you only knew how many girls swooned over Darcy!' I said, 'I didn't know you were allowed to have a heart in your group.' She said, 'Believe it or not, we fell in and out of love all the time.'

She had tried to study Arabic and had translated some short stories and poems from English into Persian – for herself, she added as an after-thought. She used the Persian expression 'for my own heart'. After a pause she added, 'And then I got married and now have a daughter.' I wondered if she had married the man of our rumours; he was a man I had no fond memories of.

I asked her how old her daughter was. She said, 'Eleven months,' and, after a pause, with a playful shadow of a smile: 'I named her after you.' 'After me?' 'I mean, she has a different name on her birth certificate – she is called Fahimeh, after a favourite aunt who died young – but I have a secret name for her. I call her Daisy.' She said she had hesitated between Daisy and Lizzy. She had finally settled on Daisy. Lizzy was the one she had dreamed of, but marrying Mr Darcy was too much wishful thinking. 'Why Daisy?' 'Don't you remember Daisy Miller? Haven't you heard that if you give your child a name with a meaning she will become like her namesake? I want my daughter to be what I never was – like Daisy. You know, courageous.'

Daisy was the character my female students most identified with. Some of them became obsessed. Later, in my workshop, they would go back to her time and again, speaking of her courage, something they felt they had lacked. Mahshid and Mitra spoke of her with regret in their writings; like Winterbourne, they felt they were bound to make a mistake about her. When she rose to say goodbye, I looked at her with some hesitation and said, 'May I ask you a rather personal question? You said you were married. And your husband?' 'I married someone outside the university,' she said. 'He is in computers. And open-minded,' she added with a smile.

She had to go, she had an eleven-month-old daughter with a secret name waiting for her at home. 'You know, I didn't think about it then, but we did have fun,' she said. 'All the fuss we made over these writers, as if what they said was a matter of life and death to us – James and Brontë and Nabokov and Jane Austen.'

The Bosnian War

From 1992 to 1995 war raged in Bosnia, defeating all attempts by the UN to broker a peace agreement in the area. Bosnia's declaration of independence from Yugoslavia in March 1992 was followed by pitched battles between Serbs, Croats and Muslims in the streets of the capital, Sarajevo, and throughout the country. The Bosnian Serbs, led by Radovan Karadzic, set out to create a Greater Serbia by bombarding the city and forcibly moving entire populations of Muslims and Croats from their homes. Their siege of Sarajevo lasted until 1994.

*After the initial burst of violence, reporters were almost the only people able to move across the different lines of confrontation. In under three years more than two-thirds of Bosnia's people were driven from their homes, and one of the most dangerous spots was at Brcko on the river Sava, where Serbs, Croats and Bosnian Muslims contested a narrow corridor round the river port. **Patrick Bishop** of the* Daily Telegraph *brilliantly evoked the scene in a routine despatch of May 1993.*

It was a fine day for killing. The mist was lifting from the meadows, giving way to sunshine, while the breeze carried the scent of hortensia blossom.

All along the lane, soldiers were turning up for work.

They came by bicycle, by foot or in cars driven by their wives. The cars stopped at the crossroads, where there was a sign saying *Ratna Zona* (War Zone). The men got out, smiling and waving goodbye, strolling the last mile to the front line.

It was still early. The fighting had not really started, just the occasional machine-gun burst drifting over the cornfield and the odd thump of a mortar.

The birds were making more noise.

The café at the crossroads had been turned into a canteen. Three men sat in the shade among ammunition boxes, peeling potatoes for the fighters' lunch. Inside, the soldiers who had been fighting all night were sleeping. A middle-aged man in a black T-shirt and camouflage pants stood, yawning, on the veranda.

'It was a bad night,' he said. 'There were enough dead.'

For once, we were hearing the story from the other side of the line. The Muslims had attacked after dark, taking Omarbegovaca village near Brcko, which commands the narrowest point of the corridor linking the Serbs of northern Bosnia with their mother country.

Each day since the war began, the area has been fiercely contested. Brcko is the corridor's choke point, the most vulnerable part of the lifeline through which arms, petrol, food and money flow to sustain the Serb communities in northern Bosnia and Croatia.

For a year, the Muslims on one side and the Croats on the other have been struggling to cut it. For a year, the Serbs have been trying to force them back. Under the Vance–Owen peace plan, the existing land link between Serbia and the northern Bosnian Serbs would be broken, and the corridor road put under United Nations control.

In breach of a ceasefire signed earlier this month, the Serbs launched an attack with tanks and artillery to expand the corridor south of Brcko.

The Muslims, despite a lack of heavy weapons, are fighting back. But the latest counter-attack faltered when Serb reinforcements from the village of Potocari went in and drove them out. Now these combatants were sleeping and it was the turn of the day shift.

Down the road came Milovan and Dragan, car mechanics in quieter times. In their well-pressed olive-green fatigues they looked like generals compared with the fashionably scruffy younger men. But they were just ordinary Serb soldiers taking their turn at the front. Milovan was sixty, with a thick head of white hair. He smiled as he heard the latest news. 'The Muslims always wait until Sundays when we are resting before they attack,' he said.

He was happy to see two Britons. 'You were our allies in the war. We expect you to be our friends still. Now only God is on our side.' Dragan was earnest and voluble. Like most Serbs in Bosnia, the main thing on his mind was the Vance–Owen plan, and he launched into a heartfelt speech. 'We should all have the right to decide what the country should be like,' he concluded. 'I for one do not want to live in an Islamic state.'

The Muslims he is fighting are his old neighbours. At some points the lines are 30 yards apart. 'I recognise the voices. We call across to each other. Sometimes we ask for news of people on the other side. Sometimes we swear at each other.'

It was time to go. Milovan and Dragan shook hands and set off down the road. Watching them walking away, it was possible to see the Serbs as they see themselves – simple, proud people, fighting for a right that the world has consistently refused to grant them.

This message was rammed home at a grim little ceremony that took place later on the other side of Bosnia. On the banks of the river Drina, the women of Ratkovici gathered to bury their dead – fifteen men and women killed in a Muslim massacre eleven months before, whose bodies had just been discovered.

General Milan Gvero, the Bosnian Serbs' second-in-command, looked at the open, black-painted coffins, in which the mourners had scattered banknotes and apples, and shook his head.

'You can't feel good at a time like this,' he said. 'But as a man, in my heart, I know what I'm doing is right – fighting for the right of the Serb nation. My people need peace, but not a peace that brings more victims tomorrow. That means that everyone has to be on their own land. We have lived here for one thousand years.' You do not have to go far to see the general's principles put into practice. The 12-mile road between the riverside shed where the ceremony took place and Bratunac is an unbroken trail of destruction. Every house is smashed and burned. Muslims used to live there.

Anthony Loyd was brought up in a distinguished military family and himself served in the British army, but he soon took up a camera and notebook instead and headed off to record some of the strangest and most brutal conflicts he could find. In the killing fields of Bosnia he experienced human nature at its worst and best, and in My War Gone By, I Miss It So, *confessed his addiction to the adrenalin rush he got from war. Here he sets the scene for his first journalistic tour during the siege of Sarajevo, in the spring of 1993.*

There was a Bosnian government army sniper positioned in one of the top floors of the burned-out tower block overlooking the Serbs in Grbavica. He was audio landmark to our days. We lived in the street below at the edge of Sarajevo's ruined parliament building in a small strip of the city sandwiched between the front-line Miljacka river and the wide expanse of Vojvode Putnika, the street dubbed Snipers' Alley soon after the war began. The area had a few benefits but they were purely relative in the overall scheme of Sarajevo's war.

Our proximity to the Serbs meant that they were seldom able to bring down heavy artillery fire upon us for fear of dropping short and hitting their own troops on the other side of the small river. The tight clustering of buildings afforded protection from automatic fire, provided you knew which alleys to run across and were not unlucky with a mortar round. It was only if you chose to leave the claustrophobic confines of this narrow template in search of food or as a release from the stifling boredom that your troubles really began. There was no way around it, if you wanted to go anywhere else in the capital you had to deal with Vojvode Putnika. Empty your mind, fill your lungs and kick out for the centre knowing that if it happened then you would not hear it, merely get smashed forward on to your face by a mighty punch. Some people never bothered to leave the area. They waited for others to bring them food, growing paler and madder with frustration by the day. Others never bothered running. They said that they were fatalists but I think they were just tired of living, exhausted by the mental effort of dealing with the random nature of the violence. Kalashnikov rounds and shrapnel might have been the city's new gods but there was no need to hand them your destiny on a plate. Even so, however fast you beat the ground you knew that it would never be faster than a speeding bullet. But most of us kept making the effort anyway, hoping it would cut us a bit of leeway with the reactions of the men on the hills above us.

I was sitting with Endre with my back to the wall of our house. It was late morning and the March sun was high and moving slowly south-west, leaving us in the wedged shadow of the building. We were indulging in Sarajevo's greatest wartime activity: smoking and hanging around hoping nothing would happen to us but that something would happen somewhere, anywhere, to break the monotony and give us a sense of time progressing, of anything progressing. The war had been going on for nearly a year and had no end in sight. The city's inhabitants were sinking into a sense of hopelessness which was catching, even for a foreigner with a way out. Our conversation followed the usual pattern: I asked lots of questions to try to get my head around the situation while Endre, a Hungarian Yugoslav, listened attentively and then began his answer. He did it the same way each time. 'Well, Antonio,' he would open ponderously, 'it's like this ...' The sudden bullwhip crack of a bullet interrupted us and we looked at the tower block. The government sniper was obviously back up there, though we could not see him, and had taken a pop at something he had seen across the river.

The two sides of the tower visible from our position almost never changed their appearance: the front was a wide expanse of black and twisted window frames, the southern side a concrete Emmental of shell-holes from tanks. There was only one time I can remember it ever looking different. Some Muslim soldiers had crawled up to the top at night and unfurled a long banner down the side of the building that directly faced the Serbs. 'DON'T WORRY BE HAPPY', it read vertically in letters each a metre high. The Serbs shot it to ribbons the next morning. I could never work out if this meant that they had got the joke or not.

After a few seconds' silence our conversation continued. Then another shot rang out. Endre paused again, this time raising an index finger in expectation of something. Across the river a machine-gun fired a burst back towards the tower, its dull popping sound following only after the whacking of the bullets chipped off bits of concrete in harmless-looking grey puffs above us. Still Endre held up his finger, waiting for something else. Again the sniper fired, only this time there was a scant second between the crack of his shot and great explosive smashings and sparks as an anti-aircraft gun riddled the top storeys of the tower in a nerve-jangling roll of sound. Silence followed the last detonation. The sniper would not fire again that day. Endre lowered his finger and turned to me smiling. 'Well, Antonio,' he began, 'that is what we call "educating fire".'

*Antony Loyd's friend and brother in reporting was **Kurt Schork** of Reuters. Schork decided to trade in work for the New York transportation agency for* *journalism, reporting the wars in the Balkans and Africa before being killed in a roadside ambush in Sierra Leone in 2000. Because he was an agency man, his name and his original copy rarely appeared in newspapers, but here is one of his most affecting pieces from Sarajevo, 23 May 1993.*

Two lovers lie dead on the banks of Sarajevo's Miljacka river ...

For four days they have sprawled near Vrbana bridge in a wasteland of shell-blasted rubble, downed tree branches and dangling power lines.

So dangerous is the area no one has dared recover their bodies.

Bosko Brckic and Admira Ismic, both twenty-five, were shot dead on Wednesday trying to escape the besieged Bosnian capital for Serbia.

Sweethearts since high school, he was a Serb and she was a Muslim.

'They were shot at the same time, but he fell instantly and she was still alive,' recounts Dino, a soldier who saw the couple trying to cross from government territory to rebel Serb positions.

'She crawled over and hugged him and they died like that, in each other's arms.'

Squinting through a hole in the sandbagged wall of a bombed-out building, Dino points to where the couple lie mouldering amid the debris of Bosnia's fourteen-month civil war.

Bosko is face down on the pavement, right arm bent awkwardly behind him. Admira lies next to her lover, left arm across his back.

As they passed Bosnian lines and headed for the Serb-held neighbourhood of Grbavica, someone shot them.

The young couple had been dead two days before Admira's parents found out. Ham radio operators in Serbia contacted them trying to confirm rumours of Bosko's death.

'I spoke to his mother then and she gave me permission to bury them together in Sarajevo,' says Admira's father.

'We want them to lie together in the ground, just as they died together,' he adds.

Frantic to retrieve the bodies, Admira's parents are bewildered by unresponsive Bosnian and Serb bureaucracies, and by UNPROFOR's hands-off policy.

Zijah Ismic claims he begged UNPROFOR to let him drive one of its armoured pesonnel carriers in to get his daughter.

He says the UN told him armour-piercing rounds from machine-guns and cannon around Vrbana bridge would go through the vehicle.

'Love took them to their deaths,' Ismic says of Bosko and Admira.

'That's proof this is not a war between Serbs and Muslims. It's a war between crazy people, between monsters. That's why their bodies are still out there.'

Nine-Eleven: New York

*The terrorist attacks on New York and Washington on 11 September 2001 marked a turning-point, not just for the US but for the world. Four airliners were hijacked – two crashed into the twin towers of the World Trade Center in New York, one into the Pentagon, and one – thanks to the great courage of the passengers – into open country near Pittsburgh. The story of that day was told at first primarily through images – a drama played out in real time on television. The words followed. One of America's most distinguished novelists, **John Updike**, was among those who saw the immense tragedy unfold in New York.*

Suddenly summoned to witness something great and horrendous, we keep fighting not to reduce it to our own smallness. From the viewpoint of a tenth-floor apartment in Brooklyn Heights, where I happened to be visiting some kin, the destruction of the World Trade Center twin towers had the false intimacy of television, on a day of perfect reception. A four-year-old girl and her babysitter called from the library, and pointed out through the window the smoking top of the north tower, not a mile away. It seemed, at that first glance, more curious than horrendous: smoke speckled with bits of paper curled into the cloudless sky, and strange inky rivulets ran down the giant structure's vertically corrugated surface. The WTC had formed a pale background to our Brooklyn view of lower Manhattan, not beloved, like the stony, spired midtown thirties skyscrapers it had displaced as the city's tallest, but, with its pre-postmodern combination of unignorable immensity and architectural reticence, in some lights beautiful. As we watched the second tower burst into ballooning flame (an intervening building had hidden the approach of the second aeroplane), there persisted the notion that, as on television, this was not quite real; it could be fixed; the technocracy the towers symbolised would find a way to put out the fire and reverse the damage.

And then, within an hour, as my wife and I watched from the Brooklyn building's roof, the south tower dropped from the screen of our viewing; it fell straight down like an elevator, with a tinkling shiver and a groan of concussion distinct across the mile of air. We knew we had just witnessed thousands of deaths; we clung to each other as if we ourselves were falling. Amid the glittering impassivity of the many buildings across the East River, an empty spot had appeared, as if by electronic command, beneath the sky that, but for the sulphurous cloud streaming south towards the ocean, was pure blue, rendered uncannily pristine by the absence of jet trails. A swiftly expanding burst of smoke and dust hid the rest of lower Manhattan; we saw the collapse of the second tower only on television, where the footage of hell-bent aeroplane, exploding jet fuel and imploding tower was played and replayed, much-rehearsed moments from a nightmare ballet.

The nightmare is still on. The bodies are beneath the rubble, the last-minute cellphone calls – remarkably calm and loving, many of them – are still being reported, the sound of an aeroplane overhead still bears an unfamiliar menace, the thought of boarding an aeroplane with our old blasé blitheness keeps receding into the past. Determined men who have transposed their own lives to a martyr's afterlife can still inflict an amount of destruction that defies belief. War is conducted with a fury that requires abstraction – that turns a planeful of peaceful passengers, children included, into a missile the faceless enemy deserves. The other side has the abstractions; we have only the mundane duties of survivors – to pick up the pieces, to bury the dead, to take more precautions, to go on living.

American freedom of motion, one of our prides, has taken a hit. Can we afford the openness that lets future kamikaze pilots, say, enrol in Florida flying schools? A Florida neighbour of one of the suspects remembers him saying he didn't like the United States: 'He said it was too lax. He said, "I can go anywhere I want to, and they can't stop me." ' It is a weird complaint, a begging perhaps to be stopped. Weird, too, the silence of the heavens these days, as flying has ceased across America. But fly again we must; risk is a price of freedom, and walking around Brooklyn Heights that afternoon, as ash drifted in the air and cars were few and open-air lunches continued as usual on Montague Street, renewed the impression that, with all its failings, this is a country worth fighting for. Freedom, reflected in the street's diversity and daily ease, felt palpable. It is mankind's elixir, even if a few turn it to poison.

The next morning, I went back to the open vantage from which we had watched the tower so dreadfully slip from sight. The fresh sun shone on the eastward façades, a few boats tentatively moved in the river, the ruins were still sending out smoke, but New York looked glorious.

'The War on Terror'

It quickly became apparent that al-Qaeda, an Islamic fundamentalist group, had carried out the attack – the first major attack on the North American mainland in its history. President George W. Bush retaliated by declaring a worldwide 'war on terror' and issuing an ultimatum to the Taliban rulers of Afghanistan to give up Osama bin Laden, the al-Qaeda leader.

*Up to that moment, Osama bin Laden was a largely unknown quantity, though the BBC reporter **John Simpson** had come across him in February 1989, when crossing the Afghan border to report on the Soviet withdrawal from the country. He and his camera team were anxious to film a report on the various mujahedin (guerrilla) groups which were then controlling the country.*

[The mujahedin] were pleasant enough to us, and welcomed the diversion we provided. At that stage in the war the different mujahedin organisations were more united, and here as elsewhere various groups were working together: the more moderate Jamiat-e-Islami side by side with the fiercely fundamentalist Hezbe-e-Islami. It was impossible to tell the difference between them: they all wore green turbans and *shalwar kameez*, and they all had AK-47s. Everyone in Afghanistan who considered himself to be a man carried an AK-47.

For a while we filmed them as they fired off their mortar rounds, cheering every time a cloud of grey smoke went up over their latest hit. I got ready to do my piece to camera while the firing went on behind me.

It was then that the figure in white appeared. He was clearly an Arab, not an Indo-European like the Afghans around us. His robes were spotless, and his beard sensational. He appeared to be in his middle twenties, though it was hard to be certain. His AK-47 was slung over one shoulder, and he had a nasty-looking knife stuck in his belt. His calf-length boots looked expensive.

I had a good view of them, because he jumped up on a wall beside me and started haranguing the mujahedin, pointing to us and getting very excited.

'Problem,' said our translator. 'He wants them kill you.'

You, you notice. It was like that ancient joke about Tonto and the Lone Ranger: 'Tonto, we're surrounded by Indians.' 'What you mean we, white man?'

There were four of us, the cameraman, sound recordist, producer and me. The mujahedin numbered around eighteen.

The harangue went on for some time, but with a certain relief I could see the man in white wasn't getting anywhere. The audience listened carefully, and considered the merits of the case judiciously. But in the end they voted along party lines: the extreme Hezbe men in favour of the proposition, the moderate Jamiat men against. It was a good job we had chosen this particular mujahedin post; there was another a few hundred yards up the road where the proportions were reversed, and Hezbe had a majority.

The Arab could, I suppose, have used his AK-47 on us, but the Jamiat group, with that sense of hospitality you always get in Muslim communities, had decided that we were their guests and that they were therefore obliged to protect us as long as we stayed with them. If he had killed any of us, the rules of the game would have obliged them to kill him. Very comforting.

Anyway, once that was settled we went back to recording my piece to camera. I had to kneel down so that the cameraman could see the mortar firing behind me, and what with the ache in my knees and the loud explosions as each round went off, I suppose I rather took my eye off the man in white. After a while, though, I became aware of another haranguing, a little further off. He was shouting at the driver of an ammunition truck.

'Says, come and run over infidel,' our friend translated, meaning me in particular. 'Says, he give $500 to do it.'

It wasn't much, and I felt obscurely annoyed at being priced so moderately. It certainly wasn't enough for the driver, who shook his head and laughed, and drove off in the direction of the road.

The figure in white ran off towards one of the archways under the road where the mujahedin slept, and we followed him over there, intrigued.

We found him lying full length on a camp bed, weeping and beating his fists on the pillow out of frustration at not being able to kill us. I almost felt like comforting him, but resisted, of course. We moved on quite soon after that: the tears wouldn't last for ever, and even $500 was a reasonable amount of money.

I never forgot his eyes, or his beard: setting one's prejudices aside, he was a splendid-looking character. We assumed he was a Wahabi, a member of the extreme Saudi Arabian fundamentalist sect which had become heavily involved in the war in Afghanistan. I had seen another member of the sect a few months earlier, as I queued up at a completely redundant Pakistani border post to show my passport before crossing into Afghanistan.

Distinctly less impressive-looking, he had hissed at me, 'If I see you across the border in Afghanistan I will kill you.'

In 2003, American and British troops invaded Iraq. One of the witnesses of the arrival of the Americans in Baghdad was a young architect who later used the Internet to send his messages, many of which were published in the Guardian *in London, round the world. Calling himself* **Salam Pax**, *the Baghdad Blogger, he gave an account of his life, and that of his family, in the Iraqi capital. This is his 'blog' for Monday, 7 April 2003.*

The Americans called it 'a show of force' and not the anticipated invasion of Baghdad. Well, it was definitely a great show for anyone watching it from a high orbit. Added to the constant whooshes of missiles going over our heads and the following explosions, another sandstorm decided to make our life even more difficult than it already is. I mean your – ahem – boogers come out red because of all the sand you enhale. Closing the windows is madness. It is safer to open the windows when the explosions start.

Since the day the airport was seized we have no electricity and water is not reliable. At times if you have a tap that is higher than 50 centimetres you won't get water from it. We turn on the generator for four hours during the day and four at night, mainly to watch the news. Today my father wanted to turn on the generator at eight in the morning, because of news of an attack on the centre of Baghdad. We sat for two hours watching the same images until Kuwait TV showed footage taken from Fox News of American soldiers in al-Sijood Palace. Totally dumbstruck. Right after that we saw al-Sahaf denying once again what we have just seen minutes ago. He kept insisting that there are no American troops in Baghdad and for some reason kept insisting that al-Jazeera has become 'a tool of American media'. Idiot. Jazeera has been obviously very critical of the American 'invasion' (they insist on calling it that) and what does the super-smart information minister do? Ostracise them some more.

I have not been out of the house for the last three days. We are now fifteen people at Hotel Pax, although it is not so safe here. Everybody expects the next move to be on the west/south-west parts of Baghdad and are telling us we will be the front line. I can only hope when push comes to shove the Americans will not be met with too much resistance and we don't end up in the cross-fire.

> *From basic training to Iraq and back again,* **Kayla Williams** *spent five years in American military intelligence – 'one of the 15 per cent of the US army that's female' – and her book,* Love My Rifle More Than You, *is tough, witty and unsparing. As an interpreter in Iraq she had contact with local communities, publishing her account of what went on in her weblog. This was eventually banned, not least because she was not afraid to disapprove of US conduct and to say so. It became the basis for her book. Here she describes visits to a shrine in Kurdistan of the Yezidis, whose religion pre-dates Islam and Christianity.*

The Yezidi shrine at this mountain site was a small rock building with objects dangling from the ceiling. There were little alcoves in the shrine where locals placed offerings and worshipped. People came and left money that anyone else could take, if someone else came who needed it more. Or people took the money to use towards the upkeep of the shrine itself. And inside the shrine there was another door to a smaller room that I never entered or saw. No one exactly explained the purpose of the shrine, but we sometimes heard accusations from local Muslims that the Yezidis were *devil worshippers*. The dangling objects appeared to have more to do with the rays of the sun, but nothing was made clear.

One day a father came to worship with his several children, and the oldest daughter in the family appeared mesmerised by me.

She was excited to see a female American because she could talk to me. It was not appropriate for her to speak to the men, but she was permitted to speak to me. And it was the first time I encountered a young local woman with whom I could spend some time talking.

She didn't know how old she was, since the locals didn't have a real way to record birthdays, but she estimated that she was about sixteen.

Our conversations were extremely stilted, given her near-absence of Arabic and my difficulty making myself understood as a result.

Her name was Leila, and we became friendly, if not friends.

She returned to the shrine with her family three or four more times while I was there, and we began to exchange gifts.

The mother never joined her family on this pilgrimage.

I noticed that all the girls in the family had tattoos on their faces, but none more than Leila. Small dots on her chin, her forehead and the sides of her face.

I tried to ask what these dots on her face meant, but there was too much of a language barrier. The only thing I could ascertain was that the girls seemed to receive more of these tattoos as they grew up; Leila's youngest sister had no markings on her face, but her other sisters had one, two and four as they got older. But whether the dots were religious or cultural, I never learned.

At another time in Iraq, when we were among the bedouin people, I noticed from a distance that the women appeared to have tattooed writing on their feet. But again I never learned what it meant; I also never got close enough to the bedouin women to read the tattoos. I was always very curious.

Besides my general interest in the locals, and my desire to get to know what the civilians were like, it was just great to see a girl. This was such a male environment otherwise. And even though our conversations were hobbled by our mutual inability to make ourselves easily understood, there was just a sense of *relief*. For me. And, I began to suspect, for Leila as well.

> *The extent of the chaos in Baghdad is depicted by another blogger, a woman calling herself **Riverbend**. By profession a computer programmer, the war and increasing fundamentalism soon make it impossible for her to work: her job, night and day, is trying to keep her family together through days and weeks of increasing violence and crime. Here she describes what happens when a friend, nicknamed A., disappears.*

At 8 a.m., I was putting the kettle on in preparation for morning tea. The house was silent but no one was asleep. No one had slept all night. E. was still pacing; my father and uncle were closed up in the living room, trying to decide on a course of action and L. was trying not to cry. Suddenly, just as I lit the stove, the phone rang. It never sounded so shrill. I ran to the living room and found that my uncle had already jumped to answer it and was barking, 'Elloo?' L. ran into the room and stood wringing her hands nervously.

It was A.'s best friend and business partner, S. He had heard from A. just a few minutes before ... he had been abducted and was being held for a ransom of $15,000. A. and S. are partners and share a small shop in a mercantile neighbourhood in Baghdad. They sell everything from Korean electrical ovens to fluorescent light bulbs and make just enough money to support their respective families. We'd be given three days to get the money – a place would be agreed upon where we'd give them the money and they'd release A. later on.

We panicked. The whole house broke down. L. fell to the floor crying and shouting that they'll kill him – she just knew they'd kill him as they were killing others. We tried to calm her down and finally decided to give her a couple of valiums to ease the stress. We sat debating what to do – go to the police? No way. In some areas, the police were actually working with abductors for a certain amount of money and there was nothing they were willing to do anyway.

We spent the rest of the day rushing to sell gold, collect money and my uncle took a broken L. to the bank to empty the account – they've been saving up to build or buy a house. A.'s parents were soon at my uncle's house and we had a difficult time breaking the news to them. His mother cried and wanted to rush home for her few pieces of gold and his father sat, stunned, chain-smoking and trying to make sense of the situation. S., A.'s friend, came over with money – looking harrowed and tired.

To make a long, terrible story short – we had the money by the middle of the next day. L. had almost lost her wits and the only way the rest of us stayed sane was with the hope that A. would soon be back at home, with us.

The money was handed over on the third day after his abduction. But no A. came back. They told my uncle and S., who had gone with him, that A. would be set free in the next couple of days. My uncle and S. came home almost in tears – as if we had sent them on a mission and they had failed us.

I can't even begin to describe the next couple of days. If it was bad before – it suddenly became worse. We hear about abductions all the time ... but actually to experience it is something else. It's like having a part of you torn away. To think that A. might not come back was more horrible than anything we'd experienced so far. Watching his parents deteriorate from one minute to the next and knowing his wife was dying a little bit inside every hour that passed by was so nerve-racking that I'd run outside every hour to breathe in some fresh air – not the stale stuff inside the house contaminated with depression, frustration and fear.

On the fifth day after A.'s abduction, we were all sitting in the living room. There was no electricity and L. had fallen into a valium-induced sort of calm. We suddenly heard a feeble clang of the gate – as if someone was knocking, but not very hard. E. jumped up, ran to the door and called out, 'Who is it?!' A moment later he ran back – it was A.... . he had come home.

I won't describe the crying, screaming, shouting, jumping, hobbling (A. was limping) and general chaos that followed A.'s entrance. Apparently, his abductors had been watching the house for the last couple of weeks. As soon as A. dropped off his parents, they had followed with two cars and forced him to the side of the road on a secluded street. Four armed men forced him out of the car, put a bag over his head after kicking him around and threw him into a minivan with some more men.

After several hours of abuse and interrogation about his assets (which they seemed to have thought much more than he actually had), they let him make a call to his business partner who was supposed to call his family for the money.

(And if you could have seen him the moment he described this – you'd know all about the tenacity of the Iraqi sense of humour – here was A., with a gash on his head, a bluish bruise on the side of his face, a back bruised with kicks and punches, feet bleeding after walking over 1 kilometre barefoot and he was cracking jokes: 'They actually only wanted $5,000,' he said at one point, 'but I was outraged – told them I was worth *at least* $20,000 – five is just an insult to my personal worth ... we agreed on $15,000 in the end.')

They had kept him in a slum on the outskirts of Baghdad where police and troops don't dare set up camp. He was transferred from one hovel to the next and at each one he says there were abducted people. Some of the abductions were political, some religious and many were for the money. He says the worst part was not being able to see anything around him, but being able to hear the others being beaten ... and anticipating another kick or punch from any random direction.

I saw him again yesterday and he still looks haggard and tired. L. says he can't sleep all night – he keeps waking in the middle of the night with a nightmare or some sort of hallucination – thinking he's still caught.

And so that's how we've been spending our last few days. It has been a nightmare and I've had to examine a lot. Everything has felt so trivial and ridiculous ... the blog, the electrical situation, the insomnia, the 'reconstruction', the elections, the fictional WMD ... politics and politicians ... I've been wondering about all those families who can't pay the ransom or the ones whose sons and daughters come home on a stretcher instead of on foot or in a garbage bag, as we heard about one family ... and I've also realised how grateful we should be just being able to make the transition from one day to the next in a situation like ours.

One of the most potent means of new media communication is through Twitter, a means of conveying short sharp reports and message through the Internet and by text messaging on phones. The presidential elections in Iran in June 2009 brought hundreds of thousands of demonstrators on to the streets across the country, in the belief that the elections had been rigged against the challenger, Mir-Hossain Mousavi. The Twitter messages gave pithy witness accounts of what was happening on the ground, and are testimony to the sense of the political earthquake that was shaking Iran. One of those collecting the 'tweets' and transmitting them to the outside world via Internet was Josh Shahryar, a professional translator who adopted the nom de plume 'Nite Owl'. At the end of June 2009, the demonstrations were at their height.

These are the important happenings that I can positively confirm from Sunday, June 21 in Iran.

1. Thousands of people took to street. People were beaten up in some parts, while in other parts; they weren't allowed to gather and were dispersed. There was a silent protest of people in front of the UN's office as well. Sporadic clashes are reported from Baharestan, Enqelab, Vanak and Vali-Asr squares. Hundreds of students continued to protest in Tehran University for the fourth straight day. There were also reports of people being attacked in the UN gathering – this has been partially confirmed.

2. The majority of Mousavi's advisors and important aides have all been arrested. He has been left with only a handful of junior political workers and is currently under effective house arrest as he not allowed to speak to journalists or make any other statements. His movement has been limited today and he did not appear at any gatherings. His Facebook account and most of the news websites affiliated with him as well as his website and websites of his supporters have more less all been either hacked or [are] now under effective government control. False statements regularly issued from the hacked accounts. Ghalam-Net can no longer be trusted and his Facebook account is currently being used by the Iranian government to place information so that the protesters can either lose hope or get violent.

3. Even in this state, however, Mousavi has continued his call for a general strike on Tuesday. He has also called all citizens to turn the headlights of their cars on from 5 to 6 pm on Monday in order to commemorate those that have been killed in the protests during the past week and the few days after. He has reportedly called upon people to go

on an indefinite strike until their demands are met if he is to be killed by government.

4. Five of Hashemi Rafsanjani's family members were arrested early on Saturday, these included his daughter Faezeh Hashemi who was among the first from his family to join the protests open on Wednesday. The government announced that they had been arrested because they were under threat of assassination by terrorist elements within the country. Four of the family members were released later while Faezeh was released late at night. No news of why they were released could be confirmed.

5. The police are continuing to find and arrest any reformists that have not been arrested in the past few days. The government-run media in Iran has released information of the arrests of at least 475 people. Yet the number cannot be confirmed or denied. What sources indicate is that more than 5,000 people have so far been arrested by the government. Correspondents of the BBC and Al-Arabiya news crew have been asked to leave the country on Monday. The photojournalist of *Life* magazine has gone missing. Overall, more than two dozen journalists within Iran are currently under arrest. The government has also increased censorship and at least four newspapers in Tehran were edited by government agents.

6. The government has branded all protesters as thugs as the national media in Iran continues to call them so through government sources. One media outlet in Iran announced that people tried to hide in Embassies on Saturday while trying to flee from terrorists. However, they are unable to account for the participation of a large number of mullahs and clergy in these protests. Here's a picture of some of the 'thug' clerics: http://i.friendfeed.com/53ae98683f0c...8d09210f908338

7. Business owners in Tehran and shopkeepers in Tehran are said to have already put their support behind Mousavi for the protests. Our sources have urged everyone in Iran to get food, fuel and other resources as soon as possible and prepare for a few days of shortage of supplies. Autobus workers have also indicated that they will join the protests and the strike now.

8. The Writers' Association of Kordistan, the Human Rights Campaign

of Kordistan and some other prominent people have also called for a strike in Kordistan province on Tuesday.

9. Tweeters indicate that anyone flying into Iran should be highly alert as the government is thoroughly checking those arriving at Tehran International Airport and any connections to Mousavi could mean an arrest on the spot. The government has also created dozens of false twitter accounts to urge people to be violent so they can have a bloodier crackdown and crush the protesters.

10. Rafsanjani has met with clerics from Qom yet again. There are wild rumors circulating as to what the outcome of the meetings will be. However, no news has actually arrived about the incident. Any claims made right now are far-fetched. However, people are slowly starting to call upon him to take action. Tweets have included messages to him, urging him to come to the plight of the oppressed. Mohammad Khatami has released condemning the violence yet again and asked for an end to hostilities.

11. The city of Tehran and cities around Tehran have yet again been hearing Allah o Akbar at night. It needs to be mentioned that most sources tell of the voices getting louder as the protests continue. Chants of 'Death to Dictator' have also been heard. And in a heartbreaking and cruel gesture, the government banned people from holding a memorial for Neda – the Iranian girl whose death by a police bullet in Tehran has sparked international outrage – in any mosque in Tehran, openly.

12. The Iranian government is aggressively trying to clamp down on internet, telephones and other communication sources. Almost all foreign TV channels are banned, getting through to Iranians on the phone is almost impossible and internet's download speed right now in Tehran is, according to one source, '375 bytes'.

Sources and Acknowledgements

Every effort has been made to contact copyright holders; in the event of an inadvertent omission or error, please notify the editorial department at Profile Books, 3a Exmouth House, Pine Street, Exmouth Market, London EC1R 0JH, for a correction to be made in future printings.

VISIONS OF THE FUTURE
Transatlantic Triumphs and Disasters
Marie Curie: *Madame Curie*, Eve Curie, trans. Vincent Sheean copyright 1937 by Doubleday, a division of Random House, Inc. Used by permission of Doubleday, a division of Random House, Inc.
Orville Wright: *The Papers of Wilbur and Orville Wright*, vol. I, ed. Marvin McFarland (McGraw-Hill, 1953).
Harry Senior, Harold Bride, Mrs D. H. Bishop: *New York Times* (19 April 1912, 17 April 1912, 19 April 1912).

Social Revolution in Edwardian Britain
J. V. Radcliffe, Anonymous: *Manchester Guardian* (9 November 1910, 5 June 1913, 28 May 1913).

Imperial Dreams in the Antarctic
Roald Amundsen: *The South Pole: An Account of the Norwegian Antarctic Expedition in the* Fram, 1910–12, trans. A. G. Chater (John Murray, 1912).

Robert Falcon Scott: *Scott's Last Expedition: The Personal Journals of Captain R. F. Scott, CVO, RN on his Journey to the South Pole* (Smith, Elder & Co., 1913).

Apsley Cherry-Garrard: *The Worst Journey in the World* (Constable and Co., 1922). Reprinted by permission of the Scott Polar Research Institute, University of Cambridge.

Ernest Shackleton: *South: The Story of Shackleton's Last Expedition 1914–17* (Heinemann, 1919).

Frank Worsley: *Shackleton's Boat Journey*, published by Pimlico. Reprinted by permission of The Random House Group Ltd.

The Balkans and the Coming of War

Edith Durham: *High Albania* (Edward Arnold, 1909).

Borijove Jevtic: *New York World* (29 June 1924).

THE GREAT WAR

How it Began

Alfred Lichtenstein: *The German Poets of the First World War* (Croom Helm, 1985). Reprinted by permission of Taylor & Francis Books UK.

Johannes Niemann: 'The Christmas Truce, 1914' from *1914–18: Voices and Images of the Great War,* Lyn MacDonald (Penguin Books, 1988). Copyright © Lyn MacDonald 1988.

J. C. Dunn: *The War the Infantry Knew 1914–19: A chronicle of service in France and Belgium with the Second Battalion, His Majesty's Twenty-third Foot, the Royal Welch Fusiliers, founded on personal records, recollections and reflections, assembled, edited and partly written by one of their medical officers* (Jane's, 1987).

T. A. White: *Ordeal by Fire: Witnesses to the Great War*, Lyn MacDonald (The Folio Society, 2001).

H. W. Nevinson: *Guardian* (14 April 1916). Copyright Guardian News & Media Ltd.

Irfan Orga: *Portrait of a Turkish Family* (Victor Gollancz, 1950).

The Western Front

Robert Graves: *Goodbye to All That* (Jonathan Cape, 1929). Reprinted by permission of Carcanet Press Ltd.

Frederick Manning: *Her Privates We* (Peter Davies, 1930).

Henri Barbusse: *Under Fire*, trans. Robin Buss (Penguin Books, 2003). Translation copyright © Robin Buss 2003. Reprinted by permission of Penguin Books Ltd.

Anonymous reporter: *New York Times* (13 April 1916).

Bill Fell: *Lost Voices of the Royal Navy*, ed. Max Arthur (Hodder & Stoughton, 2005). Reprinted by permission of Hodder & Stoughton Ltd.

The Battle of the Somme

Ernest Shepard: *A Sergeant-Major's War* (Crowood Press, 1987). Reprinted by permission of The Crowood Press.

Robert Graves: *Goodbye to All That* (Jonathan Cape, 1929). Reprinted by permission of Carcanet Press Ltd.

Cecil Lewis: *Sagittarius Rising* (Heinemann & Davies, 1985). Reprinted by permission of Greenhill Books c/o Casemate UK.

Julian Bickersteth: *The Bickersteth Diaries 1914–18* (Leo Cooper, 1995). Reprinted by permission of Pen & Sword Books Ltd.

The War in Italy

Ernest Hemingway: *A Farewell to Arms* (Jonathan Cape, 1929). Copyright © Charles Scribner's Sons 1929. Copyright renewed © Ernest Hemingway 1957. Reprinted by permission of Scribner, an imprint of Simon & Schuster Adult Publishing Group and The Random House Group Ltd.

Giuseppe Ungaretti: 'San Martino del Carso', trans. Jon Silkin, from *The Penguin Book of First World War Poetry*, ed. Jon Silkin (Penguin Books, 1981). Reprinted by permission of The Estate of Jon Silkin.

Vera Brittain: *Testament of Youth: An Autobiographical Study of the Years 1900–25* (Virago, 1978). Reprinted by permission of Mark Bostridge and T. J. Brittain-Catlin, literary executors for the Estate of Vera Brittain, 1970.

Lawrence of Arabia and the Middle East

T. E. Lawrence: *Revolt in the Desert* (Jonathan Cape, 1927).

Ronald Storrs: *Orientations: The Memoirs of Sir Ronald Storrs* (Ivor Nicolson and Watson, 1937).

Gertrude Bell: *The Letters of Gertrude Bell*, ed. Lady Bell (Ernest Benn, 1927).

The Last Days

Ernst Jünger: *Storm of Steel*, trans. Michael Hoffman (Allen Lane, 2003). Copyright © Michael Hoffmann 2003. Reprinted by permission of Penguin Books Ltd and Penguin, a division of Penguin Group (USA) Inc.

Elmer Sherwood: *Diary of a Rainbow Veteran, Written at the Front* (Moore-Langen Company, 1929).

Stanley Spencer: excerpt from his journal, as quoted in *Stanley Spencer – An English Vision*, Fiona MacCarthy (Yale University Press, 1997).

Isaac Rosenberg: 'Break of Day in the Trenches', first published in *Poetry* magazine (December 1916).

J. C. Dunn: *The War the Infantry Knew 1914–19: A chronicle of service in France and Belgium with the Second Battalion, His Majesty's Twenty-third Foot, the Royal Welch Fusiliers, founded on personal records, recollections and reflections, assembled, edited and partly written by one of their medical officers* (Jane's, 1987).

Russia: Defeat and the Coming of the Revolution

Florence Farmborough: *Nurse at the Russian Front: A Diary, 1914–18* (Constable, 1974). Reprinted by permission of Constable & Robinson.

John Reed: *Ten Days That Shook the World* (Boni & Liveright, 1919).

Arthur Ransome: *Manchester Guardian* (11 October 1921). Copyright Guardian News & Media Ltd.

A Phoney Peace

D. F. Boyd: *Manchester Guardian* (26 May 1921). Copyright Guardian News & Media Ltd.

BETWEEN THE WARS
Bright Young Things
John Dos Passos: *U.S.A.* (Constable, 1938). Reprinted by permission of
Lucy Dos Passos Coggin on behalf of the Estate of John Dos Passos.
Robert Byron: *The Road to Oxiana* (Macmillan, 1937). Copyright ©
Robert Byron. Reprinted by permission of PFD (www.pfd.co.uk) on
behalf of The Estate of Robert Byron.
Evelyn Waugh: *Labels: A Mediterranean Journey.* Copyright © Evelyn
Waugh, 1937. Reprinted by permission of PFD (www.pfd.co.uk) on
behalf of The Estate of Evelyn Waugh.

The Great Depression
Elliott V. Bell: *We Saw It Happen*, ed. Hanson Baldwin and Shepard Stone
(Simon & Schuster, 1938).
Woody Guthrie: 'Dust Storm Disaster' copyright © 1960 Ludlow Music,
Inc., USA. Assigned to TRO Essex Music Ltd. of Suite 2.07, Plaza 535
Kings Road, London SW10 0SZ. International Copyright secured. All
rights reserved. Used by permission.
Roland Blythe: *Akenfield: Portrait of an English Village* (Allen Lane, 1969).
Copyright © Ronald Blythe. c/o Rogers, Coleridge & White Ltd, 20
Powis Mews, London, W11 1JN.

The Age of the Dictators
Patrick Leigh Fermor: *A Time of Gifts* (John Murray, 1977). Reproduced
by permission of John Murray (Publishers) Ltd.
D. Sefton Delmer: *Daily Express* (22 February 1933). Copyright © Daily
Express.
Leopold Trepper: *The Great Game: The Story of the Red Orchestra*, trans.
Helen Weaver (Michael Joseph, 1977).
Duke of Pirajno: *A Cure for Serpents: An Italian Doctor in North Africa*,
trans. Kathleen Naylor (Eland Books, 1985). Reprinted by permission
of Eland Publishing Ltd.
Carlo Levi: *Christ Stopped at Eboli*, trans. Frances Frenaye (Farrar Straus
& Giroux, 1947). Reprinted by permission of Farrar, Straus & Giroux,
LLC.

The Spanish Civil War

Arthur Koestler: *Dialogue with Death*, trans. Trevor and Phyllis Blewitt (Penguin Books, 1943). Copyright © Arthur Koestler. Reprinted by permission of PFD (www.pfd.co.uk) on behalf of The Estate of Arthur Koestler.

George Orwell: *Homage to Catalonia*. Copyright © 1952 George Orwell and renewed 1980 by Sonia Brownell Orwell, reprinted by permission of Houghton Mifflin Harcourt Publishing Company.

Noel Monks: *Eyewitness* (Muller, 1955). Copyright © Daily Express.

The Chinese Revolution

Hsiao Ch'ien: *Traveller without a Map*, trans. Jeffrey C. Kinkley (Hutchinson, 1990). Reprinted by permission of The Random House Group Ltd.

Edgar Snow: *Red Star Over China*. Copyright © 1938, 1944 by Random House, Inc., copyright © 1961 by John K Fairbank, copyright © 1968 by Edgar Snow. Used by permission of Grove/Atlantic, Inc.

Anonymous: 'Atrocities at Nanking', trans. Robert Gray from www.cnd.org/ njmassacre/njm-tran/njm-intr.htm (February 1996).

THE WORLD AT WAR 1939–2945
Opening Salvos

J. R. Frier, Muriel Green, Nella Last: *Mass-Observation*, ed. Sandra Koa Wing (The Folio Society, 2007). Copyright © Sandra Koa Wing 2007. Reproduced with the permission of The Curtis Brown Group Ltd on behalf of The Trustees of the Mass Observation Archive. Copyright © The Trustees of the Mass Observation Archive.

Antoine de Saint-Exupéry: *Flight to Arras*. Reprinted by permission of The Random House Group Ltd.

Marc Bloch: *Strange Defeat*, trans. Gerard Hopkins (Oxford University Press, 1949).

C. H. Lightoller: *Dunkirk*, Arthur Durham Divine (Faber & Faber, 1945).

Henry Reed: 'The Naming of Parts', *New Statesman and Nation* 24, no. 598 (8 August 1942). Copyright © New Statesman Ltd 2008. All rights reserved.

The Battle of Britain and the Blitz

Geoffrey Wellum: *First Light* (Penguin Books, 2002). Copyright ©
   Geoffrey Wellum 2002. Reprinted by permission of Penguin Books
   Ltd and John Wiley & Sons, Inc.

Richard Hillary: *The Last Enemy: The Memoir of a Spitfire* (Copyright ©
   Richard Hillary 1942). Reprinted by permission of A. M. Heath & Co.
   Ltd.

Frank Edwards: *Mass-Observation*, ed. Sandra Koa Wing (The Folio
   Society, 2007). Copyright © Sandra Koa Wing 2007. Reproduced
   with the permission of The Curtis Brown Group Ltd on behalf of The
   Trustees of the Mass Observation Archive. Copyright © The Trustees
   of the Mass Observation Archive.

F. W. Winterbotham: *The Ultra Secret* (Weidenfeld and Nicolson, 1974).
   Copyright © 1974 by F. W. Winterbotham. Reprinted by permission
   of Weidenfeld and Nicolson, a division of The Orion Publishing
   Group, and HarperCollins Publishers.

Theodora Fitzgibbon: *With Love: An Autbiography 1938–46* (Pan Books,
   1983). Reprinted by permission of David Higham Associates, on
   behalf of The Estate of Theodora Fitzgibbon.

The Battlefield Extends

Daniel K. Inouye: *Journey to Washington* (Prentice-Hall, 1967). Copyright
   © Prentice-Hall, Inc. 1967. Copyright renewed © Senator Daniel K.
   Inouye 1995. All rights reserved. Reprinted by permission of Simon
   & Schuster, Inc.

Keith Douglas: *Alamein to Zem Zem* (Faber & Faber, 1992). Reprinted by
   permission of Faber & Faber Ltd.

The War in Italy

Michael Howard: *Captain Professor* (Continuum, 2006). Reprinted by
   permission of Continuum International Book Publishing.

Norman Lewis: *Naples '44: An Intelligence Officer in the Italian Labyrinth*
   (Eland, 1983). Copyright © The Estate of Norman Lewis c/o Rogers,
   Coleridge & White Ltd., 20 Powis Mews, London, W11 1JN.

Curzio Malaparte: *The Skin*, trans. David Moore (Harborough Publishing, 1959).

Eric Newby: *Love and War in the Apennines* (Picador, 1983), published in the USA as *When the Snow Comes They Will Take You Away* (Scribner, 1971). Copyright © Eric Newby 1971 and copyright © Charles Scribner's Sons 1971. Reprinted by permission of HarperCollins Publishers Ltd and Scribner, an imprint of Simon & Schuster Adult Publishing Group.

Joseph Heller: *Catch-22* (Jonathan Cape, 1962). Copyright © Joseph Heller 1962. US copyright © Joseph Heller 1955, 1961, renewed 1989. Reprinted by permission of Simon & Schuster Adult Publishing Group.

D-Day and After

Norman Scarfe: *Assault Division: A History of the 3rd Division from the Invasion of Normandy to the Surrender of Germany* (Spellmount, 2004). Copyright © Norman Scarfe 1947, 2004. Reprinted by permission of Norman Scarfe, c/o John Welch.

Ernie Pyle: *Ernie Pyle's War: America's Eyewitness to World War II*, James Tobin (Free Press, 1997). Reprinted by permission of the Scripps Howard Foundation.

Marie Vassiltchikov: *Berlin Diaries 1940–45* (Chatto & Windus, 1985). Copyright © 1985 The Estate of Marie Harnden. Used by permission of Alfred A. Knopf, a division of Random House, Inc.

Alan Moorehead: *Eclipse* (Hamish Hamilton, 1945). Reprinted by permission of The Estate of Alan Moorehead and Pollinger Ltd.

Kurt Vonnegut: *Slaughterhouse-Five* (Jonathan Cape, 1970) Copyright © 1968, 1969 by Kurt Vonnegut, Jr. Used by permission of Dell Publishing, a division of Random House, Inc.

Victor Klemperer: *To the Bitter End: The Diaries of Victor Klemperer, 1942–5*, trans. Martin Chalmers, translation copyright © 1998 Martin Chalmers. Published in the USA as *I Will Bear Witness: A Diary of the Nazi Years, 1942–1945* (Modern Library, 2001). Reprinted by permission of Random House, Inc.

The War in Russia

George Grossjohann: *Five Years, Four Fronts* (Presidio Press, 2005).

Vassily Grossman: *A Writer at War: Vasily Grossman with the Red Army 1941–45*, ed. Luba Vinogradova, trans. Antony Beevor . Copyright © 2005 Ekaterina Vasilievna Korotkova-Grossman and Elena Fedorovna Kozhichkina. English translation, introduction and commentary copyright © 2005 by Antony Beevor and Luba Vinogradova. Used by permission of Pantheon Books, a division of The Random House, Inc.

Guy Sajer: *The Forgotten Soldier – War on the Russian Front* (Cassell, 1999). Reprinted by permission The Orion Publishing Group, London.

The War in Europe Ends

Fey von Hassell: *A Mother's War*, ed. David Forbes-Watt (John Murray, 2003).

René Cutforth: *Order to View* (Faber & Faber, 1969). Copyright René Cutforth. Reproduced by permission of the author c/o Rogers, Coleridge & White, 20 Powis Mews, London W11 1J N.

Patrick Gordon-Walker: US radio broadcast (24 April 1945).

Anne Frank: *The Diary of a Young Girl* (The Definitive Edition), ed. Otto H. Frank and Mirjam Pressler, trans. Susan Massotty (Penguin Books, 2001). Copyright © The Anne Frank-Fonds, Basle, Switzerland 1991. English translation copyright © 1995 by Doubleday, a division of Random House. Reprinted by permission of Doubleday, a division of Random House, Inc and Penguin Books Ltd.

Curzio Malaparte: *Kaputt*, trans. Cesare Foligno (New York Review of Books, 2005).

Wladyslaw Szpilman, Wilm Hosenfeld: *The Pianist: The Extraordinary Story of One Man's Survival in Warsaw, 1939–45*, trans. Anthea Bell (Gollancz, 1999). Copyright © Wladyslaw Szpilman 1998. Reprinted by permission of Victor Gollancz, Weidenfeld & Nicolson, London, an imprint of The Orion Publishing Group and Christopher Little Literary Agency.

New Horizons, Revolutions and Independence

Rosa Parks: *Rosa Parks: My Story* (Dial Books, 1992) Copyright ©
Rosa Parks 1992. Reprinted by permission of Dial Books for Young
Readers, a division of Penguin Young Readers Group, a member
of Penguin Group (USA) Inc., 343 Hudson Street, New York, NY
10014. All rights reserved.

Patrick Cockburn: *The Broken Boy* (Jonathan Cape, 2005). Copyright ©
Patrick Cockburn. Reprinted by permission of Patrick Cockburn, c/o
Rogers, Coleridge & White Ltd., 20 Powis Mews, London, W11 1JN
and The Random House Group Ltd.

Rachel Carson: *Silent Spring* (Hamish Hamilton, 1958) Copyright ©
1962 Rachel Carson, renewed 1990 by Roger Christie. Reprinted
by permission of The Estate of Rachel Carson, Pollinger Ltd and
Houghton Mifflin Publishing Company. All rights reserved.

Penderel Moon: *Divide and Quit* (Chatto & Windus, 1961).

James Cameron: *Point of Departure* (Arthur Barker Ltd., 1967).

Alexander Solzhenitsyn: *The Gulag Archipelago 1918–56*, trans. Thomas
P. Whitney (parts I–IV) and Harry Willetts (parts V–VII), abridged by
Edward E. Ericson, Jr. (Collins Harvill, 1986, published by the Bodley
Head; Harper & Row, 1985). Copyright © 1985 by the Russian Social
Fund. Reprinted by permission of HarperCollins Publishers and the
Random House Group Ltd.

Victor Zorza: *Guardian Omnibus*, ed. David Ayerst.

Humphrey Taylor: *Drum Magazine* (21 March 1960).

Nelson Mandela: *Long Walk to Freedom* (Abacus, 1995). Reprinted by
permission of Little, Brown Book Group Ltd

Youth, Sex and Violence

Mervyn Griffith-Jones: *The Trial of Lady Chatterley*, ed. C. H. Rolph
(Penguin, 2005). Reprinted by permission of The Estate of C. H.
Rolph.

Lady Chatterley verdict, Simon Winchester: *Guardian* (3 November 1960,
31 January 1972). Copyright Guardian News & Media Ltd.

Philip Larkin: 'Annus Mirabilis' from *Collected Poems* by Philip Larkin ©
The Estate of Philip Larkin and reproduced by permission of Faber
and Faber Ltd and Farrar, Straus & Giroux, LLC.

Tom Wolfe: *New York Herald Tribune* (7 February 1964). Reprinted by
permission of Tom Wolfe, by arrangement with Janklow & Nesbit
Associates.

Hans Koning: *Nineteen Sixty-Eight: A Personal Report* (Unwin Hyman,
1988).

Simon Winchester: *The Guardian* (31 January 1972). Copyright
Guardian News & Media Ltd 1972.

Ryszard Kapuscinski: *The Soccer War* (Granta, 1990). Reprinted by
permission of The Liepman Agency, on behalf of The Estate of
Ryszard Kapuscinski, and Granta Books.

Neil Armstrong: *First On the Moon: A Voyage with Neil Armstrong, Michael
Collins, Edwin E. Aldrin Jr.* (Little, Brown, 1970). Copyright © Little,
Brown and Company, Inc. 1970. Reprinted by permission of Little,
Brown and Company.

The Vietnam War

Nicholas Tomalin: *The Times* (5 June 1966). © Nicholas Tomalin/Sunday
Times 1966.

Michael Herr: *Dispatches* (Macmillan, 2002). Copyright © Michael Herr,
1977. Reprinted by permission of Alfred A. Knopf, a division of
Random House, Inc and Pan Macmillan London.

James Fenton: 'The Fall of Saigon' from *The Best of Granta Reportage*
(Granta, 1993). Copyright © James Fenton. Reprinted by permission
of PFD (www.pfd.co.uk) on behalf of James Fenton.

Jon Swain: *River of Time* (Minerva, 1996). Reprinted by permission of
The Random House Group Ltd.

Bob Woodward and Carl Bernstein: *All the President's Men* (Quartet
Books Ltd, 1974).

A Walk on the Wild Side

W. H. Davies: *The Autobiography of a Super-Tramp* (Jonathan Cape, 1950). Reprinted by permission of Dee & Griffin for the Mrs H. M. Davies Will Trust.

Hunter S. Thompson: *Fear and Loathing in Las Vegas* (Flamingo, 1993). Copyright © 1972 Hunter S. Thompson 1972. Used by permission of Random House, Inc and The Wylie Agency, Inc.

Linda Polman: *We Did Nothing: Why the Truth Doesn't Always Come Out When the UN Goes In*, trans. Rob Bland (Penguin, 1997). Copyright © Linda Polman 2003. Reprinted by permission of Penguin Books Ltd and Jan Michael on behalf of Linda Polman.

THE AGE OF THE REPORTER
The Front Line

Brian Hanrahan: *I Counted Them All Out, and I Counted Them All Back*, with Robert Fox (BBC, 1982).

Robert Fisk, Richard Beeston: *The Times* (20 September 1982, 22 March 1988). © Robert Fisk/*The Times* 1982.

Harold Brodkey: *This Wild Darkness: The Story of my Death* (Fourth Estate, 1996). Copyright © Harold Brodkey 1996. Reprinted by permission of HarperCollins Publishers Ltd.

John Simpson: 'Tiananmen Square' from *The Best of Granta Reportage* (Granta, 1993). Copyright © John Simpson. Reprinted by permission of LAW on behalf of John Simpson.

Peter Millar and Richard Ellis: *Sunday Times* (11 November 1989). © *The Sunday Times* 1989.

Paul Rusesabagina: *An Ordinary Man* (Bloomsbury, 2006). Reprinted by permission of Baror International, Inc. and Bloomsbury Publishing.

Azar Nafisi: *Reading Lolita in Tehran* (Random House, 2003). Copyright © Azar Nafisi 2002. Reprinted by permission of Random House, Inc. and IB Tauris Publishers.

The Bosnian War

Patrick Bishop: *Daily Telegraph* (May 1993). Copyright © *The Daily Telegraph* 1993.

Index